Ideology and Power
in the Age of
Lenin in Ruins

CultureTexts

Arthur and Marilouise Kroker　　　　*General Editors*

CultureTexts is a series of creative explorations in theory, politics and culture at the *fin-de-millenium*. Thematically focussed around key theoretical debates in the postmodern condition, the *CultureTexts* series challenges received discourses in art, social and political theory, feminism, psychoanalysis, value inquiry, science and technology, the body, and critical aesthetics. Taken individually, contributions to *CultureTexts* represent the forward breaking-edge of postmodern theory and practice.

Titles

Ideology and Power in the Age of Lenin in Ruins
edited and introduced by Arthur and Marilouise Kroker

The Hysterical Male: new feminist theory
edited and introduced by Arthur and Marilouise Kroker

Seduction
Jean Baudrillard

Panic Encyclopedia
Arthur Kroker, Marilouise Kroker and David Cook

Life After Postmodernism: Essays on Value and Culture
edited and introduced by John Fekete

Body Invaders
edited and introduced by Arthur and Marilouise Kroker

The Postmodern Scene: Excremental Culture and Hyper-Aesthetics
Arthur Kroker/David Cook

Ideology and Power
in the Age of Lenin in Ruins

**edited and introduced by
Arthur and Marilouise Kroker**

**St. Martin's Press
New York**

All rights reserved. For information, write:
Scholarly and Reference Division
St. Martin's Press, Inc. 175 Fifth Avenue, New Yo
NY 10010

First published in the United States of America in 1991

Printed in Canada

ISBN 0-312-06154-4

Library of Congress Cataloging-in-Publication Data

Ideology and power in the age of Lenin ruins / edited and
    introduced by Arthur and Marilouise Kroker.
        p.   cm. -- (CultureTexts)
    ISBN 0-312-06154-4
    1. Power (Social sciences) 2. Ideology. I. Kroker, Arthur,
    1945-   . II. Kroker, Marilouise. III. Series.
    JC330.I34   1991
    320.5'09'049--dc20

                                                      90-27739
                                                      CIP

ACKNOWLEDGEMENTS

We would like to express our appreciation to intellectual and personal friends who
have supported and encouraged our work over the years: William Leiss, David Cook,
Michael and Deena Weinstein, and Frank Burke.

We dedicate this book to people everywhere
working for peace in the world.

CONTENTS

IDEOLOGY AND POWER
IN THE AGE OF LENIN IN RUINS

Arthur and Marilouise Kroker

When the Berlin Wall Finally Came Tumbling Down

What is the fate of ideology and power in the age of Lenin in ruins? Now that bureaucratic socialism stands unmasked as an actually existing ideology of state domination in all of the societies of Eastern Europe, what is the destiny of Marx's understanding of ideology as only a falsification of capitalist relations of production? And now that power in Western Europe and North America dissolves into the sign of seduction, what is to be the fate of the political subject, outside, that is, the closed horizon of both techno-capitalism and socialist realism. When the Berlin Wall finally came tumbling down, all of the old comfortable markers of political debate suddenly shattered, revealing in its wake a desperate urgency to rethinking the meaning of ideology and power in a world dominated by the eclipse of the political legitimation of state socialism and by the seeming triumph everywhere now of the rituals of primitive capitalism. The East goes Thatcherite; the West goes Green; and the United States goes virtual (technology).

Lenin in Ruins

If the twentieth century can be plunging towards its conclusion with such violent energy, that is because we witness now the simultaneous decomposition and success of its two founding moments: the search for materialist freedom and for collective justice. Not decline in the traditional sense of a final catastrophe which marks the end of one historical epoch and the beginning of another, but a new historical mode of transformation—*hyper-decline*—in which communism and capitalism can exist now as pure forms: stripped of their illusions and unmasked of their interests. Historical manifestations, that is, of what Pietr Sloterdijk has described in the *Critique of Cynical Reason* as "enlightened false consciousness." The *myths* of communism and capitalism, then, as floating signs—degree zero-points—for the cancellation and imminent reversibility of all the polarities: the mutation of the (socialist) struggle for justice into cynical power; and the materialist dream of the (liberal) flight from politics into the triumph of cynical ideology. Like "strange attractors" in astrophysics which can exercise such a deadly fascination because of their ability to *alternate* energy fields instantly, the myths of state capitalism and state communism are alternating sides of the rationalist eschatology: the symptomatic signs of the appearance of the *bimodern condition*.

Bimodernism? That is the contemporary historical situation in which the great referential polarities instantly reverse fields, changing signs in a dizzying display of political repolarization. A violent metastasis in which all the referential finalities of the political code of the twentieth century—capitalism and communism most of all—begin to slide into one another, actually mutating into their opposites as they undergo a fatal reversal of meaning. No longer justice versus the acquisitive instinct, power versus ideology, (socialist) history versus (consumer) simulation, or (economic) liberalism versus (political) democracy, but now the instant reversibility of all the referents. A fatal eclipse of the empire of the sign in which capitalism and communism do a big historical flip. Not just the myth of capitalism in desperate need of the communist "other" to sustain itself or communism as a barrier against the universalization of the commodity-form, but now communism aping the *economic* form of primitive capitalism, and capitalism taking on the *political* form of the command economy of late communism. The capitalist societies, then, as the forward frontier of the communist valorization of power; and communist societies as the last and best of all the primitive capitalisms. In one, the inspiring faith in commercial accumulation and the resucitation of law of value of the production machine; and in the other, the radical depoliticization of the population, its actual body invasion, by a totalitarian image-reservoir under the control of a cynical political mandarinate. In one, the recuperation of the productivist myth of Franklin Delano Roosevelt as a policy of economic reconstruction; and in the other, the Leninist use of all the mass organs of media manipulation as a way of coordinating private opinion with the war machine.

So then, Spengler again: but this time the *ecstacy* of the decline of the West. The history of two familiar genocides: of the (capitalist) logic of exterminism in the name of reason; and of (communist) murder in the name of collective justice.

Not capitalism and communism as fatal antagonists, but as the deepest fulfillment of the dream of the West: the dream, that is, of the universalization of the rationalist eschatology as the radiating code of politics, economy, culture and subjectivity. The one the history of the individual search for commercial freedom under the sign of missionary consciousness; the other the struggle for social justice under the code of historical materialism. The first, the penetration of subjectivity by the language of the technological dynamo; the second, the externalization of subjectivity into the public orthodoxies of socialist realism. The one a daring, but ultimately futile attempt, to mute the leviathan of politics by making democratic aspirations subordinate to liberal capitalism; the other a revolutionary effort to suppress ideology in the name of power. A history, that is, of a fatal *dedoublement* in the Western mind which, playing on the more ancient philosophical terrain of justice and freedom, created, and then destroyed, within the space of a single century two deeply entangled myths. On the one hand, the communist myth, scientist in the extreme and ruggedly materialistic in its practice, which stood (and fell) on the possibility of subordinating the demon of capitalist desire to the historical sovereignty of the State. And, on the other, the capitalist myth, individualistic in its genealogy and contractual in its social execution, which held out the possibility of maximizing human freedom by bringing the *object alive*, by, that is, creating a system of objects in which liberty would accrue to the physics of market exchanges. Like all myths which seek to solve the riddle of history, the myths of capitalism and communism suffer, in the end, the desolation of a purely *aleatory* fate: in all the socialist societies, the state acquires organicity; it actually comes alive in the political form of what Sartre has called "The Thing"—cynical ideology—and eats its political subjects; and, in the capitalist societies, the object comes alive in the consumer language of seduction—cynical power—and, like a radiating positivity, first eats space and time, and then consumes subjectivity itself. The historical myths of capitalism and communism as both suffering a common biological denouement: two big eating machines which require for their operation the radical depoliticization of the population, the softening up of the masses, that is, as a prerequisite to the libidinal feast of cynical power and cynical ideology. What Heidegger once prophecied would be the triumphant appearance of the dark language of "harvesting"—the will to exterminism—of the living energies of social and nonsocial nature as the primal of twentieth century politics.

The End(s) of History

In Modris Ekstein's *Rites of Spring*, it is recounted how during the trench warfare of World War I soldiers from both sides began on occasion to actually live in no man's land, that indefinite terrain which, belonging to no one, became a privileged imaginary country in opposition to the ruling empires of the war machine. When this was discovered, the opposing General Staffs, *both* German and British, immediately ordered the shelling of these troops, finding in their neutral presence an imminent threat to the sovereignty of the great political signifiers of the war machine.

This text consists of theorists of no man's land, occupants of the deterritorialized terrain of the intellectual imagination: standing midway between the epochal referents of power and ideology. While they have real theoretical differences, they commonly share the position of intellectual witnesses to the transformation of the *politics* of the rationalist eschatology at the end of the century. Their writings are like explosive blasts from the pent-up pressures of the weak points of the war machine: points of tension which are so unreconciled in politics and economy, that they find finally a theoretical purchase.

Ideological blasts, as in the case of the writings of Giddens, Habermas, Márkus, Baumann, Laclau and Lefort: theorisations written in the shadow of Marxism where the irreconcilability of democracy and state capitalism are put into question. Here, the political history of the twentieth century is rewritten by connecting anew the question of ideology to the reality of domination.

Power blasts, written with and against the theorisations of Jean Baudrillard, where the concern is not so much with the end(s) of history as with the final declaration of the end of history: the death of history, and of politics and society with it, as the question of ideology is sucked, like so much floating debris in the dark matter of political space, into the black hole of cynical power.

And finally, *culture* blasts–the final section on **Demon Politics**–where the epochal retheorisations of ideology and power are materialized in specific contestations with actually existing political culture. Here, the explosive energy of the theoretical imagination is poured into an examination of the ruling political questions: *ressentiment* as the basis of contemporary politics; the resurfacing of the Hobbesian calculation as the (fading) essence of American political experience; the materialization of Heidegger's "will to exterminism" as the dynamic language of liberalism today; and finally, the enucleation of women within a labyrinth of *signification*, which, just as Anthony Giddens predicted, reconnects the questions of ideology and domination.

More than a rereading of the central concepts of power, ideology and culture, the theorisations in this text have an epochal significance in representing the ways in which critical thinkers, writing at the *fin-de-millenium*, have chosen to represent the political history of the twentieth century. Here, we are confronted with three alternative histories of the contemporary century: one written under the sign of a revalorized theory of ideology; the second inscribed in the language of cynical power; and the third focussing directly on the problematic terrain of culture.

Indeed, it may well be said someday of that critical arc of neo-Marxist theorists, ranging from Giddens and Laclau to Habermas and Lefort, that, aside from sectional differences, their writings bring to a brilliant conclusion the myth of modernism, so integral to Marxian eschatology. Here, in a return to the original Marxian impulse to think ideology politically by reconnecting it to political economy, sometimes as "false consciousness" and at other times as the inscribed horizon of the law of productivist value, these theorisations repoliticize ideology by linking it to a searing analysis of the signifying practices and systemic requirements of state capitalism. Here, the Marxian project of "demystifying history" by reinverting the *camera obscura* is thought with such political intensity that the question of ideology itself is uprooted from its previous position as the transparent horizon of class domination, becoming now a critical agent in teasing out the dominations and dependencies of the system of capitalist political economy. Or, as Giddens says: "The forms of ideology are very often the modes in which signification is incorporated as part and parcel of what one does in daily life." Operating then within the parameters of the law of value, the theories of ideology represented here foreground the question of human freedom against the background of the mirror of political economy. And if they can so universally concur in the politics of democratic assent, that is because these are the last and best of all the enlightenment thinkers: intellectuals of the late twentieth century who seek to repair the broken connection of labor, reason and politics, so darkly prophecied in all of Marx's writing on the capitalist expropriation of the enlightenment dream. Rethinking ideology and domination, therefore, as a more elemental intellectual drama in which the great polarities of the dialectic of enlightenment are brought into violent collision, with the fate of democracy hanging in the balance.

It's just the opposite in the Baudrillardian scene, represented in this text by the debates on **Power and Seduction**. Here, the concept of ideology itself is put in question, as a postmodern optic is brought to bear on the death of all the modernist referential finalities. Not political economy, but a culture of signification; not the production machine, but the simulacra of consumption; not the law of value, but the *code*; not a class-driven logic of domination, but the "radical semiurgy" of the mediascape; not accumulation and the acquisitive impulse of capitalist desire, but disaccumulation and self-cancellation as the emblematic signs of seduction; and, most of all, not the "truth-referent" of ideology-critique, but the triumph of cynical power as the end of truth, and of the violent termination of history. Between, then, the neo-Marxist theorists represented in **Disappearing Ideology** and the postmodern theorists of **Power and Seduction**, there is a fundamental gap of discontinuity: a fateful point where the project of "demystifying history" under the lens of the *camera obscura* reverts into its opposite number—the writing of the disappearance of history into semiurgy under the sign of the *trompe-l'oeil*. Rejecting the critical theory of the state as itself a perspectival simulacra of the law of productivist value, the postmodern theorisation, represented most intensively by the "talisman" of Baudrillard, flips the derivative truth-value of ideology into the fatal sign which haunts it: cynical power. Here, it is argued that if there can be such an enthusiastic renewal today of the question of ideology and domination, maybe that is because ideology-critique has one last half-life as a moral reenergizer of a system of exchange-value which is dying, actually fading away, because of its lack of symbolic energy. Not ideology-critique, then, as a last barrier of democracy against a system of class domination, but as the moral rearmament of the "rationalist eschatology." A moral rearmament of the mirror of capitalism which is all the more effective because it is trapped in the illusion of political transgression: the illusionary belief that it is possible to overcome the limit experience of the rationalist eschatology by the recovery of the silenced moment of the "other." Which is to say, therefore, that between the modernist theorisation of **Disappearing Ideology** and the postmodern reflections of **Power and Seduction** there is a more fateful entanglement of the twentieth century mind on the question, not only of power and ideology, but of Nietzsche and Marx. An eloquent recounting of two opposing histories of the contemporary century: one skeptical and tragically hip but lacking a material basis in an ideologically specific analysis of the state; the other written within the parameters of the social, thoroughly entangled within the horizon of democracy versus domination, but shielded by its own reversion to nominalist epistemology from the postmodern insight of ideology as a *mise-en-scene* of the fatal destiny of cynical power.

Or maybe it's neither. Not the disenchanted universe of ideology and domination or the "reenchanted simulation" of the society of seduction, but the culture of **Demon Politics**. The culture, that is, where ideology under the sign of signification and power encoded by cynicism burn with such violent intensity that they actually take possession of subjectivity itself. A demonic culture, and a demonic politics too, which is led by Nietzsche's "ascetic priests" who work to alter the direction of *ressentiment*, and which is populated by a radically depolicitized mass, wavering between the sleep of "mechanical forgetting" and the sacrificial violence of revenge-seeking behavior. A deeply sacrificial culture which is bimodern to this extent: it exists midway between hyper-primitivism of emotions and hyper-rationalism of its controlling codes. And not a projective culture either, but one which traces a great arc of reversal: a reversion of the rationalist eschatology to its primal origins in myth; of ideology to its foundations in cynical truth; and of power to a sacrificial table of values, alternating the positions of predators and parasites.

Consequently, a third history of the twentieth century: one which does not contradict the reconnection of ideology and domination or the unmasking of cynical power, but accelerates them to such a point of violent intensity that they achieve escape velocity, revealing thereby politics at the *fin-de-millenium* as a historic wager between subjugated knowledge and cynical power.

The New World Order

If the debates among ideology (modernism), power (postmodernism) and sacrifice (bimodernism) can rehearse so well some of the main currents of critical thought in the contemporary century, that is probably because these theoretical perspectives have a purchase on the political imagination which is more projective than retrospective. Like an immense gravitational field swept into the dark vortex of the Year 2000, the theorisations of ideology, power and sacrifice retreat ahead of politics, denominating all the while the political architecture of the future. Not so much, then, a summary of key controversies in *fin-de-millenium* thought, but an early warning system of major transformations in international politics.

Maybe it is not so much Lenin in ruins now as the *world in ruins*. Not just the fall of the Berlin Wall as a fatal sign of the disintegration of Soviet empire, but as a talisman of the decline of American empire. The fatal loss, that is, with the unmasking of the myth of communist hegemony of the privileged object of sacrificial violence—the mimetic "Other"—which performed the honorific religious function of scapegoat for the burnout of the American mind.

But not for long. As a dazzling symbol of the triumph of alterity, a great magnetic shift of political fields takes place, with an instant mutation of East/West conflict to a new cold war of North against South. The Gulf War, that is, as a field of sacrificial violence for the violent regeneration of American politics, and for reaffirming faith in the equivalence of freedom and technology—the civil religion of America. What Habermas once described as the "glassy background ideology" of technology now mutates into the guiding principle of the vaunted "new world order:" George Bush's term for the coming to be of Hegel's universal and homogenous state under the hegemonic sign of the technological dynamo.

The Gulf War, therefore, as a grisly replay of the medieval crusades. A final war in which, as the French theorist Paul Virilio states in *Pure War*, there is a conjunction of the Holy War (of religious fundamentalists) and of the Just War (of the nuclear technicians).

A war which can be fought at the geographical meeting-point of the Tigris and Euphrates Rivers as if to emphasize that this is an epochal drama: the imminent reversal of the always projective logic of the West back to its primal origins in Mesopotamia. A religious war between Virilio's "dromocratic" war machine, the most intensive expression possible of the dream of the rationalist eschatology, and, in distorted form, the new "Other" of Arab nationalism. The world's first purely *designer* war: a promotional war machine which scripts in advance the whole metastasis of violence as an advertising campaign for the technological invincibility, and thus political necessity, of the "new world order."

The scene of a fatal decomposition in which all of the political tendencies from the past—ideology, power and sacrifice—rush towards their violent climax in purely inverted form: cynical ideology, cynical power, and cynical sacrifice. Consequently, the debates in *Ideology and Power in the Age of Lenin in Ruins* have, beyond their theoretical divisions, a broader literary significance as harbingers of the main contours of the nihilistic politics of the twenty first century. Third millenium politics, therefore, not as a time of cold seduction versus command socialism, but of a new world order which can be so deeply sacrificial because it is all about the harvesting of the energies of the social and the non-social universes by the "dromocratic" war machine. A time of the unmasking of ideology as domination, of power as a *trompe-l'oeil* of the cynical sign, and of sacrifice as mimetic violence against an "Other" which has only the *irreal and projected* existence of a frenzied political fantasy.

WHAT IS TO BE DONE[1]

Mark Lewis

The monuments and memorials with which large cities are adorned are... mnemic symbols...Not far from London Bridge you will find a towering and more modern column, which is simply known as 'The Monument'. It was designed as a memorial of the Great Fire, which broke out in that neighborhood in 1666 and destroyed a large part of the city ... [W]hat should we think of a Londoner who shed tears before the Monument that commemorates the reduction of his beloved metropolis to ashes although it has long since risen again in far greater brilliance? ... Yet every single hysteric and neurotic behaves like [this] unpractical Londoner. Not only do they remember painful experiences of the remote past, but they still cling to them emotionally; they cannot get free of the past and for its sake they neglect what is real and immediate.

Sigmund Freud
Five Lectures on Psychoanalysis

Cleric holding up cross, Bucharest, Romania, 1990

Cleric holding up cross to Lenin, Bucharest, Romania, 1990

Iconoclasm

It is a familiar image: The man of God raises his arms and in a series of highly symbolic gestures summons up the force and truth of The Father. It is a summoning up which will aid in the reparation or atonement of a public for its earthly sins and, more specifically, the sacrileges which, in moments of madness and hallucinatory blindness, that public has inflicted on the very image of God. Here, then, is just such a moment.

He lifts his hand, and, in a gesture somewhat denuded of seriousness by its appropriation within the Dracula film genre, holds up a cross, a defiant and defensive gesture against something which offends. But this gesture... against what? ... Against whom? The frame widens, revealing that the danger to which all these visual histrionics are addressed is, in fact, a work of art, a bronze metal statue that, until recently, occupied Piatia Scinteli in the center of Bucharest, Romania. It appears that our man of God is gesturing atop the giant granite plinth which only moments before, had been the base upon which Vladimir Ilich Lenin (an Antichrist as it turns out) had stood. Looking out and down upon the 'publics' of Bucharest, Lenin's monumentality was a sign of the very power of inscription, of the power of the symbolic in the production of political economies. I have spoken of Lenin's removal, but it is more properly, perhaps, *a certain image* that is being removed, an image in the name of which the cleric has been battling, drawing upon his own substantial register of theological iconic inscriptions. And in the context of thinking about the nature of "the public", it is worth repeating that what the cleric wishes us to avert our gaze from is a work of art, a work of art made from a certain metal—bronze—and one that figuratively depicts and represents in rather complex configurations, a man, a political leader, an ideology, a liberation, a tyranny and, very significantly, an absence.

This image of the unceremonious removal of a statue that depicts Lenin is a familiar one. All over Eastern Europe and the Soviet Union today, publics, either spontaneously or under orders, are removing images of Lenin from public view.[2] They are smashing and melting down his figure or simply taking it to a place where it may not be seen, except by appointment. In Bucharest an appointment can be made by those with an intention to purchase the said statue of Lenin: twelve tons of Bronze that the mayor, Dan Predescu, hopes will find a home in the 'West', and bring desperately needed hard currency to his city's treasury.[3] If I have taken up that suggestion, made such an appointment with Mayor Predescu, it is not simply to find an ironic humor in the idea that we might place Lenin upright again, here in the West. Rather it is to take advantage of a very particular situation, one which repeats a tradition that goes back at least as far as the French Revolution, and which allows us to think a little about the status and changing meanings of so called public works of art. These are works which, as I have argued elsewhere, inevitably perform the function of simultaneously marking out and policing the public shere.[4]

By placing the statue of Lenin in Oxford (see footnote #1), not only am I responding directly to Mayor Predescu's suggestion but, in the spirit of enstrangement that his cunning proposal would seem to include, I am also asking that we consider the general authoritative presence of public monuments and official public art—consider, that is, questions of permanence, commemoration and visibility.

The move is simple but also a little noisy. The statue that in one sense, communicates the presence of an 'alien' (a Russian) and an alien idea (Communism), looks authoritative in an absurd sort of way. It is perhaps in the disturbing space that the statue's displacement opens up, that we might begin to see—as if for the first time and in the absence of any indigenous revolution—works that have performed similar contradictory projects here in England, here in what Dan Predescu calls the West.

I have mentioned revolution, or at least the absence of one in England. I have done so because as a motif it is crucial to my discussion of public art, specifically with regard to the latter's removal, destruction and displacement. Revolutions, rebellions, uprisings, even terrorisms: each gives to public works a particular *visibility*, one that as Robert Musil has noted, is often denied them at other times.

> The most striking feature of monuments is that you do not notice them. There is nothing in the world as invisible as monuments. Like a drop of water on an oil-skin, attention runs down them without stopping for a moment...We cannot say that we do not notice them; we should say that they de-notice us, they withdraw from our senses. [5]

If Musil is certain that to produce a public monument of a 'great person' is to consign that person to oblivion, he perhaps under-estimates the continued efficacy of the monument in its ability to be *always more and less* than the figure which it ostensibly represents. The monument's invisibility is a sign of a silent interpellation, of a subtle but nevertheless pervasive marking-out of the public realm according to the logic of certain statist concerns. After all, is it not always the state which installs or permits the installation of 'public' works of art? If monuments remain silent, they only "de-notice us" insofar as they become part of the architectonic and semantic landscape. As Freud points out in his *Five Lectures on Psychoanalysis*, such a landscape will continue to be a determinant producer of identification and memory. [6]

When there is a crisis in the realm of the social—a revolution or political uprising—then the symbolic realm, of which public art is part becomes the subject of a certain re-evaluation. While we might indeed hesitate before concluding that the removal and destruction of 'hated' monuments is the only possible critical re-evaluation of the semiotics of public statuary, we need to acknowledge that the *visibility* which inaugurates such an attack is a prerequisite for any attempt to re-interpret and intervene within this area of the symbolic realm. Clearly, the impulse to attack and destroy public works is part of a general attack on the continued presence of the signs of an *ancien regime*. It is confirmation also that in moments of 'madness', publics will treat monuments and public works of art as if they were the actual leaders themselves, as if bronze effigies were literal extensions of Kings' bodies. In a report from 1871 on the destruction of the Vendome Column, for instance, *The London Illustrated News* gave this account of what happened after the column was felled:

> Three orators of the commune stood at different points in the ruin and made speeches. They treated the statue [of Napoleon] as the Emperor itself, spitting on his face, while members of the national guard hit his nose with rifles. [7] (My emphasis)

The Hungarian crowds in Budapest in 1956, may have felt that they were literally attacking Stalin himself as they smashed a statue of him, each crack of the hammer on metal and stone at once producing a delicious and murderous

3

vicarious pleasure. Without wishing to subtract from what was the eruption of a popular will by some publics, I would like to remark that at some level, such a theological belief in *the image*, in its divinity, confirms the ideology of the "King's Two Bodies."[8] This ideology has enabled despots to represent themselves as being at one with their image, an image that marks the King's history as at once secular and spiritual, of the earth and of the eternal. For the King or Emperor, his image is not so much a representation, but constitutes his very public embodiment. *The image is his power.* To deface his image is to deface him; a knock with a hammer is in some sense part of the same economy which incites the believer who would rather genuflect. Up to a point perhaps. This anyway is the paradoxical trap which the Romanian cleric unwittingly finds himself in: He holds up his cross, not to Lenin himself, but to an image which threatens to seriously undermine his own relationship to "the image", a relationship that pivots around the cleric's right to *interpret* images and to judge their authenticity (according to the laws of God). Ultimately we might conclude that what offends the cleric in Bucharest, is not so much that the statue of Lenin represents an anti-Christian current that threatens the church's survival (which, of course, in some sense it does), but rather that Lenin, like any "two bodied" ruler or King who has become synonymous with his own image, threatens to disrupt the very economy of the image which guides the church's theological belief in authenticity. For if Lenin *is* his image, then this can only de-value the equivalence which God himself is supposed to enjoy with *His image*.

This may seem a rather peripheral point, insofar as it is not necessarily clerics who are overseeing the removal of works of public art today, but rather angry and rebellious publics who quite rightly desire to have a say (albeit sometimes through simple acts of negation) in the semiotics of "their" public space. In so far as they are acting on that desire, we could tentatively say that the attempts to remove and smash certain works of art, are as much a part of the project of a public art as the discrete objects themselves. Although we may question the necessity, or progressiveness of a 'vandalism' which destroys works that during moments of social and political crisis may already be in the process of having their meanings transformed, these destructive acts are inscribed within the works as a potential from the moment that they are commissioned and publicly installed. The works' installation and destruction share the same economy. What falls outside that economy and disrupts it, are unforeseen appropriations of public art works immediately following the demise of the very power that these works were meant to re-present. Stalin's boots, remained as the container for the Hungarian flag in 1956; In Leningrad in 1918, the inscriptions on many statues were altered to reflect the revolutionary moment. That such appropriations and semiotic disruptions can occur, suggests that there is more than one possible future for the public work of art "after the fall" of the *ancien regime*.

The reason for my questioning the status of a gesture of pure negation of the image, is simply to try and understand the extent to which such an iconoclasm can unwittingly, and against its own best intentions, display an immense respect for the image. And further, how through an act of destruction, the power of the image, the power of public statuary to control and define the public realm may

4

paradoxically be confirmed. Two forms of negation need to be distinguished, two different orchestrations, if you like, of a mass iconoclasm with respect to the revolutionary and post-revolutionary moment. On the one hand, are seemingly spontaneous actions of various publics as they vent their anger and frustration on the visible signs of power of an *ancien regime*. Stalin's desecration in Budapest can be understood in this context, as can the defacement of the statue of Dzhirzhinsky by students in Warsaw.[9] On the other hand, are the planned removals of the art and images of the old political regime, where "revolutionary" governments order their destruction. In Poland today, the Solidarity government has been overseeing such a program of removal and destruction The Lenin statue in Romania was also removed by state order.

We can speculate that the iconoclasm of art's orderly removal embodies more of a respect for the image than does a public's spontaneous destruction. An inevitable consequence of such a respect might be the erection of yet more permanent statues and monuments, their 'contents' differing perhaps, but their formal precision remaining much the same. And is not the fate of such careful and 'thoughtless' formal precision, precisely the continuity of public art's terror, its "Architecture of Fear"? This may be a little pessimistic, perhaps, but let us watch the re-organization of Poland, for instance, to see if in fact today's leaders in the fight against Communism do not eventually rest their bulks, bronze cast on granite.

The question of respect (for the image) and how it is invested very differently in the two forms of removal (as well as destruction/modification) that I have proposed, leads very directly to a critical consideration of the various arguments that are often made for the retention and conservation of public monuments and other works of art. These are arguments that are predicated on an assumption that a work's meaning can change—that the semantic charge of a work from the past will be different once it has been re-appraised and displaced within the symbolic organization of the post-revolutionary state. But how is that re-appraisal and displacement accomplished? It is, as I suggested above, primarily because that possibility is already contained within the work from the start, because the work will never be the simple representation of its subject, no matter how important or trivial the latter may be.

The axis of visibility-invisibility is the determinant field across which the public work of art exacts its different meanings. In this respect, it is extremely similar to the process Freud described and named fetishism. Like the fetish, the public work of art serves (at least) two ends, the one ultimately undermining the other. The monument covers up crimes against the public in so far as it is able to temporary 'smother' the possibility of remembering specific histories in terms of the violence that engendered them; it instead commemorates a history or event in terms of a pernicious heroism or nationalism. But at the same time, the monument exists as a perpetual marker, a reminder of those very crimes. It waves a red flag, so to speak, on the site of its repressions. And when the symbolic order is thrown into crisis—revolution or terrorism—the public monument's semantic charge shifts and the work becomes less heroic in form but rather begins to take on the characteristics of a scar—literally a *permanent monument* to the original crime(s). This may be as good a reason as any for the retention of at least some works—perhaps worked on, perhaps displaced somewhat after the demise of the regimes responsible for their erection. That is the argument, for instance, of Samir Al-Khalil, in his discussion of the possible future of the *Victory Monument* in Baghdad after Saddam Hussein is overthrown or dies.[10]

Georges Bataille had much to say about this idea of the repression of social life by monuments. He wrote more specifically about architecture, but in the following quote, we can also detect the figure of the stone or bronze statue: standing upright and phallic, pretending to guard the public space when it in actual fact, it both constitutes that space and simultaneously demands that we forget by what means the latter's publicity is obtained.

> The ideal soul of society, that which has the authority to command and prohibit, is expressed in architectural compositions properly speaking. Great monuments are erected like dikes, opposing the logic and majesty of authority against all disturbing elements...It is obvious in fact, that social monuments inspire social prudence and even real fear. The taking of the Bastille is symbolic of this state of things: it is hard to explain this crowd movement other than by the animosity of the people against the monuments that are their real masters. [11]

A public monument which like architecture is to some extent the image of the social order, guarantees, even imposes that very order. Far from expressing the soul of society, monuments then, to paraphrase Denis Hollier, smother society, stop it from breathing.

Revolution

'Revolutionary' and immediately 'post-revolutionary' societies have been forced to deal with the representations of its pre-revolutionary history articulated through public art. In France, there were fierce debates over what was to happen to the public works of the Royalist regime following the revolution of 1789. Attempts were made to determine to what extent particular monuments *represented* the ideology of the past, and to therefore apportion a punishment commensurate with the degree of a work's culpability. Works of art were forced to stand trial. As was the case with all other mock trials in post-revolutionary France during the period of 'the terror', the works were often executed, destroyed before they had a chance to account for themselves.

Some revolutionaries argued that the old monuments and other works of art should be used as the building materials for new 'revolutionary' works. And this indeed was the idea that originally motivated the looting and destruction of the Royal Tombs at St. Denis when it was agreed that all the works contained there should be used in the construction of a symbolic mountain in honor of Marat and Le Peletier. Other projects of this nature involved saving some works, or at least parts of them, so that their recognizable form could be reintegrated within new allegorical projects. J.P.B. Le Brun, for instance, argued that Angier's statues of Louis III, his wife and son, should be saved so that they could be overturned at

6

the feet of David's project for *The Colossus of the People Sovereign*. He also suggested that the left foot of the statue of Louis IV from the place Vendome be saved in order to "Conserve the proportions of these monuments, which, when placed beside the French People, will show the smallness of the monuments to those that they regarded as the greatest."[12]

Others, arguing against the continued existence in any form, of any traces of the old art and public monuments and participated in an orgy of destruction, knocking down and breaking every work that offended their revolutionary sensibilities. In this rampage, they were supported by successive legislatures and officials. A Parisian police officer of the time noted that he had heard: "Complaints on all sides that the eyes of patriots were offended by the different monuments built by despotism in the time of slavery, monuments that should certainly not exist under the reign of liberty and equality."[13]

When it was detailed in the legislative assembly that the people were destroying bronze statues of Henry IV, Louis XII, Louis XIV and Louis XV, the assembly simply encouraged these actions by declaring that "It is the manifest will of the people that no monument continue to exist that recalls the reign of tyranny...the statues in public squares in Paris will be taken away and statues in honor of liberty will replace them".[14]

Into this mire of debate and unpredictable action stepped the Abbe Gregoire. Anthony Vidler has presented Gregoire's project of redeeming and saving works. In the brief summary that follows I have borrowed from Vidler's published texts on this subject.

Gregoire was a supporter of the revolution but one who argued for the conservation of old works of art and public monuments, on the grounds that they were: "transforming the symbols of oppression into permanent reminders of tyranny, forcing them to become a kind of permanent pillory".[15] By using a rhetoric that he knew would be warmly received by the revolutionary assembly, Gregoire began to formulate a notion of what he called "cultural vandalism", a kind of thoughtless and destructive behavior that was to be understood as distinct from, even contrary to correct or corrective revolutionary behavior. As Vidler points out, it is certainly a paradox that the cultural vandalism of the revolution's early years was also accompanied by an emerging sensibility towards a national patrimony embodied in historical and artistic monuments. Indeed, many have noted that for the museum to really begin to exist, it *needed* 'vandalism': the museum fed off the fragments left behind by, and saved from, cultural vandalism.

If Gregoire was opening up an entirely new discourse (on cultural vandalism and on the necessity of museums to protect against the former), his contribution to the discussion concerning the necessity of conserving works of the *ancien regime* was also part of his attempt to evince a recognition of the possible separation of the symbolic and political realms. If he argued that the old statues, for instance, could be used pedagogically—albeit by negative example—he did so primarily in order to save the objects themselves, objects that he might have believed could eventually be turned away from their tyrannical histories. That is to say, he believed that once these objects were recognized as no longer marking out, no longer smothering a public history, they might then take their place in a museum of art and antiquity. Such a museum could serve, simultaneously, the nation's need for nationalism, didacticism and moral improvement. Gregoire was beginning to articulate a sense of the discontinuity which overdetermines the symbolic realm and how that discontinuity would always already be part of any monument's history. It is a discontinuity that ultimately inscribes within the work an built-in obsolescence; and it is this built-in obsolescence which will finally allow the work to be rescued by a museum where it will take its place in the national history of a country, its patrimony of permanence.

I have strayed a long way from Lenin in order to articulate some of the contradictory investments in the historical idea of public art, of an art that is apparently more democratic, more of the people than any other. But as should be clear by now, I am suggesting that not only is this very far from the truth[16]— that public art often imposes, subjects, terrorizes—but that a sense of public art's 'opposite' —the 'private' works of the gallery, etc.—emerges in part through attempts to save public works from the anger of revolutionary publics. All of this to say that we need to be very cautious before we assign to a type of work a positive or negative epithet, simply on the grounds of its actual geographical emplacement. Indeed, some works, once 'publicly' located and then placed within the contextual confines of a museum might find themselves, in their latter history, to be less like, recalling Bataille, "dikes, opposing the logic and majesty of authority against all disturbing elements," and more truly public (in the literal sense of the word) than before. Notwithstanding this problem of posing the question of a so-called progressive public art, I think that it is possible to suggest other paradigms, other ways of conceptualizing public art And I can propose one of these now, through a return to my initial discussion of Lenin himself.

V.I. Lenin

All over Eastern Europe, every day for some months, cities have been oversee-ing the removal of busts, statues, bas reliefs and pictures of Lenin. These are images that are hated by many, hated because they are understood and perceived as synecdoches for equally despised communist regimes. But, of course, Lenin was always much more than this simple representation. And there is indeed some sense of the idea of Leninism which survives today, survives despite the whole-sale removal of his public effigies, survives the very fact that these monuments were ever built in the first place. Perhaps the removal of these massive monu-ments is not totally incommensurate with some of the original ideas of Lenin, par-ticularly those ideas he had about a revolutionary public art. This is not to say that I think that the monuments should necessarily be removed, destroyed or displaced (on this matter I can confess only to the most profound ambivalence), but what I want to recognize is that the Lenin of 1917-1918, the Lenin of "On the Monuments of the Republic"[17] might never have approved of the original erection of the bronze statues, in Bucharest or elsewhere. Insofar as this idea(lism) of Lenin can be said to be remembered today, I want to briefly examine

Lenin's relationship to the question of public art as it emerged during the immediate months after the October Revolution.

By the time of the 1917 revolution, Lenin had already insisted that art under socialism should no longer serve the elite of society, "those 10,000 suffering from boredom and obesity; it will rather serve the 10's of millions of labouring people, the flower of the country, its future".[18] In order to further this aim, Lenin proposed what he called a *Monumental Propaganda*. This was to be a so-called "people's" art, one that would become part of everyday life, assisting in the ideological shaping of a new revolutionary mass consciousness. Lenin argued that this Monumental Propaganda should be produced through the posing and installation of slogans and other "quickly executed forms." Even more important to Lenin were "the statues—be they bust or bas reliefs of figures and groups."[19] The statues were *not* to be made of marble, bronze or granite, but on the contrary, were to be extremely modest in their production, and should take advantage of cheap and readily available materials such as plaster. Lenin felt that these works should react to the moment, that their objective was always to instruct within the context of particular celebrations. Above all, wrote Lenin, "Let everything be temporary"[20]. And with these words addressed to Lunacharsky, Lenin announced the beginning of a massive project (much of it centered around May Day celebrations) to install dozens of plaster statues and busts, each one celebrating a revolutionary figure or event. Very few of these works survived more than a few months, and almost none remain in any form today, as Lenin and the artists involved must have anticipated. Some of the works were crudely executed, others crudely conceptualized, while others were extremely radical insofar as they challenged the whole notion of *permanence* with regards to public monuments and statuary. Particularly interesting is Nikolai Kolli's *The Red Wedge Cleaving the White Block* (1918). In this work Kolli seems to parody and question the whole historical project of the permanent public monument, a monument that relies on the height and unassailability of a stone plinth from which it towers over the publics that move within its domain. The plinth is also the site of the official inscription, of the command to respect of King's and Dictators. In plaster form, what Kolli is splitting open, is the very support system of all monuments. It seems to suggest the absurdity, within the revolutionary context, of erecting yet another bronze statue on the physical supports of historically inscribed tyranny—the plinths that have born the weight of cold terror.

This work by Kolli was produced within the context of other works by artists which consisted in temporary modifications and additions to existing statues and monuments. And if the revolution did produce its fair share of "cultural vandalism," it is also the case that many at the time thought that this exercise of destruction was not only unnecessary, but actually counter-revolutionary.[21] As the artist Alexander Blok put it at the time: "Even while destroying we are still the slaves of our former world: the violation of tradition itself is part of the same tradition."[22]

Not quite the Abbe Gregoire, and perhaps not sharing his archivist's imperative for conservation, but nevertheless, Blok's demand, his perception is part and parcel of a more complex and interesting approach to the art of the past. Moreover, it is an approach which I believe is not at all contrary to Lenin's own desire that contemporary public works be temporary.

Military Metal

Many of our monuments and public works of art are made from metal. Metal is cold to touch. This is a metaphor that on closer inspection constantly envelops the description of leaders, now bronze cast or engraved in metal, unimpeachable in their authority. It is a metaphor that quite literally formalizes the close association of metal figures with the cold terror they can always summon up. The text of terror, its cold economy is embodied, figured in the surplus of the king's image. Which is to say, we do not need to see it in order to see it. Metal will always remind us of this absence. Here is Pascal:

> The custom of seeing kings accompanied by guards, drums, officers and all those things that bend the machine toward respect and terror causes their face to imprint on their subjects respect and terror, even when they appear by themselves, because one does not separate in thought the persons from their retinues with which they are ordinarily seen.[23]

Not only does metal statuary have metaphoric resonances with terror which allow us to recall unwittingly the invisible retinues of power, but in the very production of bronze figures—their forging and moulding—there is an inextricable link with the very economy of the military machine. Traditionally, bronze is the material of guns and canons, and we should not be the least bit surprised that the latter have often been made by melting down up-rooted and destroyed public statues.[24] Guns can be made from melted statuary, but, equally public statuary can be produced from melted guns. The Vendome Column, erected by Napoleon to commemorate the French victory at Austerlitz[25], was covered with 425 bronze plaques moulded in bas relief which displayed some of the incidents of the Austrian campaign. The bronze, which weighed close to two million pounds, was obtained by melting down 1200 captured Austrian canons. In 1871 the column was destroyed in an uprising, and while the masonry was quickly broken up and taken away by onlookers as souvenirs, the national guard kept a protective eye on the bronze plaques—plaques which, of course, would be extremely valuable if and when they were returned to their military form.

I would like to think of Lenin's demand for temporariness, his proscription on the use of bronze, as in some sense, an intervention within this economy of military terror. Plaster will only crumble and therefore prove useless in the manufacture of instruments of war (a crucial exigency, one imagines, for a country surrounded by hostile forces just ready to turn any existing metal against the revolution, and in this context, Kolli's work would seem to have a particularly materialist resonance). Its use in the public sphere recalls the military economy of statuary at the same time as it disrupts it. It asks us to think less about the permanence of the structure—its apparent right to exist forever—and rather more about any particular work's contingent meaning, how for instance that work imposes itself in a very contradictory way. After all, as I suggested earlier, permanent monuments are often born of terror and force—they are literally imposed, and occupy spaces like an invading army—and it is not the least bit surprising, therefore, that their eventual demise should reduplicate that terror, both in the act of destruction itself and in the re-cycling of the works into yet further instruments for subjection.

There are many other examples of plaster monuments being used to address the question of military terror. Perhaps the most famous one in recent years was the Liberty Statue erected in Tianenmin Square in China. Students created not only a symbol that in its temporariness called attention to the very spontaneous and changing nature of their revolution, but they also made an ironic and critical commentary on the tradition of the public monument itself. It was, recalling Lenin, 'modest' and 'quickly executed', and importantly it also appeared to be from the wrong tradition—'statues of liberty' being so closely associated with a hostile power. Indeed, when the army stormed the square, one of the first things it did was to smash the statue. But, as it turns out the statue's reference was not so 'alien' after all. Ironically, the Red Guards had some twenty years earlier done precisely the same thing when a group of them attacked the Yellow Flower Cemetery in Canton. In the Cemetery were the tombs of the 72 martyrs of the Republic of China who were killed in the overthrow of the Ching dynasty in 1911. A large monument there had inscribed the words "liberty, equality and universal love." Nearby, there was also a statue of the Goddess of Liberty. Both the statue and the monument were violently destroyed by the guards who could not understand that liberty was not a concept born of capitalism.[26] Perhaps the plaster recall at Tienenmin Square of that earlier moment of destruction was unintentional, even largely unnoticed. However, contextualising it historically might help undermine any easy appropriation of the students' statue by the forces on the right, who are equally unable to understand that liberty is not a concept born of capitalism.[27]

Impermanence

I have strayed a long way from Bucharest, and I have done so in order to contextualise the problem of public art which is foregrounded with the removal of the statue of Lenin. I have only been able to very schematically outline some of the more obvious semantic and ideological investments in the art of public monuments, but it is these investments which I believe public art today must both examine and problematise. Perhaps a truly public art would be one that allowed different publics to make their (temporary) marks on what Bataille has called the fascist organization of public life. These works might then attempt to give air to what the statist installations have worked so hard and effectively to smother. The paradox is that as soon as these works become permanent, they tend to become the very objects which they were intended to intervene against. This is perhaps why we need to re-invent each work, each public, in order to

11

Nikolai Kolli: The Red Wedge Cleaving the White Block (1918)

make the art answerable to successive publics. This re-invention though, would ask of us something both more ambitious and subtle than the simple negation that destruction implies.

The statues and other public monuments which until very recently had occupied the streets and civic squares of Eastern Europe, were the remainders of a project which had defied Lenin's own understanding of public art. "Let everything be temporary," he demanded. Yet it took the citizens of Bucharest some thirty years before they had the right to remove the clumsy bronze statue of Lenin which had imposed itself upon the city and its publics.[28]

Against this motif of permanence and metal, of coldness and terror, I would argue that it might be more useful, at least for the moment, to take up Lenin's demand for temporariness. While I recognize that this might seem to consign contemporary radical work to oblivion (as 'historical' public works continued to exist under the guise of invisibility), I do not believe that this is necessarily cause for concern. On the one hand, questions of permanence and durability can never really be part of a radical project. For an ambition of permanency would always fail to recognize the very mutability and entirely arbitrary constitution of art's publics. Public art is literally an art creating a public, an art creating society – one that may or may not be commensurate with any real body of people in a real time or place. On the other hand, the work of research, historiography and connoisseurship will continue nevertheless: there are records, photographs, texts, witness accounts, sometimes even the actual objects. As the early street art of the Russian Revolution demonstrates: permanent bronze works they may not be but the record of their interventions, what Gregoire might have called their inevitable didactic presence, lives on.

LENIN IN RUINS

In the spirit of this observation I want to take one last look at this picture of Lenin being removed, an image which stands, I suppose, as a record of a public art project that has now entered a different (perhaps terminal?) stage in its history. When I first saw this image, I was struck with a certain sadness, for it seemed to say something about the impossibility of alternative forms of organization, the impossibility of finding a way to think of the importance of both Lenin and how some of his ideas might have been represented differently. For after all, much was made of the statue's removal in the West, and the event was used to dramatic effect as a *denouement* to the history of Communism.[29] There was, however, something about this picture which made me recall another image. The effigy of Lenin being removed by a crane bore a strong formal resemblance to the drawing by El Lissitzky entitled *A Design for a Rostrum for Lenin* (1920-24). Lissitzky's image would seem to be a reminder of the original radical impulses that motivated a certain idea of public art, an idea which I have tried to associate with the name of Lenin, but it could also stand as a kind of portention of the inevitable metal work to come.

Coda

There are two important areas which are integral to any discussion on the idea of public art and which I have hardly even touched upon in this paper. Firstly, there is, of course, the question of difference as it is obtained through the performative function of the works themselves. Literally, there are the typical divisions of labour which organize the contents of works and their locations. Sexuality and race are crucial to an understanding of these ideological divisions of labour. For instance, whether a statue is of a man or a woman, whether that sexed figure bears a name and a history or whether it is simply 'generic' are considerations of some importance. Similarly, a colonial history of Europe, for instance, could be traced simply through a mapping of where public monuments were placed and how and when they were removed. In this paper I have been unable to include any detailed discussion of these crucial differences simply because of what I felt to be the necessity to respond directly to a particular historical and political event. I do examine the question of sexual and colonial difference with respect to public art and public monuments in a forthcoming paper entitled *Public Dreams and Public Wounds*

The second area that needs to be dealt with is the question of the representation of the public work and its allegorical future. For if in this paper I have argued that works of art have become the subjects of a deep rage and anger and have therefore been attacked and often destroyed, it is also the case that these attacks have become the subjects of works of art themselves. Not only are there real events depicted (such as the felling of the Vendome Column), but there is a whole genre of works which have either anticipated, incited or simply provided the allegorical background for this type of semiotic disturbance of the public space.

Statue of Lenin being removed from Bucharest (1990)
Photo: Mark Lewis

ПРОЛЕТАРИИ

El Lissitzky: A Design for a Rostrum for Lenin (1920-24)
Photo: Mark Lewis

Notes

1. This paper is based on a talk given for the symposium *Art Creating Society* organized by Stephen Willats at The Museum of Modern Art, Oxford England in June 1990. For the exhibition that accompanied this symposium, I installed in the streets of Oxford a 1/3 scale plaster model of the statue of Lenin that was recently removed from Bucharest, Romania. Thanks to Jeff Brandt for research and building assistance. A statue of Lenin was also installed near the parliament buildings in Quebec City in November 1990. Similar statues will be installed publicly in Montreal and Toronto in 1991.

2. Other countries are also taking part in this re-organization of their public art. For instance, South Yemen which recently merged with North Yemen, has undertaken to remove all its Lenins by the end of the year.

3. This information was ascertained during a phone call to the Mayor's office in May of this year.

4. See my "Technologies of Public Art," *Vanguard* Volume 16, No. 5 (Vancouver, November 1987). Also "The Public Imaginary," by Mark Lewis, Janine Marchessault and Andrew Payne, *Parachute* 48 (Montreal, October 1987) and my "Photography, Democracy and the Public Body," *Parachute* 55 (Montreal, August 1989).

5. Robert Musil, as quoted by Marina Warner in her book *Monuments and Maidens* (London: Picador, 1987).

6. Sigmund Freud, *Five Lectures on Psychoanalysis*, New York: W.W. Norton.

7. *The Illustrated London News* (May 27, 1871).

8. E. H. Kantorowicz, *The King's Two Bodies* (Princeton: Princeton University Press, 1957). Also for an interesting critique as well as complementary text see Louis Marin, *Portrait of the King* (London: Macmillan Press, 1988).

9. Dzhirzhinsky, a Polish citizen who was the founder of the Soviet secret police, was monumentalised in metal in what used to be called Dzhirzhinsky Square (Now called Bank Square). In a celebrated incident, students climbed up the statue and painted its hands red. The Government later ordered the removal of the statue.

10. The Victory Monument in Baghdad consists of a pair of sixty foot arms which hold two swords that cross over Victory Square some 140 feet in the air. The arms are bronze cast, from the actual arms of President Saddam Hussein. Hussein's fists emerge from two heaps of helmets, each helmet from a dead Iranian soldier, with bullet holes that are stained with the blood of exploding heads. Samir al-Khalil has suggested that the monument be retained so that it can stand as a reminder of the fear and tyranny brought on by the megalomania of Hussein. al-Khalil reminds us that the West were far too hasty in their destruction of fascist public art after the fall of the 3rd Reich. See Samir Al Khalil's *Rear Window: The Architecture of Fear*, a documentary for Channel 4 Television (England); produced by Tariq Ali for Bandung Productions Ltd.

11. Georges Bataille, "Architecture," *Documents*, no.2, May 1929 (OC 1:171). As quoted in Denis Hollier, *Against Architecture; The Writings of Georges Bataille* (Cambridge: MIT Press, 1989) After quoting this passage from Bataille, Hollier suggests that we only have to look at contemporary 'government ideas' on monumentality to realize that Bataille was not 'jumping to conclusions.' Hollier finds this example in Le Monde in May 1973 from the then Minister of Cultural Affairs, Maurice Druon:

    I am convinced that one of the reasons for what we certainly must call urban decadence results from the absence in our cities of temples, palaces, statues, or anything that represents the superior facilities of human beings: faith, thought and will. An urban civilization's vitality is measured perhaps by the prestigious monuments it is capable of erecting.

12. See Claudette Houlde (editor), *Images of the French Revolution*, (Quebec: Musee Du Quebec, 1989).

13. Daniel Hermant, "Destructions et vandalisme pendant la Revolution francaise," *Annales E.S.C.*, 33 (1978), Quoted in Anthony Vidler, "Monuments Parlants", *Art and Text* 33 (Melbourne, Winter 1989).

14. *Images of the French Revolution* (ibid)

15. See Anthony Vidler, "Monuments Parlants: Gregoire, Lenoire and the Signs of History", *Art and Text* 33 (Melbourne, Winter 1989). And also Anthony Vidler, *The Writing of the Walls: Architectural Theory in the Late Enlightenment* (Princeton: Princeton Architectural Press, 1987).

16. The 'idea' of public art is currently enjoying a lot of attention by art curators and museums. Usually, their idea of being public means literally placing the work 'out on the street.' Not only is this a very narrow understanding of what forms publicity can take, but by circumventing any critical discussion of the role of art in creating a public and its historical projects in this regard, such a move often unwittingly re-duplicates the very divisions of labour and systems of control, etc., that it ostensibly sets out to challenge and undermine. For more discussion on this matter see my "The Technologies of Public Art" (ibid).

17. V.I. Lenin, "On the Monuments of the Republic" (April 12, 1918), *On Literature and Art* (Moscow: Progress Publishers, 1967)

18. V.I. Lenin, *Complete Collected Works*, V.12

19. A.V. Lunacharsky, "Lenin o Monumentalanoi propogande", *Lenin i izobrazitelnoe iskusstvo* (Moscow: 1977), quoted in Vladimir Tolstoy, "Art Born of the October Revolution", *Street Art of the Revolution* (London: Thames and Hudson, 1990)

20. A.V. Lunacharsky (ibid)

21. In the essay "On the Monuments of the Republic", Lenin does in fact 'order' that those "monuments erected in honor of tsars and their minions and which have no historical or artistic value are to be removed from the squares and streets and stored up or used for utilitarian purposes." He did however order that such a program of adjudication and removal should be done under the auspices of a special commission made up of the People's Commissars for Education and Property of the Republic and the chief of the Fine Arts department of the Commissariat for Education. together they were to work with the Art Collegium of Moscow and Petrograd. This does suggest that Lenin was sympathetic to the idea that politicians alone would be unable to decide which works were of `merit', etc., and that he felt it necessary for 'experts' to be consulted. Despite, for example, the fact that many hundreds of religious icons were destroyed, it is still the case that Lenin's approach to the art of the past was significantly more sophisticated than either the legislators of the French Revolution and many of the current 'post-communist' governments in eastern Europe. An exception would seem to be the Czech government of Havel, who recently suggested that many of the socialist realist monuments should be placed, undamaged in a forest so that 'nature' would grow around and over them.

22. Block's sensibility has, by and large, been lacking in present day Eastern Europe. However, there have been exceptions. For instance, there is a group in eastern Germany called "The Monuments of the DDR Committee" who have been arguing that none of the old public works should be torn down or destroyed precipitously. They have insisted that there be generous public consultation and that the artists of the works (if still alive)

should be included in any discussion concerning the future fate of the works.

23. Blaise Pascal, "Les Provinciales" in *Oeuvres* (Paris: Gallimard, 1950). Quoted in Louis Marin, *Portrait of the King* (London: Macmillan Press, 1988).

24. Invading armies as well as revolutionary armies have historically used the metal from statuary to help in the production of weapons. When the Germans were invading the Soviet Union, they actually melted down statues of the 'Czar and his minions' that still remained in order to help in the manufacture of guns for the campaign.

25. Interestingly enough, the Column at Vendome was built on the spot where a statue to Louis the IV had been destroyed by the revolutionaries in 1792. The original statue of Napoleon was placed on top of the column in 1810. In 1814, the Bourbons were restored and the statue was taken down. Twenty or thirty years later, under King Louis Phillipe, another statue of Napoleon was placed there, this time representing the Emperor standing on a heap of cannon balls. Napoleon III had this statue removed and instead replaced it with a reproduction of the original statue of Napoleon in Roman costume and crowned with a laurel wreath.

26. As reported in the *South China Morning Post* (August 31, 1966).

27. As many have pointed out, but seldom reported in the Western Media, as the tanks entered the square, the students stood in front of their 'statue' and sang the Socialist International. For a brief moment, then the Statue of Liberty became something else, its meaning in the context of socialist students who had built a replica of it, was transformed. You might say that its meaning was rescued from its perversion within the American market phenomenon. As Lou Reed has aptly put it, the inscription on the *Statue of Liberty* should read "Give me your tired, your hungry, your poor, and I'll piss on them." (Lou Reed, "Dirty Boulevard" on the LP *New York*, Sire Records, 1989)

28. The statue was built by the Romanian artist Boris Caragea in 1960. Caragea's design was selected after a national competition. But as anyone familiar with statues of Lenin in the Soviet Union knows, his design was simply a replica of one of the standard poses used to depict Lenin.

29. Coverage of the removal of Caragea's statue in Bucharest was given prominence on all four American networks for over three days. Images of the statue being ripped from its pedestal were overlaid with predictable and cheap dialogue about the 'end of communism'. The fact that Eastern European cranes were not up to the job and that an American crane had to be borrowed was given particular emphasis!

I

DISAPPEARING IDEOLOGY

FOUR THESES ON IDEOLOGY*

Anthony Giddens

The concept of ideology has been debated for some two hundred years within and without the disciplines of philosophy, politics and sociology. If there are such things as contested concepts, and if there were a prize for the most contested concept, the concept of ideology would very nearly rank first. Nobody can even decide how to pronounce it! Given the existence of these traditional debates and problems concerning the ideological content of ideology itself, one might think it best to throw one's hands up in despair, and discard the notion altogether. But I do not think such a reaction would be justified. I want to argue that it *is* possible to point to some modes of analyzing ideology that at least provide a framework for coping with the issues that the concept raises.

Along these lines, I wish to mention four theses, and to give at least a cursory analysis of them. Briefly, I shall claim, first, that the concept of ideology has to be separated out from the content of *science*; second, that it is *empty of content* because what makes belief systems ideological is their incorporation within systems of domination; third, that to understand this incorporation we must analyze the mode in which patterns of signification are incorporated within the medium of *day-to-day practices*; finally, that we should be critical of the "dominant ideology thesis" elaborated in different versions by such authors as Parsons, Althusser and Habermas.

My first thesis is that the notion of ideology has to be disconnected from the philosophy of science, with which in the past it has almost inevitably been bound up. The term *ideology* was coined as a positive term, meaning something like an all-embracing and encyclopaedic form of knowledge, capable of cutting through the resistance of prejudice to produce a form of certain knowledge upon which social technology could in turn be founded. As is well known, Napoleon is supposed to have reversed this perspective, treating ideology as a derogatory apellation. Ideology became regarded as "that which lies beyond the margins of science"—as the very repository of prejudice and obfuscation. "Ideology", henceforth, is supposed in some way to function as a boundary condition of science. Now I want to *reject* any definition of ideology as falsity, as non-science or as 'poor science'—the concept of ideology should not be formulated by comparing or contrasting it with the achievements of science.

In the space of these brief remarks, obviously, I don't have time to illustrate how such connections with science have been part of the history of the notion of

*Editors' note: The following three introductory contributions comprise a revised and edited version of remarks first presented to "Current Controversies in the theory of Ideology: An International Symposium," The Polytechnic of Central London, England. This section on "Disappearing Ideology" was originally commissioned by John Keane for the CJPST.

ideology. Nevertheless, I take it that the entanglements to which it leads are fairly clear. Compare, for example, the respective views of Popper and Althusser, both of whom wish to demarcate in a clear-cut fashion between what counts as science and what does not. Popper's prime examples of ideologies or pseudo-sciences—Marxism and psychoanalysis—are for Althusser precisely the type cases of sciences, of forms of knowledge which have broken free from ideology. I consider this rather comic opposition to be based upon a false starting point. I want to reject the argument that ideology can be defined in reference to truth claims. And I also want to reject the idea that ideology can be defined in terms of any specific *content* at all. The significance of these points will, I hope, become apparent when I move to my second argument.

My second thesis is this: the concept of ideology should be reformulated in relation to a theory of *power* and *domination*—to the modes in which systems of signification enter into the existence of sectional forms of domination. This can be illustrated with reference to Marx's writings on ideology. Marx wrote a great deal about ideology, and at the same time hardly anything at all. A great deal of his substantive writing, including *Capital*, is a critique of ideology, in the sense that it is a critique of political economy. But if one actually searches through Marx's writings for analyses of a concept of ideology as such—most of them appear in *The German Ideology*—there are very few sources to be found where Marx sets out a systematic exposition of the notion. In Marx one finds only various possible formulations of what the concept of ideology means. In *The German Ideology*, one can distinguish two senses in which Marx uses the term. On the one hand, there are the famous observations, discussed by Kofman and others, about how the ideologists write history upside down. The ideologists are accused of writing history as seen through a *camera obscura*, as if it were an echo of human consciousness. These kinds of comments occur frequently in *The German Ideology* and occasionally elsewhere in Marx's writings, and they imply that the way of demystifying history is to set it right way up again, by studying history as it really is.

In *The German Ideology*, however, there is another celebrated assertion about ideology, namely, that the ideas in any given epoch are above all the ideas of the dominant class. According to this proposition, the dominant class has access to notions which it can in some sense disseminate to legitimate its own domination. This version of the theory of ideology ‚connects ideology to the problem of domination. The German ideologists are seen to write history from a point of view that serves to sanction the existing forms of power in the societies in which they are the intellectual leaders. Drawing upon this second Marxian strand, I therefore propose to interpret the concept of ideology in the following way. I want to define ideology as the mode in which forms of signification are incorporated within systems of domination so as to sanction their continuance. I take it to be the type case of such a notion of ideology that sectional interests are represented as universal interests. This is the basic mode in which forms of signification are incorporated within systems of domination in class societies. In my opinion, this point is exemplified in *Capital*, where Marx tried to demonstrate that political economy is ideological insofar as it conceals the operation of capitalism as a class system. The political economists failed to incorporate an account of either the historical origins of expropriated labour or of the nature of surplus value.

My third thesis is that the analysis of ideology must come to terms with recent developments in the philosophy of language and action. Very briefly, these developments mark a transition from a philosophy of language based upon the notion that language is above all a medium of describing the world, to an interpretation of language which emphasizes language as praxis or as the 'other face' of action. Language is intertwined with everyday practices. If one acknowledges the significance of this philosophical shift, it has immediate implications, I think, for the problem of ideology. Most traditional treatments of ideology have exaggerated the importance of propositional belief claims as components of ideologies. This point can be illustrated with a mundane example. Researchers visit a factory and ask workers questions like: What do you think of the Queen? What do you think of the Royal Wedding? Do you believe that management and workers work together like a team? The researchers then imagine that they have uncovered key features of ideology by virtue of their finding that there is some agreement about the continuing importance of the role of the monarchy, etc. Now while I do not wish to deny the possible significance of this kind of finding, it does seem to me to be highly important not to limit the notion of ideology to such formulations. This is because the most subtle and interesting forms of ideology are those incorporated within day-to-day practices. While not necessarily propositional beliefs, these forms of ideology are very often the modes in which signification is incorporated as part and parcel of what one does in daily life. If I may again pursue the previously mentioned example: more important than whether or not workers agree that they and management are a team are the ways in which modes of signification serve to produce a daily world in which the work situation and economic life are treated as essentially separate from political life, from their lives as citizens. The insulation of the economic from the political I take to be one of the major mechanisms of class domination. The most subtle forms of ideology are buried in the modes in which concrete, day-to-day practices are organized. If one simply treats ideology as the content of propositional belief systems, a vast area of human action which is ideologically relevant is excluded.

My final thesis derives from the first three. I think it imperative to accept the broad line of argument which writers such as Abercrombie and Turner have suggested in attacking what they call 'the dominant ideology conception' within the social sciences. In their view, both Left and Right have greatly exaggerated the degree to which there is an ideological consensus among the majority of people in different classes, both in contemporary societies and in societies prior to capitalism. They indict Parsonian functionalism and its emphasis on the significance of a common value system as a co-ordinating mechanism of order. But they also criticize its left variant, the Althusserian characterization of 'ideological state apparatuses'. To this list I would add, somewhat provocatively, Habermas' discussion of legitimation. I think one should be as skeptical of the claim that legitimation is a fundamental mode in which the coherence of class-dominated societies is secured as of these other theories of consensual ideology. It is particularly important to be cautious about the thesis that crises of legitimation are the main sources of tension which threaten the stability of Western capitalist societies. Such a view presumes—in company with Parsons and Althusser—that social order rests upon normative consensus—that normative consensus, mixed with a little police power and coercion, is the main mechanism whereby sectional interests are held together in a class society. But there is good reason to question just such a presumption.

King's College
Cambridge
England

THE IMPOSSIBILITY OF SOCIETY

Ernesto Laclau

In these brief remarks I should like to refer to several problems which are central to the contemporary Marxist theory of ideology. In discussing these problems, it is evident that we presently live at the centre of a theoretical paradox. The terms of this paradox could be formulated as follows: in no previous period has reflection upon 'ideology' been so much at the centre of Marxist theoretical approaches; at the same time, however, in no other period have the limits and referential identity of 'the ideological' become so blurred and problematic. If the increasing interest in ideology runs parallel to a widening of the historical effectivity attributed to what was traditionally considered as the domain of the 'superstructures'—and this widening is a response to the crisis of an economistic and reductionistic conception of Marxism—then that very crisis puts into question the social totality constituted around the base-superstructure distinction. As a consequence, it is no longer possible to identify the object 'ideology' in terms of a topography of the social.

Within the Marxist tradition, we can identify two classical approaches to the problem of ideology. These approaches have often—but not always—been combined. For one of them, 'ideology' is thought to be a *level of the social totality*; for the other, it is identified with *false consciousness*. Today, both approaches appear to have been undermined as a consequence of the crisis of the assumptions on which they were grounded: the validity of the first depended on a conception of society as an intelligible totality, itself conceived as the structure upon which its partial elements and processes are founded. The validity of the second approach presupposed a conception of human agency—a subject having an ultimate essential homogeneity whose misrecognition was postulated as the source of 'ideology'. In this respect, the two approaches were grounded in an *essentialist* conception of both society and social agency. To see clearly the problems which have led the theory of ideology to its present impasse, we need to study the crisis of this essentialist conception in its two variants.

Let me turn, first, to the crisis of the concept of social totality. The ambition of all holistic approaches had been to fix the meaning of any element or social process *outside* itself, that is, in a *system of relations* with other elements. In this respect, the base-superstructure model played an ambiguous role: if it asserted the *relational* character of the identity of both base and superstructure, at the same time it endowed that relational system with a centre. And so, in a very Hegelian fashion, the superstructures ended up taking their revenge by asserting the 'essentiality' of the appearances. More importantly, the structural totality was to present itself as an object having a positivity of its own, which it was possible to describe and to define. In this sense, this totality operated as an underlying principle of intelligibility of the social order. The status of this totality was that of an essence of the social order which had to be *recognized* behind the empirical variations expressed at the surface of social life. (Note that what is at stake here is not the opposition, structuralism vs. historicism. It does not matter if the totality is synchronic or diachronic; the important point is that in both cases it is a *founding totality* which presents itself as an intelligible object of 'knowledge' [*cognitio*] conceived as a process or re-cognition.) Against this essentialist vision we tend nowadays to accept the *infinitude of the social*, that is, the fact that any structural system is limited, that it is always surrounded by an 'excess of meaning' which it is unable to master and that, consequently, 'society' as a unitary and intelligible object which grounds its own partial processes is an impossibility. Let us examine the double movement that this recognition involves. The great advance carried out by structuralism was the recognition of the relational character of any social identity; its limit was its transformation of those relations into a system, into an identifiable and intelligible object (i.e., into an essence). But if we maintain the relational character of any identity and if, at the same time, we renounce the *fixation* of those identities in a system, then the social must be identified with the infinite play of differences, that is, with what in the strictest sense of the term we can call *discourse*—on the condition, of course, that we liberate the concept of discourse from its restrictive meaning as speech and writing.

This first movement thus implies the impossibility of fixing meaning. But this cannot be the end of the matter. A discourse in which meaning cannot possibly be fixed is nothing else but the discourse of the psychotic. The second movement therefore consists in the attempt to effect this ultimately impossible fixation. The social is not only the infinite play of differences. It is also the attempt to limit that play, to domesticate infinitude, to embrace it within the finitude of an order. But this order—or structure—no longer takes the form of an underlying essence of the social; rather, it is an attempt—by definition unstable and precarious—of acting over that 'social', of *hegemonizing* it. In a way which resembles the one we are pursuing here, Saussure attempted to limit the principle of the arbitrariness of the sign with the assertion of the relative character of that arbitrariness. Thus, the problem of the social totality is posed in new terms: the 'totality' does not establish the limits of 'the social' by transforming the latter into a *determinate* object (i.e., 'society'). Rather, the social always exceeds the limits of the attempts to constitute society. At the same time, however, that 'totality' does not disappear: if the suture it attempts is ultimately impossible, it is nevertheless possible to proceed to a relative fixation of the social through the institute of nodal points. But if this is the case, questions concerning those nodal points and their relative weight cannot be determined *sub species aeternitatis*. Each social formation has its own forms of determination and relative autonomy, which are always instituted through a complex process of overdetermination and therefore cannot be established *a priori*. With this insight, the base-superstructure distinction falls and, along with it, the conception of ideology as a necessary level of every social formation.

If we now pass to the second approach to ideology—ideology as false consciousness—we find a similar situation. The notion of false consciousness only makes sense if the identity of the social agent can be fixed. It is only on the basis of recognizing its true identity that we can assert that the consciousness of the subject is 'false'. And this implies, of course, that that identity must be *positive* and *non-contradictory*. Within Marxism, a conception of subjectivity of this kind is at the basis of the notion of 'objective class interests'. Here I am not going to discuss in detail the forms of constitution, the implications and the limitations of such a conception of subjectivity. I shall rather just mention the two processes which led to its progressive abandonment. In the first place, the gap between 'actual consciousness' and 'imputed consciousness' grew increasingly wider. The way this gap was filled—through the presence of a Party instituted as the bearer of the objective historical interests of the class—led to the establishment of an 'enlightened' depotism of intellectuals and bureaucrats who spoke in the name of the masses, explained to them their true interests, and imposed upon them increasingly totalitarian forms of control. The reaction to this situation inevitably took the form of the assertion of the actual identity of the social agents against the 'historical interests' which burdened them. In the second place, the very identity of the social agents was increasingly questioned when the flux of differences in advanced capitalist societies indicated that the identity and homogeneity of social agents was an illusion, that any social subject is essentially decentred, that his/her identity is nothing but the unstable articulation of constantly changing positionalities. The same excess of meaning, the same precarious character of any structuration that we find in the domain of the social order, is also to be found in the domain of subjectivity. But if any social agent is a decentred subject, if when attempting to determine his/her identity we find nothing else but the kaleidoscopic movement of differences, in what sense can we say that subjects misrecognize themselves? The theoretical ground that made sense of the concept of 'false consciousness' has evidently dissolved.

It would therefore look as if the two conceptual frameworks which formerly made sense of the concept of ideology have broken up, and that the concept should consequently be eliminated. However, I do not think this to be a satisfactory solution. We cannot do without the concept of misrecognition, precisely because the very assertion that the 'identity and homogeneity of social agents is an illusion' cannot be formulated without introducing the category of misrecognition. The critique of the 'naturalization of meaning' and of the 'essentialization of the social' is a critique of the misrecognition of their true character. Without this premise, any deconstruction would be meaningless. So, it looks as if we can maintain the concept of ideology and the category of misrecognition only by inverting their traditional content. The ideological would not consist of the misrecognition of a positive essence, but exactly the opposite: it would consist of the non-recognition of the precarious character of any positivity, of the impossibility of any ultimate suture. The ideological would consist of those discursive forms through which a society tries to institute itself as such on the basis of closure, of the fixation of meaning, of the non-recognition of the infinite play of differences. The ideological would be the will to 'totality' of any totalizing discourse. And insofar as the social is impossible without some fixation of meaning, without the discourse of closure, the ideological must be seen as constitutive of the social. The social only exists as the vain attempt to institute that impossible object: society. Utopia is the essence of any communication and social practice.

Government
Essex University
England

LA LANGUE INTROUVABLE

Michel Pêcheux/Françoise Gadet

Michel Pêcheux: Françoise Gadet and I have recently written a book, *La Langue Introuvable*, which concerns the relationship between history, ideology and discursivity and the question of the *langue*, as professional linguists have considered it. As far as we are concerned, the reflection upon ideologies took its point of departure from the early 1960's French problematic of philosophical structuralism, a problematic which was largely organized around the question of the *lecture* (interpretation) of ideological discourses. This problematic, which at that time condensed around Lévi-Strauss, Foucault, Barthes, Lacan, Althusser, and others, not only took the form of a research programme: it was as much a polemical device aimed at the dominating ideas of the time. Three sets of dominating ideas of that time can be mentioned. First, there were the still intact "remains" of a philosophical spiritualism associated with a religious conception of *lecture*. These "remains" extended from literary hermeneutics (which pursued the "themes" through "works") to the phenomenological conception of the "project" (i.e., the projection of meaning into verbal material by the constituting power of the subject-reader)...In each case, there was actually a theological representation of a *relation* between an origin (God, the Author) and an end (the subject-consciousness) through the Text, which was in turn considered to be a more or less transparent medium of this relation. The more everyday, secularized forms of this theological *lecture*, secondly, were inscribed within the spontaneous sender/receiver figures which were becoming prominent within the human and social sciences under the many forms of "content analysis" of communication. Finally, there was "scientific" objectivism, which reacted to the above-mentioned spiritualism through reference to the *seriousness* of science and, above all, to the Theory of Information. This project sought to "objectively" treat texts as if they were a population of words, upon which one could perform a sort of quantitative, statistical demography.

The philosophical structuralism of the 1960's declared war on these spontaneous or sophisticated forms of *lecture*. It wrote such concepts on its banners as "lecture symptômale" and "discourse theory", and it issued slogans such as "specification of the efficacy of a structure on its effects, through its effects". Marx, Nietzsche, Freud and Saussure were recruited for this struggle over the definition of speaking, writing, listening and reading. As Althusser explained in *Lire le Capital*: "Only since Freud have we begun to suspect what listening, and hence what speaking (and keeping silent) *means* (veut-dire); that this 'meaning' (vouloir-dire) of speaking and listening discloses, beneath the innocence of speech and hearing, the specifiable depths of a hidden level, the 'meaning' of the discourse of the unconscious—that level whose effects and formal conditions are thought through by modern linguistics." Hereby, the strategic link between "the theory of ideology" and linguistic structuralism was clearly established. Since the point was to analyze the unconscious discourse of ideologies, structural linguistics appeared as the scientific means of escaping from the "je ne sais quoi" of literary hermeneutics. If ideological discourses were in fact the myths pertaining to our societies (and comparable to those studied by Vladimir Propp, then Claude Lévi-Strauss), it was thought possible to construct the traces of their invariant structure (the system of their functions) within the combinatory series of their superficial, empirical variations—and thereby to attain something of this structure present in the series of its effects.

The different attempts at discourse analysis which appeared at this time in France—including the programme of Automatic Discourse Analysis on which I have worked since 1967—have sought to achieve this goal through various means. Analyses of discourse tried to deal seriously with moden linguistics, and particularly with the writing of an American linguist, Zellig Harris, providentially titled *Discourse Analysis*. For a considerable time, and following the lead of the French linguist, Jean Dubois, this text served as a concrete scientific reference point for linguists involved in the field of discourse analysis. I shall not discuss here the theoretical, methodological and historiographical results issuing from this work.* I shall instead emphasize the weak point of the undertaking, such as it appears to me in retrospect, concerning the role we attributed to the notion of dominating ideology. Considering, as we did at the time, that the myths pertaining to capitalist societies constituted their *dominant* ideology, this might have led us to the questions: Does there not exist, within these same societies, other and different myths? Could these myths be reactive, contradictory, antagonistic, and even capable of revealing the existence of dominated ideologies which are subordinate to, yet distinct from, the dominant ideology?

By virtue of a return of logicism in our own practices, these questions were in fact totally by-passed in favour of a theoreticist reference to the "discourse of science" (Historical Materialism, in this case) which was conceived as a *unique* point of antagonism towards dominant ideology. At the time, of course, this was a political question, the pedagogic aim of which was to "free" the organizations of the French workers' movement (above all, the PCF) from the "myths" of dominant ideology by asserting the value of Marxist science. This was the French way of dreaming of an impossible "escape from ideology", of pretending to at last control historico-political reality itself by means of the separation of Science and Ideology (Compare Lenin's slogan: "Marx's theory is all-powerful because it is true"!)

From this point of view, it may be said that Althusser's famous article concerning "ideological state apparatuses" was an attempt at rectification which also provoked an additional blunder, inasmuch as it was almost unanimously interpreted as a work of *functionalist sociology*. In order to understand something of the question of ideology, Althusser stated explicitly that it was necessary to consider the question of ideology from the standpoint of "the reproduction of capitalist relations of production". For various reasons, "reproduction" was immediately interpreted as the eternal repetition of an identical state of affairs, and certain people even reproached him for thus identifying Marxist analysis with a pure theory of social reproduction.

Reconsidering the aim of this famous article, however, one cannot avoid being struck today by the fact that "considering the question of ideology from the standpoint of reproduction" necessarily implies, for a Marxist, also considering ideology from the standpoint of *resistance* to reproduction, that is, from the standpoint of the multitude of heterogeneous resistances and revolts which smoulder beneath dominant ideology, threatening it constantly. It thereby implies considering dominated ideologies—not as preconstituted ideological germs which have a tendency to develop themselves in such a way that they symmetrically substitute for the domination of dominant ideology but, rather, as a series of ideological effects emerging from domination and working against it

---

*Editor's note: The most important of Pêcheux's earlier writings include: *Analyse automatique du discours* (Paris, 1969); (with Catherine Fuchs) "Mises au point et perspectives à propos de l'analyse automatique du discours", *Langages*, 37 (mars 1975), pp. 7-80; and *Les Vérités de la Palice: linguistique, sémantique, philosophie* (Paris, 1975), an English edition of which appears as *Language, Semantics and Ideology: Stating the Obvious* (London, 1982). Other relevant publications and commentaries on Pêcheux's writings are included in the appendix of this issue.

through the gaps and the failures within this domination.

Althusser's discussion of "ideological state apparatuses" was *also* very much aimed at this, but probably in an overly opaque or prudent manner. In my view, the movements which developed at the end of the 1960's around school, family, religion, the social division of work, and the relationship to the environment all constitute what I call *ideological struggles of movement*. While these are very much a question of class struggle on the terrain of ideology, they should be thought of not as struggles between classes constituted as such but, rather, as a series of mobile clashes (on the terrain of sexuality, private life, education, etc.) about those processes through which the domination-exploitation of the bourgeois class is reproduced, with adaptations and transformations.

The most important theoretical consequence of this perspective, in my opinion, is that the ideological objects implied within the struggles of movement are necessarily objects of logical paradox. They have the strange property of being both *identical and antagonistic to each other*—analogous to the Ministry of Love in Orwell's *1984*, which is an undertaking dedicated to torture. Such ideological objects as work, sexual pleasure, nature, science or reason cannot be given the status of formal logical objects (if logic is considered here as a discipline of univocal communication). These objects only occur as relations of historically mobile forces, as flexible movements which are surprising because of the paradoxes they entail. These movements function as divided units, somewhat like those two Italian princes who both swore before God: "I want the same thing as my brother", while each murmured under his breath: "I want to get my hands on the town of Turin".

Any consideration of these heterogeneous, contradictory and asymmetric processes implies thinking about their relation to language (through the metaphorical shift of meaning, the paradoxes, the play on words, etc.) Such consideration must also be seen as a *constituent part* of these processes themselves—in this sense, the range of discursivity is inherent in ideological processes. By thus considering the range of discursive materialities as an area of non-connected heterogeneities which are mobile within their contradictions, the perspective of our research programmes has changed drastically since the era of philosophical structuralism. Stressing the discoveries of Michel Foucault, Gilles Deleuze or Jacques Derrida, discourse analysis is no longer a matter of reconstructing the homogeneous invariants of a structure of ideology (or ideologies). It rather explores this game of mobile discursive heterogeneities which generate the events specific to ideological struggles of movement.

All this, obviously, implies a certain conception of the relationship between historical reality, linguistic materiality and the existence of the subject: it brings into question that comfortable metaphysics which considers classes as autocentric and preconstructed objects, the subject as an active unit of an intentional consciousness, and the *langue* as the instrument of communication of this subject's expressions and actions. In this sense, more than ever before, Marx, Freud, Nietzsche and Saussure are in the forefront. They engage the pretensions of the impossible theory of semantico-pragmatic universals, a theory which floats on the horizon of our time, like a new dream of domination. This impossible theory is the most recent form of the *langue introuvable* with which linguistics (and not only linguistics) has been obsessed since its beginning.

Françoise Gadet: I should like to begin by mentioning a part-time linguist who, in addition to leading a state, considered the relationship between language and ideology: Joseph Stalin. He is well known among linguists for his paper, "Marxism and Questions of Linguistics", in which he argues about the relationship between language and social classes. As is also well known, he resolves this question by claiming that language is not a superstructure.

Stalin also deserves a reputation as a forerunner of the extended performative. This reputation is suggested by a declaration of Siniawski, a victim of Stalinism who said in front of his judges: "If we translate metaphors into real terms, it is the end of the world. We say 'darkness is falling, it's raining cats and dogs, stars shoot across the sky'. If this actually happened, the world would go to the dogs. When Lenin talked about ideological struggle with our opponents, he used metaphors. Stalin translated those metaphors into real terms, and this is how the horrors of 1937 began."

If one reads metaphors to the letter, language ends up being taken for reality, representing it without distanciation. Established as equivalent to reality, the order of language would thereby be categorical, serious, definite. Meaning would exist in itself, because it would coincide with words in the reality of an ideology. The consequences of such a conception of language are well known in the fields of politics and literature, and so I shall only consider the implications of such a position for linguistics. I should like to explain, from the point of view of a linguist interested in the question of ideology, why Pêcheux and myself dared title a chapter of *La Langue Introuvable*: "Metaphors, too, are worth struggling for". Our conception of the relationship between *langue* and reality necessarily implies a specific conception of *langue* itself, and I think this conception sheds more light on the metaphorical process, inasmuch as it raises questions about the nature of rules within language.

My starting point, metaphor, leads me to consider the topic of linguistic creativity. By "creativity" I do not so much mean the general possibility of language creation, a feature common to all languages, namely, that the language system itself allows historical displacements within the field of possible formulations. I rather wish to question at this point a common-sense conception, which approaches this problem of creativity by relating two forms of oppositions: first, the opposition between word and sentence and, secondly, the opposition between freedom and constraint.

According to this common-sense conception, it is always the word which is considered as the foundation of creativity and freedom within language. Hence, certain examples of creativity are usually mentioned: slips of the tongue, portmanteau-words, puns, metaphors, neology, the poetic play on words, the play on words proper, rhymes, spoonerisms, anagrams, and so on. Here we again encounter a lot of English expressions which assume that expression is a matter of words: to use one word for another, to weigh one's words, without changing a word, to play on words, looking for words, the right word, the power of words, not afraid of words...Most of these expressions, of course, imply the syntactic base of a sentence.

On the other hand, this common-sense conception of language considers syntax as a rigidity factor, a constraint, a limit or filter, as a process by which tight reins are kept on spontaneity. From such a perspective, a psychoanalyst reflecting upon the necessity of an *écriture* of oral material would be forced to say: "Ultimately, syntax is on the side of secondary processes". I think that such a conception of syntax is not only a consequence of an analysis made upon fixed-order languages (e.g., French or English), in which word-order is determined. It is also, and probably above all, a consequence of an imaginary reconstruction of syntax: syntax is considered as a set of imperative rules that assert what is forbidden and what is allowed—rules which take the form of *don't say that, but say this*. Any attack on this order is therefore seen as necessarily a breaking of the rules, a deviation, a standing outside of language.

Some recent works in the field of linguistics suggest the necessity of abandoning this dichotomy beteen word and sentence. Consider, for example, the reseach of Judith Milner, which is concerned with language play. She shows how playing with language negatively reveals something about language, because through the mere possibility of laughing, for instance, one behaves as if one understood something else. Playing with a language is a question of syntactic analysis. This is exemplified in the famous witticism commented upon by Freud: *Tu a pris un bain?* (Did you take a bath?) *Pourquoi, il en manque un?* (Why, is one missing?) There is here a lexical ambiguity between a full expression (*to take a bath*) and the combination of the verb *to take* and the noun *a bath*. But it is the syntactic scheme which allows this play, and consequently the witticism. Milner therefore writes: "I insist upon the fact that most of the time, playing with language, though generally considered as pure lexical ambiguity, involves in fact problems of syntactic analyzability". Similarly, another linguist (again, a woman) is working on the linguistic status of metaphor. Lacan's definition of metaphor as the substitution of one word for another is well known. She shows that this is true, but only because there exists a syntactic frame for the substitution itself. She therefore calls metaphor a fact of language with a syntactic origin. For example, the expression *son colonel de mari* (which could be translated: her colonel of a husband) can only be interpreted by a French speaker as a derogatory or ironical attitude towards colonels, through reference to the expression, *son imbécile de mari*.

These examples indicate the necessity of referring to syntactic structure, considered both as indifferent to, and responsible for, the ideological processes of language. Syntax is the basis of historical creativity. Language rules thus cannot be considered as categorical rules—in the sense that a rule must or must not apply. They must rather be seen as intrinsically allowing for ideological play and discursive latitudes. Consider an especially enlightening example: Roland Barthes' expression, *tricher la langue* (literally: to cheat the language). It is not very interesting to point out that the verb *tricher* is normally intransitive (*tricher avec la langue; tricher à un jeu*) and that it is transitive in this deviant example. It is much more interesting to emphasize that Barthes uses this verb when defining literature as a work upon language. It is also more interesting to point out that using an intransitive verb intransitively is particularly frequent in some types of discourse. This is especially the case in provocative statements used on electoral posters, as for example in this one recently used against Mitterand:

> Il a avorté nos enfants
> Il avortera la France

(literally: he aborted our children, he will abort France). Neither in the first meaning (to make a woman abort) nor in the second meaning (to make a project abort) can the verb *avorter* be used transitively. By doing so, the deviant statement gains in intensity and even violence.

To what new theoretical consequences do such reflections lead? I think the major point is that the way we think syntactically about a statement always reveals a little bit more about its meaning, because we understand it in relation to other statements, through syntactical plays of forms which are required by the former statement. In the same way, producing such statements implies a position towards language that has been described by Philippe Sollers: "I can't consider as free a being who does not strive to break within him/herself the bonds of language...".

What does this position imply about the status of grammatical rules? We argue in *La Langue Introuvable* that a certain interpretation of Chomsky's work permits such a conception of language. It is well known that one of the most important concepts of generative transformational grammar is the opposition between the grammatical and the non-grammatical. This distinction works more as a way of reasoning than as a device for separating utterances. To separate utterances would be to produce a decision about, or assign a frontier between, *what is grammatical* and *what is not grammatical*. If we assume, to the contrary, that the opposition is merely a matter of reasoning, this necessarily implies taking into account what is impossible within the *langue*, precisely in order to understand what exists within it. In my opinion, the main discovery of Chomsky's work is its comprehension of the relationship between the grammatical and the non-grammatical as a continuum or natural consistency—and not as the *langue* versus its outside, the normal versus the pathological, or the rule versus deviation. Nothing reveals an excluded sequence as excluded, except the fact that it is excluded. Therefore, there is no frontier or assignable point of language shift between the grammatical and the non-grammatical. There is only work within language, in which meaning is defined in relation to what does not make meaning, the meaningless.

To understand Chomsky this way—and I agree this is not the usual way—is in fact to raise the question of a subject's mastery of his/her *langue*: playing with rules is not the same as following the rules of a game. From our perspective, there is no "deviation"—and hence there is no "poetical" language. There is only a general process of language, working as much in the verbal learning of children, as in the everyday use of language by every speaker, as well as in its political or literary uses. Once again, Barthes presents several examples of this interplay between the grammatical and the non-grammatical. One of them seems to me especially interesting, for it presents an apparent contradiction between his *écriture* and his theoretical position. In the *Leçon inaugurale*, he writes: "In our language, I am compelled to establish myself first as a subject, before expressing the action which, because of this, will only be an attribute of the subject: what I do is only the consequence and outcome of what I am. In the same way, I always have to choose between masculine and feminine, because both neuter and any mixed gender are forbidden to me; or, again, I have to indicate my relation to another person by using either *tu* or *vous*: any emotional or social hesitation is not allowed. Thus, in its very structure, language implies a fundamental relation of alienation." These observations lead him to this famous conclusion: "Language is neither reactionary nor progressive; it is indeed fascist".

In his practice as a writer, Barthes had previously worked out the necessity of deciding on grammatical gender. In *fragments d'un discours amoureux*, in which he quite systematically avoids the discursive engendering of the partners involved in the *discours amoureux*, he uses unmarked terms (*the subject in love; the object of my love; you; we; the other; the other body*) and some nominalizations, such as *the absence, the anguish of love, imposing on my passion the disguise of discretion*. We find here discursive characteristics which, from within language, play with the necessity of language: a *ruse*, if I dare say. But the term ruse seems to imply a notion of strategy. It is, however, not the case that Barthes is the master of what he writes, as if he could translate ideological aims into *langue* or discourse. To make language work is only to play on its constraints and on its blanks—to play with the latitudes it affords.

In *La Langue Introuvable* we attempted to question the strategic position of the language master who seeks to rule over a world of statements through his own process of enunciation. Against the narcissism of successful communication, we tried to assert the historical and political value of failure. The certitude of the American joke and the anxiety of a Jewish wit provide a philosophical illustration of this difference. The joke is the reply of the small American farmer to his pastor when the latter invites him to thank the Lord for having given him such a beautiful land: "But if only you had seen this land in the state in which He gave it to me!" The witticism is the reply of the small Jewish tailor to his unhappy client who had to wait six years for the delivery of a pair of trousers and thereupon remarked that God took only six days to create the world: "All right, but look at the trousers, and look at the world...".

Ecole Pratique   Université
des Hautes Etudes   de Paris-X

SOME CONDITIONS FOR REVOLUTIONIZING LATE CAPITALIST SOCIETIES [1968]*

Jürgen Habermas

Marx was convinced that a revolutionizing of the capitalist social system of his time was possible for two reasons. First, because at that time the antagonism between the owners of the means of production and wage labourers clearly manifested itself as class struggle, i.e., the subjects themselves were becoming conscious of this antagonism and therefore could be organized politically; and, secondly, because in the long run the institutional pressure for capital utilization in private form confronted the economic system with an insoluble problem. I know that for Marx these two conditions represented necessary but by no means sufficient conditions for a revolution. However, I shall limit my discussion to them, as I believe that these two conditions are no longer satisfied under state-regulated capitalism.

The *first* condition of a politically organizable class struggle is given if the relationship between the privileged and dominated groups is founded on exploitation, and if this exploitation becomes consciously subjective, i.e., is *incompatible* with the accepted legitimations of domination. Exploitation is thus defined as the dominating class living upon the labour of the dependent class which therefore, on the other hand, can pressure the dominant class by the withdrawal of its co-operation. The dominated wage labour of the nineteenth century was in this sense an exploited class. At the same time, this relationship of exploitation was incompatible with bourgeois ideology. According to this ideology, the transactions between private individuals were supposed to be regulated through relations of equivalence of exchange and consequently unfold in a sphere emancipated from domination and freed from violence.

Secondly, the analysis of the capitalist economic system which Marx accomplished on the foundation of the theory of value, as is known, serves to prove the inevitability of system-endangering disproportionalities. As long as economic growth is tied to the mechanism of the utilization of capital in private form, the

Translated by John Keane

*Editor's note: This essay was first presented as a lecture to the 1968 Korčula Summer School, Yugoslavia. It is translated from the version which is published in *Kultur und Kritik* (Frankfurt am Main, 1973), pp. 70-86. Permission for this translation has been granted by Professor Habermas, although with two strong stipulations: first, that this essay be considered as a rough summation of themes presented elsewhere, especially in *Technik und Wissenschaft als 'Ideologie'* (Frankfurt, 1968); and, secondly, that this essay's concern with the "glassy background ideology" of science and technology be interpreted as a critical response to certain apologetic accounts of the logic and consequences of scientific-technical progress, above all, those which are to be found in the writings (during the 1960's in the Federal Republic) of Hans Freyer, Helmut Schelsky and Arnold Gehlen.

accumulation process must repeatedly come to a standstill. This periodic destruction of non-utilizable reserves of capital is a condition of revolution, because it constitutes a vivid demonstration of the discrepancy between the developed productive forces on the one hand, and the institutional framework of the capitalist social system on the other. It thereby makes the masses conscious of the insoluble system problem.

In the following, I should like to name two developmental tendencies which are decisive for the state-organized capitalism of the present time.[1] This approximate reconstruction of its emergence should make clear on the one hand why the classical conditions of revolution are today no longer present; but, at the same time, it should indicate the structural weakness of the system which presents itself as a new point of attack.

I

Since the last quarter of the nineteenth century, two developmental tendencies have become observable in the most advanced capitalist countries: on the one hand, an increase of interventionist state activity which has to guarantee the stability of the system and, on the other hand, a growing interdependence of research and technology which has made the sciences the primary productive force. Both tendencies destroy that constellation which had been unique to liberal capitalism in its developed stage.

1. The permanent regulation of the economic process through state intervention has emerged as a defence against the system-endangering dysfunctionalities of unregulated capitalism. The basic ideology of equivalence of exchange, which Marx had theoretically unmasked, has practically collapsed. The form of private economic utilization of capital can only be maintained through the state correctives of social and economic policy which stabilize circulation and compensate for market consequences. Thereby the system of domination is itself transformed. After the disintegration of the ideology of equivalence of exchange—upon which the modern natural law constructions of the bourgeois-constitutional state were also based—political domination requires a new basis for its legitimacy. Now that the power indirectly exercised within the exchange process itself has to be controlled by pre-state organised and state institutionalised authority, legitimation can no longer be derived from a non-political order, the relations of production. In this sense, the compulsion to direct legitimation in pre-capitalist societies is once again renewed. On the other hand, the re-establishment of direct political domination (with a traditional form of legitimation grounded in cultural tradition) has become impossible. Formal democratic authority in state-regulated, capitalist systems is placed under a legitimation obligation which can no longer be redeemed through recourse to the pre-bourgeois form of legitimation. This is why a substitute programmatic replaces the equivalence-ideology of

free exchange. This programmatic is oriented not to the social consequences of the market institution, but to the state compensation of the dysfunctions for free exchange relations. It links together the moment of the bourgeois ideology of performance (which of course shifts status assignment according to individual performance from the market to the school system) with the promise of welfare (with the prospect of job security as well as income stability). This substitute programmatic obliges the system of control to both maintain the conditions of stability of a total system which grants social security and chances of personal advancement and to overcome risks associated with growth. This necessitates considerable room for manoeuvering for state interventions which, in return for restrictions placed upon the institutions of private law, secure the private form of capital utilization and bind the loyalty of the masses to the capitalist form of society.

Insofar as state activity is directed to the stability and the growth of the economic system, politics now assumes a strangely negative character: it is concerned with the elimination of dysfunctionalities and the prevention of system-endangering risks, i.e., it is oriented not to the realization of practical goals but to the solution of technical problems. Through its orientation to preventive action, state activity becomes restricted to technical tasks. Its purpose is "just to keep the system going". Practical questions therefore are virtually pushed aside. I am here distinguishing between technical and practical questions. Technical problems arise with respect to the purposive-rational organization of means and the rational choice between alternative means for the attainment of given goals. Practical problems, on the other hand, arise with respect to the acceptance or rejection of norms, in our case of norms of collective life which we can—with good reasons—support or reject, translate into reality or struggle against. The distinction between technical and practical questions corresponds, I should like to add immediately, to the distinction between work and interaction. Work is a term which describes any form of instrumental or strategic action, while interaction refers to a reciprocal relationship of at least two subjects under common, that is, inter-subjectively comprehensible and binding norms.

I return to the question of eliminating essential practical substance from the politics of late capitalism. Old style politics was forced, if only because of the form of legitimation assumed by traditional authority, to define itself in relation to practical goals: interpretations of "the good life" were attached to contexts of interaction. The same was still true for the ideology of bourgeois society. Today, however, the substitute programmatic only refers to the functioning of a controlled system. It excludes practical questions and thereby the discussion of the acceptance of standards which were only accessible to democratic will-formation. For the solution of technical tasks is not dependent upon public discussion. But public discussions could problematize the boundary conditions of the system within which the tasks of state activity primarily appear as technical problems. The new politics of state intervention therefore requires a depoliticization of the mass of the population. In the same measure as practical questions are excluded, the political public sphere loses its function. The mass media assume the function

of securing that depoliticization of the masses. On the other hand, the legitimation of domination by the substitute programmatic leaves open a decisive
legitimation need: How can the depoliticization of the masses become plausible
to them? Marcuse provided an answer to this question: technology and science
also take on the role of an ideology.

2. Since the end of the nineteenth century, a second developmental tendency,
characteristic of late capitalism, has become more and more powerful: the
scientization of technology. Through large-scale industrial research, science,
technology and commercialization have been integrated into one system. It is
linked in the meantime with state-commissioned research, which primarily
supports scientific and technical progress in the military field. From there
information flows back into the domain of civilian goods production. Thus
technology and science become the primary productive force and with that the
conditions of applicability of Marx's labour theory of value disappear. It no
longer makes sense to calculate the amounts of capital for investments in
research and development on the basis of the value of unskilled (simple) labour
power, because institutionalized scientific-technical progress has become the
basis of an indirect surplus value production, compared to which the only source
of surplus value Marx considered—the labour power of the immediate
producers—has less and less importance.

This development subsequently gives rise to a strangely technocratic consciousness. So long as the productive forces were clearly connected to the rational
decisions and instrumental actions of a socially producing humanity they could be
understood as a potential with a growing technical power of disposal; they could
not, however, be confused with the institutional framework in which they are
embedded. With the institutionalization of scientific-technical progress, the
potential of the productive forces assumes a form which decreases the dualism of
work and interaction in the consciousness of humanity. It is true that social
interests still determine, as always, the direction, the functions and the pace of
tehcnical progress. Yet these interests define the social system so fully that they
are identical with the interest of maintaining the system. The private form of
capital utilization and a loyalty-securing code of distribution for social compensations are as such withdrawn from discussion. A quasi-autonomous progress of
science and technology appears as an independent variable on which the single
most important variable of the system, namely, economic growth, in fact
depends. This results in a perspective in which the development of the social
system seems to be determined by the logic of scientific-technical progress. The
immanently law-like character of this progress seems to produce the compel-
lingness of tasks to which a politics based on obeying functional needs must
respond. If this technocratic consciousness, which of course is a false consciousness, manifests itself as everyday self-understanding, then the reference to the
role of technology and science can explain and legitimize why in modern societies
a democratic process of will-formation concerning practical questions must both
lose its functions and be replaced by plebiscitary decisions about alternative sets
of leaders of the administrative *personnel.* In this sense, technology and science

today assume a double function: they are not only productive forces, but also ideologies. This also explains why the discrepancy between the forces and relations of production no longer continues to be meaningful, that is, is no longer evident in the consciousness of the mass of the population.

II

We can now return to the two structural conditions of revolution stated by Marx. The second condition, namely, that the mechanisms of capital utilization in private form as such confront the system with insoluble problems, is no longer satisfied if it is correct that the institutionalization of scientific-technical progress casts fundamental doubt upon the orthodox crisis theory, and if in actual fact, through the organisation of science as the leading productive force, space is created in which state activity can principally secure economic growth and mass loyalty through re-distribution. I do not want to go further into this possibility at this point.[2] What is of interest to me is that the first condition of the possibility of a politically organizable class struggle is also no longer necessarily fulfilled. For capitalist society has changed to such an extent—due to the two aforementioned developmental tendencies—that *two* key categories of Marx's theory of revolution, *viz.*, class struggle and ideology can no longer be so easily applied.

1. The late capitalist system is defined to such an extent by compensation, i.e., by a politics of conflict avoidance which secures the loyalty of the wage-dependent masses, that the class conflict—built into the social structure by the private economic utilization of capital now as before—is the conflict which, with the relatively greatest probability, remains latent. This conflict retreats behind other conflicts which, although also conditioned by the mode of production, no longer can assume the form of class conflicts. Claus Offe has analyzed this paradoxical state of affairs: open conflicts are more likely to be sparked by social interests the less their violation has system-endangering consquences. At the periphery of this state sphere of action, needs are pregnant with conflict because they are remote from the latent central conflict and therefore do not enjoy any priority in the warding off of dangers. Conflicts arise due to these needs to the extent with which the disproportionately spread state interventions give rise to retarded spheres of development and to corresponding tensions of disparity. The interests linked to the maintenance of the mode of production can no longer be unambiguously located in the social system as class interests. For the system of political control, which is oriented to the prevention of threats to the system, excludes just that "domination" which is exercised when *one* class subject opposes the *other* as an identifiable group.

This signals not an abolition but a latency of class antagonisms. It is true that, as empirical sociologists, we can satisfactorily demonstrate that class-specific differences continue to exist in the form of subcultural traditions and corresponding differences of not only standards of living and ways of life but also of political attitudes. Furthermore, the socio-structurally conditioned probability arises that the class of wage-labourers will be hit harder by social disparities than other groups. And, finally, the generalized interest in the maintenance of the system on the level of immediate life chances is today still anchored in a structure of privilege: For the concept of an interest completely independent of living subjects would cancel itself out. But with the warding off of dangers to the system, political authority in state-regulated capitalism has absorbed an interest in the maintenance of the compensatory facade of distribution that reaches beyond the virtualized class boundaries.

On the other hand, the displacement of the conflict zone from the class boundary to the underprivileged spheres of life does not at all imply the elimination of grave conflict potential. As the racial conflict in the United States shows in the extreme, so many consequences of disparity can accumulate in certain areas and groups that civil war-like explosions result. When not linked with the protest potential of other origins, all conflicts based solely on such deprivation are characterized by the fact that, while they provoke the system to react sharply and in a way incompatible with formal democracy, they cannot really revolutionize this system. For deprived groups are not social classes; in addition, they never even potentially represent the mass of the population. Their loss of rights and their pauperization are no longer identical with exploitation, since the system does not feed upon their labour; at most, they represent a past phase of exploitation. Yet they cannot *enforce* the fulfillment of the claims they legitimately represent through the withdrawal of their cooperation; these claims consequently have an appellative character. In the extreme case, deprived groups can react to the long term non-recognition of their legitimate claims with desperate destruction and self-destruction: such civil strife, however, lacks the revolutionary chances of success of class struggle so long as coalitions with privileged groups are not realized.

In late capitalist society the deprived and privileged groups no longer oppose each other *as* socio-economic classes insofar as the limits of deprivation remain group specific at all and do not pass directly through the categories of the population.

2. The technocratic consciousness is in one respect "less ideological" than all previous ideologies, because it does not have the power of delusion which simulates the fulfillment of interests by only compensating suppressed desires. In another respect, the glassy background ideology which fetishizes science is more irresistible and far-reaching than ideologies of the old type. By concealing practical questions, this ideology not only justifies the particular interest in domination of a certain class and suppresses the particular need for emancipation of another class—it also strikes against the emancipatory species-interest as such.

The technocratic consciousness is no rationalizing, wishful phantasy, no "illusion" in the Freudian sense of positing a non-repressive, wish-fulfilling relationship of interactions. The basic figure of just and domination-free interaction satisfactory for both sides could still be attributed to bourgeois ideologies. Founded on communcation restricted by repression, it was precisely these ideologies that satisfied the criteria of wish-fulfillment and substitute satisfaction in such a manner that the relationship of force that at one time had been institutionalized with the capital relationship could not be named as such. The technocratic consciousness, however, no longer expresses a projection of the "good life" that, though not identical with the bad reality, at least is brought into a potentially satisfactory relationship with it. Certainly both the new as well as the old ideology serve to preclude the thematization of the social base. In the past, the relationship between capitalists and wage labourers was the direct basis of social violence; today it is the structural conditions which define the functional tasks of system maintenance, namely, the private economic form of capital utilization and a political form of distribution of social compensations which secures the loyalty of the masses. Nevertheless, the old and the new ideology differ in two respects. On the one hand, the capital relationship—due to its being linked to a political mode of distribution guaranteeing loyalty—is no longer based on uncorrected exploitation and oppression: the virtualization of continuing class division presupposes that the repression on which it rests has become historically conscious and has *only then* been stabilized in modified form as a characteristic of the system. For this reason, the technocratic consciousness cannot be based on collective repression in the same way as was the authority of older ideologies. On the other hand, mass loyalty can only be produced with the help of compensations for privatized needs. The interpretation of the accomplishments which the system uses to justify itself must in principle not be political; this interpretation refers directly to the use-neutral allocation of money and leisure and, indirectly, to the technocratic justification of the exclusion of practical questions.

III

At this point, I have reached a decisive step in my argumentation. I maintain that the conditions of a politically organizable class struggle in late capitalism are not fulfilled so long as there is an effective separation of two motivational links—links that were always connected in the workers' movement and in Marxist theory—in such a way that one interest can be satisfied and the other repressed. What is being satisfied is the economic interest of consumers in socially produced goods and services and that of employees in reduced working hours; what has been repressed is the political interest of individuals, their achievement of autonomy by voluntarily participating in all decision-making processes upon which their lives depend. The stabilization of the state-regulated capitalist social system depends on the loyalty of the masses being linked to an unpolitical form of social compensations (of income and leisure time) and to ensuring that there is a screening out of their interest in the solution of practical questions concerning a better and good life. For this reason, however, the social system of state-regulated capitalism rests upon a *very weak legitimation basis*. By diverting the interests of broad strata to the private domain, the system of domination is almost exclusively negative and no longer affirmatively justified by practical goals. The depoliticization of the public sphere, which is necessary for the system and rules out a process of will-formation in radical-democratic form, discloses the strategic point of vulnerability of the system.

Before naming the forces which are directed at this point of weakness, I will at least mention the two *international* tendencies which have so far contributed instead to a stabilization of capitalism.

1. The connection between the economic stability of the developed capitalist countries and the catastrophic economic situation in the countries of the Third World can no longer apparently be apprehended today through the theory of imperialism. I do not doubt that the adverse socio-economic starting conditions in these latter countries have been generated by the imperialism of the contemporary industrial nations. There is every reason to believe, however, that relationships based on economic exploitation between First and Third World countries are tending to be replaced with relationships of strategic dependence and growing disparity. On an international level, deprivation also signifies an outrageous deprivation of rights which, however, is no longer automatically identifiable with exploitation and, in the future, will become even less so identifiable. This also clarifies why those countries which represent a past phase of exploitation today convincingly assert a certain moralization of claims against the former colonial powers.

2. The establishment of a bloc of socialist states following the Russian Revolution and the victory of the Allies over fascist Germany has created a new level of international class struggle. The military presence as well as the state socialist model of organized society exert a competitive pressure upon, and at least contribute to the self-disciplining of capitalism. The internal pressure created by the imperative to maintain mass-loyalty through economic growth and social compensations is reinforced by the external pressure of tangible alternatives. An endangerment of state-regulated capitalism will certainly not result so long as the alternative model is only represented by the form of domination of bureaucratic socialism. Nevertheless, the *immobilisme* of the 50's has fractured, and there are more frequent signs of new revolutionary developments. If the classical conditions of the revolution are no longer fulfilled, are there alternative conditions? In conclusion, I would like to respond to this question—at least in thesis form—with respect to developments within both late capitalist social systems and the international sector.

DISAPPEARING IDEOLOGY

IV

1. For the time being neither the old class opposition nor the new types of deprivation contain protest potential which tends to repoliticize the withered public sphere. The only protest potential which is currently directed at the new conflict zone by recognizable interests arises within certain groups of university and high school students. Here we can begin with three observations:

a) The protest group of university and high school students is a privileged group. They do not represent interests that immediately derive from their social position and that could be satisfied—in conformity with the system—through increased social compensations. The first American studies[3] of student activists confirm that the great majority are not status-seekers but, rather, that they are recruited from social groups of a higher status and without economic burdens.

b) The legitimation propositions of the system of domination do not seem to be convincing to this group for understandable reasons. The welfare state substitute programmatic for the decayed bourgeois ideologies assumes a certain orientation to status and achievement. According to the afore-mentioned studies, however, the militant students are less oriented to private, occupational career and future family than the remainder of students. Both their academic performances—which are frequently above average—and their social origin lend little support to a horizon of expectations which is determined by anticipated labour market pressures.

c) In this group, conflict can be sparked not by the expected *extent* of discipline and sacrifice but only because of the kind of imposed renunciations. University and high school students do not struggle for a greater share of the disposable categories of social compensations: income and leisure time. Their protest is much more directed against these categories of 'compensation' as such. The little data we have confirms the assumption that the protest of youth from middle class families is no longer identical with the generational pattern of authority conflict. The active students more likely have parents who share their critical attitudes; relatively frequently they have been raised with more psychological understanding and in accordance with more liberal educational principles than comparable groups of non-activists. Their socialization seems more likely to have been effected within subcultures freed from immediate economic pressure, and within which there has been a loss of function of the traditions of bourgeois morality and their petit-bourgeois offspring. Thus, the training for the 'switching over' to the value orientation of purposive-rational action no longer includes the fetishism of this action. These educational techniques can foster experiences and orientations that collide with the conservative forms of life grounded in an economy of poverty. From this foundation could arise a complete lack of comprehension of the meaningless reproduction of superfluous virtues and sacrifices—a failure to understand why, despite the high level of technological development, the lives of individuals continue to be conditioned by the dictates of work, the ethics of competitive achievement, the pressure of status competition, the values of possessive reification and of proposed substitute-satisfactions, and why the discipline of alienated labour and the annulment of sensuality and aesthetic satisfaction are maintained. A structural exclusion of practical questions from the depoliticized public sphere has to become intolerable to this sensibility.[4]

I admit that this perspective upends the commonly accepted assumptions of Marxist theory. My hypothesis suggests that not material destitution but material abundance is the basis upon which the petit-bourgeois structure of needs— generated for centuries under the compulsion of individual competition, and which has not penetrated into the integrated labour force—can be broken. According to this hypothesis, only the psychology of satiety of the available affluence sensitizes the population to the ideologically concealed compulsion of bureaucratized forms of work and life, within which the wealth of past generations has been acquired. If this is correct, then the revolution would not lead to the abolition of poverty but assume it.[5] On a global scale, however, the prospects for this assumption are not good. As matters stand, the protest of youth can only have revolutionary consequences if it is confronted in the near future with an insoluble system problem to which I have so far not referred. I am of the opinion that the problem which will increase in importance is that of a structurally conditioned erosion of the ideology of the achieving society. The degree of social affluence produced by an industrially developed capitalism, and the technical as well as organizational conditions under which this wealth is produced, continually increase the difficulty of even subjectively and convincingly binding the allocation of status to the mechanism of evaluating individual performance.

2. On an international level, two developments are emerging which permit conjectures about a qualitative transformation of the external pressure on the late capitalist system. Again, I should like to differentiate between relations with Third World countries and relations with socialist countries of the Soviet type.

a) There are strong resons for believing that organized capitalism as well as bureaucratic socialism are incapable of generating from within sufficient motivation to provide effective, i.e., sufficiently large development aid that is exclusively oriented to the interests of the recipient countries. It is estimated that, for this purpose, the affluent countries would have to divert 15-20% of their social product in order to close the economic gap between the poor and the affluent countries. As this is unlikely to happen, a catastrophic famine during the 80's cannot be ruled out. The extent of this catastrophe could be so large that, with respect to this phenomenon, the discrepancy between the forces and relations of production can once again become directly evident to the population of the industrialized countries.[6] Such a consciousness of the inability of the established system to solve problems of survival in other parts of the world could renew an international class struggle situation if one of these countries—I am here thinking of China—succeeded in developing an industrial potential sufficient for atomic blackmail without at the same time developing the forms of bureaucratic domination and that mentality which have hitherto always accompanied the industrialization of a society. If China, despite industrial growth, maintained its revolutionary point of departure and effectively renewed the consciousness of this beginning in each generation, the pauperized and weakened nations, which today do not necessarily have to be the exploited nations, would find an advocate. This advocate could compensate for the missing means of economic pressure through the withdrawal of cooperation by military pressure, without at the same time adhering to the sensitive rules of the game of the atomic superpowers.

b) An alternative development, which could also lead (with less risk) to an external pressure on the developed capitalist societies is in my opinion only probable if—despite the brutal repression of the Czechoslovakian reformers—an anti-authoritarian dissolution of bureaucratic socialism could soon be achieved. Only a radical democratization of the developed state socialist countries could produce a competitive model, one which makes the limits of state-regulated capitalism obvious, that is, visible to the consciousness of the currently well-integrated masses. Under the given military and strategic conditions, the superiority of the socialist mode of production cannot become effective and visible as long as both sides choose economic growth, the supply of goods and the reduction of working hours—private welfare—as the only criterion for comparison. The superiority of a mode of production should be judged according to the space it opens for a democratization of decision-making processes in all social domains.

Max-Planck-Institut für Sozialwissenschaften
München

Notes

1. Here I am repeating parts of the analysis of *Technik und Wissenschaft als 'Ideologie'* (Frankfurt, 1968); the essays from this volume were subsequently translated as *Toward A Rational Society. Student Protest, Science and Politics*, trans., Jeremy J. Shapiro (London, 1971), essays 4-6; *Theory and Practice*, trans. John Viertel (Boston, 1973), essay 4; and *Knowledge and Human Interests*, trans. Jeremy J. Shapiro (London, 1972), appendix.

2. Compare my study, *Legitimation Crisis*, trans. Thomas McCarthy (Boston, 1975).

3. S.M. Lipset, P.G. Altbach, 'Student Politics and Higher Education in the USA', in S.M. Lipset (ed.), *Student Politics* (New York, 1967), pp. 199 ff.; R. Flacks, 'The Liberated Generation, An Exploration of the Roots of Student Protest', *Journal of Social Issues*, July 1967, pp. 52 ff.; K. Keniston, 'The Sources of Student Dissent', *ibid.*, pp. 108 ff.

4. Compare the subsequent study of R. Döbert, G. Nünner-Winkler, 'Konflikt und Rückzugspotentiale in spätkapitalistischen Gesellschaften', *Zeitschrift für Soziologie*, 1973.

5. See Herbert Marcuse, *Counterrevolution and Revolt* (Boston, 1972).

6. As a consequence of more recent prognoses, I see a need to weaken my previous formulations.

ON THE GENESIS OF IDEOLOGY
IN MODERN SOCIETIES

Claude Lefort

Under the circumstances, outlining an analysis of ideology saves one the work that would be necessary for a thorough critique of ideological formations as they can be discerned in determined historical conditions. If such a critique were realized, the outline might not hold to the actual conditions, nor retain its original value. Indeed, its limitations are only too easily perceived. To present a *profile* of bourgeois ideology without reference to dates or places is to neglect many of the traits which should be taken into consideration, for example, the relation which occasionally arises between dominant discourse and the course of class conflict, the political regime, national tradition and a culture's heritage. In re-examining these articulations, several forms might come to light where previously only one was discerned, and thus the adopted perspective would not be left intact. The suspicion which hangs over the analysis of totalitarianism is no less serious. This analysis does not dissociate Stalinism from Nazism or fascism, although it does not permit one to be mistaken for another. Furthermore, nothing is said about the ideological transformations which have occurred in the USSR and eastern Europe over a period of nearly twenty years, nor is there any comment about China's very singular variant of totalitarianism. As for ideology, which for lack of a better term we describe as "invisible" (not because it actually is, but because it seems to be organized in such a way as to blur the characteristic oppositions of the previous ideology), the one which currently prevails in Western democracies is indicated rather than described. No doubt much laborious research would be necessary to uncover the discursive connections suggested here: from the center of organization to that of education, from the center of the media to social psychology, or to that of literary, philosophical and artistic expression. This latter shortcoming is all the more perceptible in that we believe it possible through this third form to discover the general properties of ideology and the principles of its transformation. Nonetheless, it can be explained, if not justified, like the outline format, by the concern to hastily revive a critique whose foundation is, at the present time, buried under the rubble of Marxism.

Indeed, it is impossible not to bring up the decay of the concept of ideology, given the way it is employed by sociologists or historians invoking scientific authority, as well as by revolutionary militants. Some have proclaimed "the end of ideology" (a formula which was immensely popular at the beginning of the

*From Claude Lefort *Les Formes de l'histoire: Essais d'anthropologie politique*, Gallimard, Paris, 1978 pp. 278-329. Appeared originally in *Textures* 8-9, 1974. An abbreviated version was published in the *Encyclopedia Universalis* (vol. XVII, Organum). Translated by Kathy Sabo in collaboration with Greg Nielsen, Université de Montréal for the *CJPST*.

sixties and which has recently been revived), convinced that the demands of industrial society gradually compel adaptation to reality and that the great doctrines no longer mobilize the masses. Others are content to denounce the decay of bourgeois ideology by invoking the powerlessness of the dominant to defend a value system which, from business to family, formerly governed the functioning of institutions to their own benefit. Still others, from a different perspective, see all thought as ideology; faced with their adversaries, they do not hesitate to lay claim to a proletarian ideology, as if each class interest, in itself determined, found direct and coherent expression in language.

In the first case, ideology is reduced to the *manifestation* of a global project of societal transformation; that is to say, actually to the explicit discourse of a party—communist or fascist (or one of their variants), whereas the question as to how it arose from the crisis of bourgeois ideology and why the latter is able to profit from a general thesis on the organisation of society disappears. In the second case, the present dominant ideology is identified with bourgeois ideology, defined by traits which were formerly attributed to it by the Marxist movement. In this way, with regard to the decay of bourgeois ideology, it is not possible, in principle, to perceive the signs of a transformation. Thus, one yields either to the myth of a revolution in progress, at the point of bursting out, or to the myth of an "unofficial" domination and exploitation, unable from that point to recognize their legitimacy or to be recognized as legitimate. Finally, in the third case the concept of ideology retains no trace of the initial meaning which supplied its critical force: ideology is reduced to ideas which are defended to assure the victory of a class, to a good or bad cause whose nature one knows or could know, and whose agent one knows or could know oneself to be.

In one way or another, the split between an order of practice and one of representation, which Marx's work leads us to examine, is ignored; or perhaps "concealed" would be a better choice to emphasize that it is not a question of the distortion of a concept. Rather, in a misappreciation of the problem of ideology, an ideological blindspot shows itself; just as the lack of comprehension of the problem of the subconscious would not stem from an error in the reading of Freud, but from a new resistance to discovery which would threaten the subject's certitudes.

Thus, by means of remarkable ruse, ideology has come to designate almost the contrary of its original meaning. Formerly referring to a logic of dominant ideas, concealed from the knowledge of social actors and only revealing itself through interpretation and in the critique of utterances and their manifest sequences, it has today been reduced to a corpus of arguments, to the apparatus of beliefs which provides the visible framework of a collective practice, identified with democratic liberal discourse for some, or with Leninist or Stalinist discourse (indeed, Maoist or Trotskyst) for others, or even with fascist discourse just as they are presented.

To reopen the path to a critique of ideology, to the examination of the present, is not to return to the original purity of Marx's theory. Such a step would be doubly illusionary, first of all, because strictly speaking, there is no theory of ideologies in Marx's work; his analyses are ambiguous and to make use of his work, one must interpret it. Secondly, the present can only be decoded if one questions the principles which control its intelligibility. In addition, returning to Marx's undertaking can retrace his procedure only *at a distance* and include the examination of the thought about ideology in the examination of ideology itself. The distance proves to be considerable, given that Marx only conceived of ideology as "bourgeois ideology", and that we are led to recognize it in other forms, and moreover, to understand the principle of its transformation. Nonetheless, we must stress the fact that Marx did not make bourgeois ideology into a product of the bourgeoisie. Rather, he leads us to relate it to social division and to link its origin to that of a historical formation—as he terms it, "the capitalist mode of production"—which he concluded to be different from all previous formations grouped together in the category of "pre-capitalism".

Our outline takes the following conception as its starting point: it confines ideology to one type of society, and thus formally challenges the application of the term to a feudal, despotic, or stateless structure in which the dominant discourse draws its legitimacy from reference to a transcendent order, and does not admit the notion of social reality intelligible in itself, nor, at the same time, the notion of a history or nature intelligible in itself. On the other hand, we clearly break with Marx's conception from the moment that we no longer deal with ideology as a reflection, when we attempt to uncover its work and think of formation and transformation together, that is to say, we attribute to it the ability to articulate and rearticulate itself, not only in response to the supposed "reality", but in face of the effects of its own masking of reality. It must be emphasized then, that this break concerns not only the conception of ideology, but the conception of mode of production, or the Marxist definition of the locus of reality.

The society whose specificity Marx conceives by contrast to all previous formations comes into being with the schism of capital and labour. Class oppositions are condensed in the antagonism between bourgeoisie and proletariat; the separation of the State and civil society responds to the necessity for a power which represents the law in everyone's eyes, and which has the means of generalized restraint. Detached from the dominant class, the State tends to put its general interests ahead of the particular interests of one or the other of its parts and to maintain the obedience of the dominated. Simultaneously, the fragmentation in sectors of activity (each tending to develop according to the image of its autonomy) is created as a consequence of the growing division of labour and from the necessity of specialists taking charge of the social needs of bourgeois domination (the political splits from the economic at the same time as the judicial, scientific, pedagogic, aesthetic sectors, etc., define themselves). In this society, the conditions for the unity of the socialisation process are already set out. Capital, without men's knowledge, already embodies materialized social power, whereas with the increasing abstraction of labour, a class arises which is more and more homogeneous and which tends to absorb all the exploited strata. However, this latent unity can only be realized by the negation of the division, a negation whose driving force rests in the revolutionary class, in a praxis where its productive force and its struggle against exploitation are articulated. The contradictions which derive from the accumulation of capital and from the separation of the various sectors of activity within the overall structure, the gap between them, their unequal development, social struggles (above all class struggles, but also those between groups linked to specific interests and practices), all these make capitalist society an essentially *historical* one, that is to say, destined to a continueal upheaval of its institutions, to give birth to new things and to undergo the explicit experience of the real as history.

In terms of such a description, ideology becomes in turn a separate domain; it constitutes a world of ideas in which an essence of social reality is represented; oppositions of all orders are changed into determinations of the universal, domination is changed into an expression of the law. The affinity between the political and the ideological is evident: just as power splits from a totally divided society to embody the law's generality and to exercise physical restraint, and as it simultaneously transposes and misrepresents a class's domination, so does ideological discourse separate itself from all the forms of social practice, to embody the generality of knowledge and to exercise the force of persuasion; it transposes and misrepresents at the same time as an idea, the reality of domination. Indeed, the political and the ideological, when all is said and done, are not intelligible unless one recognizes both the incompletion of the socialization process and the possibility inscribed *in reality* of this completion, to which communism gives real expression. But whereas the political is still determined within the limits of the socialisation process, ideology achieves in the imagination that unity which only real action, the negativity of labour and of proletarian praxis, will bring about.

As fruitful as it may be, this analysis (which certainly does not summarize all of Marx's thought) misrepresents the symbolic dimension of the social domain. It is impossible, in our view, to deduce the order of law, of power or of knowledge from relations of production; impossible also to reduce the language in which social practice is articulated to the effects of the labour-capital division. These relations and effects are only constructed, only developed according to *conditions* which we cannot possibly place on the plane of reality. Instead, that which is labelled as such opens up to humanity, becoming organized and comprehensible only once the signs of a new experience of law, power and knowledge are put in place, once a mode of discourse is installed in which certain oppositions, certain practices, actually *manifest*, that is to say, link with each other and potentially contain a universal meaning, in allowing a regulated exchange between thought and action.

According to Marx, the progress of exchange and the progressive instituting of the market go back to the origins of capitalism; however, the market practice confronted limits which prohibited its generalisation, despite its considerable expansion and the maturity of its techniques in other social formations (in China for example). These obstacles formed part of the symbolic system, a configuration of signs of law, power and knowedge which did not allow the disassociation of social relations and personal dependence. Also noticeable at the origins of the accumulation of capital was the naked violence of the dominant who tore their means of production from the peasants' hands and reduced them to the status of a pure labour force. However, what Marx calls the original sin of capitalism also applies to his own theory, because the violence born of the new mode of production was not mute; it was supported by a representation of cause and effect, whose articulation was deprived of meaning under other social conditions; it became part of a discourse capable of finding the criterion for its coherence within its limits, and which could become the pivot of an articulation of the law and reality.

No description of the changes which have occurred in production, exchange and ownership can explain what is brought into play with the formation of the modern State. The *stage* of social reality *appears* where political power is confined within society, as the instrument which unifies it, where this power is supposed to originate through its action. Represented on this stage is the institution of social reality; in the events which are acted out there, in the relations which are created between individuals and groups, the framework of reality can be located.

Although power is brought within the boundaries of space and time where social relations are articulated and is thereby disaligned with regard to the law which it represents, this does not mean that it becomes actual power. If it were to appear as such, the indications of social identity would be abolished. However, it is true that the power is exposed to this threat as soon as its representation is involved in the institution of social reality; not only appearing as if generated in the society, but in appearing as a founder, since it is henceforth deprived of any indication of its own foundation, removed from the order of the world from which it drew the assurance of its function. Thus, it can only be established under the sign of the law if it always re-establishes itself, that is to say, by employing a *discourse*—where the difference between the one and the other, and the difference between "saying" and what is said arise from the identity of the social subject. This discourse is itself ambiguous, unable to be determined as the product of power without, in turn, falling to the realm of fact, unable as well to relate to a transcendent guarantee without losing its properties. In its exercise, it is thus concerned with producing its "truth", with affirming its *power of discourse*, in order to deny its determination as discourse of power. This ambiguity is such that the power is for the first time shown to be simultaneously localized and non-localizable. It is non-localizable in that it arises at the intersection of two actions which refer to each other, which are generated by the society that power generates. However, it is necessarily localized insofar as it is tied down to the domain of social reality.

The disentangling of the social and world orders goes together with the disentangling of the political and the mythical-religions; but, by the same token, it also goes with that of the political and the non-political *within* the social order. The differentiation of economic, judicial, pedagogical, scientific, aesthetic practices, etc., which are developed, not as actual practices (in the pores of society according to the Marxist metaphor), but as practices which put social reality as

DISAPPEARING IDEOLOGY

such into play, is only clarified under these conditions. Simultaneously, this differentiation is that of social discourses, "particular" discourses, but ones which are concerned with claiming a universal truth. The oscillation which is indicated between the discourse of power and the power of discourse includes the possibility of a disjunction between power and discourse. In other words, each particular discourse reveals its power, not only at a distance from institutionalised political power, but in contradiction to the determination of power represented in itself, insofar as it is joined to a singular practice where social division is found. Thus each discourse tends to set off in search of its own foundation; in the discourse's exercise itself, a relation is formed with knowledge, whose limits are not actually determined, in the sense that a general knowledge of the social order and the order of the world in conjunction with the power of the State is lacking. That the diverse discourses are interrelated in no way means that they can be condensed into one, because the truth is that they are not only contemporarily instituted in function of one experience; they participate in the institution of social reality and decode it through the effect of the disarticulation of power and the law and their own differentiation, each referring back to itself in elaborating its differences.

With such a process, the question is not to attribute the *cause* to the *fact* of the modern State. In doing this, we would be victims of the same illusion that we denounced in Marx's work; we would only be transferring to another level the determinism which Marx was tempted to place at the level of the relations of production. As well, we could say that the characteristics of the modern State are only determined in a system where knowledge reveals its differentiation, where discourse reveals its alterity (instead of speech being organized through the exterior pole of the Other), events whose origins were put forward by the humanism of the Renaissance. If, however, we label as political the "form" in which the symbolic dimension of social reality is uncovered, it is not in order to give greater importance to relations of power, among others, but rather to make it understood that power is not "a thing", empirically determined, but indissociable from its representation, and that the experience made of this, simultaneously experience of knowledge and the mode of articulation of social discourse, is constitutive of social identity.

In this perspective, the break with Marx goes so far as to touch upon what is for him the final question: the future unity of the process of socialisation *in reality*. The question of unity overshadows that of social identity which could not arise in reality; it implies its defection and marks the insertion of the practice in the order of language.

From the moment we refuse to define ideology with regard to a supposed reality, it demands a new interpretation. We can only define it by recognizing the attempt belonging solely to modern society to conceal the enigma of its political form, to cancel the effects of social and temporal division which are generated to restore the "real". In this sense, we do not grasp it as a reflection, nor through the practice which it would reflect. It is exposed by its own workings: in response to the "institution" whose finality is to bring the indetermination of social reality back to its determination.

The transformation of ideology allows us to better understand its formation because the contradiction which is present is revealed there: it cannot realize itself without losing its function, nor can it go to the limit of the affirmation of reality without the threat of appearing in its externality to the practice and instituting discourse from which it arises to defuse the conflicts.

It is true that in attempting to present here the logic of the transformation of ideology, the outline suffers from being an outline rather than a first draft of a full analysis, from its rigid construction rather than from a lack of precision. The role which we give to the contradiction leaves us open to the accusation of Hegelianism. Nonetheless, it should be noted that this contradiction is not concerned with history, with the future of "Spirit", but only brings to light the genesis of the social representations of concealment. The principles of this genesis can be deciphered because in accordance with the same task, through repetition, the movements of discourse are carried out in the historical process.

The Problem with Marx

Marx's procedure was entirely different from that of contemporary Marxists. He did not possess an inherent sense of the distinction between the ideological and the real; rather, he developed it. We cannot forget that the critique of German philosophy, and most importantly that of Hegel, controls his initial interpretations of social structure, and that in *Capital*, moreover, the critique of the illusions of the bourgeois economy and the market forms the basis for the discovery of the unity of social labour and the process of value formation. Being only too familiar with his method, neither can we underestimate the audacity of an attempt to pinpoint the signs of a logic of deception in all the dominant modes of representation, and notably in philosophical discourses where a radical critique of established ideas is demanded. Finally, we cannot fail to observe that in his work, the distinction between reality and ideology is articulated with the implicit distinction between knowledge and ideology—and that this latter distinction prohibits attaching the terms of the former to the plane of objective knowledge. It is actually when he demonstrates, in his *Critique de la philosophie de l'Etat de Hegel*, the extravagant mechanics of Hegel's philosophical system, that Marx acquires for the first time an understanding of ideological phenomena. There, he reveals the attempt to substitute an ideal origin of the State for its real origin. This becomes a process of inverting reality, the transposition in space of the theory of contingent socio-historical determinations, and the imaginary solution to existing contradictions—in effect, a process of idealisation. But more importantly, he reveals the action of the fulfillment of knowledge which turns in on itself, simulating the conquest of totality, and which conceals from itself the fact of its own creation, thereby effacing the division between thought and being. We must recognize that in ideology (it is of little importance that the concept has not yet been clarified, the outline of its constituent elements has been brought to light), a triple denial is effected: the division of class, linked to the division of social labour; the temporal division, the destruction-production of forms of social relations; and finally, the division of knowledge and the practice which it reflects, and from which it is instituted as such. In addition, when Marx analyses the State and the bureaucracy and no longer their Hegelian representation, and when later, forgetting the *folie* of the philosophical system, he only concerns himself with understanding that of the capitalist system, it is in order to bring to light the same process. The discourse within the institution supports the illusion of an essence of society; it wards off a double threat to the established order, arising from a society which is at once divided and historical. This discourse must be recognized as rational in itself, a closed discourse which, while masking the conditions of its own production, claims to reveal that of empirical social reality.

Our aim is not to analyse Marx's thought. If this were the case, it would then have to be agreed that his distinction between knowledge and ideology only carries the seeds of the critique of any discourse claiming to define the real in a refusal to recognize the conditions which assure its externality. It would also have to be agreed that he himself yielded to the temptation of this position by investing the positive sciences with the certitude of which he had divested philosophy. Yet, it is important to briefly reformulate Marx's problem, to unearth it from the dogmatic commentaries which have covered it, in order to assess the theoretical conditions which he has imposed upon us as well as the limits beyond which we must go if we wish to take up his interpretation again in examining contemporary societies.

This problem is posed in terms which preclude the reduction of ideology to bourgeois discourse, and thus prohibit exclusively retaining its function of mystification, justification and conservation in the service of class interests. Marx has amply emphasized this function, notably in *The German Ideology*, but it is only intelligible if ideology is first considered in relation to its focus: social division. Marx implies that a society cannot continue to exist as a human society unless it creates a representation of its unity—unity which, in reality, is witnessed in the relation of reciprocal dependence of social agents and at the same time is belied by the separation of their activities. Thus, even though social division is not determined in the universal division of class (that of the bourgeoisie and the proletariat), the existence of "limited social relations" implies the projection of an imaginary community under cover of which "real" distinctions are determined as "natural", the particular is disguised under the traits of the universal, the historical erased under the atemporality of the essence. The representation in which social relations are embedded indicates in itself a position of power, since the imaginary community governs over the individuals or separate groups and imposes behavioural norms upon them. In this sense, the overlying universal inserts the dominated into his condition and assures the position of the dominator. Nonetheless, the point of view of class domination and that of the "representation", however related they may be, do not coincide. Analysing Asiatic depotism, Marx observes that the prince embodies the imaginary community above the dispersed rural communities. The "real" power—which can be located, in practice, by the signs of command (control of bureaucratic apparatus), constraint (recruiting of peasant labour for war or state objectives), and exploitation (imposing a surplus value on agricultural production)—this empirically determinable power is held in a representation which reflects and conceals social division (the absolute distance between master and enslaved people symbolically transposes the untransformed separation of rural communities). Still, it is true that this is an extreme case, since the bureaucracy only exists as a class through the mediation of the despot. It is also true that his discourse (be he god, demi-god, or divine representative) tends to become confused with the discourse of the universal. The indications which Marx gives pertaining to class formation in *The German Ideology* are even more suggestive. He brings to light a division between individuals such as they are determined in a collective relation, in function of their common interests with regard to a third person, and these same individuals defined as members of a class, receiving their identity as "average individuals", find themselves belonging to a "community". Detached from the real activity of the division of labour, and hovering above the individuals, this "community" effaces the third person, and thus becomes the essence of social reality. In this perspective, the class itself, unlike the economic category to which it is attached, shows itself to be held in the ideological process. Furthermore, the analysis of *The 18th Brumaire* discloses that its formation as the dominant political class implies a denial of the temporal difference, a refusal to recognize the present; camouflaging it under the characteristics of Ancient Rome proves to be a necessary condition for bourgeois revolutionary action.

Social Division is not in Society

If this is the path which Marx seems to open up, there can be no doubt that he also closes it off. In effect, it would be impossible for him to follow such a course unless he claimed to determine the nature of social reality through the positive sciences, yielding to the illusion of an intrinsic development attributed to the observer, and unless he argued in accordance with a superficial opposition between production and representation. Admittedly, it must be recognized that the concept of production is considerably expanded in Marx's writings. He notes that men do not produce only the tools necessary to meet their needs, and these being met, do not only produce new needs; they also produce their social relations. It can indeed be said that even language results from production, since Marx admits that it appears with the necessity for commerce between men, and that in short, he envisages its development by relating it to the communication model—individual to individual or group to group—which is one aspect of social relations. Nonetheless, the use of this concept, however widespread, constantly guarantees a natural evolution of humanity. It is true that man produces the instruments of his production and his social relations at the same time; what is produced is, in turn, a productive force. In this way, he is also a product of what he produces, but the idea of production being self-production does not free him from a mechanism. In the last analysis, the social state proves to be a combination of terms, of which the identity (be it a necessity, an instrument, a linguistic sign, labour, its individual or collective agent) is unquestionable. From such a perspective, the concept of the division of labour itself refers to a basic fact, certainly in Marx's eyes, to a fact of evolution, but one which lies within a field already covertly developed in such a way as to give the impression that the elements are naturally determined. Nothing could be more significant in this respect than Marx's effort, in *The German Ideology*, to trace the origins of the division of labour, and his assertion that primitively it was none other than the division of labour in the sex act. There, without doubt, Marx's positivism shows itself. The argument assumes precisely that which escapes explanation: a division of the sexes such that the partners would naturally identify each other as being different, so coming to reflect upon this difference, and be represented as man and woman. It becomes clear that this is not a simple deviation of interpretation when, in the same section of *The German Ideology*, as Marx enumerated the three fundamental conclusions of the history of humanity, procreation is presented as the act of production of the family, of the double relation man-woman and parents-child. In the same way that copulation is seen to be the primitive model of cooperation and social division, procreation is considered to be the model of the historical production of humanity. In both cases, there is a negation of the articulation of the division—between sexes or generations—with the actual "thought" of the division, which cannot possibly be deduced from the former since it is implicit in the definition of the terms. It is the symbolic order which is negated, the idea of a system of oppositions by virtue of which social "figures" can be identified and articulated in relation to each other, that is, the relation between the division of social agents and the representation. In other words, Marx refuses to recognize that social division is also originally the division of the socialisation process and the discourse which articulates it.

Criticizing Marx in no way leads us to assert the primacy of the representation nor to fall back into the illusion which he denounced of an independent logic of ideas. Neither does it distract us from the task of discovering the mechanisms which tend to assure the representation of an imaginary essence of the community. On the contrary, we are striving to understand them, but without yielding to the naturalist illusion. Such an attempt presupposes that we no longer confuse social division with the empirical division of men in the operation of production. We cannot determine it any more than the division of the sexes in an objective space which would have pre-dated it; we cannot relate it to positive terms inasmuch as they arise as such, even in its activity. Social space is established, we must assume, with the division, and this only insofar as it is visible to itself. Its differentiation through relations of kinship or class, through the relation between state and civil society, is indissociable from the action of discourse at a distance from the supposed reality, a discourse which states the order of the world. It is therefore impossible to take up a position which would comprehend the totality of social relations and the workings of their articulations. Similarly, it would be impossible to include the totality of historical development, to establish a beginning and an end to social division, as that would then be concealing from ourselves our own involvement at the level of discourse already brought into play in the division. This blindspot would prompt us to take our representation as being real in itself.

At this point, the limits of Marx's thought seem to be indicated by his treatment of the process of representation as if it were a result of the ventures of cooperation and division, as if this reality were determined on the natural level of labour. Thus, he could not avoid confusing the ideological and symbolic orders, reducing discourses such as the mythological, religious, political, judicial, etc., to the projection of "real" conflicts into the imaginary, and lastly, lowering the signs of law and power to the empirical plane, thereby transforming them into social "products".

The Imaginary and the "Historical Society"

This critique must be even further developed. To state that the institution of social reality is simultaneously the appearance to itself of the social reality gives rise to a certain ambiguity because one is then tempted to picture the emergence of discourse on social reality as emerging from the social space, thus simply reconstituting a more sophisticated version of sociologism. In actual fact, the ambiguity is already present when we speak of the "discourse on social reality" as if it were possible to perceive it as such, to include the discourse which declares the order of the world as well as the one which declares the physical order in it, as if the question of social division, even freed from empiricism, included in itself that of the division of man and the world and also that of the division of the sexes and generations; especially as if it were possible to reduce the question of the origins of man and the question of birth to a question of origin as it appears in society through myth or religion. In each epoch, men's discourse is ruled by a metasociological and metapsychological question. We misunderstand it first of all by believing it possible to enclose it within certain limits; but still more seriously when, in consequence, we forget that the discourse on social reality does not coincide with itself in the social space where it acts and where, at the same time, it is instituted. Finally, we misunderstand it in forgetting that what it articulates assumes the fact of its own articulation, or, in other words, that the labour of division and institution is "older" than that of the social division and institution. Thus Marx's limit is sharply brought out in attempting to envisage social reality from within the boundaries of social reality, history from within the borders of history, man from man and with a view to man. It is thus brought out in attempting to evade, not the relations between man and "nature" (because he speaks of it continuously in order to assure himself of an objective determination of man in a naturalist perspective), but rather the relation of man, the social, history, to what is in principle beyond reach, from which he is generated and which remains implicit in him.

Through becoming aware of this limit, we are encouraged to reformulate the conditions of ideological analysis. As we have already stated, it is not possible to determine ideology with regard to a "reality", whose traits would be taken from positive knowledge, without losing the notion of the operation of the constitution of reality, and without placing ourselves in the illusionary position of overlooking Being. On the other hand, we can attempt to understand how, in a given epoch, the dominant discourse acts in such a way as to conceal the process of social division, or that which at present we also call the process of generating social space, or still, the *historical*, in order to make it understood that social division and temporality are two aspects of the same institution. Undoubtedly, it will have to be admitted that such a discourse, inasmuch as it is placed in social division, in its action of describing the social space can only be opaque to itself. But it is an altogether different matter to state that it bears a knowledge whose principle is hidden from it, and that it acts according to the demands of concealing the traces of social division, that is to say, according to the demands of the representation of an order which would assure it of the natural determination of its articulation, and with it, of the articulation of social relations *here* and *now*. As the institutor, the discourse is without knowledge of the institution, but insofar as it is concerned with averting the threat that the manifestation of a gap between being and discourse hangs over it, that of the backlash from this experience, it actively becomes the negator of the institution of social reality; it is a discourse of occultation, in which symbolic indicators are converted into natural determinations in which the statement of social law, the statement of world law and that of physical law come to mask the inconceivable link between the law and the statement, the dependence of the law on the person who utters it and the dependence of the utterance on the law.

Nonetheless, we must immediately become aware of the conditions under which it is possible to grasp this distinction. In effect, it assumes that the institution of social space has become perceptible to itself, in such a way that the instituting discourse cannot efface its tracks through the imaginary. In other words, it assumes that social division and historicity in themselves have come to question this in such a way that the occultation's work remains subject to their effects, that in its failures, in the continual attempt to correct them, through its conflicts, it allows that which we can now call *reality* to appear, *reality*, to indicate that it is a question of that which indeed exposed the impossibility of concealment. In this sense, examining ideology confronts us with the determination of a type of society in which a specific imaginary realm can be located.

Although Marx, as we have just pointed out, was tempted to convert social division into the empirical division of classes, and yielded to the illusion of a determinism which would govern the series of modes of production, it is still to

57

him that we owe the idea of modifying the imaginary realm. In effect, by opposing the capitalist mode of production to all previous ones, he glimpsed the peculiarity of a mode of institution of social reality in which the effects of the division and historicity can no longer be neutralized through the representation. In seeking to define Asiatic despotism (to which we have already referred), he actually weakens its construction, since he asserts that this social formation tends to reproduce itself as such, independent of all events such as wars, migrations, changes in dynasties; that the economic and social organization is as if paralysed due to the absolute separation of the imaginary community and the rural ones. In so doing, he prompts us, first of all, to doubt the respective functions of production and representation, by leaving it to be assumed that the first is subordinate to the second. Even though he persists in presenting despotism as an imaginary function which grafts itself onto the reality of the division of labour, he cannot, at the same time, avoid admitting that it has a symbolic effectiveness (which is attested to by designating the mode of production in non-economic terms); but especially, through an extreme case he clarifies a distinctive trait of all the pre-capitalist formations. The assertion that their mode of production remains essentially conservative in spite of all the historical differences, that the division of labour and social relations always tend to crystallize there and to resist the change factors, is in fact only intelligible if one recognizes the full effectiveness of the symbolic device which, owing to the separation of two positions— that of law, discourse on social reality, the power which is at once bearer and guarantor of this discourse and the place of actual social relations—makes possible the placement of the established order between social groups and agents in the world order, and thus diffuses the effects of social division. This is a device whose particular task is to assure the conditions of occultation without allowing the question of an opposition between imaginary and real to arise. Actually, reality only shows itself to be determinable insofar as it is assumed to be already determined, in accordance with an utterance which, mythical or religious, attests to a knowledge whose actual activity of knowledge, technical invention, interpretation of the *visible*, cannot bring the foundation into play. The discourse is indeed instituting; it orders the possibility of an articulation of social reality. However, it defines the oppositions as "natural", and thus defines the status of the dominant and dominated in kinship and class relations owing to the concealment of social division behind the representation of a massively asserted division, of another world, of a materialized invisibility. We can only grasp the extent of this operation if we understand that in one sense it realizes a possibility which forms part of the institution of social reality, by making it appear that this institution is not a social fact in itself, that the question of social space is, from the beginning, a question of its boundaries or its "outside" (just as the question of the body is that of its origin and its death), that the discourse is not only the product of men, but that they are articulated in it. We are definitely transgressing the borders of Marxism again in rejecting the idea that myths and religions are simple human inventions, but only in order to follow in its wake, to attempt to picture a model in which the symbolic device is such that the concealment of social division coincides with the actual power of blocking its effects and the concealment of the historical coincides with the actual power of barring the path to change, or of containing its development.

If we venture to conceive of the genesis of the different types of social formations, we must make certain corrections in these propositions. The differences between the structures of a primitive society, those of Asiatic despotism, the ancient city-state, and European feudalism are so great that treating them as variants of one model might appear to be an arbitrary decision. From our perspective, we are in particular constrained to neglect an essential articulation: that between power and discourse on social reality—an articulation, however, which can only become visible through the activity in which the pole of the law is disassociated from the pole of the utterance, and where the contingency of the utterance and its function of occultation venture to appear. It must be admitted that there is no criterion which could distinguish the imaginary from the real where the place of power is held "empty" and where relations are organized according to its neutralization, whereas when the power is linked to men's actions and shifted out of position with regard to the law, the possibility of this distinction is already opened up. In spite of this, in all cases, the origin of discourse on the order of the world, on the order of social reality, proves to have been conceived *elsewhere*.

Marx himself only conceives of this model (whatever his claims to developing a theory of the evolution of humanity) from the starting point of his analysis of the capitalist mode of production. In discovering that the latter is essentially "revolutionary", that is to say, not subject to chance, but in itself a generator of events which continually modify established relations, Marx is led to generally oppose two types of social formations.

Let us briefly recall the two traits which, in Marx's eyes, characterize modern society: on the one hand, the unification of the social domain through the generalization of exchange and of the reduction of all concrete labour to abstract labour; on the other hand, the division of labour and capital, the concentration of the means of production and the formation of an ever-increasing mass of social agents, reduced to the simple possession of their labour power. Undoubtedly, these two traits are indissociably linked: society tends to refer to itself in all its parts, or in the language of the young Marx, the "reciprocal dependence" of all social agents tends to be achieved insofar as a cleavage is effected for the first time between two antagonistic poles whose relation brings into play the identity of everything. Thus, the social space tends to appear within its own limits (and not with reference to another locus from where it would be visible) as soon as all the divisions become subordinate to a general one, when kinship and territorial relations, and more generally, relations of personal dependence, are all dissolved, and when each of the two terms of the division, by the negation of its contradiction, refers to the unity of social reality. Certainly these operations are not symmetrical, given that although the mass of workers realizes the negation by representing the image of the collective Producer (who is only recognized in the abolition of the division), capital, on the other hand, the embodiment of social power, is only achieved through enlarging the division and by representing the image of a class destined to the fantasy of being a universal class as a *particular* class. The orgin of ideology takes its place in this process as an attempt to represent the universal from the particular point of view of the dominant class. The singularity of this attempt stems from the fact that it is entrenched in the social division, that it results directly from it. As we have already stated, this attempt cannot be interpreted in terms of collective psychology, but rather as the sign of a logic which is part of the institution of social reality; from the moment that the division no longer finds its expression in the division of the world of production and the world of representation, but rather is represented within the world of production itself, that is to say, is hidden behind the image of an immanent rationality in reality. In this sense, the singularity of the attempt also lies in the fact that it comes to terms with the activity which frees capital from all the limitations imposed by the limited social relations, and which invests it, as a socialized system of exploitation, with an unlimited power of objectification and rationalization of production. The ideological process differs from the religious process not only in that the former tends to develop within the confines of social space, but also, in so doing, it becomes intricately linked with "scientific" knowledge, knowledge which lays claim to the self-deciphering of reality. On the other hand, the ideological process is just as radically distinguished by the fact that it is subject to the effects of an incessant social upheaval generated by capitalism, in which the institututions, mentalities, and collective behaviours are modified, in which the centers of power shift, in which the bourgeois strata, which drew their income and power from different sources, enter into opposition; by the fact, then, that it must accomplish its task of concealing the division by modifying its own statements or by simultaneously having recourse to a multiplicity of representations in order to seal the cracks opened by the change in the "rationality of reality". Thus, the singular relation between ideology and historical society is exposed. The imaginary is no longer part of the symbolic device which tends to define the institution of social reality in referring the detail of social organization to a discourse which is split from it. Insofar as the question of the genesis of social reality from its own locus arises (the mastery of this genesis, the means of denying and containing it being concealed), a new type of discourse then comes into being, concerned with abating the oppositions and breaks at the dual level of time and space. In other words, ideology is the sequence of representations whose function is to re-establish the dimension of the "ahistorical" society within the historical society.

Once again, taking from Marx's language, the idea of "conservation" fulfills a strategic function in his interpretation; in all pre-capitalist formations, the mode of production is conservative, whereas in capitalism the ideology is conservative and is assigned the task of concealing the revolution which resides in the mode of production. Marx undoubtedly sensed that in this latter case, the imaginary is segregated from the institution of social reality, due to the manifest breakdown of every symbolic system susceptible to mastering this institution. Marx, like Feuerbach, can indeed continue to consider religion as a typical expression of ideology; but, in demonstrating that religion has emigrated into social relations, he partially perceives the specificity of ideology: the tacit recognition of historicity, the division, and even the implication of the representation in that which it represents. He partially realizes that in modern societies, the process of the imaginary goes hand in hand with an unprecedented experience of "reality" as such. In aiming at this distinction resulting from the real and the imaginary, he acquires the ability to return it to social formations within which it would be indecipherable. But this ability is sustained by the illusion which is at the center of modern society, that the institution of social reality can explain itself. Marx grasps the principle of ideology as the specific mode of the imaginary, but he continues to suppose that it can be reduced to the concealment of *something*: class division, division of labour and capital, of the State and civil society, of the historical present and its tasks. He does this without ever going so far as to consider that if it actually insures this concealment, it is ordered and supported by a principle of occultation which has been substituted for the one which governed the symbolic device of all the pre-captialist formations; the impossibility of a discourse on social reality being generated in a locus other than its own.

We cannot confuse ideology with the refusal to recognize this impossibility which, from a broader perspective, is the same one which is confronted by all discourse in modern societies, in that each discourse is seeking its own foundation. In addition, today we would not say that Marx's thought is ideological any more than we would say the same of any other work to which we attribute the power of institution in modern times. Moreover, social discourse and not only that which relates to theoretical works, cannot be considered as ideological for the simple fact that it is developed in the face of such an impossibility. In addition, we consider the argument which discredits the principles of democratic discourse in reducing them to utterances of bourgeois democracy to be a false creation, although we do point out the impossible attempt to place the institutor in the instituted. With just such confusion, the critique of a fraction of the *intelligentsia* is developing at the present time. All around, it sees the signs of ideology, and multiplies its condemnations of political discourse as such, of economic, judicial, philosophical or pedagogical discourse, without being able to assess what has been brought into play and what still is each time there is an attempt at contact between instituted knowledge and the institutor owing to its inability to succeed; such an attempt turns the discourse into a "workplace", whose effect is to keep open the lines of questioning which are at its roots, in spite of all the arguments which are asserted. In this sense (the paradox being only apparent), this mode of discourse, in the activity which condemns it to a certain blindness, attests to that which is beyond the grasp of action and knowledge, a relation to the enigma of the institution. If we were to take as ideology the discourse which confronts the impossibility of its self-genesis, this would mean that we would be converting this impossibility into a positive fact; we would believe in the possibility of mastering it; we would again be placing ourselves in the illusionary position of overlooking discourse in order to "see" the division from which it emerges, whereas the discourse can only reveal this in itself. On the contrary, we maintain that ideology is organized by a principle of occultation which strays from its task: it indicates a return of social discourse upon itself, suppressing all the indications which would tend to destroy the certainty of the social being: signs of historical creativity, of the unnamed, of what is concealed through the action of power, of what breaks apart through the scattered affairs of socialization; signs which make a society, or humanity as such, estranged from itself.

As we have stated, such is the nature of ideological discourse already discerned by Marx, but deceptively related to a hidden reality (the state of the division of labour determined by that of the productive forces); it is a second discourse, following the track of the instituting discourse which does not know itself, and under the latter's influence, attempts to simulate a general knowledge of reality as such. This discourse, then, develops in the affirmative mode, the mode of determination, generalization, reduction of differences, of externality regarding its object; as such, it always implies the point of view of power which guarantees an actual or possible order and which tends toward anonymity to attest to a truth imprinted in things. This second discourse draws nothing from its own depths; that is how Marx can justify his observation that ideology has no history. But it would be incorrect to consequently assume that the discourse is linked to a determined ensemble of utterances.

We have already noted that this dependence with regard to the instituting discourse has several effects. In the first place, it tends to take hold of the signs again in order to incorporate them into its concealment of the historical. It accomplishes this in such a way that the "modern" representation (we will return to this point) is at its highest point of effectiveness in masking the temporal difference. In the second place, it tends to achieve the homogenization of the domain by taking in hand the questions which arise in accordance with the differentiation of social space and conflicts of a class and group in order to diffuse them. Thus, the demarcation of a political practice, which we are in no way led to describe as ideological as such, gives rise to a particular discourse which actively elaborates the image of political essence (whether this is to maintain its rationality or its final irrationality is not important). This operation repeats itself, starting from the determination of a judicial, aesthetic, or pedagogical practice; its effectiveness lies in the fact that the same schemas goven in each discourse, that each one leads to another and constitutes one link of the general discourse on social reality. Yet it is equally true that the different layers, each in accordance with the conditions in which it is placed and its particular aspirations, come to speak a language at the service of "rationality" and "reality", of the concealment of any temporal or spatial break, whose effect is to insure the complementarity of representations in an epoch. Thirdly, the attempt to compensate for the shortcomings of the general discourse, always subject to the impossible mastery of the instituting one, imposes a successive recourse to disparate schemes of explanation, logically incompatible, although one model evidently predominates. Different social agents are not alone in sharing the task of ideological discourse; it is destined to move its references to feed its justification—for example, references to the past and future, to ethics and technical rationality, to individual and community. In this sense, it is forced to make the most of what it has, to adapt itself to heterogenous versions in order to retain the effectiveness of its general response.

Nonetheless, these remarks are not sufficient. Even thus corrected, the proposition that ideology has no history might well be misleading, because it hides the contradiction which ideology confronts, and which orders its transformations. As well, it may conceal from us the logic of the imaginary in historical society. We can find the driving force of ideological changes, not only in a "real" history, as Marx believed; to some extent, the necessity for its reorganization is determined by the failure of the process of concealment of the institution of social reality. Because ideology cannot operate without showing itself, that is to say without being exposed as a discourse, without letting the gap appear between this discourse and its object, it implies an evolution in which the impossibility of erasing its tracks is reflected.

Bourgeois ideology, which Marxists persist in confusing with ideology in general—prisoners that they are of an empiricist schema which reduces it to a determined state of class division—only constitutes one instance of it. Indeed, it is in examining the signs of its failure that the genesis of totalitarian ideology is brought to light. In discovering the boundaries of the latter, we may also obtain some indication as to the mechanisms which govern the imaginary in contemporary western societies and whose effectiveness supposes both the exploitation and the neutralization of the totalitarian attempt.

The So-Called "Bourgeois" Ideology

Everything that we have said concerning the general properties of ideology applies to bourgeois ideology. At its peak, in the nineteenth century, it is possible to discern a social discourse external to social reality, a discourse governed by the illusion of an explanation of reality from within the real, and which tends to present itself as an anonymous discourse in which the universal speaks of itself. Whatever support this discourse finds in certain epochs and for certain strata of the dominant class, it is subject to the ideal of positive knowledge and expressly or implicitly challenges any reference to another locus where knowledge about social reality and world orders would collect. But we must not forget the singularity of the device through which ideological discourse attempts to fulfill its function. Actually, it is organized by means of a split between *ideas* and the supposed *real*. The externality of the other locus, linked to religious or mythical knowledge, is erased, but the discourse only refers back to itself through the detour of the transcendence of ideas. The text of ideology is written in capital letters, whether it is a question of Humanity, Progress, Nature, Life or key concepts of bourgeois democracy inscribed on the pediment of the Republic, or even of Science, Art, as well as Property, Family, Order, Society or Country; it can be a conservative or progressivist version of bourgeois discourse, or a socialist or anarchist version of antibourgeois discourse. This text carries the constant signs of a truth which determines the origins of facts, which encloses them in a representation and directs the argumentation. The determination of an order of appearances is asserted or maintained through the transcendence of the idea; or more generally, the possibility of an objectification of social reality opens up, no matter what point of view is adopted.

The double nature of the idea as representation and norm, however, cannot be overemphasized; neither can the double character of the argumentation, which attests to a truth in reality and to the conditions of action in conformity with the nature of things. Moreover, an essential articulation of ideological discourse stands out in the function expressly attributed to the rule. Once again, the same model remains from conservatism to anarchism: a body of dictates is constructed, whose application is conditioned by knowledge and action. The strength of the rule, which provides the assurance of reality and intelligibility wherever and however it is interpreted, is ascertained from political or economic discourse to pedagogical discourse. In this sense, discourse on social reality can only maintain its external position with regard to its object by presenting the image of the rule's guarantor, who, through his existence, confirms the idea's incarnation in the social relation. The guarantor's position is itself explicit. He is part of the representation; a whole ensemble of images is employed where traits of the bourgeois, the boss, the minister, the family man, the educator, the militant, etc., appear. Undoubtedly, at one extreme of ideological discourse, authority tends to be hidden behind the power of the idea; however it is true, then, that this power becomes inordinate, that science is claimed through this power with greatly increased vigor and that if the particular determinations of social agents are sometimes engulfed by it, the image of man as universal man effectively comes to support the truth of the rule in socialism and anarchism.

Let us take note of the fact that the representations of the idea, of the intelligible sequence of facts, of the rule, of the master holding the principle of action and of knowledge, presume a singular type of discourse destined to display itself as such. The discourse on social reality asserts itself as discourse; it is very significantly modelled on pedagogy. This characteristic brings to light the distance, which too is represented, between the speaker, wherever he may be situated, and the *other*. We do not mean to say that discourse emanates from an agent or a series of agents who would only be representatives of the dominant class. Insofar as it is presented as discourse on social reality, extracting itself from the social, ideological discourse develops impersonally; it conveys knowledge which is supposed to arise from the order of things. But it is essential for it to clarify at all levels the distinction between the subject, who is established by his articulation with the rule, who expresses himself in stating the rule, and the *other*, who, not having access to the rule, does not have the status of subject. The representation of the rule goes hand in hand with that of nature, and this opposition converts itself into a series of manifest terms: for example, the "worker" is represented opposite the bourgeois, the uneducated man opposite the cultured one, the uncivilized man opposite the civilized, the madman opposite the sane one, the child opposite the adult. Thus through all the substitutions, there is a natural being whose image supports the assertion of society as a world above nature. This is the device by which social division is concealed: the position of indicators which allow the determination of the difference between social and sub-social, order and disorder, world and "underworld" (a difference which is of no importance in "pre-capitalism" when the social is perceived from another locus, from an order beyond it) in such a way as to permit the identification and mastery of that which reality conceals from discourse. Thus the latter is able to cover up the question of its genesis, or that of the institution of social reality (which amounts to the same thing) by laying out the boundaries of that which is foreign to any creation this side of the institution, by taking into account an overgrowth of irrational facts whose thrust must be checked. Indeed, it must be repeated that this representation is contested in antibourgeois discourse, but the latter shares, and even broadens, pedagogical aims. It tends to confine itself to a counter-discourse which determines the present irrationality's image and reduces the *other* to the malevolent figure of the dominator—he is no less haunted by the illusion of a transparency of the society's right for itself.

As we have already suggested in calling to mind Marx's analyses, the strength of ideology, in the model which we are broadly sketching, stems from the fact that the discourses, whose homology we have pointed out, remain disjointed. Let us repeat that ideology follows the lines of the institution of social reality; if it provides a general "response", the latter does not arise uniquely in one place. It is multiplied according to a differentiation whose principle Marx vainly imputed to the division of labour which cannot in itself be considered as the driving force of change, and which undoubtedly would rather have to be linked to the division of political power and the law, and as its result, to the activity of segregating the instituitons and social discourses which underlie them. Thus an ideological discourse cuts across the situation constituted by the determination of the state, business, the school, the asylum, of modern institutions in general; it cuts across the tracks of determined spaces in which measurable relations between given agents are organized. Thus taking as a point of departure a historical articulation, ideological discourse occasionally presents the image of a necessity of essence. Doubtless each attempt is only possible because it draws on all the others. There is a constant give and take between the processes of legitimation and dissimulation implemented: however, "knowledge" is not concentrated at one sole extreme, and in this sense a gap between power and discourse is preserved everywhere and always. The task of homogenizing and unifying social reality remains implicit. For this reason, the possibility of a shift or even an inversion of utterances is always open, or in other words, of contradictory versions which, in spite of conflict, insure an identity of reference for social agents.

However the conditions which assure bourgeois ideology's effectiveness also hold the possibility of its failure. Assuredly, to explain its decay, it would be necessary to go beyond its limits, to examine history, but we only propose to highlight the internal contradictions of ideology which compel it to modify itself in order to continue fulfilling its function in historical society.

Judging by a widespread Marxist argument, the decay supposedly results from the fundamental contradiction of ideological discourse and *real* practice which becomes more and more perceptible to the eyes of the dominated. The argument is too well known to require summarizing, and it is known to have found strong support in Leninist criticism of "formal democracy" whose mystification is gradually discovered by the masses through oppression. While a certain amount of truth must be attributed to it, one is led to wonder how reality comes to appear, if it is sufficient to look at the lived experience of a class in order to conceive of the formation of a social discourse which would gradually weaken ideology's hold. This question is all the more important if we consider the societies in which formal democracy has collapsed: we must agree that it yields its place not to a *real* democracy, but to totalitarianism.

The Marxist interpretation seems to be more fruitful when it emphasizes the internal contradictions of ideological discourse. The necessity to state propositions of universal value and, at the same time, to provide a representation of the established order justifying class domination would have the effect of destroying its apparent rationality, and would prohibit it from ever going to the limits of its assertion. Hence, it would give rise to criticism even in its practice, and to a counter-discourse on each of its levels. Marx, as we recall, suggests in *The 18th Brumaire* that bourgeois discourse responds in its own way to the division of labour. The intelligentsia specializes in the worship of abstract truths; it maintains the illusion of an essence of humanity which does not admit the image of particular interests; it speaks the language of poetry, while the political representatives of the bourgeoisie speak in prose. According to this, as soon as the order is threatened, the latter remain alone on the stage. Although he sees them as the realistic spokesmen of the dominant class, placing their discourse in ideology does not exceed the limits of his analysis. Though they take measures which unequivocally manifest the defense of class interests, they still make use of a language which claims to explain things, to state the law of reality and the reality of the law. The concept of ownership, of the State, or labour or the family is no less ideological than those of a humanist intelligentsia. Moreover, if one or another of the intelligentsia's concepts, such as "equality", finds itself relegated to certain circumstances because it might give a toehold to revolutionary demands, the "prose" could never completely break with the "poetry"; discourse on liberty always comes to back up discourse on ownership just as discourse on justice always comes to support discourse on order. As well, without touching the conflicts which tear the agents from ideological discourse, one could deal with this discourse generally to analyse its oppositions and to demonstrate that there is not one idea which could be formulated, not one argument developed in its service, whose assertion does not require an idea or an argument contradicting them. The discourse covers up incompatible representations; it lives on the "horrible mélange" of the image of an unconditional individual beside that of an unconditional society, on the alliance of an artificialist and mechanistic thought with one that is substantialist and organicist. Furthermore, since it is essential for it to explain itself as discourse on social reality, and as it continually names things, through the effect of its internal conflicts, it unknowingly generates the divergence of social reality and discourse.

Yet if we want to determine the extent of the contradiction without forgetting that it stems from the impossible project of a discourse which claims to present the transparency of social reality, and as social discourse, to be discourse on social reality, we must examine precisely that singular property of bourgeois ideology of realizing itself by procedures such as the utterance being nearly perceptible to itself, the statement being almost defined, the image of the speaker being nearly visible, whereas at the same time, everything is supposed to dissolve into social reality's quasi-appearance to itself, because in itself, the internal contradiction does not destroy the discourse. As we have pointed out, it gives the discourse its strength; it develops an articulation between opposing terms, assuring the possibility of saying everything, or, to employ a more contemporary vocabulary, of "rehabilitating" everything, even the most subversive. On the other hand, ideology is undermined by its necessity to produce ideas, which are presented as transcendent with regard to reality at the same moment as they determine it or only seem to express it. Nothing is more remarkable than this process: the idea of ownership or of the family cuts across the fact of ownership or of the family. The latter is not silent; there is no institution which does not organize itself in a language activity. But we have to deal with a language of the second power, which seeks to distance itself with regard to the first and which attempts to avert the danger within it, resulting from the fact that speech circulates in the latter, differentiating the agents from each other at the same time as it relates them, and only settling in accordance with an activity in which the possibility and the limits of exchange are brought into play, a venture whose conditions *and* effects escape the institution. The idea of the family encloses the fact of the institution and implies the belief that its conditions of possibility and its limits are conceivable from within it. The question of the family then, arises through the effect of the representation. It does not arise from the simple fact that there is a limited kinship network; as Lévi-Strauss justly observes, this supposes speech, knowledge, sometimes highly developed reflection of its principles of organization, but not a *view* over the institution which circumscribes it as such, within the social domain, at a distance from others. The differentiation of functions, of roles, the hierarchy of rights, in no way supposes that there is a *view* over the father, mother, child, or, as we would suggest, an intensification of the representation, owing to which an essence emerges, or in this case, an imaginary social relation which amounts to the same thing.

Without doubt, it would be a commonplace to say that the idea of the family is formed through opposition to the contingency of the institution which has become almost perceptible; however, it is already less trite to remark that this contingency is not abolished, but displaced through the effect of the idea, that the latter, whose function is to conceal it, is immediately marked by it, and that finally, a limitless activity is set in motion, an activity attributable to a sequence of ideas to remove the contingency's effects from the utterance. This is a task of argumentation, of justification, which, as we have already observed, is itself represented in ideology; it presents the image of rationality extricating itself from reality (it is of little importance, it must be made clear, that it ends up concluding on the irrationality of human nature). This task's only check is its sudden abolition in returning to the basic utterance of the idea, that is to say, to the assertion that the institution is sacred: the family, the social unit, at the foundation of society. The idea, then, is realized as pure transcendence, and it is known that this realization is in response to a potentiality of ideological discourse wherever it acts. The latter tends to retreat towards a point of certainty where the necessity for speaking is annulled. It is haunted by tautology. The words "family", "ownership", "society", as well as "liberty", "equality", "progress" or "science" condense a knowledge that does without any justification. But the point of certainty is untenable—the transcendence of the abstract idea— because what is sought cannot be attained. It is beyond social reality, a certainty about social reality as such, a referent whose loss is precisely at the origin of ideology. This referent, then, could not be adapted to the utterance of ideas, according to which it could not develop a discourse on social reality, envisaged as determined space. The idea could not therefore fall back on itself without a reappearance of the necessity to produce its foundation by taking hold of signs which, in the supposed reality, attest to it. We would note that this operation implies a recognition of the difference between what is and what is said. In this sense, then, the discourse knows itself as discourse and chooses to represent itself as such because in so doing, it maintains the illusion of a mastery of its origin and of its own space. Paradoxically, it is the ostentation of the language which allows the concealment of the enigma of its genesis, or that which we have called the question of social division. Yet the consequence of this phenomenon is no less noteworthy: if fascination answers to ostentation, it is equally true that the discourse shows itself, finds itself threatened with being perceived as actual discourse.

An analogous contradiction can be pointed out in the status conferred upon the rule and the authority which is supposed to support it. The social universe, it must be remembered, is a universe of rules, and there are no rules which, even in the absence of repressive apparatus designed to make them respected, do not imply a knowledge of the prohibited and the dictated. Yet, in ideology, the representation of the rule is divided from the actual operation of it. Assuredly, this split is accompanied by profound modifications in the relations actually maintained between social agents, but let us set aside this difficult problem in order to consider only the phenomenon of the representation. Perhaps this problem is best observed, as we have already suggested, within the context of pedagogy, and particularly in the learning of a language. Actually, the dominant myth is that language can be mastered by going back to the principles of its construction, defined by grammar. The rule is thus extracted from an experience of the language, determined, made fully visible, and is supposed to control the conditions of the possibility of this experience. The enigma of the language, whether it is internal and external to the speaker, whether there is an articulation which he does not control from himself to others, marking a return to himself, is concealed by the representation of something "external" to the language, from where it would be generated. We know that in its original state, this illusion has reached its highest point when Jesuit education prohibits the use of one's first language at school and imposes an artificial Latin in order to promote a means of persuading one that speech is generated from the rule. Even though this illusion cannot stand up to the demands of a child's socialization in historical society, it brings to light the whole logic behind a representation of pedagogy which claims to overcome the insurmountable difference between the institution of knowledge and the knowledge of the institution. Once again, we uncover the ambiguity of the representation, as soon as the rule is stated, because exhibiting it undermines the power which the rule takes upon itself to introduce into practice. This inordinate power must, in fact, be shown, and at the same time, must owe nothing to the activity which makes it appear. To be true to its image, the rule must be abstracted from any question concerning its origin; thus, it exceeds the operations which it controls. Its power is to confer upon the subject a right to speak, to know, to control his action; whereas lacking the rule, the subject is not only deprived of the means of expression or knowledge, but literally dismissed, that is to say, thrown outside the network of the institution. But to be true to its image, the rule must also prove its validity through usage; it is constantly subject to the demonstration of its effectiveness and is thus contradictorily represented as a convention. Only the master's authority allows the contradiction's concealment, but he himself is an object of representation; presented as a defender of the rule, he lets the contradiction appear through himself. On the one hand, he embodies an authority which does not have to explain itself, or as we say, by divine right, while on the other, he expresses signs of his competence.

We can now point out in all sectors of the social domain the configuration which is made particularly visible by education. Not only the representation of education, but also the representation of literature, of painting or of philosophy implies the same set of contradictions. To avoid the ambiguity which is so widespread today (and which takes its place in a new form of ideology), in passing, let us repeat: we cannot hold a *view* of the historicity of education, of philosophy, of literature, or of painting, etc., which would save us from the question brought into play in their institution; we can only speak of the representation which comes to overshadow the latter each time, to attempt to cancel its effects and to simulate a domination of the socialization process, owing to a determining of the instance of the rule and the instance of the master. Yet, let us not hesitate to expand this analysis. In the context of production enterprises, one must point out the dissociation of the institution and representation, of social discourse implied in the practice and the discourse on social reality which claims to determine its principles in presenting the image of the director, who, on the one hand, holds an authority of divine right, while on the other, retains a certain degree of competence, and in exhibiting the image of the rules, retains a body of dictates in which are expressed an unconditional knowledge of industrial organization and the mundane conditions of human labour's productivity.

The ideological discourse which we are examining has no safety catch: it becomes vulnerable when attempting to make visible the place from where social relations would be conceivable—both thinkable and creatable; it is vulnerable in its powerlessness to define this place without letting its contingency appear, without being condemned to slip from one position to another, without thereby making perceptible the instability of an order which ideological discourse must raise to the status of the essence. In observing it, we are perhaps in a better position to understand why this discourse, in its project to extract itself from social reality and to affirm itself as discourse, can only remain scattered, and why its task of implicit generalization of knowledge and implicit homogenization of experience could disintegrate, faced with the unbearable burden of the ruin of certainty, of a wavering of the representations of discourse, and consequently, of a division of the subject. Claiming its discursive power, it never coincides with the discourse of power; it manifests in itself the position of power. However, whether the latter is the power of the actual or potential government, or one of its countless substitutes, this discourse represents it, exposes it to the *other*'s eye, but is not structured or unified under the principle which would condense the multiplicity of statements into the same assertion and would relate them to the same guarantor. We have already noted that ideological discourse has no safety catch; that is to say that it finds itself constructed in such a way that it is marked by the absence of a guarantor of its origin. In responding to the question of its origin, ideological discourse is ordered; however, it changes itself, shifts within its limits. This is the cost at which power operates in the effectiveness of social relations.

Totalitarianism and the Crisis of Bourgeois Ideology

Through the phenomenon of totalitarianism, we can distinguish the specific traits of bourgeois ideology, since the latter's contradiction is reflected in it. To some, it may appear outrageous to treat as variants of the same model fascism and Nazism, on the one hand, and on the other, that which is called communism, but which, in fact, only constitutes a bureaucratic society's discourse. Nonetheless, we speak of totalitarianism without taking into consideration the differences of regime, which in other respects are highly significant, because our sole concern is to clarify a general aspect of the genesis of ideology.

In totalitarianism, the process of occultation of the institution of social reality seeks to complete itself. In Nazism, it is not essentially a matter of the resurrection of a system of values coming from pre-capitalism, and challenged by bourgeois society, even though evidently there is an attempt to return to the representation of a communal order, based on a relation to the earth, blood ties, and personal dependence, a representation which has continued to survive at the edge of bourgeois ideology in all the forms of conservatism. With communism, it is not essentially a matter of attempting to insert universalist values of bourgeois society into reality, by destroying the form of particular interests at all levels of social activity. However, this project evidently is part of its enterprise, and is rooted in the history of the proletariat's revolutionary struggles within the capitalist world. The formation of totalitarianism is only intelligible if one recognizes the "response" which is brought to the problem of the division of ideological discourse and the process of socialization, or that which we readily call the historicity of social reality. The illusion stems from a social discourse which, implicated as it is in practice, invests it with a general knowledge. This knowledge is always maintained in an external dimension by bourgeois ideology, and wherever it operates, it emits signs of its unity, and thus signs of the homogeneity of the objective domain. Thus the limits of sectors which were formerly expressly recognized, such as the economic, political, judicial, pedagogical, aesthetic and even scientific, are obliterated. The assertion of the identity of reality, as it appears, seeks to turn back on itself from any particular statement; it feeds a passion for tautology and simultaneously, the quest for a totalization in the explicit is substituted for the labour of occultation of bourgeois discourse, whose particular quality was to leave the generalization in the latent. Whereas the latter tends to make the essence of its discourse perceptible to itself, and as such remains out of alignment with respect to power, totalitarian discourse acts with the conviction of being imprinted on reality, and of embodying the potentiality of a continued and general mastery of its articulations. In this sense, it is entirely political discourse, but it denies the particular fact of the political and attempts to achieve the dissolution of the political in the element of the pure generality of social reality.

More precisely, totalitarian discourse denies all the oppositions taken in hand by bourgeois ideology in a representation which each time was made to diffuse their effects, and which threatened the foundation of each term in exposing it to the necessity of explanation. Before anything else, totalitarian discourse effaces the opposition between the State and civil society; it is dedicated to bringing to light the presence of the State throughout social space, that is to say, to transporting, through a series of representatives, the principle of power which informs the diversity of activities, and which includes them in the model of a common allegiance. Yet we must not lose sight of the fact that the discourse does not carry out this operation within the limits of a commentary which exploits its distance with regard to the real in order to point it out in its entirety. Rather, it diffuses itself in the network of socialization; it develops systems of signs whose *representative* function is no longer discernable; it takes hold of actors and places them within these systems in such a way that the discourse (almost) speaks through them and (almost) abolishes the space which is indeed indeterminate, but always preserved between the articulation and the utterance in bourgeois ideology.

The masses are the instrument *par excellence* of totalitarianism, through which the consubstantiality of the State and civil society is manifested. At all levels, they embody the principle of power; they spread the general norm which

71

provides the assurance of a sort of reflection by the society of itself, and, simultaneously, the assurance of its polarization towards a goal, delivering it from the silent threat of the inertia of the instituted, making its identity perceptible through the imperative of activism. But the practice and structure of the Party cannot be distinguished from the discourse whose center it would be (other than by showing the contradictions within which it operates and which it conceals at all levels). Just as all those who fulfill the same function at a more specific level—unions, associations for young people, women, intellectuals, etc. —this representative acts in practice precisely in accordance with the demand of the representation; it figures in the relations which arrange the unity within it that it guarantees before the ensemble of society. In itself, it is a system of signs which allows the formation of a hierarchy, the production of a cleavage between the apparatus and the base, the directors and the executors, the partitioning of activity sectors, in the simulation of transparency to itself of the institution, of a reciprocity of decisions, of a homogeneity of the political body.

In this sense, ideological discourse tends to become discourse of the Party—the discourse on the Party being only a detachment of the latter, although it is absolutely essential to it and marks the limit of the enterprise to which we will return. Nothing brings this phenomenon into focus better than the forming of a new type of social agent, the militant, an image through which can be seen the subject's position within the discourse that he is supposed to speak. The militant is not in the party as if in a determined milieu with visible borders; he is in himself a representative of it; he draws from its source the possibility of freeing himself from conflicts to which he is exposed by his participation in different institutions governed by specific imperatives of socialization, the possibility of embodying the generality of social reality. As a bearer of the representation, the militant accomplishes his function by constantly reflecting that which is organized independently of him in the supposed system of social reality. At the same time, he establishes himself as possessing power and knowledge; he controls the worker, the peasant, the engineer, the pedagogue, the writer; he profers the norm, concentrates the powers of *activism* and finds the vocabulary and syntax of his discourse imprinted in himself in such a way that he forms himself in the operation of ideology.

To the necessity of collecting social discourse in itself beyond all division, of welding together the scattered images of man in bourgeois society, of grasping the key to open all the doors of social structure, and to focus attention on all the forms of economic, political and aesthetic activity, of entering into possession of a general knowledge, of joining all these experiences to one pole of truth, the necessity is added of effacing itself, faced with the anonymity of the idea, of the argumentation, of the rule, of the supreme authority, all of which appear welded to each other. The militant type only completes the full expression of the attempt to efface the difference between individual and society, between the particular and the general, between the private and the public. The principle image is that of the indeterminate man, who finds his definition as fascist or communist: a pure social agent whose adherence to a class only provides a Western modality of his insertion into the total society or is even expressly challenged in a pure denial of an internal schism of this society. There can be no doubt that in this respect, "communist" totalitarianism succeeds most effectively in exploiting the mechanisms of ideology. It is not enough to reject class determination; this totalitarianism goes so far as to give form to social relations in which traits of the dominant class become less and less distinguishable until they dissolve into the image of a purely functional hierarchy, whose members would each be linked, step by step, to the central focus of socialization, the edges of the division between dominator and dominated.

Yet whether it is a matter of fascism or communism, one can see at work a logic of the identification whose motivating force is the cancellation of conflicts which develop in accordance with oppositions peculiar to bourgeois society. Whereas in the latter, the power of the representations is maintained by a constant shifting of the "solution", of a putting off of the contradiction due to a gap between the instances of discourse, in totalitarianism, there is a basic assertion of the identity of the representation and reality, a condensing of the terms of the contradiction into images which reflect each other. In the first, the discourse acts according to constant compromises between the principle antagonists, whereas in the second, it seeks its effectiveness in a general response which would exclude the traces of the question. But the success of the latter would be unintelligible if it could not bring to light the signs of the totality in the detail of social life. Indeed, the mechanism of identification acts in a modern society which reveals differentiation, internal opposition, change, at each of its levels of activity; not only the effects of the division of labour must be taken in hand, but also those of the segregation of socio-cultural spaces. The attempt itself to efface the opposition between the State and civil society, and to render the indivision of the political and non-political visible supposes that the logic of the norm appears in the form of social relations here and now, that is to say, that a system of articulations is put into practice in accordance with which the power is able to reduce itself without running the risk of being divided.

In subjecting all spheres of society to the imperative of the organization, ideological discourse, be it fascist or communist, is assured of mastering oppositions which develop from and within each other, and it is able to reduce the distance to its object. Indeed, the representation of the organization allows the difference between the subject and the law to be concealed, a difference which is open in the activity itself of the institution, and which implies the possibility of linking the latter either to a human action (whether the focus is situated in the individual or in the group) or to a transcendent principle. In one sense, the organization obliterates the traces of the social subject, whatever the modality of its appearance; it does not efface the positivism of an empirically determined subject, whether it is the dominant class, the dominated class, or the producing individual, but it does conceal the question of the subject as such, a question in which a relation between oneself and the other is always brought into play at the same time as a relation to the law. Thus the organization, in representing a system of operations which would assign their definitions to the agents and their relations, makes the general antagonism between the dominator and the dominated invisible, an antagonism which arose with bourgeois society in the context of production. But simultaneously, this system appears as a pure construction, as a global operation sustained by itself, and in this sense, as a pure manifestation of human Logos, as a pure manifestation of the socialization put into practice, of an institution in action, only dealing with itself, polarized towards the totality. The representation of the organization tends to be achieved in the process of the organization itself because the latter is organized on the illusion of knowledge of social reality, which is manifested in the network of operations where the agent belongs.

The dependence of totalitarian ideology with regard to bourgeois ideology is shown by the fact that it grasps two principles, a radical artificialism and a radical substantialism, which remain juxtaposed in bourgeois ideology. It welds them together in the assertion of a society which would be thoroughly active, concerned with assuring its *functioning*—a human factory, and as such, turned in on itself, in possession of its foundation. Evidently, totalitarianism draws its faith in the organization from capitalism, but while it finds itself thwarted by the necessity of representing the social domain's differences, this faith spills out in response to the threat of the disintegration of this domain and makes the organization the essence of social reality. But it still must be emphasized that the new ideology implies the vision of a *center*, from which social life is arranged; a center which is transferred from one sector of civil society to another, but which holds power and knowledge at the heart of the State apparatus. The organization's discourse, organized so that anonymous knowledge directs the thought and practice of its agents, is only supported by constant reference to the authority in which the decision is concentrated. With this double condition, the contradiction of bourgeois ideology is overcome by the concept of the total State; the organization's network demonstrates that nothing is lost in the activity of socialization which implies the exteriorization of social discourses and practices; the self-identity of power exposes the origin of the norm.

Fascism and communism, let us repeat, stem from a meta-sociological interpretation. Any attempt to analyse them as empirical, socio-historical formations comes up against a limit, however rich the information may be, because it does not take into account the question of social existence, of the historical as such, which is brought into play in totalitarianism. The latter is neither an accident in the development of industrial capitalism, nor an aberration for which psychology can provide the key: it achieves a potential found in social reality from the moment that its institution can no longer be conceived or contained by a discourse which seeks its origins elsewhere. Moreover, the greatest error is to see in it only a variant of despotism, even more so since Stalin's power, as Hitler's, resembles that of a despot, and perhaps even more: both draw on the archaic sources of Germanic culture and the Asiatic world; a singular history is inaugurated with totalitarianism. It is not the resurrection of a political system which comes to make do with industrial society, but an attempt to close the social space from the imaginary center of its institution, to make reality and appearance coincide here and now. The despot and his bureaucracy govern over society, but their strength is the sign of a transcendent strength, a sign of *externality* for man. Totalitarian power, Nazi or Stalinist, is diffused in the representation of the organization, and it exercises the fascination and terror of representing precisely the entire non-divided social reality, inhuman discourse as absolutely human.

Such, at least, is the pole towards which totalitarianism ideology tends, but in going beyond the contradictions of bourgeois ideology, it continues to come up against the impossibility of fulfilling itself. In its turn, it lives under the threat of the effects of social division, as our description has suggested. The bureaucracy's ideal is the anonymity of social discourse, the manifestation of rationality in the organization, the placement of the subject in the logic of fascism, in the logic of communism, such that its language only appears as nonsensical. Yet for it, the representation of the center of the decision is no less essential, a power which asserts itself in full confidence, beyond all dispute. The joining of the two representations is only possible if the oppositions of power within the bureaucracy are ignored, as well as the exclusion of the majority of those without power from the ruling apparatus. The strength, as well as the weakness of bourgeois ideology lies in the fact that discourse on social reality, in its articulation (an articulation which is always perceptible) to a real or potential position of power, does not coincide with social discourse, nor with the discourse of power, that it can thus pass through different centers and can be opposed to itself without being destroyed. On the other hand, totalitarian discourse has no room to manouver; it does not allow a separation of subject and discourse and it requires its identification with power and with those who hold it at the highest echelons of the State. Doubtless this analysis is extreme; there is no conjuncture, even at the height of totalitarianism, where the removal of the subect in the discourse can be effected, nor is there complete identification with the master. A *parallel* exchange of words carries the signs of the separation and the difference. But the fact remains that the oppositions cannot be transcribed symbolically: they must be absolutely rejected, or failing that, terror is substituted for discourse.

Generally, the contradiction of totalitarianism stems from the fact that on the one hand, power is doubly hidden, as a representative of the undivided society and as an agent of the organization's rationality. On the other hand, power appears in the undivided society, unlike in any other society, as a repressive apparatus harbouring sheer violence. This is not a contradiction between the representation and the fact, hence, even our formula must be corrected: terror is not simply substituted for discourse; it is spoken, it sweeps along a fantastic argumentation whose effect is to close the intolerable gap between subject and discourse. Still, it must be added that this enterprise cannot be interpreted as a simple response to events which would disrupt the established order. As the history of Stalinism evidently shows, the image of power as terrorist power, as an inordinate power, has a necessary function. Through it as well, men reveal their dissolution into the general element of social reality, that is to say, they reveal the contingency of any particular determination regarding the law proferred by the master—the absolute master of the State, but also his representatives at all levels of the hierarchy and in all sectors of activity. However, with slipping from one position of power to another, a principle of instability is introduced, which might make the mechanism of domination visible. If, in bourgeois ideology, the danger is that the power is exposed to derision, in totalitarian ideology, it runs the greater risk of arousing horror. As the effects of the contradiction are developed, it is true that means of defence are put into place to attempt to reinforce the ideological discourse's cohesion.

Thus, after Stalin's death, his example is used to represent and to denounce the excess of power over rationality—this is the function of personality cults— whereas at the same time, the example of the petty bureaucrat is used to represent and denounce an excess of irresponsibility over the just impersonality of decision. But these defences attest to the latent crisis of the system of bureaucratic representations. It is no less instructive to pinpoint the vulnerability of the bureaucracy in the face of all kinds of events, from both the economic and cultural orders, which elude the prediction of the directors and which are likely to manifest a breakdown of the general norm, here and now, that is, a failure in the workings of the organization. In one sense, the elaborations on social reality are inexhaustible faced with the social event. Actually the articulation of the discourse to power and to law is such that "reality" cannot question it; its access is strictly controlled by the representation, however, this representation requires signs of the organization's effectiveness. The power is not mirrored in the hierarchy but in structures where social action and social aims must be attested to, where, more profoundly, men must discover their common existence in the pure dimension of social action oriented towards a social purpose. Thus, the signs of production, for example, feverishly displayed, are supposed to provide the continued proof of the dominant discourse's validity in reality. In short, a double necessity is imposed, to absolutely include and to absolutely exclude the social event, to imprint it onto the organization's logic and to absolutely deny it as a force of disorder. The extent of the contradiction would not be measured if it were forgotten that totalitarian ideology is created in "historical society", that is to say, let us reiterate, in a society which cannot be rooted in a representation of its limits, which is, in principle, open to the question of its future, destined to excessiveness, to conflict, which, in each of its parts, experiences the effects of changes in the others, a society where the internal differentiation, the gaps between practices and between representations go hand in hand with its history. The bureaucratic fantasy is to abolish the historical in History, to restore the logic of a "society without history", to match the institutor and the instituted, to deny the unpredictable, the unknowable, the continual loss of the past through the illusion of a social action, transparent to itself, which would control its effects in advance, and which would maintain continuity with its origin.

However strong the illusion, it is apt to be refuted. Undoubtedly, the refutation is, in turn, concealed; the breakdowns in planning, for example, are attributed to bureaucratism, to the residual inertia of the social body, to the mania for regulations. Again one must be persuaded that the representation of bureaucratism is no less ideological than that of social action; it is an essential component of the system, whose function is to support the power of the rule in its coinciding with the instance of power and to bring its corruption back into the presence of parasitic agents. But apart from the rule standing out excessively wherever rationality is supposed to show itself, the total logic of the organization "can" appear as a logic of the absurd. It is true that ideology has another means of defence more effective than denouncing bureaucratism to resist the backlash from the power's decisions, or more generally, from social reality. The attempt to assure its mastery of the social space is supported by the representation of the enemy: an enemy who could not be presented as an opponent, but whose existence strikes at the integrity of the social body. Moreover, the enemy does much more than personify the adversity, or, as it is often observed, serve as a scapegoat.

In a society which does not tolerate the image of an internal social division, which claims its homogeneity beyond any actual differences, it is the other as such who acquires the fantastic traits of the destroyer; the other, however he is defined, to whatever group he belongs, is the representative of the *outside*. Although in bourgeois ideology, men's essence is affirmed with regard to a sub-humanity (even though the latter is relegated to the depths of society and is never so far down into "nature" that it does not pose the problem of its management, because it is perceived *in* society), totalitarian ideology is maintained by the exclusion of an evil agent, the exclusion of a representative of the anti-social. The effectiveness of the representation could not make one forget that it does not have the supreme disposal of its effects. It tends to circumscribe the other's place, but does not achieve this due to a generalized denial (which we have amply emphasized) of the difference between the subject and social discourse. Any sign of this difference risks denouncing the subject as the enemy. The alterity cannot be encircled; the image of the concentration camp is not enough to disarm it. The individual, wherever he must enter into the discourse of power, reveals the possibility of his exclusion. Insofar as he shows himself able to speak, he is exposed as potentially guilty. In this sense, the bureaucratic world continues to be haunted by insecurity, even though it is wholly organized to represent a bastion of security, to maintain a community in the certainty of its cohesion. The assertion of total social reality does not get rid of the fantasy of self-devouring; totalitarian discourse effaces the externality of the idea; discourse on social reality tends to be absorbed into social discourse; it effaces the externality of power; the State tends to carry out its fusion with civil society; it effaces the externality of the rule; the organization tends to be sufficient to transmit rationality; it effaces the externality of the other, social division is concealed. However, the externality returns; discourse on social reality is threatened with appearing as generalized illusion, as discourse in the service of power, simply masking oppression.

IDEOLOGY AND POWER

The Invisible Ideology

Totalitarian ideology prevails in a large part of the world; thus, a rigorous analysis should take into consideration the specific traits it assumes in certain countries, and particularly in China. As well, it should consider the modifications which have come about in the USSR and in Eastern Europe during the last fifteen years. In our eyes, the observable differences in time and space do not call into question the coherence of the system. An understanding of this system, we noticed, allowed us afterwards to distinguish that which constitutes the specificity of bourgeois ideology. At present, it must be added that it equally clarifies the formation of the new ideological discourse in Western democracies of our time.

Our conviction is that this discourse continues to exploit a system of representations which reached its full effectiveness in the second half of the nineteenth century, but that this system is no longer at the center of the imaginary. This hypothesis makes no claim to originality; an already extensive critical sociology—notably to which the names Marcuse, Whyte, Roszak and Baudrillard are attached—has brought to light the function now fulfilled by the themes of the organization, of social communication, of membership in a group, of consumption, etc. Since these ideas are no doubt familiar to the reader, we need not elaborate them here. On the other hand, we should emphasize the relation that contemporary discourse maintains, both with totalitarianism, and with bourgeois ideology, the way in which it is part of the general genesis of ideology. Although occasionally the totalitarian finality of this discourse has been justly emphasized, it has hardly been perceived that its formation attests to a "reflection" of the contradictions which haunt totalitarianism, to an attempt at forestalling the threat hanging over social existence, the project which would reveal the representation of homogenization and unification of social reality. This project, let us emphasize, is attached to its opposite, thereby cancelling the distance between discourse on social reality and social discourse, placing the first within the second. It is indeed this enterprise which is repeated in the new ideology, but it is dissociated from an assertion of totality, brought back to a latent state, and in this sense, is rearticulated to the principle of the system of bourgeois ideology, in which a displacement of imaginary formations was required, their conflict tolerated, and compromises constantly worked out. Concealing the distance between the representation and the real, which jeopardizes bourgeois ideology, and renouncing the achievement of the representation in the form of totalization of the real, constitute, in our view, the double principle which organizes a new logic of dissimulation.

If the affirmation of totality, notably in communism, is operated with the necessity of rejoining the State and civil society, of discarding the image of a fragmentation of power and its decline to the order of actuality, it implies, we observed, that the ideology's discourse is transformed into the power's discourse; this affirmation exposes it dangerously by revealing the divided instance of decision and coercion and the features of the master, not only at the top of State bureaucracy, but through its multiple "representatives". A new strategy is developed to represent a society sheltered from this hazard. Certainly, the term "strategy" evokes the action of a subject who would enjoy the freedom of defining the best means of dissimulation. However, we have said often enough that the old ideology was not that of the bourgeoisie, so that we could not be accused of accepting the illusion that it would have become the ideology of a new class, for example, the technocracy, as some like to claim. The strategy to which we are referring designates the ruses of the imaginary, a process which, although unaware and "without history" in the sense that Marx intended, nonetheless takes into account the effects of knowledge and history and inserts them into new configurations at the service of a task which actually remains unchanged.

Thus the group, constructed as a positive entity, regarded both as expression and aim of social communication, comes to screen the separation of the apparatus of domination and the majority of those without power. The representation of the group's structure, indifferent to the conditions which dictate the status of its members, tends to exclude from its domain the question of origin, of legitimacy, of rationality, of oppositions and hierarchies instituted in each sector. A new faith is invested in this representation: a "mastery" of social reailty in the experience of socialization itself *here and now*, that is to say, within the perceptible borders of each institution, in each situation where man finds himself placed according to the "natural" necessity of production or, more generally, of economic activity, but also of pedagogy or leisure, as well as political, union, or religious practice. So many analyses have been devoted to the phenomenon of human relations in industry, to the expansion of group techniques in a wide variety of organizations, to the practice of seminars, information conferences, to the spreading of social psychology in businesses, schools and hospitals, that it would be useful to linger over the ideology of social communication. Yet the function fulfilled with regard to this by the great instruments at its service, radio and television, is no less instructive. Without them, the new system of representation would certainly be non-viable, because it is in propagating itself, not only from one particular place to another, but each time from an apparently circumscribed focus to an apparently indeterminate focus, it is through the effect of its reply, indefinitely multiplied from the private pole of the institution to the public pole of information, that ideological discourse attains the generality necessary to its task of homogenization of the social domain in the implicit. With the incessant development of public debates, encompassing all aspects of economic, political and cultural life, ridiculing everything from the most trivial to the most revered, an image of reciprocity is imposed as the image of social relations itself.

This image is doubly effective because simultaneously the communication is valued independently of its agents and of its content, and the *presence* of individuals is simulated: a head of state confides his difficulties to someone designed to listen, or this listener, from the masses, but duly appointed, bears the contradiction to a minister or questions an expert designed to answer him, etc. This performance goes so far as to make the actors' identities perceptible.

Undoubtedly we have there one of the most remarkable forces of the imaginary: to absorb the personal element into the impersonal discourse which presents the essence of social relations, but substantiating the illusion of a living speech, a subject's speech, when in fact, the latter is dissolved into the ceremony of communication. It is an illusion because the limits of the debate are determined outside of its visible domain; the leader's neutrality conceals the principle of its organization and in the end, those who hold the power are presented on the same plane as those whose fate they decide behind the scenes.

We would still not take into account the full extent of the phenomenon if we were to become obsessed by the manifestly political aspects of social communication. The effectiveness of discourse such as that transmitted by radio and television lies in that it is only partially explained as political discourse—and it is precisely from this that it acquires a general political importance. Everyday things, questions of science and culture are what support the representation of an achieved democracy where speech would circulate freely. The signs of this circulation are ostentatiously produced, whereas the statutes remain crystallized according to oppositions of power. In no other epoch has there been so much spoken: discourse on social reality served by the different modern means of communication is carried away; it is overcome by a dizzying infatuation with itself; nothing escapes conferences, interviews, televised debates, from the generation gap to traffic flow, from sexuality to music, from space exploration to education. This narcissism is not that of bourgeois ideology, since the new discourse is not articulated from above; it employs no capital letters; it feigns to propagate information, even pretends to question; it does not overshadow others at a distance, but includes a representative in itself, presents itself as an incessant dialogue, and thus takes the space between the *one* and the *other* to make a place for itself. Through this operation, the subject finds himself (almost) accommodated in the system of representation in an entirely different mannner than in totalitarian ideology, since at present he is invited to incorporate the terms of all opposition. At the same time, he is accommodated in the group—an imaginary group in the sense that the power is taken away from men to conceive of the real activity of the institution by participating in it, by confronting their relation through differentiation.

In this sense, the remark we made about the implication of the personal in the impersonal is clarified. This event again indicates the distance taken with regard to totalitarian discourse. The latter tends to dissolve the personal element, because it does not tolerate the image of a dispersion of the centers of socialization, nor does it permit an experience of the subject in a particular place that escapes from the general norm. But this dispersion no longer strikes at the integrity of the representation of social reality from the moment that the subject finds himself captured by his own image in the network of socialization. Thus the television screen only materializes an impalpable screen on which a social relation is projected, a relation sufficient in itself insofar as it condenses the double representation of a relation in itself and a relation between people. One could measure, for example, the effectiveness of a course of action which, from commercials to political or cultural programs, provides the repeated illusion of an *entre-nous*.

The informant's speech is placed at the pole of anonymity and neutrality; under this condition, it diffuses an objective knowledge, whatever its nature, but simultaneously, it makes itself singular, mimics live speech, assumes the attributes of the person to assure its conjunction with those addressed, who, in spite of their numbers, of their separation and ignorance of each other, will each find himself personally reached and mutely assembled owing to the same proximity to the speaker. In this sense, the most banal program is an incantation to *familiarity*; in mass society it installs the limits of a "small world" where everything occurs as if each person were already turned toward the other. It provokes a hallucination of *nearness* which abolishes a sense of distance, strangeness, imperceptibility, the signs of the outside, of adversity, of alterity. Let us note in passing that it is amazing to occasionally see people strolling down the street or sunbathing on the beach, transistor radio glued to the ear, or to see homes in which the television or radio are on constantly, even without the presence of those who turned them on; no other phenomenon better demonstrates the imaginary dimension of communication. The latter provides the assurance of a social link, at a distance from its reality; it provides a background, an accompaniment—just as the music of the same name, which, however, is only a variant of generalized communication—and this background is the foundation, this accompaniment is the lining continuously spun from the intolerable fact of social division. The certainty of the communication could, if necessary, be sufficient, given that in actually removing himself, the subject remains in his network. It is of little importance that he stops watching or listening: his personal ghost is in place, once and for all, in the *entre-nous*.

What appears in this *entre-nous*, air freshener or an increase in prices, highway deaths or feminism, is not of great importance. More important is the power to infer a primordial relationship which could not be brought into play in the discourse's operation and the possible oppositions of its agents. The faith in social communication and in the attachment to a group still leaves room for the idea of social division when even this is camouflaged, that is to say, passed off as a failing of a dialogue between individuals or classes, or a break in the cohesion. On the other hand, the representation of the social relationship is unconscious, the *entre-nous* assures the staging of the communication as well as the subject's involvement in the group. This involvement requires neither its being the aim of the group in its actuality as a valid group, nor an identification with the power which is supposed to represent its unity. At the level of the *entre-nous*, the "we" is not asserted but presupposed, destined to invulnerability from remaining invisible. No doubt a political leader is led to proclaim "We liberals...", "we men of progress", or "we socialists", just as the speaker on the air, outside of a political context, proclaims "We the French"; but this "we", however effective it remains, is secondary, because arranged prior to his statement are the conditions of a network in which agents are linked to each other through being deprived of the marks of their oppositions as well as those of discourse as discourse.

Only these conditions allow ideological discourse to be constantly buried in the socialization process, and simultaneously create the illusion that, in principle, nothing is concealed from communication. The dispute is centered on ideas, on particular agents, that is to say, precisely on what appears, on that which lives on bourgeois ideology, on its ineradicable residue, and (for all that) on the representation of oppositions, absolutely necessary to sustain the dialogue. Yet what escapes, or tends to escape the dispute is the fantasy of reciprocity, according to which everything is shown to be open to discussion, visible, intelligible, because such indeed is the ultimate effect of the occultation of the division: the image of a discourse without limits in which everything comes to appear. One can understand, consequently, that this discourse feigns to ignore prohibitions; since it invades the social domain, it abolishes all the distances contrived by bourgeois ideology. it introduces sexuality, violence and madness into the *entre-nous*; it effaces the division between the ordinary world and the depths of society; it ignores the danger of nature. Similarly, this trait distinguishes it from a communist discourse which, ever haunted by the representation of a total social reality, of a flawless body, does not tolerate an attachment to signs which would strike at its integrity, which supports itself by multiplying taboos about subjects which escape social controls. This discourse is distinguished, too, by its aptitude for letting its agents speak instead of restricting the granting of speech, defending itself against the violation of its space by simulating within itself a place for the contradictor.

The system's effectiveness simultaneously supposes the representation of the discourse's scientificity. In one sense, the latter was found at the heart of bourgeois ideology; but with it, science still represents a visible pole. Discourse on science exists at the same time as an exploitation of science in order to elaborate social reality. In the context of industrial production itself, a knowledge of the rationality of labour is defused, a knowledge which is displayed, but which is also circumscribed within the limits of a ruling apparatus. Taylorism, as is known, will eventually give it its full expression. Assuredly, the persistence of the old ideology must here again be recognized, but even more so, the extent of the modifications which have occurred must be measured. Firstly, the locus of the enterprise must be considered, not to determine the features of its actual transformation, but in order to examine the representation. It is the representation of the organization, one which is not a product nor an application of science, but which embodies it, and whose formula is not the property of the managerial class but is inscribed in reality. This representation no longer tolerates the division of directors and those who execute their directives, nor the division of human labour and means of production; it links all the terms by effacing their subordination, in order to articulate them within a structure which would function in itself, through rational imperatives, and independently of men's desires and choices. The image of the instances of decision and restraint, the image of the rule, are covered by the law of the organization. This law coincides with the organization's discourse; it is concealed from the subject's view, although here and there they reveal absurdity in the details of programmed operations. Its effectiveness lies in that it is not perceived as external; just as the effectiveness of the discourse which transmits it lies in the fact that it is not constrained to appear as discourse on the organization, or that the latter, having just been expressed, only represents a part of the former, and leaves as implicit its validity and legitimacy. This inference of the law and discourse is only possible because the agents find in them the form of their established relation, because their action and cooperation are supposed to be prefigured in the model of the organization. But it would be a mistake to think that the relation between individuals is reified, to use the Marxist expression; the model tends to convert the subject into the "organizational man", as Whyte indicates. In other words, what is considered as real becomes the organization; indications of a rationalization in itself of social reality, and those of his own identity are provided according to a supposed knowledge that the organization holds *over him*.

Again, it must be emphasized that this representation is not circumscribed within the limits of the production enterprise. It is propagated in all the great social establishments, in commercial enterprises, in public and private administrations in the universities, in hospitals.

The organization's discourse is not realized in the totalitarian fantasy. We have already noted its limits. Yet it is important to point out the support given to it by the diffusion of the representation of science outside of the context which we have just mentioned. This representation does not allow itself to be localized. In it is invested a generalized belief in the self-intelligibility of social reality and the self-intelligibility of man. In other words, at the level of objectivity, the distinctions essential to bourgeois ideology tend to be effaced: those of nature, of the psyche, and of the society. In particular, it is impossible to appreciate the range of the organization's discourse and how it is preserved in the implicit without pointing out the work effected by the human sciences. As Marcuse has rightly noted, the official discourse of psychology and sociology is governed by artificialism, operationalism and formalism. The psyche, society and culture are commonly defined as systems; the general model of an organization, of the personality's functioning is imposed by the concepts of social integration, communication, tension and regulation, in the simplest or the most sophisticated versions.

Truthfully, if we wished to develop the analysis of the various forms of ideology, it would be necessary to examine the unique contribution (even more so in that they are often presented as anti-ideological criticism) of literature and literary theory, of philosophy or aesthetics. There is a search for a language which makes the question of its genesis perceptible, which no longer accepts the assurance of the narrative, the novel, the image, the theory, the assurance of a natural distance between a supposed subject and a supposed object, a language which departs from the established lines of reading and writing, of the viewer and visible, of the author and the other, which welcomes the departure of meaning, the break of origin, as Merleau-Ponty would say. This language is applied to deciphering unconscious structures in which desire and thought are at work before any thought or desire takes form. In short, all that gives strength to the instituting discourse finds itself hidden under the new illusion of a machinery of the text, of thought, desire, the illusion of a game in itself, of difference, of the "real" suppression of the subject, sense, origin, history. It is an illusion which gives substance to new indications, which is maintained by eluding the hazards of the unconquerable division between the one and the other, between sense and nonsense, between the space of the work and that of the world, between what is within and what is without, an illusion which, in all modes of writing, results in a technique of illegibility, which significantly tends to abate the danger of interpretation, providing the process of occultation which governs the organizations's discourse with its precise response.

But since we must be content with only a glimpse of these contributions, let us rather emphasize psychology, because it operates, not at the periphery, but at the center of the new ideology. Indeed, how can one fail to see that it is psychology which provides the organization with the representation of a knowledge about the subject, which feeds the illusion of the agent's evaluation, not of his aptitude, but of his personality. It places this illusion in the materiality of a battery of tests, questionnaires, and maintenance guides, in an apparatus claimed to be scientific, whose triple function is to determine the image of the "organizational man", to make him appear to himself through knowledge of the other, and to conceal the image of those in power by generating the illusion of an impersonal norm.

Undoubtedly, one could justly note that the entire system of education, and not only psychology, is organized according to a capacity to measure knowledge and imposes the self-image of an evaluated individual. It must also be observed in passing that one of the dominant themes in modern pedagogy, self-evaluation, is among the most effective for obliterating the educator's presence and for invisibly imprinting the power's discourse. In any case, diploma-worship— independent of the education system's efforts to procure the "socially necessary" agents for the world of the organization—generates, in the entire range of society, the individual's identification with the agent of knowledge.

Even though it is more particular, psychology's action is no less decisive, because through it, the imaginary "personality" arises: a system decipherable for the other, or since the other takes refuge behind science, one which would be offered to the understanding of the organization. For the rest, the psychologist's place in the system of education cannot receive enough attention. Even very young children are affected by testing. The psychologist's knowledge penetrates them already at this age, in order to imprint upon them the mark of inaptitude or deviance. He is slowly substituted for the educator, to displace the relation to the law, to ward off the visible blow of authority, and to link sanction to the decree of a neutral and anonymous force.

Moreover, it is impossible not to examine the great staging of scientificity developed by radio, television and the printed media. The incantation to social communication is doubled by one to information. We cannot underestimate the hold of the experts' knowledge, or of the servants of scientific vulgarization, who, day after day, dispense the truth about child education, for example, about the couple, sexuality, the secrets of the organism or of space. It is not only the magic of the *entre-nous* which renders everything speakable; there is also the magic of objectivity. One feature of the system which must not escape our attention indicates again the distance taken with regard to totalitarian ideology. The borders of knowledge are not represented, nor is it necessary for them to be. If everything can be pronounced, the indefiniteness of what is said must be noted; thus its perpetual newness. Totalitarianism insures itself against the hazard of a fragmentation of time through the stark assertion of a historical truth, which makes the development of the present from future progress (in such a way that there are always only certain utterable things within the borders of the established order, and that the unknown is domesticated, circumscribed to the level of what is known). Where it acts in that way, the new ideological discourse again takes hold of signs, cultivates them, in order to efface the historical threat. As social communication is content to be realized here and now, knowledge is exhibited here and now, bearing the solutions to the secret of nature, the secret of man, arousing a fascination with the present. Not knowing, then, signifies not coinciding with the times, not coinciding with social existence as it is manifested. It signifies incurring the society's tacit sanction, excluding oneself from legitimate social bonds.

"Newness", then, is nothing more than the materialized proof of temporal difference, of the historical, and thus of its concealment behind the illusion of a difference in time, of a masterable distance from the present to the past, of a conquerable relation to the present as such. Invisible once again is the operation which diffuses the effects of the institution of social reality, which attempts to prohibit the question about the sense of the established order, the question about *potentiality*. Whereas potentiality is linked to desire, whereas it brings into play the refusal of experience, newness blocks the view. In other words, it is the rattle which an infantilized group tries to grasp or catch, always a motion behind the appearance of the object they are to know. Once again we must not neglect to associate with the mania for newness at all the borders of organizations, the mania manifested (especially in France which is exemplary in this respect) by the circles of intelligentsia, devoured by the fear of not producing or not grasping that little thing which carries the guarantee of the death of the past and of the fullness or splendour of the present.

In conclusion, we hold that it is from this perspective that the function of ideology in consumer society could be interpreted. Too many analyses, in the context of a critical sociology, perpetuate ambiguity in overemphasizing the consumption practice. It may not be possible to conceive of this practice without linking it to the genesis of historical society. We may only be able to attempt to interpret through this phenomenon the signs of the institution of social reality, of which no one is the instigator, and we may not be able to do better than to question a world in which our own identity is given to us. On the other hand, the representation which haunts the consumption practice is open to criticism precisely in that it arises from the institution's actions to conceal it, that it develops a "response" destined to conjugate the insecurity engendered by the differentiation and the "not knowing" of the differentiation in space and time.

Baudrillard has shown in depth that the consumer product, whatever its nature, does not exercise an attraction in order to respond to some need whose origin can be located in the individual or group. It becomes the representative of a "system of objects" in which are related the demand, the satisfaction and the articulation of the signs to each other, in such a way that it turns back on itself and presents the illusion of social reality as such. In this sense, the discourse of consumption condenses the representation of the organization and of communication. It introduces a universe where the difference between producer and product is effaced through the appearance of an independent network of objects and where the difference between someone and someone else is simultaneously effaced through the appearance of a common adherence to the same world. Yet it still must be noted that what is consumed is incessantly new, the representative of a difference in time which feeds desire by simulating an indefinite return to the desired object, at the precise moment where the desire is held by the representation. This simulation, once again, indicates an attempt to represent the historical, to make change invisible by determining the visible.

Nonetheless, by holding to these observations we might miss the essential ideological function of consumption discourse, because the illusion it substantiates is that of a world where man perceives only signs of men. It is a world whose space is open to any route, where all is perceptible provided that one has the means, a world where vision, the manipulation of objects, activity are multiplied by an instrument without obstacle, and are as if fitted to something all-visible, all-manipulable, all-explorable. We need only consider the advertising which presents us with the house of our dreams, ready to welcome us, key in the door; it summarizes a very long discourse on social reality which teaches that the things of the outside are there, within, that the universe is arranged for man, that nature is the environment. There, ideology reaches the limit of its task; it puts the great wall in place, but makes it invisible, saves itself having to make a statement about whole man and the total society.

But although ideology achieves its task, must we think that its contradictions are resolved? How could they be if it is true that historical society is that society which undermines any representation of its institution?

The more that discourse on social reality seeks to coincide with social discourse, the more it applies itself to mastering the unmasterable activity of the institution, to taking hold of the signs of the institutor, and the more it runs the risk of losing the function assumed until then by ideology; the legitimation of the established order, not only that of a regime of ownership, but that of reality as such; it generates the conditions for a questioning which (in the East as well as the West) is aimed beyond the expressions of power and exploitation, at the indices of socialization in the modern world, and which brings the question of the *Other* and *Being* back into focus.

Paris, France

CONCEPTS OF IDEOLOGY IN MARX*

György Márkus

There is surprising agreement concerning the significance of Marx's theory of ideology, inasmuch as it is generally regarded as one of his major contributions both to a general social theory and to philosophy. Through the introduction of this theory, Marx is said to have seriously contributed to a fundamental reorientation—an historically and socially oriented "turn"—in the treatment of problems concerning human knowledge and cognition. This agreement about the historical importance of the theory nevertheless goes hand in hand with an almost complete disagreement about the content of these significant views. Both Marxist and non-Marxist interpretations of the Marxian concept of ideology seem to disagree about even the most elementary questions concerning its meaning. Does the notion of ideology carry a negative-pejorative emphasis, or is it in this respect value-neutral and therefore capable of being applied to Marx's own theory, which could in turn be characterised (at least in its intentions) as a "scientific ideology"? Does science, including the natural sciences, represent the principal opposite of ideology, or is it just one of the forms of its manifestations? Is the theory of ideology essentially a *genetic* one, dealing above all with problems concerning the historical origin of ideas regarded as *effects* of other causes? Or is it a *functional* theory that basically deals with problems related to the effects which ideas and their systems—treated as relatively independent *causes*—can and do have in other areas of socially significant behaviour? To all these, certainly very basic, questions one can find widely differing, even diametrically opposed, answers.

The situation becomes even more paradoxical if one turns from the secondary interpretative literature toward those perhaps more significant writings which attempt to continue the tradition initiated by the Marxian conception of ideology. On the one hand, it seems unclear how these theories can appeal to a common ancestry at all, since they deal with quite divergent, almost unrelated topics. In the so-called concept of "ideological state apparatuses" developed in structuralist Marxism by Althusser, for instance, the term "ideology" refers essentially to the functioning of such institutions as the family, the school system, the Church, and the mass media. In the works of Marxists such as Lukács or Lucien Goldmann, however, ideology almost exclusively denotes the paradigmatic products of high culture—great philosophical systems, exemplary works of art, the historically most significant social and economic theories, and so on. On the other hand, and despite the radically divergent problematics they deal

---

*This is an expanded and revised draft of a lecture first presented at the Department of Philosophy, New School for Social Research, New York, April 1981.

with under the common name of ideology, both of these views have one thing in common, namely, that their standpoint is strangely irreconcilable with the best known, so to say "introductory", statement of Marx on ideology: it is not ideas which make or transform history, because ideas are mere sublimates of material life activities in the heads of individuals. So Althusser regards the ideological state apparatuses as organisations through whose operation the empirical individual first becomes constituted as the allegedly active subject in society; these apparatuses are ascribed a determining role in the reproduction of the dominant system of social relations. Analogously, representatives of so-called humanist or historicist Marxism—especially following the historical trauma of Fascism—have either underlined the emancipatory potential of (at least some) products of autonomous high culture, or (like Adorno and Horkheimer) they have emphasized that the loss of the autonomy of high culture has been one of the basic causes of a foreclosure of real possibilities of emancipation in modern society.

I have referred here, essentially for rhetorical purposes, to the vagaries which mark the history of the reception and interpretation of the Marxian conception of ideology, to find some justification for a renewed attempt to disentangle an old and rather boring question: What did Marx mean by "ideology"? But the problems just indicated may perhaps also provide some initial support for my own emphasis on the complexity and heterogeneity of the theoretical concept of ideology as it is actually used within the texts of Marx. I shall try to argue in the following that Marx deployed this concept in distinctly different contexts, for different purposes and that, accordingly, this concept has recognizably different meanings in his writings. And while the *three* different meanings of ideology I shall try to distinguish are clearly interconnected, any attempt to perceive these as various aspects of a unified broader approach contains not only some significant *lacunae*—a fact indicated by Marx himself—but may well also contain some inner strains which are not so easy to overcome.

I

If one turns to the very texts of Marx in which he either directly addressed (or at least alluded to) the problematics of ideology, it becomes rather evident that the term is most frequently used in a critical, directly *polemical* way. In *The German Ideology*, for instance, the concept of ideology invariably has a negative, what is more, *unmasking* meaning. It designates those philosophical and social-political theories which conceive ideas and their systems as the mainsprings of historical progress. Ideological theories transform themselves—and thereby their creators, the intellectuals—into the hidden demiurges of history. True, at some points Marx seems to operate even in these polemical contexts with a broader concept, one that embraces all those cultural objectifications which history by reference to some metahistorical, eternal principle in general (thus the Feuerbachian theory of religion is regarded as ideological since it explains religion in terms of an ahistorical human essence). But, fundamentally, the critique of ideology in this sense means the "unmasking" of any attempt to demonstrate the supremacy of spirit in history.[1] The concept of ideology is a polemical tool directed against all variants of *historical idealism*. In opposition to this idealism, Marx poses his theoretical and, above all, practical materialism: it is not theoretical transformations of interpretations of the world, but the practical transformation of the material life conditions of society and the material life-activities of products that constitutes the terrain of decisive social struggles through which the fate of human progress is resolved. This is precisely the (rather simple) point of the famous, and often over-interpreted, metaphor about the *camera obscura*: in ideologies, as in a *camera obscura*, everything appears upside-down because—*per definitionem*—ideological systems of belief suppose themselves to be the ultimate determinants of human material activities whereas, in real life, the practically enacted and institutionalised relations between producers constitute both the ultimate source and the criterion of efficacy for the culturally elaborated systems of social belief.

To this concept of ideology corresponds a definite intellectual practice—that of critically *unmasking* beliefs through a demonstration of their social determination and genesis. In these polemical contexts, Marx employs a genetic method of critique of ideologies, the essence of which consists in the reduction of systems of thought to the conscious or unconscious social interests which they express. To discover behind the haughty phrases about the transcendent power or eternal rule of ideas, the hidden sway of well-defined—but completely unthematized—narrow class or group interests is to radically refute their validity. And it is in the context of this criticism as unmasking that ideologies appear—perhaps at first glance in a contradictory way—both as alien to real-life speculations and as transpositions of the dominant material relations of power into the realm of thought. By transforming definite social interests into the requirements of human reason as such, these systems of thought contribute to the stabilisation of the given relations of social domination: the fixation of belief becomes a mode of legitimation.

It is possible that by borrowing the term "ideology" from the last representatives of the French Enlightenment, Destutt de Tracy and his small philosophical coterie, Marx indicates an awareness about the traditions and roots of his own conception. Whatever the case may be, it is clear that his polemical, unmasking concept of ideology stands in a relation of direct continuity with some elements in the heritage of the Enlightenment, particularly with its "critique of prejudices", conceived as socially induced deformations of reason. So one can trace back—as Hans Barth actually did—the intellectual ancestry of this concept to the Baconian criticism of the idols of marketplace and theatre—or even further, to the sophists and to Greek enlightenment in general. But one should also add that Marx is the *critic* of this tradition as well as its continuator. From the standpoint of his theory of ideology, a criticism of prejudices in the name of an impartial reason or an eternal and normatively conceived human nature is itself deeply ideological. Marx's polemics against the hidden interests constituting and determining the systems of ideology are not conducted in the name of an ahistoric rationality allegedly able to overcome all historical limitations; they are instead conducted in the name of historically and socially defined, concrete and "limited" needs and sufferings which are produced and induced by the same social interests. In the contexts we are speaking about, the theory of ideology to a large extent provides a criticism, even a self-criticism, of the "professional consciousness" of intellectuals who, as "producers of ideas", are bent on ascribing a mythical efficacy to their own activity. In this way they create for their own activity a bogus legitimation, and thereby they render themselves incapable of understanding its real social determination and function: through this lack of critical self-awareness they become—often quite unwittingly—apologists of a given, pre-fixed system of social domination and injustice.

II

If this polemical unmasking concept of "ideology" is the most frequent, preponderant one in Marx's writings, there are, however, passages in his works where the same term acquires another, *systematic-explanatory* meaning. One has only to look at the famous *Preface* to the *Contribution to the Critique of Political Economy*, to see an example of this non-polemical type of meaning. Here ideology clearly designates not a specific, criticizable type of socio-philosophic theory but a much broader range of human activities: definite branches of "cultural production" (*geistige Produktion*) and their products, and a corresponding level of social interaction and conflict. The main function of this explanatory, essentially *functional* concept of ideology is to provide a *part* of the answer to the question Marx already posed in *The German Ideology*: How, and through what mechanisms do the ideas of the ruling class become the ruling ideas in society? This question is evidently equivalent to the Weberian problem of how systems of social rule are legitimated under conditions of inequality and exploitation.

At this point one "philological" remark is pertinent. In the whole corpus of his writings, as Korsch pointed out, Marx never applied the term "ideology" to the phenomena of everyday consciousness. For him (and in opposition to many latter-day Marxists), the social domination of the ideas of the dominating class is primarily not the result of the latter's monopoly over the means of dissemination of ideas; it is not a matter of indoctrination into a definite type of culture produced aside from everyday practical life and only intellectually superimposed over its actors. On the contrary, it is Marx's theory of the social determination of everyday thinking which provides the basis both for an answer to the question posed above and for an understanding of the functional role of ideologies in society. It is therefore necessary to elaborate briefly on this point, which can be designated as a theory of "false consciousness"—a term which of course appears only in Engels.

DISAPPEARING IDEOLOGY

According to Marx, a social system like capitalism, at least in some negative sense, is *self-legitimating*. Through the very working of its socio-economic mechanisms it produces in the individuals caught up in its practices a matrix of thought, a way of directly perceiving and interpreting social reality which systematically excludes the possibility of its overcoming, both through imagination and action. I am referring here of course to the Marxian theory of *fetishism* which is primarily discussed in his later economic writings. In these writings, Marx argues that for those who are engaged in the market activities of selling and buying—i.e., practically every member of a capitalist society—social relations with other individuals inevitably appear as relations between things; what is more, these anonymous social functions assume the appearance of matters which are seemingly contingent upon free individual choice. This personification of social roles constitutes the reverse side of the fetishistic reification of social relations. This distorted and mystifying way of understanding the world in which individuals live and act is not primarily the result of some specific process of acculturation in the sense of the transmission to, and appropriation by, individuals of some institutionally fixed "doctrines". Rather, it is the direct outcome of the *experienced life-activities* of the concerned individuals. Marx certainly did not deny the role of language, and generally that of a broadly conceived inherited culture in the formation of "false consciousness". As a matter of fact, he was keenly interested in the social function of language, though his remarks on this count hardly go beyond a somewhat naively historical etymology. But he did insist that the "bewitchment of intellect" primarily derives not from "language idling" but from historically constituted life-conditions. What he underlines again and again is the fact that fetishistic modes of thought "arise from the relations of production themselves", that they are the "direct and spontaneous outcomes" of the elemental social practices of individuals. These forms of thinking directly fix and merely generalize the practical life-experiences of the *isolated* social actors; fetishistic forms of thinking enable individual social agents to orient themselves *successfully* within the given system of social relations, which are taken *as a fixed prius of their life*. Undoubtedly the Marxian theory of fetishism is heavily infected by the Hegelian terminology of "appearance", which refers not to mere semblance, but to a "false reality", a form of immediacy in which reality itself distortedly "expresses" and "manifests itself" ("sich darstellt", as Hegel wrote). This poses a whole series of disquieting problems, and not only highly abstract, philosophical questions concerning the feasibility of an ontological theory of truth which, *prima facie*, seems to be implied by Marx's terminology. His constant insistence that fetishistic perceptions and notions are not mere "illusions" and errors of a confused thinking, that the categories of bourgeois economy are "socially valid, and therefore objective forms of thought" for this whole historical epoch, *also* contains the completely straightforward idea that these forms of thought are not merely socially produced and determined, but are in fact *pragmatically effective*, and in this sense real, valid and "correct". Individuals caught up in these relations can successfully orient themselves within their given framework only in these terms. If they go shopping and do not want to squander their money, for example, they *have* to treat the price of different commodities as if it were a property independent of the utility of these commodities: only by comparing relative prices with relative utilities can individuals make a "reasonable" choice, a "good buy". This also means that the knowledge that the price of a commodity is solely the phenomenal form of its value, and that the latter is dependent upon socially necessary labour time, and so on, is about as relevant to a "good buy" as the detailed knowledge of quantum electro-dynamics is to someone exchanging a blown fuse.[2]

In addition, and indeed behind this pragmatic efficacy of false consciousness, there lies hidden its *social effectivity*, its capacity to foreclose the possibility of a rational *collective transformation* of the given social conditions. Just as fetishistic ideas successfully guide isolated individuals in their effort to assert their private interests *within* these given relations, so these ideas also render the totality completely opaque, transforming it into a matter of unintelligible naturalness or technical necessity. In this sense, fetishism represents for Marx the manifestation on the level of everyday thinking of that gulf between societal and individual possibilities, the progressive widening of which is seen as one of the basic tendencies of that whole "pre-history" he designated as *alienation*. To use Marx's own examples: as long as one conceives price or value as a mystical, "natural" property of things themselves, the very idea of a society where objects of utility do not function as commodities remains inconceivable; as long as wages are understood as remuneration for labour done, one can formulate the demand for fair, equitable wages but not even imagine a society where human productive activities would be posited in some other social form than that of wage labour; and so on. The fetishistic categories which "invert" the real relations and make them "invisible" are not only expressive of thinking which unreflexively accepts the social world as given: these absurd "category mistakes" of spontaneous everyday understanding also systematically *exclude* the possibility of a totalizing reflection both upon the historical-practical constitution of this world and the social determination of this way of thinking. And since these categories constitute that natural language of imagination and thinking within the framework of which individuals form and articulate their practical intentions, expectations and motives, they thereby acquire a truly causal efficacy. False consciousness is not a passive reflex of the "surface relations" of a society which is somehow constituted and reproduced independently of this consciousness; this consciousness is a necessary factor in the creation, reproduction and unintended, socially unconscious transformation of this society. One quotation from the *Grundrisse* illustrates this point. Speaking about the early forms of mercantilism, Marx emphasizes that while money fetishism is an absurd "illusion about the nature of money and blindness toward the contradictions contained within it", it has also been "an enormous instrument in the real development of the forces of social production", precisely because "it gave money a really magic significance behind the backs of individuals".[3] This is why Marx's own theory of fetishism is above all a critique of everyday consciousness—primarily of the consciousness of its own subject and addressee, the working class. By unravelling the social determinations of spontaneous social awareness, Marx attempts to foster a theoretical impulse towards the acquisition of real self-consciousness. In the last instance, of course, this self-consciousness can be attained only in practice, since the ultimate overcoming of fetishistic thinking is not a matter of knowledge, but of the creation of collective practical alternatives, in the light of which the unintelligible natural-ness and mystical immutability of present-day social institutions are dissolved.

If it is this conception of "false consciousness" which provides the foundation of Marx's answer to the question concerning how the ideas of the ruling class "normally" rule the whole of society, it is nevertheless evident that the theory of fetishism does not constitute the whole of Marx's answer. To be sure, in a negative sense capitalism as a system of social domination tends to legitimate itself. But even though a spontaneous, fetishistic mode of thinking renders radical and rational criticism impossible, it is at the same time too confused, fragmented and self-contradictory to insulate itself from practical-intellectual criticism. Moreover, when the automatic mechanisms of market production do not ensure the undisturbed reproduction of the underlying social relations, the fetishistic categories also tend to lose their pragmatic validity and effectiveness. During those periods of economic crisis, the web of "appearances" tends to dissipate and the relations of social domination manifest themselves in relatively naked form. The mere reproduction of everyday life-practices is not sufficient to legitimate capitalism—precisely because this reproduction process is itself punc-tuated by objective tensions and disturbances.

This is the point where the explanatory-functional concept of ideology enters into the architecture of Marx's social theory. Institutionally disseminated sys-tems of ruling ideas are seen by Marx to systematize the confused and chaotic conceptions of everyday thinking, to lend a degree of logical coherence to their fragmented structure, to explain away (and thereby apologize for) the most widely encountered experiences that contradict the seeming self-evidence of fetishistic categories. The Church, the Church-dominated school system, and various political and juridical institutions are the social organisations which Marx most frequently connects with the fulfilment of this task. Thus, in his later writings, Marx sometimes applies the term ideology to analyze the functioning of these institutions, whose personnel are described in turn as "the ideological strata of the ruling class".[4] These institutions are nevertheless conceived by him as mere transmitters and propagators of ideas which are elaborated elsewhere—in the sphere of cultural production, of high culture conceived as an internally differentiated branch of the overall social division of labour. In general it is these cultural-"spiritual" objectivations belonging to the spheres of religion, philos-ophy, social theory, political economy and art—but not natural science, it should be noted—which Marx regularly designates by the common name of ideology. These are the forms, as Marx states in the *Preface*, in which men become conscious of their social conflicts and fight them out.

Despite the fact that Marx extends the concept of ideology to all these activities and their social function in general, his attitude towards this wide range of cultural creations is in fact markedly differentiated. In the most elaborated and best-known case of his critiques of ideologies, that of the critique of bourgeois economy, this differentiation is unambiguously stated and of serious importance for Marx's own economic theory. While Marx repeatedly and emphatically states that bourgeois economy as a whole is a form of ideology, he at the same time directly counterposes the "scientific" economy of the classics (above all, the Physiocrats, Adam Smith and Ricardo) to the apologetic pseudo-science of "vulgar" economy. (This fact also clearly indicates that, for Marx, being scientific and being ideological in a given context are not mutually exclusive enterprises.) The same type of distinction can be observed if one compares Marx's critique of the young Hegelians with his repeated criticisms of Hegel: not only is the tone of these criticisms strikingly different but, more importantly, so also is the whole method of criticism itself, and in ways which definitely parallel Marx's different attitudes toward, say, Smith and Malthus. Even in Marx's sparse remarks about art—compare his treatment of Eugene Sue and Balzac—one can find a similarly drawn practical distinction.

At the risk of overinterpretation, I would suggest that Marx consistently distinguishes between what can be called "ideologies of the historical moment" and ideologies that represent epochal cultural values.[5] Concerning the first (e.g., vulgar economy), the situation is rather clear. These are cultural "products" which directly provide the intellectual material for those (aforementioned) institutions which disseminate ideas that serve immediately apologetic purposes. The claim to (scientific, philosophical or artistic) truth of these ideologies is a mere veneer that conceals their defence and articulation of specific, narrow, particularistic interests which are tied to the immediate, practical realities of the present.[6] It is in relation to these ideologies that Marx adopts the type of criticism earlier characterised as "unmasking": the reduction of the content of views to a specific configuration of interests. If one merely glances at Marx's truly voluminous criticisms of Hegel or Ricardo from this viewpoint, it is immediately striking how little Marx applies to them this method of "explanation through interests". Certainly, he characterises them as theoreticians of *bourgeois society*, as representing its standpoint. Yet Marx refers to the specific, concrete situation and interests of, say, the German bourgeoisie in the early nineteenth century only in cases where he intends to indicate and explain some internal inconsistency of the Hegelian theory of the state and *not* the theoretical kernel and significance of Hegel's philosophy.

At this point two questions arise. On the one hand, how, and on the basis of what criteria, does Marx draw this distinction between two types of ideology? And, on the other hand, what is the social significance of these cultural creations here described as "epochal cultural values"? In a sense, these two questions are closely interrelated. True, the distinction which Marx draws between, say, vulgar and classical economy is to a considerable degree based on accepted and "trivial" cultural criteria. In his critique of Malthus or Smith, Marx spends an enormous (one is inclined to say, disproportionate) amount of space to prove their lack of originality or even outright plagiarism, the presence of eclectic confusions or logical contradictions, the missing explanatory power in regard to elementary observations concerning regularities of economic life, and so on—a fact worth mentioning if only because it suggests that he treats as self-evidently valid these inherited criteria of evaluation specific to, and accepted within, a given sphere of cultural activities. But such considerations certainly do not exhaust his criticisms. For it is actually the way Marx criticizes those works which in fact meet these elementary criteria that best demonstrates what constitutes for him their significance, what makes them ultimately a "cultural value".

There is a definite methodological parallelism (to which della Volpe has already drawn attention) between the Marxian critiques of Hegelian philosophy, on the one side, and that of the classics of English economy, on the other. First, in all these cases Marx actually departs from the criticism of a *method of thinking*. This is rather self-evidently so in the case of Hegel, but one should remember that his whole analysis of Smith's system is also embedded in an unravelling of the contradictions between his dual, esoteric and exoteric modes of explanation, while the discussion of the Ricardian economy departs from a dissection of the analytic method of the latter.[7] And in all these cases he actually attempts to demonstrate how a definite way of thinking results in the exclusion of a definite problematics, in the failure even to state questions of a definite type. So Marx argues that the seemingly innocent, common sense empiricism of Ricardo prevents him from raising theoretical questions about the socio-historical genesis of the value-form itself; Ricardo is logically forced to accept (as self-evident) the value- and commodity-character of objects of utility, as if they were the inevitable, "natural" characteristics of any economy based on a developed system of division of labour.[8] Similarly, the idealist hypostatization of self-consciousness in Hegel is treated by Marx as necessarily leading to an identification of alienation with the materially objective character of human activities and, in the final analysis, with human finitude as such—and thereby inevitably excluding the very ability to imagine its practical overcoming.

What makes the work of Ricardo or Hegel epochally significant, what makes these thinkers theoretical representatives of a *type of society*, and not merely ideologues of a definite social group in a given country at a given moment, can be summed up in the following three points:
1. Their unthematised, taken-for-granted assertions and premises appear not as arbitrary assumptions, but as necessities of thinking, as outcomes of a *method*, of a definite type of "logical constraint".
2. At the same time, the "unconscious" presuppositions of their systems actually express, fix in thought, some fundamental characteristics of capitalist society; these presuppositions are related not to some momentary constellation of particular interests within this society, but to its essential life-conditions. It is these latter which they elevate—through their methodically unfolded logic—into universally binding norms or, alternatively, into untranscendable natural necessity.
3. These thinkers not only consistently ("cynically") follow through their own consequences, but also attempt to solve intellectually—from their fixed point of departure—a whole range of problems and contradictions which are

manifested in the everyday life of this society. The "creativity" of such works of culture is not to be found merely in their individual originality, but primarily in their strenuous effort to overcome in thinking those conflicts of real life which challenge and potentially undermine the universal validity of their silently adopted principles. In this sense they do not simply parade interests as universal ones; rather, they attempt to *universalise* those interests which dominate the given form of social life. Insofar as they succeed in this attempt, they make explicit and manifest the definite *limits* of a thinking which takes for granted and posits as unalterable the basic conditions of existence of a given type of society. These works of culture are not only intellectual, but also *historical-paradigmatic closures of thought*. They must therefore be unravelled or critically overcome if thinking about *another* future is to be freed, if this future can be claimed not only as a desirable utopia, but also as rational possibility.

In these senses, the Marxian conception of ideology is not merely a form of social explanation; it also represents a definite type of hermeneutics, a "hermeneutics with emancipatory intent" (to borrow an expression suggested by S. Benhabib). The essence of this emancipatory hermeneutics cannot be reduced to the search for some "sociological equivalent" to the point of view presented in any text. The critique of ideology as hermeneutics of course insists on the insufficiency of a merely "immanent reading" of the text, for it demands a comprehension and interpretation of the transmitted cultural tradition which situates this text in its own social-historical context. But it does so with the aim of discovering in the "classical" texts themselves those "unconscious presuppositions", those unreflected "prejudices" which both structure and set a limit to the possibility of rational discourse within them. Marx offers a hermeneutics which posits the constraint of concepts as a consequence of the constraint of circumstances, a hermeneutics which is guided by the intention of contributing to the removal of the second through the removal of the first. According to him, only this type of reading can, in one and the same act, capture the original *meaning* and the real historical *significance* of a text, and thereby realize the classical hermeneutical postulate of Enlightenment: to understand a work better than its own author did.

III

I have tentatively indicated two types of contexts in which the concept of ideology occurs in Marx and, corresponding to them, the two meanings this term acquires in his writings. But there is also a third one which—in contrast to the polemical-unmasking and explanatory-functional uses of this concept—I will designate as the *critical-philosophical* sense of ideology. When discussing the overall results and consequences of the divorce between manual and mental labour underlying the whole course of historical civilisations, Marx sometimes employs or implies a concept of ideology which seems to refer not to specifiable works (which are either unmasked and criticized or interpreted through historical explanation) but, rather, to a *definite type of culture in general*, and to a definite way of understanding cultural objectivations which is, according to him, both deceptive and at the same time "adequate" to this type of culture. "[T]he autonomisation of thoughts and ideas is only a consequence of the autonomisation of personal relations and contacts between individuals. . . . [N]either thoughts, nor language constitute a realm of their own; they are merely *expressions* of real life."[9] The critical edge of this implied conception of ideology is directed primarily against any comprehension of cultural creations which perceives them as *representations* which "correspond" to reality (or embodiments of equally transcendent values), which thereby acquire an allegedly timeless validity. To this conception Marx counterposes a view of cultural objectivations, which are analysed as *expressions* of the active-practical life-situation of definite (actual or potential) social agents who may acquire through these life-forms a consciousness of their historically situated needs and potentialities. In this sense culture never constitutes an autonomous realm of values *over* practical and social life. In the final analysis, it is an articulation of the conflicts of this social life, whose ultimate function consists in making the solution of these conflicts possible.

The apparent autonomy of high culture from social life is, in one sense, *the* ideological illusion, the illusion of a culture which in its totality functions as ideology. For the ultimate and hidden preconceptions, and the fundamental problem-content of any work of culture, always remain determined and circumscribed by those practical possibilities and attitudes that are open to the typical social actors—its potential addressees—under the given conditions of their existence. So when Marx is engaged in the age-old practice of all philosophers—explicating the "true meaning" of the philosophical tradition in his own language—he invariably insists upon a translation of even the most abstract and timeless problems and categories into the *practico-historical*. In his view, the speculative question concerning the relationship between matter and spirit ultimately refers to the practical problem concerning the relation of physical and mental labour; the philosophical phrases about "substance" should be deciphered as attempts and proposals to clarify the possible relationship between human activities and that system of inherited objectivations which for every generation constitutes the ready-found *prius* of its life.

The ideological illusion that high culture is autonomous is in another sense stark reality: the reality of a society in which high culture has become a sphere divorced from the life of the majority, where both its creation and enjoyment is the privilege of a few. Cultural elitism is not merely a problem of education and the dissemination of learning: its overcoming demands a dismantling of its ideological transposition, which in turn requires a new culture which directly and openly addresses itself to the problem of real-historical life, a culture which adjudicates mundane conflicts not from the vantage-point of an eternal truth bestowed by an impartial judge, but from the point of view of a committed participant. The realisation of philosophy is possible only through its overcoming *as* philosophy. And it is characteristic that Marx—always at great pains to avoid designating the natural sciences as "ideology"—seems at some points to implicate them, insofar as their *cultural form* is concerned, in the same type of criticism. "Science [he writes concerning the development of the machine production that compels the inanimate limbs of machinery, by its very construction, to act as a purposeful automaton] does not exist in the consciousness of the worker, but acts upon him through the machine as an alien power, as the power of the machine itself....The accumulation of knowledge and skills, of the general productive forces of the social brain, is thus absorbed into capital, as opposed to labour, and therefore appears as an attribute of capital...."[10]

In this broadest, critico-philosophical sense, ideology is the culture of an alienated society where goal-realisation and goal-positing—the criticism of previously transmitted meanings, the performance of socially codified, meaningful tasks, and the creation of new social meanings—become radically divorced from each other. Humans therefore do not have—either individually or collectively— control over the general results of their own activities and the ensuing direction of their own development. Ideology is an alienated form of social self-consciousness, since it brings historical conflicts to awareness only by transposing them into what appears to be a sphere of mere imagination and thought. Social tasks and possibilities which can be *solved and realised* only in practical collective activity therefore assume the form of eternal questions to which some religious, philosophical or artistic *answer* is sought. Critique of ideology in this sense is a critique of cultural objectivations which confronts them with their real life-basis, against which they assert their autonomy and which therefore remains for them hidden and unreflected, an externally imposed barrier to imagination and thought. Conversely, this critique of ideology also—and perhaps primarily— assumes the form of a critique of this life-basis by confronting it with its paradigmatic cultural objectivations. Critique of ideology is a critique of a form of social existence in which the awareness of social needs and possibilities can be achieved only in a sphere divorced from, and contrasted to, life, a sphere that has to remain a mere "culture", a value and ideal which is both unattainable and irrelevant for the overwhelming majority.

IV

This very cursory overview perhaps succeeds in indicating that the three meanings of ideology which seem to be equally present in Marx's *oeuvre* are not completely independent and isolated from each other, but are at least vaguely unified both in their practical intent and in the theoretical framework they all ultimately presuppose. However, no discussion of Marx's views on ideology is adequate, even in a minimal sense, if it fails to mention at least those "gaps" in his conceptions to which in some measure and on some occasions he himself draws attention. Two problematic gaps seem to be of paramount importance in this respect.

In a footnote to *Capital*, Marx makes the following remark: "In fact it is much easier to discover through analysis the earthly kernel of the misty creations of religion than, in the opposite way, to develop from the actual relations of life in question the form in which they have been apotheosized. This latter method is the only materialistic, and therefore scientific one."[11] This passage again makes abundantly clear that Marx's own idea of a critique of ideologies is in no way identical with a reductionist, sociological explanation of the *content* of certain cultural creations. But this remark also brings sharply into relief a requirement whose fulfilment in Marx's own theoretical practice seems to be rather problematic: the need for an historical explanation of *cultural forms* themselves, of *genres* like religion, art, philosophy, science and their various subdivisions. That the internal division of culture into various types of practices is a changing historical phenomenon which at the same time, and in each historical moment, presents a number of normatively fixed possibilities and criteria for creative activities, is undoubtedly a major problem which a theory of ideology (especially in its broadest, critico-philosophical sense) cannot by-pass. One can enumerate a number of Marxian observations that may be related to the question so posed. These observations include his discussion of the origin and general character of speculative philosophy in *The German Ideology*; his note in the *Grundrisse* (one that hardly goes beyond Hegel, admittedly) about the animosity of bourgeois society toward definite forms of art such as epic poetry; his highly interesting, though dispersed and unsystematic, remarks in his various economic manuscripts about the social preconditions of the emergence of political economy as science; and so on. However, all these observations have not only a highly schematic, but also a rather accidental character. They certainly do not indicate how the problem, so energetically stated by Marx, can and should be approached in general terms. This absence of an answer to the problem of cultural genres is all the more significant, because in his own critical practice—as I indicated above—Marx does seem to accept as self-evidently valid those criteria of evaluation which (in the nineteenth century) were inherent and tied to the predominant cultural forms. In a sense it would be true to say that—especially in his later writings—Marx seems to take inherited cultural genres for granted, and that this makes his "philosophical" concept of ideology as the culture of an alienated society rather (and at least) indeterminate. It was only a much later generation of Marxists—one which included Lukács and Goldmann, Benjamin and Adorno— who directly faced the problem of cultural genres, though predominantly with reference to the arts alone.

The second problem is not completely unrelated to the first, and can again be introduced with a quotation from Marx. At the end of his somewhat enigmatic and abruptly terminating methodological discussion in the *Grundrisse*, he states the following: "The difficulty lies not in the understanding that Greek art and epic are bound up with certain forms of social development. The difficulty is that they still afford us artistic pleasure and in a certain respect they count as a norm and as an unattainable model."[12] It is again clear that this "difficulty" is much broader and more profound than the given example. For the "functional" concept of ideology in Marx sometimes rests upon an account of the paradigmatic character or *epochal significance* of cultural creations. These paradigmatic creations are seen to articulate the limits of imagination and thought which are bound up not with momentary, passing group interests, but with the essential, structural characteristics of a whole stage of social development. But this conception advanced by Marx has its limits—it remains strictly historical. As it stands, it does not account directly for the fact that, at least in some cultural genres like the arts or philosophy, some of the cultural heritage of past epochs (the social conditions of which we may even have difficulty reconstructing) preserves its significance for the present cultural practices of creation and reception alike. This problem—that culture may exert a living relevance far beyond its original epoch—certainly cannot be solved by merely referring to the now elementary observation that the list of "classical" works itself undergoes deep changes in the history of cultural transmission and reception: this fact certainly indicates that a theory of cultural tradition ought to be an *historical* one, but it does not render such a theory superfluous.

Marx's own short answer to this "difficulty" seems to be contradicted by this now elementary observation. However, this is not the only and the most disconcerting feature of his reply. In general, he answers the question about the persisting artistic significance of some ancient Greek works by referring to the specific place Greek antiquity occupies in the history of human development as such. This antiquity is seen to represent the "normal childhood" of humankind, "its most beautiful unfolding"; its manifestations—as childhood memories in general—therefore exercise upon us an "eternal charm". Leaving aside Marx's (indubitable) Europocentrism, this reply, if taken literally, is suggestive of a most disturbing application of the biologic imagery of "maturation and growth" to history. Clearly, this would lend an openly teleological character to the whole Marxian conception of social progress. Perhaps one should interpret this statement much more liberally, above all by connecting it with an Hegelian, hermeneutical concept of memory as *"Er-innerung"*. This was actually Lukács' project: He in his late *Aesthetics*, developed a conception of art as the collective memory of humankind by drawing upon this formulation of Marx. But even granting this most liberal and imaginative interpretation, the difficulty indicated by Marx seems to be much broader and more general than any answer along the lines proposed by him is able to solve. Marx does not account at all for the different role tradition plays (and the different form it takes) within different cultural genres; that is, he ignores the specific form of historicity immanent within, and characteristic of, distinct cultural forms. Since the function of inherited tradition is an important aspect and component of the often-discussed problem of the "relative independence" of ideology, the question essentially left open by Marx becomes of paramount theoretical significance.

DISAPPEARING IDEOLOGY

V

It is certainly justified to indicate at this point that Marx never intended nor claimed to create a *systematic theory* of ideology. The heterogeneous and mostly critical uses he made of this concept can be seen in retrospect to have enclosed a definite field of investigation and to have suggested/outlined an essentially unified theoretical approach to this field. No doubt, to speak about "gaps in Marx's theory of ideology" implies a critical judgment according to a criterion—comprehensiveness—which is in this case certainly inappropriate. It is, however, justified to ask whether the failure of this theoretical approach to account adequately for some of the most comprehensive and striking characteristics of the domain it encloses indicates more than a mere lack of (perhaps never intended) comprehensiveness. Are not the "gaps" I have mentioned more than mere *lacunae*? Are they not expressions of internal strains within the conception itself?

A short essay certainly cannot answer this question. But since no one, whose interest in Marx is not solely antiquarian, can simply neglect it, I would in conclusion like to suggest some considerations that may be relevant to such an answer. Without further explanation, I will take up one problem, in respect of which the internal consistency of the Marxian conception of ideology has been very often queried, and to which the earlier exposition has also referred. This is the question of the relationship between ideology and the natural sciences.

As has already been indicated, Marx had rigorously avoided applying the term "ideology" to the *content* of the theories of natural science, even though his criticism clearly implicated both the cultural-institutional form of their development and the character of the social application of their results in contemporary capitalist society. In fact, though he was completely aware of the historical connection between the emergence of the natural sciences and the capitalist mode of production,[13] he consistently chose to characterise natural scientific *knowledge* in explicitly *universalistic*—rather than historico-socially specific—terms. He described it, for example, as "the general cultural" [*geistige*] product of social development"; as "the product of the general historical development in its abstract quintessence"; as (in contradistinction to co-operative labour) "universal labour"; as "the general productive force of social brain"; and as "the most solid form of wealth, . . . both ideal and at the same time practical wealth".[14] Now it certainly can be argued that the use of such universalistic metaphors indicates a serious inconsistency within a theory which, insisting that consciousness never can be anything else but the consciousness of an existing historical practice, underlines the social determination and historical embeddedness and limitation of every system of ideas. According to this argument, the treatment of natural sciences as "non-ideological" must be regarded as one of the signs of mere evasiveness, as a specific instance of a flight from the untenable or undesirable relativistic consequences of a thoroughgoing historicism which renders the whole conception of ideology in Marx beset by internal contradictions.

101

As it stands, this criticism seems to me invalid, for it falsely constructs the problem to which the Marxian theory of ideology addresses itself. This problem is not that of the historicity of all thinking in general. Rather, the Marxian theory is concerned with those specific social-historical conditions which make it impossible for thinking to recognise self-reflectively its own historical constitution and which thereby lock this thinking into a system of categories or images that both justifies and attempts to perpetuate its very historical limitations. Marx takes it for granted that there is no thinking "without preconditions", that all systems of ideas—natural scientific as well as "ideological"—are historically situated and therefore also limited. It is equally evident to him that the mere form of scientificity, understood as the satisfaction of a set of purely epistemological or methodological criteria, is never able to ensure by itself the exclusion of the possiblity of an "ideological closure". He distinguishes theories of natural sciences from forms of ideology not because he ascribes an ahistoric validity to the former, but because he wants to distinguish two different—and by virtue of their different *social* constitution and functions—opposed processes of historical change in the broad field of culture. On the one hand, natural sciences are historical, in the sense that they exist as an uninterrupted process of critical inquiry in which earlier theories become constantly replaced by more abstract-general and more exact ones on the basis of an ever-expanding experimentation and observation that is both constantly spurred on and at the same time controlled by the experiences and requirements of productive material practice. It is this organic link of the natural sciences with the everyday practical results and experiences of the process of production that ultimately ensures that their historical change takes the form of an intellectual progress, *viz.*, the *accumulation and growth of knowledge*. The concept of ideology, on the other hand, explains why such progress cannot be observed in other fields of cultural creativity. The concept of ideology indicates that, in antagonistic societies, individuals can reach the level of social *self*-consciousness (as distinct from the social consciousness of their relation to nature) only by making deliberate choices between cultural objectivations and world-views whose struggle and dispute cannot be resolved by purely intellectual means, and whose historical alteration therefore cannot be conceived according to a model of accumulation and growth.

Marx's distinction between natural science and ideology is therefore not only internally coherent, but also in complete accordance with some of the most fundamental and pervasive conceptual distinctions that belong to the basic framework of his theory of history: the distinction between material content and social form; between the productive forces and the relations of production; and, in general, between the practical relations of humans to nature and the relations of social intercourse between humans, a distinction which he at the same time identifies with the axes of continuity and discontinuity in history. The contrast between the natural sciences and ideologies can thus be seen as the consistent application of these principal dichotomies to the field of cultural production proper.

So the problem indicated by certain critics hardly proves Marx guilty of any direct inconsistency. Nevertheless, a simple outline of his (largely implicit) "solution" to this problem raises a number of rather disquieting questions. First, such an outline makes clear that at least some of the particular presuppositions of the Marxian concept of ideology are rather immediately tied to a nineteenth century view of scientific progress which is nowadays difficult to defend. One must not necessarily accept the viewpoints of Feyerabend or even Kuhn to apprehend that the conception of scientific development as a unilinear, cumulative growth neither fits the historical facts, nor is defensible in view of the complex interrelationship between observation and theory in the natural sciences. From a contemporary perspective, Marx seems in particular to have missed the point that the natural sciences' explicitly empirical basis does not render their historical situatedness transparent, primarily because the fundamental underlying paradigms in terms of which their empirical data are constructed can be clearly recognized as such only after some alternative and competing ways of interpretation have been offered. Secondly, a reconsideration of the Marxian conception of ideology indicates the extent to which it is embedded in a theory of historical progress which sustains itself upon a key dichotomy between the continuous growth in human mastery over nature and the discontinuous transformations in the relations of broadly conceived social intercourse—a theory of progress which today can be addressed with many questions.

But the problem under discussion here not only indicates difficulties concerning the relationship between the particular details and the most abstract-general presuppositions of the Marxian view. It also makes comprehensible Marx's rather strange combination of a radical philosophical criticism of the total culture of bourgeois society as alienated-ideological with the unquestioned acceptance of the validity of inherited cultural criteria, above all those of the sciences. There is no doubt that, at least in his late *oeuvre*, Marx conceived his own theory in conformity with the cultural model of the natural sciences emancipated from the domination of capital. Directly connected with the everyday life-experiences of its social addressees, theory makes these experiences comprehensible in their historical specificity and necessity, and thereby, at one and the same time, is converted into "true science" capable of unlimited progress (since it makes its own historical presuppositions transparent as "empirically observable and verifiable states of affairs") and a "popular force".

Not only Marx's uncritical attitude toward the cultural form of the natural sciences makes his program of a consistent "scientisation" of the cognitive content of the cultural heritage theoretically suspect. This weakness appears also to have its reverse side, namely, the Marxian theory's essentially "negativistic" conception of everyday consciousness. It seems to be more than accidental that the Marxian theory of everyday consciousness, at least as far as its systematic achievements are concerned, lays all the emphasis on the necessarily fetishistic character of everyday thinking in capitalist society in general. Theory can locate the emancipatory impulses of its own subject and addressee, the working class, only in the form of *unarticulated* needs, frustrations and anxieties or, more usually, in that of *"objective* interests". It thereby by-passes the problem that even "spontaneous" resistance to capitalist society finds its expression in definite cultural forms. (It was Gramsci who first faced the problems involved in this phenomenon.) The Marxian theory of ideology therefore in fact assimilates the relationship of critical theory and its addressees into the model of "learning a science". This in turn seems to revoke the radical conception of the critical theory itself. Marx's near-contemptuous attitude to everything that today would be labelled as "working class culture"—consider his dispute with Weitling—rather dramatically illustrates this point.

But, above all, the problems associated with this program of overcoming the "illusions of ideology" through a simultaneous "scientisation and popularisation" of theory and culture in general are of a practical nature. If the shibboleth so often heard today—"the crisis of Marxism"—has any meaning at all, it should designate a whole historical process whose end result we are now facing. This process is one in which, in a situation of deep and generally recognised social crisis, Marxist theory enjoys an unprecedented "scientific" (i.e., academic) respectability, while at the same time its theoretically "respectable" (intellectually honest and serious) forms have no impact or connection with radical social movements of any kind. In a sense, the history of Marxism has turned full circle. In these times, Marxian theory has reproduced that initial situation which it so confidently set out to change—the complete divorce between theory and practice. If one is inclined, however, to trace back (at least partially) this failure to the original self-interpretation of the theory—to its lack of critical reflection upon itself as a specific cultural form—one should also remember that the historical experience of radical attempts to challenge directly the autonomy of high culture in the name of social emancipation have proved to be equally negative, and often even much more disastrous. These challenges to autonomous high culture have been assimilated into the dominant institutional forms of cultural production and reception with conspicuous ease (as in the case of many artistic experiments and movements: Brecht, surrealism, etc.); or (as the case of the Bolshevik program of the "politicization" of culture indicates) they have resulted in the transformation of high culture into ideology in the crudest sense—into sheer apologies for the existing relations of dominance and oppression, which as a consequence become culturally desolate. To understand this history, to "apply" the theory of ideology to the theory of ideology itself, today seems to be a necessary and unavoidable task.

General Philosophy
University of Sydney
Australia

Notes

1. *Marx-Engels Werke* (Berlin, 1958), vol. 3, p. 49 (hereafter cited as *MEW*).

2. I should indicate at this point that fetishism—the historically specific form of everyday con-

sciousness under capitalism—does not for Marx represent the sole type of socially induced distortions of experience and interpretation of the world in which individuals immediately live. In relation to pre-capitalist societies, he makes at least fleeting references to the "idolatry of nature" as an historical phenomenon analogous to fetishism. As the third volume of *Capital* makes clear, this idolatry involves both the personification of natural forces and things upon which human activities are still dependent *and* the corresponding naturalisation of social roles, in which relations of personal dependence and bondage manifest themselves.

3. *Grundrisse* (Berlin, 1953), pp. 136-137.

4. See, for example, *MEW*, Vol. 26, 1, pp. 145-146, 256-259.

5. This abbreviated terminology is certainly quite alien to Marx. The only place (to my knowledge) where he explicitly formulates a contrast resembling the one drawn here is in his criticism of Storch (*MEW*, vol. 26, 1, p. 257; see also p. 377), where he distinguishes the "ideological components of the ruling class" from its "free cultural-spiritual (*geistige*) production". From the standpoint of his whole theory, this latter (and certainly accidental) designation is rather questionable, and is therefore not used here.

6. See, for example, Marx's general characterization of vulgar economy in *MEW*, vol. 26, 3, pp. 430-494.

7. Cf. *ibid.*, vol. 26, 1, pp. 40-48, 60-69; vol. 26, 2, pp. 100, 161-166, 214-217; vol. 26, 3, pp. 491-494, 504.

8. The following formulation is rather typical of this train of thought in Marx: "Classical economics pear as bearers of the latter, the various fixed and mutually alien forms of wealth to their inner unity and to strip them of that character due to which they stand side by side, indifferent toward each other; it seeks to comprehend the internal interconnection apart from the multiplicity of forms of appearance...In this analysis, classical economics now and again falls into contradictions; it often attempts to accomplish this reduction and to demonstrate the identity of the source of the various forms directly, without mediating links. However, this necessarily follows from its analytic method, with which the critique and comprehension inevitably begins. It has no interest in genetically developing the various forms, only an interest in their analytic reduction and unification, because it departs from these forms as given premises...Classical economics ultimately fails, and is deficient because it conceives the *ground-form of capital*, production directed towards the appropriation of alien labour, not as a *social form*, but as the *natural form* of social production—a mode of comprehension for the discarding of which it itself clears the way" (*ibid.*, vol. 26, 3, pp. 490-491).

9. *Ibid.*, vol. 3, pp. 432-433; see also *Grundrisse*, pp. 82-83.

10. *Grundrisse*, pp. 584, 586.

11. *MEW*, vol. 23, p. 393.

12. *Grundrisse*, p. 31.

13. See, for example, *ibid.*, p. 313: "Just as production founded on capital creates, on the one hand, universal industriousness—i.e., surplus-labour, value-creating labour—so it creates, on the other hand, a system of general exploitation of the natural and human qualities, a system of general utility. Both science itself and all the physical and mental qualities appear as bearers of the latter, while there appears to be nothing *higher-in-itself*, nothing legitimate-for-itself outside this circle of social production and exchange...Hence the great civilising influence of capital...For the first time, nature becomes a mere object for humanity, a mere matter of utility; it ceases to be recognized as a power for itself; and the theoretical knowledge of its autonomous laws itself appears merely as a ruse to subjugate it under human needs, either as an object of consumption, or as a means of production."

14. The first of two quotations appear in *Resultate des unmittelbaren Produktionsprozesses*, Marx-Engels Archiv (Moscow, 1933), vol. 2, vii, pp. 156 and 160; the reference to "universal labour" is found in *MEW*, vol. 25, p. 114; the last two sentences are taken respectively from *Grundrisse*, pp. 586 and 439.

IDEOLOGY AND THE *WELTANSCHAUUNG* OF THE INTELLECTUALS

Zygmunt Bauman

It has often been noted that the word "ideology" in its nearly two centuries long history underwent a truly bewildering semantic change, acquiring in the end a meaning exactly contrary to its original connotation. Indeed, what more antagonistic semantic domains are there than truth and falsehood; science and common-sense beliefs; impartial, lasting knowledge and shifting, narrow-minded prejudice?

The oppositions are so dazzlingly evident that they easily cast similarities in a deep shadow. What is lost in this contrast is the question of continuity—more importantly, the question of a semantic field which the two apparently antagonistic meanings of "ideology" share. This question may seem strange to a generation brought up to think of the unfolding of ideas in the undialectical terms of Thomas Kuhn's "paradigm", which identifies logical contradiction with the mutual exclusiveness of underlying world-views. The question appears more obvious, even imperative, if instead of paradigms we think in terms of Michel Foucault"s "discursive formation", which is defined by its remarkable capacity of "giving birth simultaneously and successively to mutually exclusive objects, without having to modify itself".[1]

One can think of a number of reasons for placing the utility of the concept of discursive formation well above that of "paradigm". The most obvious reason is that this concept helps to reveal the genuine dialectics of thought—its continuity, the semantic interdependence of oppositions, the mutual determination of objects allegedly subject to independent logics, and so on. But there are other reasons as well. The evident fact of the on-going communication between separate languages, so baffling from a Kuhnian perspective, appears all but natural. It becomes clear that far from being mutually exclusive, different "forms of life" are often members of the same discursive community and must acknowledge, even if only obliquely, their joint membership by engaging the other form in a competition. Above all, the discursive-formation perspective brings into relief the social mechanisms behind the unfolding of thought. If in the Kuhnian world society appears only to interfere with the smooth unfolding of the play between theory and evidence, the idea of discursive formation reveals society and its authority network as the sole material content of the articulation and delimitation of objects of discourse and the dispersion of statements which it contains and legitimises. One could say that Kuhn's idea of the paradigm remains from the beginning to the end *inside* the discursive formation of ideology, which is the object of this essay—while Foucault's methodology offers the sought-after chance of stepping outside this formation so as to scrutinise and codify the rules which made possible its emergence.

But to return to our proper subject matter: it is the main contention of this essay that the problematics of the theory of ideology, with all its bizarre turn-abouts and convolutions, can best be understood within that typically modern discourse of power which is associated with what has come to be described as the "civilising process". This process has been variously analyzed in the past as the triumph of reason over ignorance; as the victory of sweetness and light over crude and uncouth existence; as the displacement of brutality and barbarism by politeness and gentle habits; as law and peaceful order replacing the fist and the pandemonium of universal war; as the taming of passions by civility and self-control. With a measure of emotional detachment, more becoming of the academic mode, the process has been characterized as the rise to dominance of instrumental rationality over irrational behaviour; as the trading off of a part of freedom for a partial security, and the concomitant harnessing of aggression; as the imposition of the courtier's ideal of *l'homme honnête*, and later of *l'homme éclairé*, upon successively lower rungs of the status ladder.

The descriptions vary in the size and importance of the aspect of the process they capture. But none seems to grasp the main link in the long chain of historical transformations which Western European society went through in the course of the last three-and-a-half centuries. If the main link is the one which articulates all the others into a continuous chain, and thereby contains the key to the interdependence of all units of the totality, then the gradual emergence of the new form of management of the socially produced surplus seems to be a promising candidate.

This form was indeed revolutionary and set the era of "civilisation" or industrial capitalist society apart from the previously dominant type of society. In this old type, surplus value was extracted from the producers, so to speak, in leaps and bounds, say, once or several times during the annual cycle of the predominantly agricultural production, in the form of rent, or a tax, tribute, or tithe. Owing to will or fear or both, the producer had to be made to part with a portion of his product. Once he had done that, he could be (and had to be to keep the process of production going) left alone. It was largely irrelevant for the circulation of surplus how he went about his daily business, how he administered the activities of his body and soul. The only thing which mattered—the production of surplus—was quite adequately taken care of by the double pressure of the natural cycle and the threat of what Ernest Gellner once called the "Dentistry State"—a state specialising in extraction by torture.

The advent of manufacture and the factory system, and later of market exchange integrating ever-lower rungs of the social ladder, ended this relatively simple method of surplus management. The extraction of surplus ceased to be the only task of the dominant class. Now it was to assume responsibility for the very production of surplus; producers could not be left alone and relied upon for the administration of their productive activities. Later on, with the spread of the market, they had also to be induced to organize their life-process in a way befitting willing and pliable consumers.

DISAPPEARING IDEOLOGY

These two different systems of surplus management were brought into being by two different types of power. The first type was to remain external and remote; its remoteness, or not-of-this-worldness, was heavily underlined by the sacralisation of the royal reign, which ceremoniously reproduced the immutability of the eternal order of supremacy. This supremacy boiled down in practice to the upward flow of agricultural surplus. In Georges Duby's words, the whole system of feudalism could well be portrayed "as a method of keeping the stomachs of the barons and their retainers full".[2] Beyond these requirements, it was of little consequence what customs or habit ruled the daily life of the food suppliers. This was—if judged by the later standards—a time of rich and robust folk culture, which the Church, exacting and meticulous in its support for the divine rights of the earthly powers, was amazingly happy to leave to its own resources.

The second type of power is much more complex. It needs to secure not merely the extraction of surplus once in a while, but the extraction of a *continuous* effort, day by day, hour by hour—an effort which is ruled by the rhythm of an external and often meaningless logic. Worse still, a commodity consumer, unlike a mere tax-paying subject, has to be a choice-making animal who will make the right choices. Hence he must be made responsive to externally manipulative stimuli if his choices are to become equally manipulable and by the same token predictable. This new task requires—to employ Foucault's distinction—a "power of discipline", rather than the old type of "sovereign power". The object of the new type of power is not the wealth or the goods possessed or produced by the subject, but directly his labour, time and mode of life. It is the body and the soul of the subject which are to be manipulated. "This new mechanism of power"—to quote Foucault—"is more dependent upon bodies and what they do than upon the Earth and its products. . . . It is a type of power which is constantly exercised by means of surveillance rather than in discontinuous manner by means of a system of levies or obligations distributed over time".[3]

Thus, the new power reaches parts former powers could not reach. It penetrates deeply into the mundane daily activities of its subjects. It makes a bid for the totality of their bodily actions. This aim cannot be achieved with the old means. It certainly cannot be attained with the help of the distant, invisible king-God, symbolising the intractable order of the universe; it cannot be recalled periodically, on the day when the levy or the tithe are due for payment. The new power must employ new resources.

The new, much more ambitious, ubiquitous, all-penetrating order cannot rely on the ritual invocation of the divine rights of the sovereign. It can rule only in the name of the norm, of a pattern of normality, with which it identifies itself. Since normality means in the end a continuous rhythm of bodily exertion and the unbroken chain of repeatable choices, it can be maintained only by a dense web of interlocking authorities in constant communication with the subject and in a proximity to the subject which permits a perpetual surveillance of his life-process. Old forms are transformed into such authorities, and new authorities are brought to life. Thus families and sexual functions of the body are deployed in the new role: churches become teachers of business virtues and hard work; factories and poorhouses join forces in instilling the habit of continuous effort; idiosyncrasy and non-rhythmical life is criminalised, medicalised or phychiatrised; individualised training by apprenticeship or personal service is replaced with a uniform system of education aimed at instilling universal skills and, above all, a habit of universal and continuous discipline. No single power is now total, like that claimed by the absolute monarch. This web of authoritative relations nevertheless reaches the kind of totality no power had dreamed of reaching before. It now legislates for the whole of the individual's life, though the legislation is exercised surreptitiously by developing within the individual a tendency to a specifically patterned conduct. The sovereignty is always self-confined. There are no limits to the greed of the norm.

This is the origin of Freud's "garrison in the conquered city". Contrary to what Freud implied, this garrison is not an inescapable effect of social life, a universal sediment of the eternal struggle between the prerequisites of the "life in common" and intractable selfishness of the biological essence of man. It appears to be, instead, a historical event and a human accomplishment. It was brought into being by a concerned, though uncoordinated, action of a plethora of crisscrossing and overlapping authorities, alongside the emergence of the new bourgeois order of society. These authorities were established through a discourse which spawned numberless variants and transubstantiations of the essential opposition between the human and the animal.

"Disciplinary power", which aimed at the drill, regimentation and routinisation of the human body, was not, of course, an invention of the seventeenth century. It was, rather, its discovery. The universal control-by-surveillance employed for centuries—effectively, though matter-of-factly, by communities and woven in the thick and tightly knit tissue of the reproduction of quotidianity—was now lifted to the level of public consciousness, articulated as a problem calling for conscious design, specialised institutions, and their re-deployment in the relationship between classes. It reached the consciousness level once the communities (whether parishes, guilds or villages) and their essentially unstretchable resources became insufficient as the means of the reproduction of quotidianity. The masses of "unattached" people—vagrants, vagabonds, "dangerous classes"—were the first categories to "be seen". By virtue of remaining outside the network of communal surveillance, these groups, so to say, made visible what had been unseen before; they prompted action where customs and unreflected practices had ruled before. These people had to become the concern of societal agencies, of legislators, of centrally administered organs of coercion. But the latter were singularly unprepared for the task, never before having been engaged directly in the reproduction of daily life. Communities lost their grip on quotidianity—but no other agency, for the time being, was prepared to step into their place. This crisis of power was the basis of the Hobbesian question, "How is society possible?", and it found its response in the entirely new role assigned to the Prince.

The Prince was now to be in charge of the surveillance power. The communal practice of "I watch you, you watch me" was articulated as a postulate of one category of people watching another. Disciplinary power turned into the vehicle of the asymmetry of class relations. Great numbers of people were now seen as having to be assisted (and, if necessary, goaded) to become "truly human"; a few were to adjust themselves to the new role of tutors and guardians of the process. It was essentially this new historical constellation, and the power crisis it generated, which strengthened the popularity of a great number of related concepts (civilisation, *Kultur*, *Bildung*, refinement, ideology, enlightenment, etc.). As we will see later, these concepts tried to capture and articulate this new situation—in a way which was unmistakably tainted with the group experience of the articulators. This disciplinary power sought to totally assault and virtually destroy popular culture; it sought the cruel repression of popular rebellions, of traditional (but now redefined as "deviant") conduct, of popular festivals, of heterodox beliefs and of "witchcraft"—a process brilliantly documented for France by Muchembled and, for England, by Stephen and Eileen Yeo.[4] In the course of this struggle, the human condition acquired a new conceptualisation. It appeared now as a drama of Manichean forces of passion and reason, of the crude and the refined, of the beastly and the human. "Rule over the fish in the sea, the birds of heaven, and every living thing that moves upon the earth" was no more a gift of God to be enjoyed in peace. The subjugation of the animal *in* man came to be a major concern for humans. One had to lift oneself to the human condition; being a human came to be a task, an accomplishment, a duty.[5]

Three aspects of this new conceptualisation of the human condition deserve special comment:

1. The "duality" of human nature is seen to have a vertical dimension. The two antagonistic constituents of the self are conceptualised as stages of a process: through hard work and constant vigilance, one is to be displaced and replaced by another. Man becomes an unfinished product or, rather, raw stuff to be shaped and moulded into a human form. He becomes an object of activity, variously called culture, civilisation, *Bildung*, refinement—all these nouns, as Lucien Febvre pointed out,[6] originally connoted a transitive activity and not (as was later the case) achieved states of being.

2. Vertical and processual in its application to the life cycle of the individual, this duality is employed synchronically and horizontally in thinking about groups in their reciprocal relations within societies, or about relations between societies themselves. The human-animal dichotomy is projected upon the superiority-inferiority relations between collectivities or categories: adults and children, men and women, sane and mad, civilised and barbarians, gentlemen and the masses. In the vocabulary of the Enlightenment, the masses were described as "les bêtes-féroces, furieux, imbéciles, fous, aveugles". As Voltaire wrote in his note-books, "The people will always be composed of brutes;. the people is between man and beast".[7]

3. There is a third element invisibly present in the dichotomy of *homo duplex*: the positing of an agent in the passage from passion to reason, and the guarding of the supremacy of the reasonable over the passion-bound. The nature of this

agent is determined by the nature of the basic dichotomy. It is an agent simultaneously enlightening and repressing, benevolent and high-handed, offering the light of reason but applying a harsh medicine for the good of those reluctant or too indolent to accept the offer willingly. Superior knowledge and superior force, guidance and discipline, reason and power, come together as they do in the symbolic unity of the patriarchal father. Knowledge and power are meant for each other; disaster follows their divorce. For Diderot, "instruire une nation, s'est la civiliser; y éteindre les connaissances, c'est la ramener à l'état primitif de barbarie". According to Condorcet, "ce n'est point la politique des princes, ce sont les lumières des peuples civilisés", which will guarantee peace and progress on earth. A half century later, Guizot would castigate England for its emphasis solely on social development, with dire neglect for the refinement of spirit, and Germany for the reverse blunder: the failure to incorporate its thought into the business of social administration.

It was within this discourse constituted by the opposition between reason and passion that the concept of ideology was originally articulated, and it is there that it remains firmly entrenched. To Destutt de Tracy, commonly acknowledged as the person responsible for the coining of the word, ideology was to be a meta-theory of the moral and political sciences and of the "great activities which immediately influence the prosperity of society". The significance of ideology would consist solely in its practical applications; its many concerns would be united by the power of action, all of them bent on enhancing. Power would be the content and the consequence of all the tasks ideology would have to put in front of itself: the science of communicating ideas, of entrenching logic in human conduct, of forming morality, of regulating desires, of education—in short, all the tasks of uniting the efforts of the human arts in "regulating society in such a way that man finds there the most help and the least possible annoyance from his own kind".[8] The Institut Nationale, created to cultivate ideology as the practical science of the regulation of society, declared a public competition on the topic "What are the institutions for establishing morality in a people?" Tracy, Volnay, Cabanis, Laplace, Chénier and other members of the Institut, the leading lights of post-revolutionary Paris, gathered around the salon of Madame Helvétius, knowing well what the answer should be. Tracy in fact noted the answer on the margins of his reading of Spinoza: the good and bad tendency of our will is always directly proportional to the extent and exactitude of our knowledge. Knowledge is power over will. The idea of ideology implied confidence in the essential malleability of popular culture in the hands of the legislator, and in the crucial role of the ideologist in the legislator's effort to create a conscious, rational, ideological order.[9] Now, with the revolution triumphant in the name of reason, the time had perhaps arrived to realise the dream expressed by d'Holbach in his *La politique naturelle*: "Enlightened policies insure that every citizen will be happy in the rank where birth placed him. There exists a happiness for all classes; where the state is properly constituted, there emerges a chain of felicity extending from the monarch to the peasant. The happy man rarely considers leaving his sphere... The people are satisfied as long as they do not suffer;

limited to their simple, natural needs, their view rarely extends beyond". By offering "the most help and the least possible annoyance", ideology was to help the legislator by enlightening his policies.

If the dichotomy of passion and reason implies that man, unless taught and trained, may well act against his own good interest, then it also implies a profound lack of preordained coordination between needs and wants. Needs are what reason dictates; wants are what passion prompts. The subordination of wants to needs is therefore a task which may, and should, be accomplished for the sake of man himself—"in his best interest". From its very birth, the idea of ideology as the scientific code of enlightened policy allowed for the possibility that making people happy may involve forcing them to abandon their wants, making them do what they would rather not.

The distinction between wants and needs therefore constitutes the discourse of power. This distinction does not, by itself, determine political alignments— the attitude of support or dissent towards a specific power structure in the here and now. It provides, however, for the possibility of both attitudes. It allows for an account of the human condition as "knowing not what they truly need"; or "wanting what they truly do not need"; or "wanting not what they truly need". It opens up a number of interpretations, some readily classifiable as conservative, others as revolutionary. The gap between wants and needs may be accounted for by reference to the inbred or native obtuseness or selfishness of particular collectivities, which cannot lift themselves by their own resources to the level of a genuine understanding of their conditions. The same gap may also be explained by manipulation, conspiracy, deception by existing powers, or by the barriers to self-awareness entailed in the immediate context of life-business. The interpretations may lead to conclusions likely to be plotted on the opposite extremes of the political spectrum. All of them, however, remain *inside* the same discursive formation: the discursive formation of disciplinary power.

This discourse establishes the indispensability of an external factor in the process leading to the discovery of, and the submission to, the dictate of reason. It also delegitimises the authority of the individual or a group of individuals in determining the action which reason requires. It denies the self-sufficiency of man in finding out about and following the advice of reason. By the same token, it establishes the necessity of power as a positive or negative, but always irremovable, element of the human condition. The rationality of the latter is incomplete without power. So is man's urge toward the good life. Metaphorically speaking, in the secular version of the search for the meaning of life (i.e., where salvation is re-phrased as the good life), the discourse of ideology parallels the Catholic, in contrast to the dissident Churches', conceptualisation.

But the power that the concept of ideology calls into being and legitimises is not any power. As with all power, it is concerned with making people do what otherwise they would not, or allowing them to do what they evidently are not doing. But the kind of power generated and sustained within the ideological discourse achieves this change in human behaviour by specific means. These means belong to the category of persuasion. They invariably consist of the supply of information and the argument. They are conversational means. They operate through a debate in the course of which a modification of the partner's motives, mental map or imagination is sought. The modification is to be attained through either legitimation of evidence or interpretation heretofore illegitimate, or through the delegitimation of currently accepted evidence and interpretations. In both cases, the essential strategy is to change the beliefs of the partner. The debate which is to accomplish this is envisaged as inherently asymmetrical. It is waged between the knowing and the ignorant; between teachers and the taught; between those who enjoy a certain privileged access to good knowledge and those who have not sought, or do not seek, such access.

In short, the drama of ideology is played in the world of ideas. As Destutt de Tracy put it in his *Mémoire sur la faculté de penser*: "Nothing exists for us except by the idea we have of it, because our ideas are our whole being, our existence itself". Ideas make the world we know; ideas may therefore change this world. The ideological discourse establishes ideas as power; and power as the administration of ideas.

In this perspective, the allegedly radical change of meaning which the word "ideology" has undergone since the heyday of the Institut Nationale seems much less dramatic. This change certainly did not involve an abandonment or even a substantial transformation of the original discursive formation. The change did not go far beyond a mere terminological re-shuffle. This verbal shift was all the easier and more convenient for the discrediting of the term "ideology" in the wake of the famous condemnation of ideology by Napoleon after Malet's abortive conspiracy of December 1812. ("We must lay the blame for the ills that our fair France has suffered on ideology, that shadowy metaphysics which subtly searches for first causes on which to base the legislation of peoples, rather than making use of laws known to the human heart and of the lessons of history.... Indeed, who was it that proclaimed the principle of insurrection to be a duty? Who educated the people and attributed to it a sovereignty which it was incapable of exercising?") Having characterised the concept of ideology as a straightforward power-bid, Napoleon rendered difficult, if not fully ineffective, further attempts to legitimise it in terms of the impartial sovereignty of reason. From that moment on, any self-confessed preaching of ideology was inextricably associated with power disputes. More often than not, particularly since the Mannheim-induced renaissance of the word, ideology was now cast on the side of wants rather than needs, partiality of interests rather than universal truth, self-inflicted or enforced error rather than sound judgment, the contingent "is" rather than the compelling "ought". But the structure of the discursive formation within which this terminological reversal took place remained intact. Indeed, the very continuity of this structure rendered the reversal possible.

For a sociologist, then, a central task is to locate the structurally determined group experience which lent itself to being articulated into a *Weltanschauung* presupposed by the concept of ideology; to find a group which could proclaim with reason and conviction, with Destutt de Tracy, that "our ideas are our whole being, our existence itself" (or, for that matter, with Marx—that "ideas turn into a material force once they capture the masses"). Not unexpectedly, the search turns towards intellectuals—people who, in Lewis Coser's words, "live for, rather than off, ideas".[10]

A full study revealing the resonance between the discourse of ideology and the group experience of intellectuals would of course require an extended and detailed documentation covering both the macro-social circumference of the phenomenon and its micro-social structure. I have to confine myself here to an inventory of such attributes of the intellectual mode of life as may assist the explanatory understanding of the emergence, and sustenance, of the conception of the world as a battle of ideas waged between reason and error, a battle in which the men of ideas play the role of generals. I must leave aside the particular circumstances of eighteenth and early-nineteenth century France, Germany, or Russia, where three different but related varieties of intellectuals were sedimented in the widening gulf between outlived power structures and a new network of social dependencies and reciprocities. In these countries, it suffices to note that there emerged a legitimation gap which created a demand, and an opportunity, for these intellectuals to appear as free-lance actors in the drama of power.

The crisis of the traditional forms of political sociability (by which I mean the organised mode of relations between subjects and the rulers) rendered them incapable of securing the kind of continuous discipline the emergent social order required. This legitimation gap was subsequently filled by *sociétés de pensée*, the focal points of new political sociability developing within the empty shell of the old. The new sociability was founded, in the words of the French historian François Furet, on that confused thing called "opinion," which was generated in cafés, salons, lodges, societies, and individual colleges integrated by correspondence. Separated from all practical levels of power, the individuals engaged in the domain of sociability-by-opinion perceived its impotence as the unhampered and uncompromising rule of thought. Untroubled by cumbersome practicalities of social action, and never confronted with the necessity of humiliating compromise or trade-off or the need to accept grudgingly the possible while dreaming of the ideal, they could (and they did) conceive of a social world subject solely to the rule of reason. Not for the first and not for the last time, marginality conceived of itself as sovereignty. In the domain of sociability-by-opinion, nothing counted but the power of persuasion and the authority of argument. Only wisdom, incarnate in compelling logical wizardry, could command there. Cafés and salons were parliaments permanently in session. The debate was continuous. There was nobody present except participants. It seemed that only the power of thought guided the course of the debate; no privileges of birth, rank, or money were allowed to intefere with the ultimate victory of better argument.

The unmistakable and distinctive quality of intellectual groupings—variously referred to as the intellectual style, or mode, or culture—can thus be traced back to the emergence of a self-monitoring community of men engaged full or part-time in argument about issues somewhat detached from the concerns and preoccupations of their more mundane, banausic activities. This phenomenon has received the fullest analysis to date in Jürgen Habermas' impressive study of the structure of "the public sphere". As Habermas indicates, the community in question was constituted by the activity of discussion. This development was virtually unprecedented. A community constituted by discussion was likely to conceive of the world as a predominantly verbal activity. Such a community was also prone to attach to its argumentation a peculiar potency to influence and alter the state of things; it tended to conceive of *lexis* (the activity of talking) as *praxis*, or action. The way in which the intellectual community was formed and sustained goes a long way towards explaining its specifically intellectual bias in favour of thought as well as its latent tendency to play down the limits imposed upon the potential of thought, definition, motive, or will by elements of reality which resisted being "verbalised away".[11]

There were other features of the group-constitutive debate which help us to understand the conception of the social world as a battle of ideologies. The intellectual debate was seen as being waged outside the context of those mundane, self-interested concerns which engaged the participants at other times in their capacity as "private persons"—as household heads, property managers, breadwinners. An invisible wall seemed to rise between the two roles the participants played in their lives. They entered debate as private persons, but the debate required—and implied by the sheer fact of being carried out as a debate—that the rules which governed their private actions were to be declared irrelevant for the duration of the debate. In consequence, the dependencies which so evidently confined their freedom in mundane life seemed (counterfactually) to stop short of the debating chamber. If debate were to go on and pursue its declared objective—the conviction of truth—then the participants were to be forced to agree not to recognise their external constraints. They were to relate to each other solely through arguments aimed at common themes. Whatever relative superiority emerged during the debate was supposed to be fully explicable in reference to the strength of the argument advanced; no other criteria of superiority or inferiority were allowed. Social position, status, power connections and other properties which constituted the private identities of the participants were either silenced or proclaimed unrelated to the topic at hand. The politics of equality provided the experiential basis from which the ideas of "species being", "man as such", "the essence of man" or, indeed, "pure reason", were perpetually generated.

As might be expected, the fictitous assumptions and the counterfactual rules of the debate which constituted the intellectual mode of life were first applied and entrenched in fields relatively remote from the concerns of daily life; or, rather, in those fields which were only weakly controlled by the powers-that-be, and which were therefore capable of being easily annexed and self-governed. Such fields came to be known in the eighteenth century as "art" or, sometimes, "culture". It was over these weakest links in the chain of established power that the debating public first asserted its authority, establishing an early prototype of the "Yenan republic" in which it could deploy and test its own rules. Debating societies, salons, cafés, were simultaneously the conquered territories and invading armies. What came to be known as culture was a hypostatized mode of life that these armies administered within their territories. Inasmuch as art and culture had been constituted (as had everything else conceived within the intellectual mode) as "meaningful" or "significant"—and not merely useful or efficient—objects and actions, they were seen to be natural and undisputed domains of intellectual authority. Since rarely challenged by alternative powers, art and culture appeared to be administered by the rules of argumentative consensus. Their evaluation seemed to claim no other ground but that of an achieved consensus always renewable in a free debate between equals. It was this quality of consensus-producing debate—its purity and freedom from foreign contaminants—which was generalised as the philosophical principle of objectivity of judgment. As John Stuart Mill was to say, "[the] beliefs which we have most warrant for, have no safeguard to rest on, but a standing invitation to the whole world to prove them unfounded".[12]

This valuation of objectivity seemed safe and sound in a debate which was the whole world; it was less secure in a world which refused to be a debate. If intellectuals were ever to use in wider battles the armour forged by the smithy of cultural argument, if they were ever to move beyond the confines of their "Yenan republic", they had to confront the task of re-negotiating fields other than culture—fields like economics or politics, which were under the control of different authorities, but which were nevertheless capable of being conquered by terms similar to those already worked out for the articulation of the domain of art and culture.

Naturally, the intellectual mode of life complete with its counterfactual assumptions served as the starting point of this re-negotiation. The substance of the re-negotiation was the universal extension of the principle of objectivity, which was understood to be the monopoly of argumentative consensus in the grounding of legitimate beliefs. The principle of objectivity demanded, for example, a rejection of the principle *cuius regio, eius religio*. It militated against the criteria of individual or group utility. It was, in essence, conceptualised in opposition to any non-intellectual power over the authority of argument. The moment the intellectual mode of life stepped over the boundary of its proper, self-administered enclave, its matter-of-fact, unproblematic rules of consensus reached the level of conscious articulation in such oppositions as objectivity and bias, reason and interest, universal truth and selfish ends. The various opposites all reflected the new experience of a resistance of alien forms of power to authority grounded in the intellectual way.

For a community constituted by discussion and argument, all other groups or structures appear as so many obstacles to the smooth unraveling of argumentative consensus. The limits imposed on intellectually administered authority are experienced as the stubbornness of counter-beliefs; as unwholesome and obstinate ideas which would not stand that test, which was binding within the "liberated territory" of argument. This amazing refractoriness of not-properly-grounded beliefs could be understood only as an effect of the breaching of rules which, if applied, would soon disclose these beliefs' groundlessness. This self-understanding of argumentation preceded inquiry; as such, it was immune to the test of refutation. Each successive failure to stamp out the beliefs which did not pass muster was seen as another confirmation that the understanding was correct and "objective" in the first place.

The idea of breaching the rules brings the rules themselves up to the level of consciousness. The counterfactual assumptions which underlay the exercise of authority inside the intellectual community were now codified into a set of stipulations which the world at large was supposed to observe. This codification took the form of the vision of "undistorted communication". Given this name quite recently by Jürgen Habermas, this vision in its essence has been upheld for a very long time in a variety of circles: in post-Marxian diagnoses of false consciousness; in claims about the ideological impact of daily life or state ideological apparatuses; in Weber's concept of the ideal type, which postulated the possibility of knowledgeable actors rationally pursuing their interests; and, more generally, in the universal belief that ignorance equals error and that error derives from the insufficient control of reason over conduct. In this sense, Habermas' vision of "undistorted communication" crowns some two centuries of negotiation guided by the intellectualist utopia of the world re-made after the pattern of intellectual community, a world organised as an unbridled debate and grounded on the principles of equality, power of argument and the openness of consensus to scrutiny and criticism.

The two successive meanings commonly attached to the word "ideology" marked (and perhaps still mark) the role assigned to the secular powers-that-be in bringing about the realisation of this intellectualist utopia. Sometimes these powers have been trusted as the major levers of change; sometimes they are cast, in disappointment, into the role of villains of the piece, i.e., as the very source and agent of ignorance. The most dramatic changes in the perception of political authority have not, however, modified the essential features of this world-view. On the contrary, the continuity of this *Weltanschauung* organised by the intellectualist utopia is the very condition which makes feasible the above-mentioned fluctuations of meaning of the concept of ideology.

The perception of the world as a battle between reason and error—as a "civilising" struggle of reason against passion, of true against false interests, of needs against wants—reserves the word "ideology" for either side of the barricade and articulates men and women as bundles of motives. These motives are represented as the principal objects of social action. Action upon motives, aimed at their alteration, is articulated as the main lever of social change as such, indeed—for all practical intents and purposes—as social change itself. By the same token, individuals, groups or institutions devoted to the dissemination of ideas and thus acting upon motives, are cast in the role of the subjects of change—as its principal initiators and agents. Among such individuals, groups or institutions a special role is allocated to those who have a privileged access to reason and operate reliable methods of correcting erroneous judgments. In a world conceived as a permanent "learn in" or "teach in" session, such individuals, groups or institutions are related to the rest of society after the pattern of teachers.

The concept of ideology belongs, in sum, to the rhetoric of power. It is in full harmony with the modern form of power as a disciplining force. But within this modern form it articulates the power struggle as seen from the perspective of the intellectual mode of life. In its pragmatic repercussions, the concept of ideology articulates the intellectualist bid for authority; it conceptualises the world in a way which locates the intellectuals alongside the strategic boundaries where problems, interests and programmes are delineated and verbalised. To conclude in this way is not to draw conclusions about the cognitive usefulness of the concept of ideology. The concept, as I have tried to show, is interwoven with the type of social reality it attempts to capture. It was born as a response to a new historical situation and then became a factor in promoting one of its resolutions. The question of "cognitive relevance" in the sense of truth as correspondence does not, therefore, arise. What has been emphasised—in opposition to many recent and highly fashionable denunciations of the theory of ideology—is that the questioning of the concept of ideology makes sense only as the questioning of the specific socio-historical constellation with which the concept has been inextricably intertwined. This constellation of disciplinary power is an historical development which the "ideological" perspective takes for granted: it "naturalises" its products and never looks beyond the universe which it has constituted. Conservative or radical in its current political applications, the perspective of ideology is bound to remain within the horizon drawn by a social system in which the asymmetry of power is the indispensable vehicle of social reproduction.

Within this horizon, no doubt, the ideological perspective tends to illuminate some aspects of social reproduction better than others. Among the factors confining and channelling human agency and its choices, it brings to light pressures variously called "socialization", "cultural influences", "distorted communication", "propaganda", "linguistic deprivation", or "false consciousness". Yet it leaves pre-discursive practices of bodily drill in the shadows. Inadvertently, the perspective of ideology translates the political issue of the relationship between the controllers and the controlled into the theoretical issue of the relationship between enlightened reason and ignorant superstition.

University of Leeds

Notes

1. Michel Foucault, *The Archeology of Knowledge* (London, 1974), p. 44.

2. Cf. Georges Duby, *L'économie rurale et la vie des campagnes dans l'occident mediéval* (Paris, 1962), p. 98.

3. Michel Foucault, *Power and Knowledge* (Brighton, 1980), p. 104.

4. Robert Muchembled, *Culture populaire et culture des élites dans la France moderne (XVe-XVII^{e}siècles)* (Paris, 1978); Stephen and Eileen Yeo (eds.), *Popular Culture and Class Conflict* (Brighton, 1981).

5. Cf. Paul Clavel, *Les mythes fondateurs des sciences sociales* (Paris, 1980), p. 38: "the rationalists of the 17th century knew that man cannot be fully reduced to reason. . . .Between the order of reason and this of drives and passions, there was an abyss. An individual incapable of conforming to the advice of his judgment leads a dissolute life and creates disorder which society must contain. Nobody doubted that people can behave like animals. . . .If man's ways cannot be amended, the only solution is to isolate him from the society he threatens. The age of reason was also an age of confinement".

6. Lucien Febvre et al., *Civilisation, Le mot et l'idée* (Paris, 1930), pp. 9-10 and the note on p. 48.

7. Quoted after Harry C. Payne, *The Philosophes and the People* (New Haven, 1976), p. 29.

8. Emmet Kennedy, *Destutt de Tracy and the Origins of "Ideology"* (Philadelphia, 1978), p. 47.

9. *Ibid.*, pp. 66, 68.

10. Lewis Coser, *Men of Ideas* (Glencoe, Ill., 1970), p. viii.

11. Jürgen Habermas, *Strukturwandel der Öffentlichkeit* (Neuwied and Berlin, 1962).

12. J.S. Mill, *On Liberty* (London, 1884), p. 72.

II

POWER AND SEDUCTION

CYNICAL POWER: THE FETISHISM OF THE SIGN

Arthur Kroker and Charles Levin

The whole chaotic constellation of the social revolves around that spongy referent, that opaque but equally translucent reality, that nothingness: the masses. A statistical crystal ball, the masses are "swirling with currents and flows", in the image of matter and the natural elements. So at least they are represented to us.

J. Baudrillard
*In the Shadow of the
Silent Majorities*

C'est le vide qu'il y a derrière le pouvoir, ou au coeur même du pouvoir, au coeur de la production, c'est ce vide qui leur donne aujourd'hui une dernière lueur de réalité. Sans ce qui les réversibilise, les annule, les séduit, ils n'eussent même jamais pris force de réalité.

*J. Baudrillard
Oublier Foucault*

Talisman

The representative problem of modern French thought is the problem of representation. The whole movement of thought in France has been toward the specification of representational features not reducible to subject and object; and then the rediscovery of energy (desire), force (differance) and power within the terms of the language paradigm itself. But, as the articles to follow all suggest, the structuralist and post-structuralist programmatic attention to representations has achieved only ambiguous insights into the power of representations as such. A synoptic review of the structuralist tradition indicates that the founding premises were never outlived and indeed that they always acted as the gravitational centre for later ventures. It is almost as if structuralism and post-structuralism together form a kind of closed universe of discourse in which questions are interesting but like Hegel's night the answers are indistinguishable. Once entered, such a universe is difficult to escape; yet the postmodern project has achieved the coherence of a hermeneutical tradition with the ineluctiblity of a rite de passage. The journal has chosen the work of Jean Baudrillard as a talisman: a symptom, a sign, a charm, and above all, a password into the next universe.

New French Thought and the Metaphysics of Representation

The critique of the Metaphysics of Representation depends paradoxically on the assertion of the autonomy of representations. This peculiar turn of ideas takes us back nearly a century to Nietszche's pragmatism: all world views are arbitrary because they are all equally motivated. The same problem emerges in the modern controversy of the sign. Where in the chain signifier-signified-referent-reality does one find the determinate link that guarantees communicable reference? Is it "reality" — so that language is reduced to a collection of tokens? Is it in the "signifier", reducing reality to a blurred hyle? Or is it somewhere in the middle, in the regions of the illusive concept or of naive realism? What gave Baudrillard his leverage in this debate was his awareness that the basic formalization of the meaning process (Saussure, Jacobson, Lévi-Strauss, Lacan, Althusser) was in fact a vicious circle of motivation-immotivation designed to exclude the act of reference while retaining the value of the referent. Post-structuralism saw this too, and proposed by way of solution the simple non-value of value and the non-meaning of meaning. Baudrillard's work was allied to this, but remained independent in certain crucial respects. He did not deny a certain necessity to the formal abstraction of the sign-logic, but he saw this as a historical concatenation (thematized in terms of the commodity), rather than as a universal condition of experience and language. From the vantage point of Baudrillard's critique of the political economy of the sign, he was able to argue that the heirs of structuralism, in their haste to expunge the vestiges of naturalism, had naturalized the arbitrary, the aleatory and the contingent, thereby creating a new ideology, an ideology without content — an ideologist's ideology.

In the nineteen–sixties, the various attempts to formalize the logic of representations in social anthropology, linguistics, poetics, marxism, and so on, conveyed a markedly positivist ethos. Yet, however rigidly defined they were, the language models heralded as the unifiers of all science actually discouraged a complete regression to nineteenth-century Positivism. Perhaps it was this narrow and continuing scrape with the Positivist temptation that generated the most fruitful tension within the structuralist movement as a whole. Structuralism never succeeded in establishing itself as a purely formal method; yet the original project has remained implicit in the unshakable assumption that an exclusive attention to the problem of representation can produce a new, non-metaphysical, thoroughly agnostic paradigm. The sheer resilience of this belief-system has obscured the fact that structuralism could only save itself from the internal threat of positivism by returning to metaphysics — this time in the form of an intimate (d)enunciation of it. What has remained constant throughout, concealed in the rigor of its attention to representation, is the metaphysical desire to determine the nature of the reality alluded to and falsified in the representational systems under structuralist scrutiny. The specific concern with semiotic, differential, textual, oppositional, decentred, rhizomatic and molecular models is designed from the outset to guarantee certain statements about the nature of the context within which representation happens. Each model attempts to preclude the question of its context on the grounds that such a question can only be answered with another model — and so each model builds within itself as its own predicate the model of its context and possibility of reference. The result is a theoretical trope which declares that reality is always going to be a model and that this model will try to foster the illusion that it is grounded in or tending toward something outside itself. The general picture is similar to what Michel Serres called (without intending to raise any problem) "an isomorphic relation between force and writing."

POWER AND SEDUCTION

The critique of the Metaphysics of Representation is based on the assumption of a deductive (or structural) causality: the representer and the represented are always preceded as effects by their representations as cause. Thus, deconstruction, schizo-analysis and genealogy return us, in spite of their own warning, to the determinate linearity of the cause-effect sequence. Indeed, the more one looks at post-structuralist developments, the more one is impressed with the movement's failure to break with the past. Henri Lefebvre referred to structuralism as the "New Eleatism" because it resembled in its naive scientistic phase the classical idealization of the concept as pure generative form. Ricoeur called Lévi-Strauss' structuralism "Kantism without a subject." And if there was a repudiation of the phenomenological and Hegelian traditions at the beginning, these soon returned, like the repressed, in the form of all the neo-structuralist problematics of the body and desire in the work of Derrida, Foucault, Kristeva, Lacan, Deleuze and Barthes. This was not only a resurgence of dangerous materiality; it was felt that these issues could be accomodated within the generalized model of terminological combination and exchange. Everything fitted into a new Master Metaphor of production through marking or inscription (the body's action upon itself?). The Nietszchean revival opened a gap in social-philosophical discourse for the "return to Freud," and so Freud was quickly structuralized. The "seething cauldron" was turned from a 'content' into a 'form', from a drive into a signifier (which retained the force of a drive), and from something which is substituted into the principle of substitution itself. Yet in spite of the influential claims of the Lacanian language model, the post-structuralist version of Freud usually meant a recuperation of instinctual atomism and its attendant nineteenth century energy and engineering models. Those hoary representations of representation in general, tended to be exclusively epistemological efforts to discover the irreducible particles or "constituent elements" of Being. Lévi-Strauss's tabular cultural unconscious and Lacan's master-slave theory of desire were fused and generalized. Everything was seen in terms of the laws of combination and substitution. The microphysics of power, the primary polytextual perversity, and various speculative libidinal dynamics all participated in the original excitement of the Freudian scientific imaginary. The Deleuzian version is especially remarkable in that it presents a theatre of industrial strife in which the personalities of the actors are expressed as machine-like apparatuses whose experiences of others take the form of infantile part-object relations, breaks, flows, grafts, disjunctions and displacements. Any attempt to grasp the idea of another person out of all this is condemned as an Oedipal repression of the levelling flow of libido, whose ideal representation is the "rhizomatic" spread of grass. Like structuralism before it, the more recent French thought is a powerful agent of reduction. It tries to constitute a unified field in which all "effects" are in principle accounted for before they happen. There is something bureaucratic about this: indeed, the scribal models allude to the bureaucratic forms of power. Foucault's power is the omnipresent police state: Fascist, rigid, controlling. It appeals to social scientists. The Derridean model is more like a parliamentary democracy:

ambivalent, flaccid, and obfuscating. It appeals to the literati. One is infinitesimally efficacious, the other, indefinitely absorptive.

Structuralism absorbs difference by making everything different in the same way and for the same reason. The post-structuralist gesture extends and realigns the structural field, but in so doing, it only intensifies the procedures of reduction and abstraction. In Derrida's deconstruction of Lévi-Strauss (*Of Grammatology*), post-structuralism performs this operation directly on the body of its predecessor. The redoubling of the method emerges as an effort to expunge systematically any residues of informality still apparent in the structuralist analysis. Thus, what appears to us in Lévi-Strauss as schematic rationalism and a naive realism of the concept, strikes Derrida as "anarchism", "libertarian ideology", and "Anarchistic and Libertarian protestations against Law, the Powers, and the State in general . . . " (131, 132, 138). In Derrida's example (*Tristes Tropiques*), Lévi-Strauss is trying, rather clumsily, to think the otherness of the Nambikwara: he does this in terms of the oppositions non-writing/writing, Festival/State, community/bureaucracy, speech/coding, etc. Derrida points out that these oppositions have already been absorbed, that writing is (always already) everywhere, and that the Nambikwara are consequently the Same. Every suggestion of their difference is dissolved into the metaphysic of presence. Against the thesis of colonial violence, Derrida advances the arche writing — the immemorial "unity of violence and writing." (106) The whole operation is achieved by what Derrida himself calls the "aprioristic or transcendental regression." (135) The terms of every problem are reduced to an a priori structure of indifference: a field of formal features is delineated and prepared for "incission." Henceforth, any hints of difference in the text to be constituted can be redesigned as the effect of the play of signifiers, so that reference is centripetally trapped. It is a method of "mimesis and castration." (*Positions*, 84)

Given the power of these uniform fields of seamless interrelationality, it is less surprising that Baudrillard, with one eye on the social terrain, the other on successive waves of metatheory, has begun to conceive the only possibility of difference, otherness and the symbolic, in terms of a violent eruption. Baudrillard has been too often misunderstood on this point, for it is natural to assimilate this commotion (as opposed to theoretical "conjuncture") of his work to the Gallic theme of the epistemological break, transgression, reversal and rupture. But there is an important distinction, which follows on the Baudrillardian conception of difference and otherness in the Symbolic. It is in these terms that we may be able to perceive, through reflection on Baudrillard, the outline of a group of important questions which perhaps only structuralism could have raised, but which it has also suppressed in the sameness of its answers. If the continuity of structuralism has been to establish a General Isomorphology, which can only be achieved through progressive formalization, whether positivistic or metaphysical, then the Critique of Logocentrism and the Metaphysic of Representation would appear to have been undermined from the start. In fact, insofar as the whole antilogocentric project came to be tied to a reflection on "ontological difference" (Heidegger), it was bound to fail, for difference and "alterity" are not likely to be secured ontologically, any more than they may be perceived or appreciated with the tools of formal epistemology alone. This problem arises in Lacan's work, where the symbolic is grasped through the ontic-ontological distinction of the Phallus, a kind of Ur-signifier which "inserts" the subject into the field of language by inaugurating a serial process of substitutions. Here Lévi-Strauss's idea of meaning as an instantaneously generated network serves to absorb the problem of the other (the symbolic) into the combinatory matrix (Patrix?). In contrast, the theme of difference for Baudrillard is neither epistemological nor ontological in the schematic structuralist sense, but social and psychological. In order to secure this domain beyond the purview of formalization-rationalization, Baudrillard defined the symbolic in opposition to the substitutive logic of the sign. The "critique of the political economy of the sign" thus emerged from the standpoint of an irreducible social symbolic excluded from formal fields of coded signification. The uniqueness of this approach was that it allowed Baudrillard to resituate the critique of representation (and logocentrism) in terms of the suppressed question of the relation of the model to reality. Seizing on the ontological ambiguity of the language paradigm, Baudrillard answered this question by developing the theme of operationalization in terms of structures of social signification. (*L'Échange symbolique et la mort*)

The most powerful metaphor in Baudrillard is precisely the loss of metaphor with the advent of a science of "meaning". The ultimate representation, the apotheosis of the subject-object dialectic, then appears as the imaginary deflation of all symbolic tension — a kind of materialization of rationalism through the actualization of the model. In the radical form of this thesis, however, the difference of the symbolic is dissolved in the sign's absorption of otherness, a development which entails nothing less than the "end of the social" and the expiry of measured critique (*In The Shadow of The Silent Majorities*) Baudrillard is forced to shift the burden of his symbolic stance onto the category of ambivalence. This allows him to recover the expressive dimension of symbolic exchange, but at the cost of having to view the latter as the immanent principle of self-destruction at work in all social forms. This explains Baudrillard's return to the mode of a skeptico-transcendental critique of worldly representational illusions: a sort of theory and practice of anamorphosis. (*Les stratégies fatales*)

Baudrillard's Double Refusal

Baudrillard is like Nietzsche to this extent. Each of his writings are works of art which seek to arraign the world before poetic consciousness. In Baudrillard's theorisations, there is a certain return to a tragic sense of history, and this because his imagination moves just along that trajectory where nihilism, in its devalorized form as a critique of abstract power, is both the antithesis of and condition of possibility for historical emancipation. Baudrillard's tragic sense derives directly from his understanding of our imprisonment in the carceral of a cynical power, a power which works its effects symbolically; and which is, anyway, the disappearing locus of a society which has now passed over into its opposite: the cycle of devalorisation and desocialisation without limit.

But if Baudrillard can be so unsparing in his tragic vision of abstract power as the essence of modern society, then this is just because his theoretical agenda includes two great refusals of the logic of referential finalities: a devalorisation of the social; and a refusal of the autonomous historical subject.[1] More than, for example, Foucault's theoretical critique of a *juridical* conception of power which reaffirms, in the end, the privileged position of the social in modern culture, Baudrillard has taken structuralism to its limits. Baudrillard's thought seizes on the essential insight of structuralist discourse: the eclipse of Weber's theory of rationalization as an adequate basis for understanding modern society, and the emergence of McLuhan's concept of the exteriorization of the senses as the dynamic locus of the modern culture system.[2] Baudrillard's theorisation of the meaning of consumer society begins with a radical challenge to sociology as an already passé way of rethinking society as a big sign-system, and with a refusal of the priviliged position of the politics of historical emancipation. The ambivalence of Baudrillard is just this: his culture critique (*la société de consommation*, *De la séduction*) is the degree-zero between the historical naturalism of Marxist cultural studies (Baudrillard's structural law of value is the antithesis of Stuart Hall's ideology as the "return of the repressed") and the sociological realism of critical theory. Against Habermas, Baudrillard (*In the Shadow of the Silent Majorities*) reinvokes the sign of Nietzsche as the elemental memory of the tragic tradition in critical theory. Against Foucault, Baudrillard (*Oublier Foucault*) nominates a purely cynical power. And beyond Marxist cultural studies, Baudrillard breaks forever with a representational theory of ideological hegemony. Just like the bleak, grisly, and entirely semiological world of Giorgio de Chirico's *Landscape Painter*, Baudrillard's thought introduces a great scission in the received categories of western discourse. And it does so just because all of Baudrillard's cultural theory traces out the *implosion* of modern experience: the contraction and reversal of the big categories of the real into a dense, seductive, and entirely nihilistic society of signs.

1. The Devalorisation of the Social

> A speechless mass for every hollow spokesman without a past. Admirable conjunction, between those who have nothing to say, and the masses, who do not speak. Ominous emptiness of all discourse. No hysteria or potential fascism, but simulation by precipitation of every lost referential. Black box of every referential, of every uncaptured meaning, of impossible history, of untraceable systems of representation, the mass is what remains when the social has been completely removed.
>
> J. Baudrillard
> *In the Shadow of the Silent Majorities*

128

POWER AND SEDUCTION

Baudrillard is explicit in his accusation concerning the death of the social, and of the loss of the "referent" of the sociological imagination. It's not so much that sociological discourse, the master paradigm of the contemporary century, has been superceded by competing ensembles of *normative* meaning, but, instead, that the privileged position of the social as a positive, and hence normative, referent has suddenly been eclipsed by its own "implosion" into the density of the mass.

> The social world is scattered with interstitial objects and crystalline objects which spin around and coalesce in a cerebral chiaroscuro. So is the mass, an *in vacuo* aggregation of individual particles, refuse of the social and of media impulses: an opaque nebuala whose growing density absorbs all the surrounding energy and light rays, to collapse finally under its own weight. A black hole which engulfs the social.[3]

Two, in particular, of Baudrillard's texts — *l'effet beaubourg* and *In the Shadow of the Silent Majorities* — trace out, in an almost desparate language of absence, that rupture in modern discourse represented by the reversal of the positive, normalizing and expanding cycle of the social into its opposite: an implosive and structural order of signs. This is just that break-point in the symbolic totality where the "norm" undergoes an inversion into a floating order of signs, where strategies of normalization are replaced by the "simulation of the masses",[4] and where the "hyperéalité de la culture"[5] indicates a great dissolution of the space of the social. Baudrillard's theorisation of the end of sociology as a reality-principle, or what is the same, the exhaustion of the social as a truth-effect of a *nominalistic* power, privileges a violent and implosive perspective on society. "Violence implosive qui résulte non plus de l'extension d'un système, mais de sa saturation et de sa rétraction, comme il en est des systèmes physiques stellaires".[6]

In the text, *In the Shadow of the Silent Majorities*, Baudrillard provides three strategic hypotheses (from minimal and maximal perspectives) about the existence of the social only as a murderous effect, whose "uninterrupted energy" over two centuries has come from "deterritorialisation and from concentration in ever more unified agencies".[7] The first hypothesis has it that the social may only refer to the space of a *delusion*: "The social has basically never existed. There has never been any "social relation". Nothing has ever functioned socially. On this inescapable basis of challenge, seduction, and death, there has never been anything but *simulation* of the social and the social relation". On the basis of this "delusional" hypthesis, the dream of a "hidden sociality", a "real" sociality, just "hypostatises a simulation". And if the social is a simulation, then the likely course of events is a "brutal de-simulation": "a de-simulation which itself captures the style of a challenge (the reverse of capital's challenge of the social and society): a challenge to the belief that capital and power exist according to their own logic — *they have none*, they vanish as apparatuses as soon as the simulation of social space is done".[10] The second hypothesis is the reverse, but parallel, image of the delusional thesis: the social, not as the space of delusion undergoing a "brutal de-simulation", but the social as *residue,* "expanding throughout history as a 'rational' control of residues, and a rational *production* of residues". Baudrillard is explicit about the purely *excremental* function of the social, about the social as the "functional ventilation of remainders".[12] It's just the existence of the social as itself "remainder" which makes of the social machine "refuse processing"; a more subtle form of death, indeed the scene of a "piling up and exorbitant processing of death". "In this event, we are even deeper in the social, even deeper in pure excrement, in the fantastic congestion of dead labour, of dead and institutionalised relations within terrorist bureaucracies, of dead languages and grammars. Then of course it can no longer be said that the social is dying, since it is already the accumulation of death. In effect we are in a civilisation of the supersocial, and simultaneously in a civilisation of non-degradable, indestructible residue, piling up as the social spreads."[13] The third hypothesis speaks only of the end of the "perspective space of the social". "The social has not always been a delusion, as in the first hypothesis, nor remainder, as in the second. But precisely, it has only had an end in view, a meaning as power, as work, as capital, from the perspective space of an ideal convergence, which is also that of production — in short, in the narrow gap of second-order simulacra, and, absorbed into third-order simulacra, it is dying."[14] This, then, is the hypothesis of the "precession of simulacra", of a "ventilation of individuals as terminals of information", of, finally, the death of the social ("which exists only in perspective space") in the (hyperreal and hypersocial) "space of simulation".[15]

> End of the perspective space of the social. The rational sociality of the contract, dialectical sociality (that of the State and of civil society, of public and private, of the social and the individual) gives way to the sociality of contact, of the circuit and transistorised network of millions of molecules and particules maintained in a random gravitational field, magnetised by the constant circulation and the thousands of tactical combinations which electrify them.[16]

2. The Refusal of Historical Subjecthood

Baudrillard also has a hidden, and radical, political agenda. His political attitude is directed not against, the already obsolescent "perspective space of the social",[17] but in opposition to the ventilated and transistorised order of the simulacrum. In the now passé world of the social, political emancipation entailed the production of meaning, the control of individual and collective *perspective,* against a normalizing society which insisted on *excluding* its oppositions. This was the region of power/sacrifice: the site of a great conflict where the finalities of sex, truth, labour, and history, were dangerous just to the extent that they represented the hitherto suppressed region of use-value, beyond and forever in opposition to a purely sacrificial politics. In the perspectival space of the historical, power could be threatened by speech, by the *agency* of the emancipatory subject who demanded a rightful inclusion in the contractual space of political economy. A politics of rights depended for its very existence on the valorisation of use-value as a privileged and universally accessible field of truth/ethics; and on the production of the emancipated historical subject as an object of desire.

With Baudrillard, it's just the opposite. His political theory begins with a refusal of the privileged position of the *historical subject*, and, what is more, with an immediate negation of the question of historical emancipation itself. Baudrillard's is not the *sociological* perspective of disciplinary power in a normalizing society (Foucault) nor the *hermeneutical* interpretation of technology and science as "glassy, background ideology"[18] (Habermas). In this theoretic, there is no purely perspectival space of the "panoptic" nor free zone of "universal pragmatics".[19] Baudrillard's political analysis represents a radical departure from both the sociology of knowledge and theorisations of power/norm just because his thought explores the brutal processes of dehistoricisation and desocialisation which structure the new communicative order of power/sign. In the new continent of power/sign (where power is radically semiurgical): the relevant political collectivity is the "mass media as simulacra"; the exchange-principle involves purely abstract and hyper-symbolic diffusions of information; and what is at stake is the "maximal production of meaning" and the "maximal production of words" for constituted historical subjects who are both condition and effect of the order of simulacra.[20] It's just this insistence on responding to the challenge of history which draws us on, trapping us finally, within the interstices of a vast social simulation: a simulation which make its *autonomous subjects* only the strategic counterparts of the system's desparate need, given its previous disfiguration of the *social* and of the *real*, for the surplus-production of meaning and of words.

Now, Baudrillard's world is that of the electronic mass media, and specifically, of television. His nomination of television as a privileged simulacrum is strategic: television has the unreal existence of an imagic sign-system in which may be read the inverted and implosive logic of the social machine. The "nebulous hyperreality" of the masses; "staged communications" as the modus vivendi of the power-system; the "explosion of information" and the "implosion of meaning" as the keynote of the new communications order; a massive circularity of all poles in which "sender is receiver" (the medium is the massage: McLuhan's formula of the end of panoptic and perspectival space as the "alpha and omega of *our* modernity"); an "irreversible medium of communication *without response*": such are the strategic consequences of the processing of (our) history and (our) autonomous subjectivity through the simulacra of the mass media, and explicitly, through television. In a brilliant essay, "The Implosion of Meaning in the Media",[22] Baudrillard had this to say of the *intracation of the mass media in the social* or, more specifically, the "implosion of the media in the masses":[23]

131

> Are the mass media on the side of power in the manipulation
> of the masses, or are they on the side of the masses in the
> liquidation of meaning, in the violence done to meaning, and
> in the fascination which results? Is it the media which induce
> fascination in the masses, or is it the masses which divert the
> media into spectacles? Mogadishu Stammheim: the media are
> made the vehicle of the moral condemnation of terrorism and
> of the exploitation of fear for political ends, but, simultaneously,
> in the most total ambiguity, they propogate the brutal
> fascination of the terrorist act. They are themselves terrorists,
> to the extent to which they work through fascination... The
> media carry meaning and non-sense; they manipulate in every
> sense simultaneously. The process cannot be controlled, for
> the media convey the simulation internal to the system and
> the simulation destructive of the system according to a logic
> that is absolutely Moebian and circular — and this is exactly
> what it is like. There is no alternative to it, no logical
> resolution. Only a logical *exacerbation* and a catastrophic
> resolution.[24]

Baudrillard's refusal of the "reality" of processed history is based on this
hypothesis: the new information of the electronic mass media is "directly
destructive of meaning and signification, or neutralizes it." [25] Information, far
from producing an "accelerated circulation of meaning, a plus-value of
meaning homologous to the economic plus-value which results from the
accelerated rotation of capital",[26] dissolves the possibility of *any* coherent
meaning-system. Confronted with this situation of the "doublebind" in which
the *medium is the real and the real is the nihilism of the information society*, our
political alternatives are twofold. First, there is "resistance-as-subject", the
response of the autonomous historical subject who assumes the "unilaterally
valorized" and "positive" line of resistance of "liberation, emancipation,
expression, and constitution . . . (as somehow) valuable and subversive".[27]
But Baudrillard is entirely realistic concerning how the "liberating claims of
subjecthood" respond to the nihilistic demands of the information order of
mass media.

> To a system whose argument is oppression and repression, the
> strategic resistance is the liberating claim of subjecthood. But
> this reflects the system's previous phase, and even if we are
> still confronted with it, it is no longer the strategic terrain: the
> system's current argument is the maximization of the word
> and the maximal production of meaning. Thus the strategic
> resistance is that of a refusal of meaning and a refusal of the
> word — or of the hyperconformist simulation of the very
> mechanisms of the system, which is a form of refusal and of
> non-reception.[28]

POWER AND SEDUCTION

Against the emancipatory claims of historical subjecthood, Baudrillard proposes the more radical alternative of "resistance-as-object" [29] as the line of political resistance most appropriate to the simulacrum. To a system which represents a great convergence of *power and seduction*, and which is entirely cynical in its devalorisation of meaning, the relevant and perhaps only political response is that of *ironic detachment.*

> This is the resistance of the masses: it is equivalent to sending back to the system its own logic by doubling it, to reflecting, like a mirror, meaning without absorbing it. This strategy (if one can still speak of strategy) prevails today because it was ushered in by that phase of the system.[30]

Baudrillard thus valorizes the position of the "punk generation": this new generation of rebels which signals its knowledge of its certain doom by a *hyperconformist simulation* (in fashion, language, and lifestyle) which represents just that moment of refraction where the simulational logic of the system is turned, ironically and neutrally, back against the system. Baudrillard is a *new wave* political theorist just because he, more than most, has understood that in a system "whose imperative is the over-production and regeneration of meaning and speech",[31] all the social movements which "bet on liberation, emancipation, the resurrection of the subject of history, of the group, of speech as a raising of consciousness, indeed of a 'seizure of the unconscious' of subjects and of the masses" [32] *are acting fully in accordance with the political logic of the system.*

Notes

1. Baudrillard's theoretical agenda in relationship to French post-structuralism and critical theory is further developed in A. Kroker's "Baudrillard's Marx", mimeo.

2. Michael Weinstein in a private communication to one of the authors has suggested this important insight into "exteriorisation of the mind" as the structuralist successor to Weber's theory of rationalisation.

3. J. Baudrillard, *In the Shadow of the Silent Majorities*, New York: Jean Baudrillard and Semiotext(e), 1983, pp. 3-4.

4. *Ibid;* p. 6.

5. For Baudrillard's most explicit discussion of the simulacrum, see "L'hyperréalisme de la simulation", *L'échange symbolique et la mort*, pp. 110-117.

6. "C'est l'euphorie même de la simulation qui se veut abolition de la cause et de l'effet, de l'origine et de la fin, à quoi elle substitue le redoublement". *L'échange symbolique et la mort*, Paris: Éditions Gallimard, 1976, pp. 114-115.

7. J. Baudrillard, *In the Shadow of the Silent Majorities*, p. 68.

8. *Ibid*; pp. 70-71.

9. *Ibid*; p. 71.

10. *Ibid.*

11. Ibid; p. 73.

12. *Ibid*; p. 77.

13. *Ibid*; pp. 72-73.

14. *Ibid*; pp. 82-83.

15. *Ibid.*

16. *Ibid; p. 83.*

17. *Ibid.*

18. Baudrillard's refusal of the "perspectival space of the social" is aimed directly at Foucault's theorisation of the closed space of the "panoptic". Baudrillard's closing of the ring of signifier/signified or, what is the same, his theorisation of simulacra in conjunction with the structural law of value breaks directly with Habermas' hermeneutical interpretation of ideology.

19. Against Habermas *and* Foucault, Baudrillard theorizes a non-representational and non-figurative *spatialized* universe.

20. J. Baudrillard, "The Implosion of Meaning in the Media", as translated in *In the Shadow of the Silent Majorities*, pp. 95-110.

21. See particularly, "Requiem for the Media", *For a Critique of the Political Economy of the Sign*, pp. 165-184; and "The Implosion of Meaning in the Media". p. 101.

22. *Ibid.*

23. *Ibid*; p. 103.

24. *Ibid*; pp. 105-106.

25. *Ibid*; p. 96.

26. *Ibid*; p. 97.

27. *Ibid*; p. 107.

28. *Ibid*; p. 108.

29. *Ibid.*

30. *Ibid*; pp. 108-109.

31. *Ibid.*

32. *Ibid*; p. 109.

WHEN BATAILLE ATTACKED THE METAPHYSICAL PRINCIPLE OF ECONOMY[1]

Jean Baudrillard

Continuity, sovereignty, intimacy, immanent immensity: a single thought in the work of Bataille, a single mythic thought behind these multiple terms: "*I am of those who destine men to things other than the incessant growth of production, who incite them to the sacred horror.*"

The sacred is *par excellence* the sphere of "*La part maudite*" [the accursed share] (the central essay of this seventh volume of Bataille's works), sphere of sacrificial expenditure, of wealth [*luxe*] and of death; sphere of a "general" economy which refutes all the axioms of economy as it is usually understood (an economy which, in generalizing itself, overruns [*brûle*] its boundaries and truly passes beyond political economy, something that the latter, and all Marxist thought, are powerless to do in accordance with the internal logic of value). It is also the sphere of non-knowledge [*non-savoir*].

Paradoxically, the works collected here are in a way Bataille's "Book of Knowledge," the one where he tries to erect the buttresses of a vision which, at bottom, doesn't need them; indeed, the drive [*pulsion*] toward the sacred ought, in its destructive incandescence, to deny the kind of apology and discursive rendition contained in "*La Part maudite*" and "*La Theorie de Religion.*" "*My philosophic position is based on non- knowledge of the whole, on knowledge concered only with details.*" It is necessary, therefore, to read these defensive fragments from the two antithetical perspectives [*sur le double versant*] of knowledge and non-knowledge.

The Fundamental Principle

The central idea is that the economy which governs our societies results from a misappropriation of the fundamental human principle, which is a solar principle of expenditure. Bataille's thought goes, beyond proper *political* economy (which in essence is regulated through exchange value), straight to the *metaphysical* principle of economy. Batailles's target is utility, in its root. Utility is, of course, an apparently positive principle of capital: accumulation, investment, depreciation, etc. But in fact it is, on Bataille's account, a principle of powerlessness, an utter inability to expend. Given that all previous societies

---

Georges Bataille, *Oeuvres Complètes*: vol. VII. Paris: Gallimard. 618 pp.[2]

knew how to expend, this is, an unbelievable deficiency: it cuts the human being off from all possible sovereignty. All economics are founded on that which no longer can, no longer knows how to expend itself [*se dépenser*], on that which is incapable of becoming the stake of a sacrifice. It is therefore entirely residual, it is a limited social fact; and it is against economy as a limited social fact that Bataille wants to raise expenditure, death, and sacrifice as total social facts--such is the principle of general economy.

The principle of utility (use value) blends with the bourgeoisie, with this capitalist class whose definition for Bataille (contrary to Marx) is negative: it no longer knows how to expend. Similarly, the crisis of capital, its increasing mortality and its immanent death throes, are not bound, as in the work of Marx, to a *history*, to dialectical reversals [*péripéties*], but to this fundamental law of the inability to expend, which give capital over to the cancer of production and unlimited reproduction. There is no principle of revolution in Bataille's work: "*The terror of revolutions has only done more and more [de mieux en mieux] to subordinate human energy to industry.*" There is only a principle of sacrifice—the principle of sovereignty, whose diversion by the bourgeoisie and capital causes all human history to pass from sacred tragedy to the comedy of utility.

This critique is a non-Marxist critique, an *aristocratic* critique, because it aims at utility, at economic finality as the axiom of capitalist society. The Marxist critique is only a critique of capital, a critique coming from the heart of the middle and petit bourgeois classes, for which Marxism has served for a century as a latent ideology: a critique of exchange value, *but an exaltation of use value*—and thus a critique, at the same time, of what made the almost delirious greatness of capital, the secular remains of its religious quality:[3] investment at any price, even at the cost of use value. The Marxist seeks a *good use* of economy. Marxism is therefore only a limited petit bourgeois critique, one more step in the banalization of life toward the "good use" of the social! Bataille, to the contrary, sweeps away all this slave dialectic from an aristocratic point of view, that of the master struggling with his death. One can accuse this perspective of being pre- or post-Marxist. At any rate, Marxism is only the disenchanted horizon of capital—all that precedes or follows it is more radical than it is.

What remains uncertain in the work of Bataille (but without a doubt this uncertainty *cannot* be alleviated), is to know whether the economy (capital), which is counterbalanced on absurd, but never useless, never sacrificial expenditures (wars, waste ...), is nevertheless shot through with a sacrificial dynamic. Is political economy at bottom only a frustrated avatar of the single great cosmic law of expenditure? Is the entire history of capital only an immense detour toward its own catastrophe, toward its own sacrificial end? If this is so, it is because, in the end, one cannot not expend. A longer spiral perhaps drags capital beyond economy, toward a destruction of its own values; the alternative is that we are stuck forever in this denial of the sacred, in the vertigo of supply, which signifies the rupture of alliance (of symbolic exchange in primitive societies) and of sovereignty.

POWER AND SEDUCTION

Bataille would have been impassioned by the present evolution of capital in this era of floating currencies, of values seeking their own level (which is not their transmutation), and the drift of finalities [*la dérive des finalités*] (which is neither sovereign uselessness nor the absurd gratuitousness of laughter and death). But his concept of expenditure would have permitted only a limited analysis: it is still too economic, too much the flip side of accumulation, as transgression is too close to the inverse figure of prohibition.[4] In an order which is no longer that of utility, but an *aleatory* order of value, pure expenditure, while retaining the romantic charm of turning the economic inside out, is no longer sufficient for radical defiance [*au défi radical*]—it shatters the mirror of *market* value, but is powerless against the shifting mirror [*le miroir en dérive*] of *structural* value.

Bataille founds his general economy on a "solar economy" without reciprocal exchange, on the unilateral gift that the sun makes of its energy: a cosmogony of expenditure, which he deploys in a religious and political anthropology. But Bataille has misread Mauss: the unilateral gift does not exist.[5] This is not the law of the universe. He who has so well explored the human sacrifice of the Aztecs should have known as they did that the sun gives nothing, it is necessary to nourish it continually with human blood in order that it shine. It is necessary to challenge [*défier*] the gods through sacrifice in order that they respond with profusion. In other words, the root of sacrifice and of general economy is never pure and simple expenditure—or whatever drive [*pulsion*] of excess that supposedly comes to us from nature—but is an incessant process of challenge [*défi*].

Bataille has "naturalized" Mauss

The "excess of energy" does not come from the sun (from nature) but from a continual higher bidding in exchange—the symbolic process that can be found in the work of Mauss, not that of the gift (that is the naturalist mystique into which Bataille falls), but that of the counter-gift. This is the single truly symbolic process, which in fact implies death as a kind of maximal excess—but not as individual ecstasy, always as the maximal principle of *social exchange*. In this sense, one can reproach Bataille for having "naturalized" Mauss (but in a metaphysical spiral so prodigious that the reproach is not really one), and for having made symbolic exchange a kind of natural function of prodigality, at once hyper-religious in its gratuitousness and much too close still, *a contrario*, to the principle of utility and to the economic order that it exhausts in transgression without ever leaving behind.

It is "in the glory of death" [*à hauteur de mort*] that one rediscovers Bataille, and the real question posed remains: "*How is it that all men have encountered the need and felt the obligation to kill living beings ritually? For lack of having known how to respond, all men have remained in ignorance of that which they are.*" There is an answer to this question *beneath* the text, in all the interstices of Bataille's text, but in my opinion not in the notion of expenditure,

137

nor in this kind of anthropological reconstruction that he tries to establish from the "objective" data of his day: Marxism, biology, sociology, ethnology, political economy, the objective potential of which he tries to bring together nevertheless, in a perspective which is neither exactly a genealogy, nor a natural history, nor a Hegelian totality, but a bit of all that.

But the sacred imperative is flawless in its *mythic* assertion, and the will to teach is continually breached by Bataille's dazzling vision, by a "subject of knowledge" always "at the boiling point." The consequence of this is that even analytic or documentary considerations have that mythic force which constitutes the sole—sacrificial—force of writing.

Translated by David James Miller
Purdue University

Notes

1. Jean Baudrillard, "Le Livre de la quinzaine: Quand Bataille attaquait le principe métaphysique de l'économie," *La Quinzaine littéraire* 234 (1-15 juin 1976): 4-5.

2. Translator's note: Only two essays from this seventh volume have been translated into English—"Le sacrifice" (dated 1939- 1940), a portion of *La Limite de l'utile* (an abandoned version of La Part Maudite); and "Notice autobiographique" (dated 1958). Both essays have been translated by Annette Michelson and appear in *October* (Spring, 1986) respectively as "Sacrifice (pp. 61-74) and "Autobiographical Note" (pp. 107-110).
A number of Bataille's works have been translated into English. In addition to *Visions of Excess* (Minnesota 1985), translated by Alan Stoekl, these include: *Literature and Evil* (Urizen Books 1985; orig. 1957), translated by Alastair Hamilton, and *Death and Sensuality: A Study of Eroticism and the Taboo* (Arno Press, 1977; orig. 1957).

3. The "Puritan mania of business" (money earned is earned in order to be invested ... having value or meaning only in the endless wealth it entails), in that it still entails a sort of madness, challenge, and catastrophic compulsion—a sort of ascetic mania—is opposed to work, to the good use of energy in work and usufruckt.

4. Destruction (even gratuitous) is always ambiguous, since it is the inverse figure of production, and falls under the objection that in order to destroy it is first necessary to have produced, to which Bataille is able to oppose only the sun.

5. Marcel Mauss, *The Gift: Forms and Functions of Exchange in Archaic Societies*, trans. Ian Cunnison (London: RKP, 1954).

BAUDRILLARD'S SEDUCTION

Brian Singer

> Peut-être fallait-il arrêter cette
> hémorragie de la valeur. Assez de
> radicalité terroriste, assez de
> simulacres—recrudescence de la
> morale, de la croyance, du sens. A bas les
> analyses crépusculaires!
> *Les stratégies fatales*

The following essay was written to come to terms with an abiding fascination with the work of Jean Baudrillard. To be fascinated implies, at least at a first moment, that one is attracted to something despite oneself, that one is drawn in wide-eyed with all belief suspended. Many times I have put his work down, sometimes violently, only to return charmed, nay seduced by the sublime irony of Baudrillard's sense of the absurd. Having recently translated one of his more pivotal works, *Seduction*, I find myself compelled to explain this fascination, with all its accompanying ambivalence, and explore its implications. Perhaps the reader shares this fascination, in which case s/he may recognize something of his or her own contrary reactions in my own, and will wish to share my line of questioning. Or perhaps the reader has never read Baudrillard. Perhaps the reader refuses to read his works because of their language, style, fashionability or politics. In this case the reader may consider this as an incitement and a guide to reading Baudrillard, for he cannot, I submit, be approached naively and read like any other author.

The book *Seduction* presents itself as an attack on the notion of truth, its pretensions and imperialism. A post-modern common-place, to be sure. But this is no mere defense of relativism, with its multiple or partial truths. Nor is it a search for some metaphysical fissure that would render the idea of Truth impossible, yet insurmountable; nor even the uncovering of some motive that would reveal the search for truth as our ultimate illusion. Here the strategy is different, and possibly more radical. Call it nihilism if one will, but only if this is not the last word.

Truth, Baudrillard begins, is associated with the realm of depths, and is to be attacked along with all the other figures of depth: that of the essence behind the appearance, the unconscious desire behind the symptom, the true nature behind the artifice, the sphere of production beneath the superstructure, the relations of force or power beneath the ideological or normative shell—in short, all the "realities" unearthed by science, interpretation, critique or some combination thereof. In opposition to truth with its underlying reality lies the realm of appearances. And the book presents itself as a defense of appearances—including frankly illusory appearances—against depths. Seduction itself involves the play of appearances, their manipulation, their mastery.

Immediately one will ask, no doubt, how one can speak of appearances without seeking to account for them in terms of some underlying truth? And a somewhat different question, how can one write a piece of "sociology" that does not seek to penetrate the social surface in order to extract some deeper truth about society? (Note, we will be speaking here of something more than a work of sociology fiction which, if it follows the general canons of mimetic representation, demands the appearance of truth, that is, verisimilitude).

Consider a first response, one that directly addresses the first question while directly appealing to the problem of seduction. Seduction, if it serves to master reality, does so not by narrowing the gap between reality and appearances in order to eliminate the latter and act directly on the former. On the contrary seduction acts indirectly, widening the gap by manipulating the appearances in order to trick one's sense of "reality." Those who act in accord with the underlying reality signalled by the appearance, or who follow the "truth" of their desires, find themselves entrapped by their own search for a transparent truth. In this sense the indirect method, by virtue of its playfulness, artfulness and agnosticism, subverts the functioning of the solemn truth of depths. The manipulation of appearances has a backhanded superiority over the the direct manipulation of reality because capable of having the last laugh.

One may, of course, respond that the "real truth" behind the appearance of truth constructed by the seducer lies with the strategy consciously produced by the latter. But what if the seducer is seduced by his/her own game, and finds that s/he has little control over his/her strategy? What if both seducer and seduced are seduced by the realm of appearances such that it is the latter that determines "reality" (as opposed to reality determining appearances)? What if large areas of society operated according to a seemingly non-conscious, unmotivated logic of seduction? Must one think that appearances are merely an extension, alibi or front for something that lies beneath? Can they not convey imperatives or determinations (that is, a power, and a potentially superior power) of their own? Beyond the truth *behind* appearances can we not speak about a truth *of* appearances?

But then are we really talking about an attack on the notion of truth? Are we not simply supplementing one truth with another, that of depths with that of appearances? Is Baudrillard not simply telling us that we can no longer simply claim that society functions according to some underlying logic, whether functional or conflictual, teleological or aeteological, or that texts embody some underlying intention or structure... that we must also look at the play of surfaces, the strategies the latter embodies, the possibilities it affords. The science (or hermeneutics) of depths can no longer reign supreme. It will have to make room for a second branch of knowledge dedicated to analyzing the "truth" of appearances and (why not?) a third that examines the play between depths and appearances. One then imagines the first moving vertically in an attempt to decode the social text, the second moving horizontally to examine the latter's recodings, while the third would move between the two, examining their conjunctions, intrusions, interferences and inversions—in short, their "communication." The pretensions of the first may be severely curtailed, but the final result will not be so radical. The content will have changed but the project, its finality relative to a notion of truth, will have been preserved intact.

Baudrillard, however, is not (or is not simply) seeking to establish a new, supplementary area of study, even one that throws a curve at all knowledge as heretofore constructed. By speaking of appearances in and for themselves, (that most visible of spheres which remains, nonetheless, outside the vision of the social sciences), he is not seeking to add a new field to the store of knowledge, one that, admittedly, is full of ironic inversions and subtle revenges. To claim the latter would be to miss the deep pessimism of his epistemology and, even more, the deeply pessimistic character of his analysis of present tendencies relative to epistemology. In effect, for Baudrillard history has epistemological effects: it is not just that science or knowledge have a history, but that the very terms science or knowledge suppose as ontological preconditions—here terms like appearances, depths, truth and reality—are also to be radically historicized. With the ultimate claim being that the tendencies of the present are such that these terms can only be sustained with increasing difficulty. More particularly, the problem, according to Baudrillard, is that the distinction between appearances and depths is collapsing, and that, as it were, from both sides.

Consider first the appearances collapsing into reality. Suppose the enlightenment dream is being realized and we are living in an increasingly transparent society, a society without secrets or areas of darkness, without veils, blinders or illusions, a society where what was hidden is becoming visible and all that is visible is, as a result, becoming substantial. It would be a society of appearances because without underlying realities. It would be a society where all appearances would be real, equally real and, accordingly, equally unreal. (One often encounters in Baudrillard social utopias—and theoretical utopias—shipwrecked by the logical extension of their premises to their ultimate realization).

Now consider the other side of the coin, reality collapsing into appearance. Suppose the appearances substitute themselves for the underlying reality and become that by which we gauge what is "truly real" in place of (or in the absence of) any real functioning referent. In this case one has moved beyond a world of verisimilitude, where appearances appear real, into a world of simulation, where appearances appear more real than reality—what Baudrillard calls the "hyper-real"—because "reality" as we experience it is modelled on appearances (rather than appearances being modelled on reality). Again one confronts a society of appearances (in the form of simulated models), where appearances are "real" and "reality" (as expressed in the hyper-real) appears as the most significant of "illusions."

In both cases, whether reality collapses into appearances or vice versa—and the two cases are indistinguishable in their consequences—the very meaning and value of truth begins to fade. And how could it not fade given the loss of the underlying reality of a referent with which to anchor appearances? One's very sense of reality teeters when confronted with an excess of unassimilated (and unassimilable) information, or with a host of hyper-real images which pre-construct the "reality" of desire, not to mention the quasi-compulsory visibility of a confessional culture. History does not simply affect epistemology; in the living future of the present it is seen to subvert the very possibility of epistemology, particularly in its quotidien forms. And with truth losing its meaning and value, it only follows that meaning is losing its meaning and value its value. With all the notions that these terms nourished beginning to fade in tandem. The value and meaning of the social and the political, not to mention social or political action, of history and the event, of sex, war... with each book the list of "referents" destined to disappear grows longer. On the horizon of Baudrillard's radical historicism, the vanishing points are to be taken literally—even as these "referents" are sometimes denied their substance less in terms of a fade-out than by way of their parodic excess. As such, an analysis of the realm of appeareances provides, at best, an anti-climactic, funereal truth (as if the owl of Minerva were turning into a vulture, even as it was flying away). Again one wonders: if with the disappearance of any underlying reality, meaning and value are withering away along with truth, how then can one write a work of sociology? Indeed one wonders how one can write anything at all?

And yet, to state the obvious, the work has been written and it is, if not sociology, then social theory. In order to understand the apparent paradox of its writing, let us begin by saying that Baudrillard is not (or not primarily) concerned with writing a work of "truth." He is more interested in throwing down a challenge to those who are so concerned. To all those "social scientists" who believe themselves to be explaining something of society by reference to its underlying reality, Baudrillard is saying that they are not (because seduced by and entrapped in their own theoretical simulations) and that they cannot (because the underlying reality they are proposing to describe, for all intensive purposes, no longer exists). And that he himself, by not trying to write such a work, will write something that resonates our present predicament with much greater force. In short, he will beat them at their own game. Though by so doing he will have changed the rules, for writing social theory will now truly be a game. And consequently, we the readers will, without having entirely left the "real," familiar world, find ourselves entering a very different terrain, with different expectations and different stakes. This becomes immediately evident when one considers the absence of that tone of high seriousness that generally marks works of social theory. Baudrillard's writing is, by contrast, hilarious—and this despite its *fin de siècle* (or *fin de millénaire*?) melancholia.

Consider something of the nature of this "game." The first thing to note is that concepts take on a different character, with a new, strategic value. In most works, and independent of the theoretical modality, concepts are constructed as instruments of interpretation that enable one to penetrate below the surface obstacles constituted by appearances (be they composed of false objects or false concepts) to the reality below. By contrast, Baudrillard treats concepts as all surface; for he, as it were, brackets their referents—that is, the underlying reality to which refer—and thus their truth value. (It is as though one were being placed before an inverted version of the phenomenological inversion). In effect, just as

POWER AND SEDUCTION

Baudrillard is claiming that society is becoming all surface, he tends to treat concepts as though they were all appearance, and thus had a reality of their own. One can, to be sure, perceive a structuralist influence here: the signs or concepts being constituted less in relation with their referents than with other signs or concepts. The bracketing, however, proceeds beyond the referent to the signifieds, the meanings themselves, thus freeing the concepts from too serious a concern with their finalities, whether descriptive, interpretative or explanatory. And once they have been delivered from the ballast of referent and function, Baudrillard is free to play with them, to call upon their symbolic resources (though not, as in Lacan, with reference to an unconscious), combine them in new ways, place them in new logics and, more generally, put them to flight. Does he believe in what he is saying? The implication here is that, with the truth value of the terms momentarily bracketed, the question is beside the point (at least at a first moment). Thus one should not be surprised to see him trying out, one after another, different, even contrary hypothesis, without any of them being either rejected or retained. (Think of the multiple us of the words "or else"...—as in the book's second page). Or consider more generally the conceptual escalation to theoretical extremes. For once they have lost anchor the concepts are able to circulate with breath-taking rapidity in a manner simultaneously declamatory and poetic. The contrast with more conventional forms of social analsysis could not be more blatant. Where most theorizing, with its unassuming prose, holds to a steady course in order to move ever closer towards its object and carress its details, here the looking glass has, as it were, been turned the wrong way round. One finds oneself pushed away from the objects under analysis, forced to observe them from an astonishing distance, and in rapid succession. The velocity of the text's movements is dizzying, and it appears a miracle if any underlying substance sticks.

Nonetheless, even when the concepts are in rapid motion, something of their reference and meaning must necessarily be retained (even if on occasion one finds oneself dragged willy-nilly by a runaway metaphor). After all, to bracket a concept's truth value is not to deny the latter, which returns, as it were, almost immediately. If the text is to make any sense at all, if it is to be more than just sound and fury, something must stick, if only by association. It is as though the process Baudrillard describes—the hemorrhaging of truth and meaning—is simultaneously a premise of his writing. But by the same token, this writing also supposes, if it is to retain even a shadow of sense, that the process is never complete, that "society" can never be completely bloodless—only anemic. It is not just that this societal anemia enables the concepts to lose much of their referential weight, or that the relation of societal anemia to conceptual lightness provides the work with much of its social resonance. It is because of this relation, presumably, that we are able to learn something about society from reading Baudrillard, but often, as it were, on the wing. Perhaps we should not speak here of "truth" but of "truth effects." For what we "learn" sometimes appears as a kind of serendipitous byproduct of the conceptual play, whereby suddenly we glimpse something in a completely untoward and unexpected manner. One finds oneself gasping: between two commas one could easily drive

143

an expository truck; single sentences could easily be turned into books. This is, no doubt, part of the work's fascination, its vertigo.

However, one cannot stop here. It is not just in terms of its conceptual play, but in certain of its larger traits that the work breaks (and breaks with) the "laws" of doing social science and takes on the character of a game (as the author himself describes it, most notably in the chapter in *Seduction* entitled "The Passion for Rules"). One might wish to see the apparent lack of concern with truth, or with the referentiality supposed by the notion of truth, as reflecting the book's game-like character (games do not have an external truth: their "truth" is entirely immanent, which is to say they know neither truth nor falsehood). Or one might see as indicative of its ludic nature the fact that the book avoids the single-minded character of a linear and cumulative progression, but instead seems to jump from topic to topic while simultaneously circling in on itself, with a prose that sometimes takes on a repetitive, almost ritualistic quality. But most of all, the game-like quality of the writing is to be seen in the relation it establishes with the reader—a relation that can best be described as a duel. Baudrillard is constantly throwing his readers' challenges—challenges to their credibility, challenges to their tolerance.

It must be clearly stated that there is something in his work to upset everyone. One finds for example a defense of astrology (and in another work, of the arms buildup). Even more typical is the brutal assault on feminism, psychoanlysis and Marxism (though in the latter case one is merely dealing with the after-shocks of *The Mirror of Production*), not to mention structuralist semiotics and the Deleuzian politics of desire (all the currents of the right-thinking left, all those who would be on the side of truth, justice, history and the Revolution—in short, all his potential readers). Baudrillard's attacks are often quite "deep," but they are never in depth; they are always rapid, almost scattershot, often bold, sometimes outrageous.

Consider some of the different, but interrelated strategies of these attacks. First, there is the rejection of the radicality of intellectual currents under attack. They are, it is claimed, secretly complicit with what they would criticize: they are part of the same imaginary, they hold to the same logics and reveal the same blind spots (Marxism shares with market ideology a naively utilitarian view of the object, feminism shares a phallocentric dismissal of appearances, etc). Second, there is the rejection of the ontological foundation on which the current seeks to ground itself and acquire its critical leverage: (use value is not a natural property of the object, but the other face of exchange value; feminism, at least in the version parlayed by Luce Irigaray, swims in a simulated biology, etc). Third, there is the denial of the very object of the school (there is no unconconscious; there is only one sex and it is masculine), or at least of its continued existence (there is no longer any desire, only sex, which itself is being neutralized by the violence of pornography), or perhaps only its continued relevence if it still exists (the sexual difference is becoming less significant socially because defined biologically; the social is brain-dead, but artificially maintained on a life support system to maintain the warmed-over corpse of a political project). Fourth, one must speak of the play of reversibility, whereby upper and lower, dominant and dominated, manipulator and manipulated, knower and known are made to exchange places by way of all the subtly ironic strategies that play with appearances so as to ensure that things are not what they seem (the mute impermeability of the masses as a strategy of resistance to the despotism of enlightenment, frigidity as a subversion of male desire). And last but not least—for implicit in all of the above—there is the quick, continuous, theoretical outbidding, often followed by the mirror play of reverse hypothesis (e.g., there is no longer a working class, nor is there a revolutionary subject, nor any subject whatever, whether collective or individual... and if the subject is disappearing, the object must be too... but then maybe the object is seeking its revenge and claiming the position, autonomy and sovereignty of the subject, and this outside all reference to "alienation").

The rapidity of the analysis, the exaggerated character of the claims, the fast and loose experimentation with theoretical propositions, the apparent unconcern with logical or any other form of consistency, not to mention the content of what is being said—all this is shocking. A fact that is perhaps in itself shocking. After all, we have been told that in this age of post-modernism cultural modernism is passé, and precisely because it has lost its capacity to shock—in which case, social theory may well be the last refuge for cultural avant-gardes (which might explain the attraction of Baudrillard for artistically inclined circles). One certainly does sense in Baudrillard a pleasure of transgression, even as he tells us that such pleasures belong to an earlier period, when the law still held sway and deviance had not yet been banalized.

The point here is that Baudrillard is not to be taken literally (how can he be taken literally, when he tells us that nothing else can?). He has created an artificial, simulated space within which to play his hand (and games suppose the most artificial and simulated of spaces because they require no reference to a reality outside themselves). This is not a political space (which, without excluding a certain gamesmanship, must seek its foundations in notions of law, justice and, yes, truth, incompatible with a ludic universe). As such, it is somewhat beside the point to respond to it politically. Even less helpful would be to respond simply with outrage, and refuse to read any further. One cannot take up the challenge by quitting the game, while trying to change the rules would be equivalent to cheating.

Of course one might ask, why play at all? Presumably, because the game is not simply a joke. Because it is not without seriousness, because there are what I termed earlier "truth effects," because the text resonates beyond the printed page, because the attacks often hit their target, because the stakes are "real"— because, in short, it is more than a game. How then does one play? How does one respond to Baudrillard's challenge? Simply by purchasing and reading the book? But presumably, by purchasing the book, we are in a somewhat better position than those who dared the absurd by responding to the advertisement that asked one to send a dollar. And presumably, by reading the book, we are doing more than subjecting out intellectual convictions and good conscience to the thrills of an avant-garde rollercoaster ride? There must be some way to respond actively. It cannot simply be that Baudrillard is duelling with himself while we, the readers, look on dumbfounded, absorbed in that newest of spectator sports, social theory.

Before, however, one can respond, even indirectly, to the problem of "reading Baudrillard," one must take another look at his analysis and its impact on what for him must be the problem of writing. Such a query must necessarily include another look at games as they are played both within and without the text.

Throughout his work, Baudrillard sets up a series of interconnected oppositions—truth vs. illusion, depth vs. appearance, production vs. seduction, the law vs. the game-rule, to name the most important. And in each case the second term, which has almost always been denied, derided or treated as frivolous, is recovered and, indeed, celebrated. Now Baudrillard is rescuing and reviving these terms not so much because he holds that the first term cannot exist without the second (at least some of the oppositions, as noted earlier, are collapsing: appearances are becoming reality and reality becoming all appearance); nor because he believes that their opposition holds the promise of some dialectical overcoming (the collapse of the opposition between appearance and reality is producing an ob-scene world—one might, perhaps, speak here of a regressive dialectics). The second term is not, or not necessarily, residual relative to the first, that is, constituted by its opposition to the dominant principle, and thus formed by and reflective of the latter. For Baudrillard the opposed terms each have their own "logic" and so form two different universes which, though they may "communicate," are fundamentally incommensurable. In other words, the world of truth, reality, production, law and desire is shadowed by a parallel world of appearance, illusion, seduction and games which can be exalted in a manner both forceful and ironic by virtue of its "logical" autonomy. But then the question becomes, if the second world has been for so long occluded by the first, particularly in the realm of social theorizing, how did Baudrillard discover it, let alone explore its continents? If it appears so residual within the present, how has he been able to endow it with its own principle?

At this point one is brought face to face with a terrible nostalgia. Over and over again one is referred to a notion of the primitive (which in previous works was conveniently condensed in the concept of "symbolic exchange"). The primitive here acquires its critical leverage not as a point of origin that would give some anthropological foundation to the human adventure, but as a point of maximum alterity which speaks of societies that operated according to altogether different principles, independent of all the master schemata of truth, representation, equivalence or desire so familiar to us. With the primitive Baudrillard would conjure up a time when rituals commanded social being, games were at the heart of social life, seduction was omnipresent (not just relative to the other sex, or other people, but to the gods), words could be delivered of their meaning in incantation, and death (and fate) could be willingly challenged and embraced. In other words, for our author the primitive represents that state where the "world" formed by the "second terms" functions with maximum autonomy and maximum effectiveness.

Once recovered in its full integrity, signs of the continued existence of the logic of this other world can be detected within the present, in however a

146

transfigured form. Indeed such is the occasion of many of Baudrillard's most brilliant *aperçus*. But note, the "logic of seduction" is recovered not just where one would most expect it—in courtship rituals, advertising, and entertainment—but also in those areas where one should be least expected to find it, that is, in those areas most invested by notions of truth, power and justice—the macro-realm of politics, as well as the micro-realms of inter-personal communication, sexuality and self (Baudrillard has not entirely forgotten Foucault). In these latter areas the logic of seduction often appears, as one might expect, to form a shadow world which, although dismissed and disparaged, haunts our conceptions of order and coherence, secretly subverting their claims. But just as often in Baudrillard's analysis, this logic appears to quit the shadows and move to center stage, leaving the other "real world" with only a secondary, cardboard existence. And this is no simple trick of perspective, for according to our author we are entering a brave, new and ludic world.

Consider the fate of politics. It is not simply that politics is no longer what it seems; it is that we no longer live in an era of politics. During the era of politics the fundamental terms of the political imaginary, the terms that give politics its value and meaning—terms like power, law, justice, equality, the public good or the people—still retained their force. Let it be noted that these are "transcendent" terms (and cannot be identified with the reality of society); they form a sort of mirror ideal above society by which the collective gathers itself together, attempts to establish its identity and orientations, determine its actions and give itself the means to carry out these actions. (And as such, these terms are constitutive of and participate in the distinctions between appearances and depths, illusions and realities, truths and falsehoods—and the concern with repression and liberation they entail—which Baudrillard would attack). If one then speaks of a democratic politics, one must add that these terms are not only without positive reality; they are without any definite content, the latter being subject to continuous debate. As a result they give rise to the expression of a division internal to society, whereby the principles supposedly constitutive of that society are subjected to constant questioning and conflict. Now suppose that another social "logic" emerges, in part as a response to, or better, as a way of avoiding any response to the underlying uncertainty of the era of democratic politics, and the public debate, social action and political conflict it calls forth. And that this new "logic" infiltrates the political scene, draining it of its substance and energy, leaving it only a shell of its former self, while imposing on the social order at large a very different mode of operationality, with very different motivations, concerns and stakes. This, of course, is Baudrillard's claim, with the further claim being that this "logic" is not without links to that "primitive" logic of seduction noted above, with the prominence it gave to games and the play of appearances.[1] If as was suggested, Baudrillard is seeking to recover a world long neglected, then "history," one might say, is on his side, and the anthropological nostalgia becomes prescient of a living future. But the repressed returns in a very different form, with a troubling, parodic character.

We have already noted that, according to Baudrillard, we live in a world of appearances, but these appearances are of a radically changed character. They no longer sit astride some invisible and underlying reality; they are becoming reality for us—which is to say that our sense of reality is now modelled on appearances, that ours is a simulated reality made to appear real. In this sense appearances are losing their illusory, imaginary and even representative character; for instead of maintaining their distance from reality, they would overtake reality in the models of the hyper-real. Within this world of appearances, one can speak of seduction (in a world of appearances one cannot but speak of appearances) but it too will have a radically changed character. No more the games of passion with their unpredictable outcomes and high stakes. No more that hot seduction subversive of one's sense of reality. One must speak instead of a soft seduction, one that acts as a social lubricant to the consumer society, rationing off minimal gratifications in homeopathic doses. Such seduction does not involve the mastery of illusions (thus supposing the difference between appearance and reality); one is less entrapped by illusion than absorbed by the simulated models of a reality that would would model the apparent reality of our desire. In effect, the collapse of the distinction between appearance and reality is accompanied by the collapse of that between the pleasure and reality principles. Which in turn must be considered the beginning of the end of that perspectival space within which the self situates its relation to others and their difference, and by incorporating the perspective of others, situates itself and its limits. If one then pushes this hypothesis further, with its elimination of the mirror state (and thus of all relational alterity of self and other), one imagines a radically "narcissistic" or "digital" universe where communication becomes ubiquitous and instantaneous, but also empty and circular, an endless proliferation without external mediation. It is at this point that one begins to perceive the ultimate triumph of a ludic world. But the games played here are those described by game theory—the formalized expression of all possibilities under limited conditions—while the "play" is that of a cybernetic universe—the modulation of a network of multiple connections and disconnections—all in the name of a search for maximization, whether that of operational efficiency or sensual plasticity. Such a world can barely be called fun. Its games do not enchant; they leave the "player" absorbed, transfixed by a numb fascination or by what Baudrillard terms at one point "a psychedelic giddiness."

Earlier I suggested that Baudrillard would combat the truth of depths by speaking of the superficial reality of appearances. But what is the sense of this combat when truth no longer attaches itself to an underlying reality, when it is appearances that alone are true because the apparent heir to the sovereignty of the real? In the face of such a situation, one might switch strategies, and instead of counterposing superficial truths to the deeper realities (discovered by science, interpretation or critique), quit the realm of truth and reality altogether by entering what in principle is the "un-real" and "un-true" realm of games. But what is the sense of such a feint when the blurring of appearance and truth has produced a ludic reality, and one in which games have lost their defiant and subversive character? A situation all the more problematic when one is not simply writing about games; what one is writing is itself a game. When, in other words, the way the book is written (and the way it is to be read) is made to reflect and respond to the content of what is written. But then how can one write a seductive work that would ensnare and entrance its readers when the character of seduction has become so degraded? How can one challenge one's readers when the reading public, its tastes shaped by the televisual media, has become impervious to reflection? How can one even communicate with this public when the language it understands systematically denies all alterity? Or put in another way, what sort of analytic strategy can one devise to counter the rose-coloured nightmare one is attempting to deconstruct? What sort of theoretical response might retain its subversive charge in the face of a world drained of substance, meaning, value and difference?

In this regard there are, I believe, two very different, even contrary responses in Baudrillard's work. The first moves as far outside the cold seduction of the digital universe as possible, towards that point of maximal alterity, the seduction of a primitive world... and that without moral tergiversation. How else is one to interpret the theoretical embrace of the terms of ritual and sacrifice, and the cruel, fatalistic world it implies? And what about the discussion, most notably towards the end of *Fatal Strategies*, of a universe determined not by universal laws of cause and effect, or those of chance, nor some combination thereof, but by the always particular, charmed and for us, senseless "logic" implied by predestination? As if the world of games would still, by virtue of some final irony or desperate hope, secretly reign supreme. Are we to see this as the hidden determination beneath a transparent world? Or as the dialectical reversal at the end of the end of history? One has the impression that Baudrillard is here creating a myth in the full sense of the word, and that this myth is a gamble in the Pascalian sense—the unreasonable but necessary belief in an invisible and sacred principle that holds the fate of each and all of us in the balance.

The other response moves in the opposite direction, towards that which it describes, appropriating its materials and extending its logic in the hope of imploding it from within. Baudrillard's analysis is extreme and describes a world that is "going to extremes". Throughout he details a sort of logical flight forward whereby, in the absence of the anchorage of referents, finalities, limits, laws or rules, some principle is "doubled," producing an unreal and disconcerting excess. Thus reality is made more real than real in the simulations of hyper-reality, speed becomes faster than fast as it reaches the point of instantaneity, obesity takes one beyond fatness (to take an example from *Fatal Strategies*), and pornography renders sex more than visible while neutralizing it by its excess. Such an "escalation to extremes" involves both a logic of proliferation—before all the exorbitant "images" of reality, sex, speed or flatulence, one can only reply that it is "too much"—and a logic of disappearance—the disappearance of (the meaning and value of) reality, sex, the body, movement and distance. In effect, within the space of his text, Baudrillard is creating a simulation model of a trajectory identified with present-day tendencies, speeding it up, which he can then watch with what must be a mixture of pleasure and horror as it all collapses in on itself. And in the process he has managed to write something that is truer than true, something that he might call an "ecstatic" truth (ecstasy being defined at one point in *Stratégies fatales* as "the vertiginous super-multiplication of formal properties"). Perhaps this is where Baudrillard is upping the ante and throwing down his ultimate challenge, daring the logic to go beyond the point where it can be meaningfully sustained and becomes absurder than absurd. Perhaps this is how, in his imagination, he would seduce and destroy the unreal reality he feels so estranged from, by calling on its resources to trap it within its own movement. Perhaps by its very fatalism such a strategy is (primitively) seductive.

In many ways this is the more satisfying response, and yet does it not threaten to become one with what it describes—a simulacrum of the dystopia of the living future? Does it not, by virtue of its conceptual self-referentiality begin to turn in on itself to the point where it turns to an incantatory prose and begins to lose all meaning? With its theoretical escalation to extremes and its hypothetical exhaustion of all alternatives in the mirror-play of reversibility, does it not deny itself all stakes in the forecast of an unalterable doomsday scenario? And is not the latter not just another one of those banal apocalypses, one of those catastrophes without consequences, which we are, as Baudrillard himself recognizes, so eager to consume in this pre-millenial era? After all the rapid-fire analytic connections and disconnections that play so fast and loose with meaning and value, doesn't the reader emerge from the book in a giddy theoretical daze? And what is the nature of the fascination? How many of those who are attracted to the work are left literally speechless, in a state of "somnambular euphoria"?

When beginning to write this essay, I told myself that I would be venting my own ambivalence relative to Baudrillard's work. But now that I am nearing the end I am convinced that the ambivalence is immanent to the work itself. Though written in extremes, it perhaps allows of only equivocal responses. If its claims were to be taken too seriously, or too literally, by either author or reader, then the former should have found it impossible to write the book, and the latter to read it. On the other hand, if the claims could simply be denied, the book would be less than uninteresting. Yet it remains fascinating: a work of sociology that violates all the canons of social science, a work of ethics that would dispense with morality, a radical work that would be without hopes. A work that would reject the very idea(l) of truth, but supposes a residual truth for its impact. And that would quit reality to enter the "unreal" space of games, but as a game would reflect the space that it has quit. It is a work that would shock its readers though they be rendered insensible by the saturation of obscene images; that would challenge its readers though they be inoculated to all but the most formal (and least antagonistic) of dualisms; and would communicate even as communication is increasingly being reduced to what one eighteenth century utopian termed the "language of the bees." A work that resonates with the irreality of the real, that fantasizes a world without fantasy, and would play in ways that it declares obsolete. A work that bemoans a world of simulation, and would then produce a radical simulation of theory. A work whose major concepts are, like so many tops, sent spinning at such a speed that they would disappear from human history. Simultaneously agonistics and agnostics, augur and agony, it is a marvelously impossible book. Something one can neither accept nor reject. A work that both attracts and repels, absorbs and torments. In a word, the perfect postmodern fetish.

Sociology
Glendon College

Notes

1.   I said earlier that one could not respond to Baudrillard's texts politically. The reasons are not simply "epistemological" (he is not writing about the underlying reality of society, nor is he writing a work of politics—his writing is a game) but also "historical" (the political scene no longer has any meaning in the present and, therefore, nothing can be expected of it). To be sure, this continuous tacking between "epistemology" and "history" can produce for the would-be critic a very slippery, even duplicitous text.

SIGN AND COMMODITY: ASPECTS OF THE CULTURAL DYNAMIC OF ADVANCED CAPITALISM

Andrew Wernick

It is no accident that Marx should have begun with an analysis of commodities when, in the two great works of his mature period, he set out to portray capitalist society in its totality and to lay bare its fundamental nature. For at this stage in the history of mankind there is no problem that does not ultimately lead back to that question and there is no solution that could not be found in the solution to the riddle of the commodity-structure.

> G. Lukacs
> *History and Class Consciousness*

Ideology can no longer be understood as an infra-superstructural relation between a material production (system and relations of production) and a production of signs (culture, etc.) which expresses and marks the contradictions at the "base". Henceforth, all of this comprises, with the same degree of objectivity, a general political economy (its critique), which is traversed throughout by the same form and administered by the same logic.

> Jean Baudrillard
> *For A Critique of the*
> *Political Economy of the Sign*

I

Baudrillard and Frankfurt

In the affluent conformism of the post-war boom, and now again in the post-60s disillusionment of our own mean-spirited and re-disciplined times, critical social thought has revived the Frankfurt School's spectre of a capitalism that has finally mastered its own historicity and so liquidated any endogenous capacity it may once have had for redemptive self-transformation.

It is perhaps noteworthy that the latest avatars of this gloomy entelechy have emerged not from Germany, the land of its birth, but from France; and, at that, from among an intellectual generation that cut its teeth on a polemic against humanized Hegel and dedicated itself thereafter to the philosophical dismantling of all the other crumbling remnants of Western logocentrism.[1] The reasons for this strange paradigmatic cross-over are partly political. In post-Hitler Germany, the neo-Kantian and anti-Romantic turn taken by critical theory under Habermas and his followers was predicated on the recovery of evolutionary optimism. That (West) German thought since then has been able to sustain this liberal mood is in some measure due to the relative persistence in that country of the extra-Parliamentary activism initiated during the 60s. In France to the contrary, May 68 was a bolt from the stars, as deliriously festive and

152

total as it was ephemeral: hard even to recall in the business-as-usual normality which so rapidly and depressingly followed. Faced afterwards with a choice between the PCF (and *Union des Gauches*) and Gaullism, it is not surprising that radical French theory should begin to display signs of ultimatism and despair.

But besides these matters of context, French thought in its moment of deconstruction has also come to display profound conceptual parallels with the earlier enterprise of negative dialectics. Both reflect the outcome of a would-be synthetic meditation on Marx, Nietzche and Freud; both share a mortal fear of the social world's ideological self-enclosure; and both exhibit a modernist determination to demolish systematicity, even at the level of critique itself. For that reason, and despite their otherwise irreconcilable epistemic differences, post-structuralism today enjoys an almost privileged access to the previously inadmissible (because Hegelian and anti-objectivist) terrain of Horkheimer, Adorno and Marcuse, and thus also to those thinkers' tragic reading of modern history as the story of Enlightenment's ineluctable progress towards total unfreedom.

Perhaps the clearest and certainly the most sociologically explicit instance of what one might call neo-Marcusian reasoning in contemporary French thought is the work of Jean Baudrillard.[2]

There is admittedly a world (i.e. an ontology) of difference between Marcuse's one-dimensional society and Baudrillard's code-dominated order of generalized exchange. In the praxis-based categories of the former it is instrumental reason which is identified as the glacially reifying agent; whereas in the latter, founded on a neo-Durkheimian anthropology of moral reciprocity, the culprit is commodity semiosis and the universalized commutability of values. But at a deeper level these critical visions converge in their common projection of advanced capitalist society as a model whose fixed determinations propel the collectivity towards a kind of slow but painless spiritual death. Baudrillard, like Marcuse, has also tried to provide psychoanalytic ground for this dystopian teleology by demonstrating its consonance with the morbid promptings of a systematically repressed desire.[3] Likewise, Baudrillard's sociological investigations into mass-mediatized consumerism, the main substance of his *oeuvre*, essentially pursue lines of enquiry previously opened up by the Frankfurt School. The guiding assumptions are identical: that the mass cultural instance has become crucial to social reproduction, that it represents indeed a strategic built-in mechanism for ensuring the social order's real statis through all the incipient upheavals it continues to induce, and that this is why the Revolution (if the term retains any meaning) has perhaps permanently missed the historical boat.

There is no doubt that Baudrillard's exploration of these themes is path-breaking. His problematization of what one might call commodity semiosis in the age of televised repetition represents in many respects a significant advance over Benjamin, and certainly over the North American mass society critics he also appropriates. More than any other contemporary thinker he has succeeded in placing the changed articulation of culture and economy in advanced capitalist society firmly on the theoretical agenda. But ultimately, I would argue, the theoretical power of his analysis is restricted by the same quasi-fatalistic circularity that vitiated the Frankfurt School's original civilizational lament. In Derridian terms: however decentred and indeterminate, the code that has allegedly triumphed is nevertheless a logos, particularly when identified with death; and such an ascription must itself fall prey to the suspicion of logocentrism. Otherwise put: we do not escape the identity principle simply by identifying the *weltgeist* as a corpse.

More pragmatically, any representation of social reality as culturally (and therefore politically) enclosed in the unidimensionality of a singular psychic space — with Baudrillard this is structural, abstract and at the second degree — is vulnerable to the counterfactual experience of 'actual' history. Theory must be adequate to explain and account for global disturbances like those of the 60s which shake the system of hegemony to its foundations. It is also important to explicate the normal play of cultural and moral politics — struggles over sexual, familial, aesthetic, religious, etc., modes and symbols — which continually mediate, sometimes explosively, the hierarchical force-field of competing material self-interests.

On this score, perhaps, it might be claimed that Baudrillard is in fact somewhat less undialectical than some of his Frankfurt forebears. Whereas in *The Dialectic of Enlightenment* it is critical theory itself which must bear the full weight of opposition,[4] his own anthropological ontology of symbolic exchange comes close to endowing even the wholly reified world of *la société de consommation* with a principle of *internal* contradiction. Symbolic exchange, in the primordial forms of gift, festival, and sacrifice, can no more be repressed than language; and so the more the 'structural law of value' dessicates social space, the more its unsatisfied reciprocities, invested with repressed libidinal energy, come to haunt all the corners of social life, threatening constantly to disrupt the repetitive dumb-show that has come to monopolize the stage. Hence, for Baudrillard, the Days of May. And also, the profound significance of even such trivial occurrences as the great New York graffiti outbreak in 1972,[5] and (in a darker vein) of that more permanent round of media-attuned symbolic-come-actual political violence to which the Western world has become accustomed over the past two decades:

> In the face of purely symbolic blackmail (the barricades of 68, hostage-taking) power falls apart: since it lives off my slow death, I oppose it with my violent death. And it is because we live off a slow death that we dream of a violent one. This very dream is intolerable to power.[6]

But if Baudrillard's social topology does provide a space for otherness and by the same token for crisis it nevertheless takes for granted that the prospect of class upheaval has passed and that capitalism's contradictoriness has come to be confined to the plane of its cultural determinations. Occluding the play of interests and *contra* Marx, transformation is only imaginable in this perspective as the quasi-magical irruption of *symbolic politics* so that we are left wondering whether Baudrillard has abandoned all hope of there being any actual exit from capitalism at all. Moreover, the antagonism he posits between symbolic and semiotic exchange[7] is pitched at so abstract indeed metaphysical a level that the whole theoretical construct, despite itself, effectively replicates the historical closure that forms the 'real' object of its critique. In this sense, however self-critically, Baudrillard's sociology remains trapped within the order of the simulacrum. Far from having smashed that mirror, his deconstruction of political economy serves ultimately only to shift its angle; so that where it once reflected the code of production it now reflects the code of the Code in a metapsychological simulation of the fourth degree.[8] Correlatively, and beyond a certain level of increasingly poetic abstraction, Baudrillard's formulations leave the mediated and conflictual institution of commodified culture in real history, and the actual politics to which that process gives rise, deeply in the theoretical shade.

Now what is noteworthy about the Baudrillardian circle, beyond the profundity of the pessimism which motivates it, is that it derives from a conceptual reduction at the centre of what is at the same time its most incisive socio-historical insight: namely, that in late capitalism sign and commodity have fused, giving rise to a new form of object (the sign-commodity) and a new order of domination (the ensemble of institutions and discourses which make up consumer culture) neither of which operate any longer according to the dictates of a strictly capitalist (i.e. economic) logic.

The problem is that in thematizing this development Baudrillard has conflated two quite different aspects of the process: the transformation of signs into commodities, ultimately represented by the rise of the culture industry, and the transformation, *via* mass marketing, fashion and status competition, of commodities into signs. It is the latter which interests him, providing as it does a framework for analyzing how the sacred and socially essential realm of symbolic value has been effectively evacuated by public discourse. But the other moment, the penetration of culture by the commodity form, which to be sure also has far-reaching consequences for systemic integration, needs to be separately considered. Not only does Baudrillard fail to do this, but by palming the commercial dimension of post-industrial cultural formation under the sign of the Sign, his attention is deflected from any direct consideration of the cultural dynamics associated with the broader and always ongoing process of commodification as such.

If, then, the Baudrillardian problematic is to be potentiated as the starting-point for a fresh round of enquiries and reflections on our historical situation, its crucial elisions must be addressed, and the totalism of the model correspondingly deconstructed in the light of the complexities which that would introduce. It is in that spirit, and with the admitted risk of falling back into the swamp of second-order, i.e. political economic simulation, that the following very preliminary considerations are put forward. Above all, their main aim is to open up the question of how, besides providing the basis for a new (post-class?) mode of hegemony, cultural commodification and the impact of commodification on culture can create the space for a kind of politics.

II

Commodification as cultural provocateur

The expansionist principle built into the accumulation process, wherein market survival necessitates growth, has created a form of society whose development to an unprecedented degree has followed a path of constant upheaval and self-overhaul. Evidently, and here too capitalism has changed, the material contradictions of class and economy analyzed at length by Marx by no means exhaust the list of pertinent effects. For besides generating an ever more elaborate, differentiated and at the same time internationalized play of interest antagonisms, and mediating it throughout, capital has also tended to make socio-cultural waves as its imperatives and modalities have steadily imposed themselves and their restless dynamic over the entire surface and depth of social life.

The waves that have emanated from capitalist dynamism at the point of production are perhaps the most familiar aspects of this process. Since the dawning of industry it has been clear that the technological revolution ushered in by the Renaissance and installed by market society at the permanent centre of its production process was bound to transform not only the physical and social environments but the character of experience and the nature of ideology as well. The meditations of classical sociology on industrialism, bureaucracy and secularization were fixed precisely on that point; and critical theory's own rich discourse on technocracy, scientism, and instrumentality has in turn radicalized the analysis and incorporated it into the conventional weaponry of anti-capitalist critique. More recently, the rise of linguistic interests and the incipient obsolescence of print have led a non-Marxist current of thinkers culminating in Innis and McLuhan to push the question to a still deeper level by considering the cultural impact of ever-advancing technology within the communication process itself.

However, much less attention, and certainly less than deserved, has been given to the equally profound effects of capitalism's parallel but distinct tendency to extend the range of the price-system and the commodity form *per se* as a universal model for social relations. Even when posed moreover this issue has proved difficult to disentangle from the former, cross-cutting, problematic of technique. Thus, Lukacs' pathbreaking theory of reification effectively assimilated Marx's category of commodity fetishism to Weber's category of instrumental rationalization; and Benjamin's formative theses on the crisis of art similarly devolve, in the end, on a purely technological point. For all his semiological conflations, Baudrillard's singular achievement in developing and updating this line of thought has been finally to confront the cultural impact of commodification on something like its own, economically concatenated, ground: in terms, that is, of how an expanding circulation process has transformed the nature of social exchange.

But if Baudrillard has thereby helped emancipate the critical theory of culture from its one-sided pre-occupation with *techne* he has maintained its one-sidedness in another respect by thematizing the cultural dynamics of commodi-fication (which he disdains to examine in any but its most contemporary forms) exclusively from the perspective of that process's conservative moment. Behind the problematic of contained consciousness to which his figuration of the sign-economy responds lies an archaic and paradoxically economistic formula according to which systemically derived ideology functions solely to pacify contradictions that emanate just as solely from interest antagonisms at the base. In Baudrillard's case, adhesion to this schema is contradicted by his explicit rejection of the orthodox class paradigm, and so here the occlusion of commodification's disruptive cultural moment actually leaves a logical gap.

To be intelligible, any system of hegemony must be understood in terms of what threatens it. But what threatens the social order guaranteed ideologically by the Code? Not, apparently, class conflict; and the *revanche* of symbolic exchange is itself a contingency beyond the scope of all control. We are left then with the mere tautology of a structural law of value for which self-replication — *la répétition* — is simply a mode of being. Missing from Baudrillard's account, in short, is an appreciation of how the whole normative apparatus of the sign-commodity, publicity and consumer culture is mobilized, at least in part, to manage the cultural tensions provoked by that same extension of the commodity-form which produced the one-dimensional world of consumerism itself. An analysis of the latter ought properly to begin therefore by considering in what these former might consist. In the first instance, let me suggest, the cultural tensions of commodification take the form of conflicts and struggles over mundane ideological values; and they are provoked all along the seam of economy and and culture where the market's lust for expansion rubs up against pre-existing forms of normativity and moral value.

It would be misleading to represent this dialectic, as both conservative and radical opponents of the advancing market have been prone to do, in terms of a simple opposition between an amoral force and a moral object. For the freedom of commodities to circulate and the freedom of buyers and sellers to exchange what they will without external interference acquires the force of a moral argument; one whose central principle, the autonomized individual, rests its appeal on a whole ideological tradition, stretching from Reformed Christianity to contemporary libertarianism. This is not to deny that "personal freedom," like all ideologies, can be championed in stunningly obtuse or cynical bad faith. There are, rather, two points:

First, the social relations of commodity production — which in their immediate operation always centre on the nexus of exchange — are thoroughly saturated in the medium of normativity, without which they could not function. The market, as Durkheim would say,[9] rests on a moral basis. His argument can be extended. Established commerce requires not only that the *terms* of trade be contractually agreed upon, but also that there be a social consensus over *what* is for trade and over the *conditions* under which (if at all) that trade is allowed to take place.

Correlatively, and this is the second point, the constant advance of the market into symbolically loaded sectors of social life precipitates at the ideological level in each significant new instance a binary counterposition of pro-market liberalism and anti-market conservatism, communalism, nationalism, familism, etc., whose respective supporters fight like football teams to establish a succession of symbolic lines beyond which (temporarily at least) neither the market nor its enemies are allowed to encroach. Outcomes, whether in the form of truce, compromise or complete rout by one side or the other, are periodically arbitrated by the state on the terrain of law.

The perennial Canadian contest between partisans of free trade and protectionism provides a kind of paradigm case. Symbolically at stake in continental economic integration is the reduction, break-up and de-auratisation of a so-to-speak nationally sacralized signifier. Mainstream policy debate has been conducted in that context as a pragmatic but ideologized negotiation between nationalists and liberals over the extent to which the boundary of the border should be emphasized or de-emphasized in the face of a mounting circulation of goods, capital and information which constantly threaten to erode it. The point is not just that economic politics are lived out as ideology, but that the economic process has ideological ramifications which create the basis in itself for a form of politics.

From the very beginnings of capitalist development the sphere of consumption, originally and without irony conceived as private and public leisure,[10] has been especially subject to the eruption of such conflicts; and the more so the more an expanding productive complex has been able to extend and cultivate the range of enjoyments from orgasm to esteem that money there can buy. The court-imposed sumptuary laws of late Medieval absolutism and the seventeenth century puritan ban on theatre provide early as it were Thermidorean examples. More latterly, the growing sex and drug industries, each inconsistently and fuzzily divided into licit and illicit zones, have provided advanced capitalist society with its own nodal points of cultural tension.

Whether and in what degree to permit the commercial circulation of (addictive) stimulants and (degrading) sexual services in fact touches modern culture on a particularly sore nerve: our chronically inconsistent attitude towards the gratification and control of somatic impulse. Daniel Bell has even argued that this motivational ambivalence, which he attributes to a deepening antagonism between the emergent norms of leisure and work, represents capitalism's primary cultural contradiction.[11] His model of the problem is simplistic and ignores the role of consumerized commodification in its genesis. Nevertheless it remains true that particular issues of permissible consumption (today, par excellence, those pertaining to pornography and censorship) can resonate deeply with broader issues of social reproduction.

POWER AND SEDUCTION

It is precisely for this reason that the market, and still more the volatile liberal individualism that is its ideological shadow and harbinger, have such a dangerous edge. The normative limits, in some cases taboos, against which they press are not merely (in fact decreasingly) traditional survivals but symbolic markers of operant mechanisms of control. For the same reason, the moral issues of circulation tend to get linked up, and at the limit generalize on the plane of an ongoing social contest which draws in all the major ideological institutions and players over how the axial principles governing instituted normativity as a whole are to be defined.

Market pressure to shift the moral boundaries, to some degree a necessarily discontinuous process, always runs the risk of opening up a radical cultural space. But such openings, when order is finally restored, can themselves prove merely to have facilitated the passage from one matrix of market-regulating obediency to another. Such indeed has so far been the main axiological drama of post-war North America: first, the establishment of a surplus-repressive cultural hegemony; then its ultra-liberal dissolutions; and then, with suitable adjustments and continuing instabilities, "the return of traditional values" (to quote a 1976 liquor ad) and normalization.

If in late capitalism market penetration at the point of consumption (i.e. of private life) has become the main axis of what we can call circulation politics this is because the development of consumption as a productive force has replaced the geographical extension of the industrial system as the central motif of economic growth. Nevertheless it should be emphasized that analogous modalities of conflict continue to be generated at the point of production also. (A rigorous distinction needs to be made here between the properly cultural contradictions that attend the displacement of natural by exchange economy and the political-economic ones that flow from the economic inequality and exploitation which the market organization of production comes to install. We may think of the former contradictions as processual, the latter as structural, except that, just as in the case of the commodification process at work in the sphere of consumption, the normative inertia against which the spread of commodified production must contend has synchronic significance in the wider process of social reproduction as a whole).

The cultural dynamic associated with the initial establishment of capitalist production is of course largely played out. Artisanal ideals, local particularisms and traditional kin structures have lost their vitality in the industrialized heartlands and only resist the expanding system at its Third and Fourth World margins. However, even on mature capitalism's internal frontier, there are still two respects in which the market penetration of production is incomplete and continues to generate major cultural perturbations.

The first concerns the spread of economic exchange relations into such relatively (or ambivalently) non-commodified sectors of social activity as religion, the family, higher learning and the arts. In none of these diverse instances is the persistence of a pre-capitalist mode of association and work a mere case of culture-lag, for that mode is vital to their functioning as well as to

159

the authenticity on which the credibility of their various products depends. Under the circumstances the market, whether through example, through the emergence of fully commercialized rivals, or through the actual mobilization of material interests, can only advance slowly. As it does so what comes to be established on each institutional site is a semi-permanent force-field of conflicting pressures internalized by the actors themselves (clergy, housewives, students, artists, etc.) as role-conflict and externalized as tendency struggles between competing moral/ideological currents and movements over the relative virtues of liberal accommodation and traditionalist hostility to the forces of progress.

These frictions are hard to regulate from above. Indeed they are exacerbated by the ambivalence with which they must be officially regarded. On the one hand, the charter values of Truth, Knowledge, Love, Beauty, etc., ceaselessly activated in value-transmitting institutions by the irritant of creeping commercialism, play an important rhetorical role in capitalism's traditional legitimation as a civilizing force; but when roused they can also function as genuine transcendentals that provide troublesome reminders of loss, supercession and difference. Thus, for the churches of the West, where Christianity was thought to have been tamed, the rise of TV evangelism and other quintessentially business enterprise forms of priestcraft represents not merely an economic threat in the competition for congregations[12] but a repulsive counter-pole of 'bad religion' against which countervailing currents of increasingly radical transformism have been driven to define themselves. As one important corollary the previously cosy relation between organized religion and the capitalist state has begun to be radically upset.

Another, and perhaps more primordial, level at which structural resistance to the market penetration of production relations provides ongoing cultural conflict concerns the pressing into circulation of that strangest commodity of them all: labour-power. Quite apart from the shattering of traditional ties and attendant socio-cultural explosions that greeted the initial establishment of a mass-market for 'free labour', conflicts have continued to arise thereafter by virtue of that dynamic propensity of the market to redefine all work-functional energy as commercially available, regardless of the instituted status of its alienable owners. The resultant ideological dialectic is analogous with the one already described in the case of commodification at the point of consumption, except that here the codings at issue mark human agents, and indeed at the very juncture of their literal inscription within the differential orders of wealth and power.

Also, the process can cut more than one way. Where the change in status implied by the commodification of labour-power represents real demotion or loss of autonomy (one thinks here of small family farms and independent professionals) it will naturally be opposed by those affected in the romantically conservative name of the symbolic order thereby displaced. But the reverse can occur when labour market participation provides the basis for rescuing ascribed social categories (women, Catholics, blacks, etc.) from the even more subordinate status, outside the real world of exchange-economy, to which they would otherwise be culturally relegated. Here resistance to the expanding labour market comes from those already in it, while its newest recruits appeal to exchangist ideology against the continued application to themselves of the old, discriminatory norms.

Within the labour market itself, these latter, reflecting pre- (or trans-) capitalist hierarchies of race, age and gender, crystallize out as so many mechanisms of dominant group protectionism; which function to ensure that insofar as inferiorized categories are not excluded from paid employment altogether, they enter its equivalence system on markedly non-eqquivalent terms. The point here, as with the contradictions of commodification in general, is that over and above the material conflicts they provoke, such instances of unequal exchange are shot through with ideological contradictions which can become active in their own right. 'Minority' movements for equal opportunity that get blocked tend to radicalize by transvaluing that which has set the collectivity they represent stigmatically or condescendingly apart. Conversely, cultivation of cultural identity among the oppressed can trigger struggles for justice.

The ideological contradictions attending the application of equivalency norms to women in the face of patriarchal gender ascriptions have been particularly dense and slow to resolve. As early as the 1780's, Mary Woolstencraft showed how the abstract egalitarianism of possessive individualism could provide the basis for a critique of patriarchal restrictions on legal rights; and since then successive waves of feminist agitation, bolstered both by the gradual delegitimation of explicit male supremacism and by the increasing *de facto* normality of extra-domestic female employment have extended the battleground to every sphere of life. However, even more than in the case of racism, which frequently articulates with deeply rooted imperial/national legitimations of the state, the freedom of women to circulate on the same economic and social terms as men has also been resisted not just because it challenges an entrenched system of power and privilege, but because the patriarchal ideology that justifies that resistance (always circling around the claim that women are somehow "different") has continued, through all the vicissitudes of cultural liberalization, to play a crucial role in the maintenance and motivation of capitalist order. At this level, the need to sustain effective social mechanisms of biological reproduction has functioned largely as an alibi not only for the continued valorization of an asymmetrical gender code but also for the maintenance of the hierarchical family/class system which that code underwrites.

In the biblically resuscitated imaginary of early industrialism, the cultural identification of wage-labour with the 'masculine' roles of breadwinner and household head played a crucial pacifying role — over and above its various economic advantages to capital — by securing for the subordinated male worker a kind of compensatory, Adamic self-respect. At first, lacking the cumulated cultural force to wage a direct attack on the triadic fortress of family/church/school erected to protect this productivist nexus, the women's movement and the equivalency principle it championed gnawed away instead at juridicial inequalities in the fields of family law, civil rights and the franchise. Later, as the fortress began to collapse under the weight of more technically and socially developed conditions, it became possible for second wave feminism to crash over the sacred boundaries of hearth and home and finally confront the eternal verities of constructed gender difference at their intimate institutional source.

Here as elsewhere, however, capitalist modernization brings no guarantees of fundamental progress. For the displacement of work-centred religio-morality by and within the theatre of consumerism merely shifted the register of generic contradictions without ceasing to engage intractable issues of global integration and control. In this respect, it is of more than token significance that the book by Friedan[13] which did so much to popularize the modern women's movement in North America was based on an insider's critique of fashion magazines. Above all, it was the entry of signs, particularly iconic ones, into mass commercial circulation which gave patriarchal ideology a new lease on life by facilitating the spectacular passage of ideal femininity, as abstract signifier of status and desire, from the esoteric world of art to the ubiquitous iconography of mass culture and publicity. In that realm, the mythological female has come to embody not just the reward and condition for work but the promised happiness of consumption as well. Thus we see how a ruse of commodification has evolved a new obstacle to the process wherein the egalitarianism implicit in universalized market exchange strives, ever more powerfully, for independent realization.

The dialectic of course does not simply terminate in the victory of the *Playboy* syndrome; and a quarter century of feminist and market pressure, the latter operating by way of a pseudo-equalizing extension of sexual objectificatin to the male, has begun to seriousy undermine consumerism's heavy masculinist ethos. Sexual bias will only finally be eliminated from consumer culture when the commodity's pleasure principle has become (dysfunctionally) polymorphuous. So, even on the second-order plane of media imagery, the structural character of the contradiction is likely to persist.

III

The sign-commodity and hegemonic regulation

The cultural provocations of commodification and the politics of normativity to which they give rise do not unfold in a vacuum but in a field already indexed to issues of hegemonic regulation and already occupied by that whole range of institutions from political parties and churches to showbiz and schools which are engaged in the collective formulation and dissemination of values.

There is no absolute sense in which any of these ideological apparatus can be considered structurally dominant[14] since their forms of influence are incommensurate and there is always a degree of free play between them in which the relations of inter-institutional force can radically and conjuncturally alter. Nevertheless there is one institutional complex within the superstructural configuration of advanced capitalism which can claim some kind of significative priority in that it is through the omnipresent refractions of its lens (in every sense a screening) that the whole process of cultural formation is continuously and publicly represented; and this is the one comprised by the (for the most part) commercially operated organs of mass communication along with all the related industries for the production of news, publicity and entertainment. In addition to its importance within the game of capitalist self-maintenance this sector is also significant systemically as the very incarnation of the commodity-form's seductive penetration of culture. And so it is precisely here, in the repressive desublimations and codifying biases of the culture/consciousness/sign industry that we confront the puzzle of commodification's other, i.e. conservative, integrative, dimension; and with that puzzle, as I have suggested, the broader mystery of how the universalizing commodity in its articulation with the cultural process establishes automatic mechanisms to regulate the normative disorder it simultaneously helps to provoke.

The automatic character of mass consumer culture's ideological operation needs to be stressed for it is the very hallmark of its work, an unprecedented indication that here at last is a consciousness-shaping institution which by its very nature functions functionally and can never get wholly out of hand. Explanations of this functionality in terms of class political manipulation — evocative phrases like Ewen's 'captains of consciousness' spring to mind — miss the point entirely. The rise of Madison Avenue, Disneyland, Tin Pan Alley and the whole corporate capitalist dream machine marks a decisive shift away from personalized ideological powers and the emergence, to the contrary, of a fully programmed cultural sphere wherein, to use Laingian terms, 'praxis' on both sides of the production/consumption divide has been effectively super-ceded by 'process.'[15] In effect, the powerful ideological inflection of commercial mass culture, whether in the direct form of culture-for-sale or at the second degree as selling-by-culture, is no more than a by-product of the accelerated circulation and increased surplus it makes possible. That inflection has therefore to be accounted for in the same way: in terms of the culture industry's inner economic determinations and the effect of these on its manner of processing and representing potentially hot cultural materials.

Baudrillard's crucial refinement of this thesis is that at the most basic level the ideological element of mass-mediated culture is determined by the interplay established there between mass-produced signs and mass-produced commodities; and, further, that this new alignment of sign and commodity is responsible not only for its systematically biased content but also, and more fundamentally, for bias in its very mode of signification as well. The saga of the sign he unfolds reads like a post-modernist update of alienation theory. Infinitely replicable, displaced from symbolic time and place, converted into commodities in their own right, signifiers become free to float independently of any organic communicative process; and in that condition like landless proletarians they rejoin social reality artificially in the form of the semiotically-endowed mass consumable commodity. Finally, as arbitrary markers linking the corporate game of product differentiation to the consumer merry-go-round of status and fashion, the signifying elements of design, packaging and promotion are drained of meaning in the self-referential play of their coded differences, which is exactly how, in deadening abstraction, they come to rule. Consciousness, in Baudrillard's account, is not so much falsified as headed off at the pass: the media factories of commercial semiosis prevail, in his pregnant phrase, by "fabricating non-communication."[16]

Without denying that such a tendency towards enforced meaninglessness is relentlessly at work, it would be premature however to declare it complete. Even advertising copy has become a zone of ideological controversy, and outraged responses to media stereotypes of women and ethnic groups testify to their continuing referential power. This being so, the axiological content of mass-mediatized culture, and not just its semiological or, for that matter, sensory forms, remains relevant to an understanding of its cultural effectivity.

In fact at the level of communicative substance, the semio-economic determinations of the culture industry *doubly* stamp its effluvia as token-bearers of a would-be pacifying ideology. On the one hand, the subject-object inversion prescribed by their consistently consumerist mode of address occults class and makes a world without capital unimaginable. On the other hand, the pseudo-reconciliations of gender, nature/culture etc., made possible on that mytholo-gical basis, and positively reinforced by the premium placed on popularity values, serve to exorcize culturally-based sources of conflict as well. The former of these mechanisms, consumerism, is perhaps too familiar to require further elaboration. But the latter, which might be dubbed the middle-of-the-road effect, does call for some comment: not only as a comparatively unexamined topic,[17] but also because the consensualist modality of mass culture holds the key, or so I would argue, to the riddle of the commodity's limited but effective capacity for cultural self-control.

With respect to this issue, Baudrillard's insistence on the centrality of commodity semiosis within the mass cultural ensemble while not wrong is unhelpful, and further clarification depends on our disentangling the relation he condenses between that moment, represented by publicity, and its obverse, the commodification of signs, represented by entertainment. What we discover in fact is that within this same complex duality the order of effectivity is here reversed: in the case of cultural tension management as opposed to that of consumerist inversion it is entertainment rather than advertising that provides the dominant paradigm for a type of normative intervention which the culture industry, just by virtue of what it is, is driven to make.

The golden rule of show business is not to antagonize the audience, for that is the hand that feeds. Indeed, its members should be positively stroked, both as the fine people they are and for the decent or at any rate normal values they hold. To be entertained is above all to be made to feel good. Where the audience is live, local, and socially homogeneous, the collective totems must be very precisely acknowledged; but the more mass and therefore ideologically diverse it is, the more general the level of conventionality to which appeal must be made. Where there is not merely diversity but conflict, the task of flattering and in the same moment defining the collective identity of the audience is particularly difficult. The most cliché-ridden depths of popular mythology must then be plumbed, and awkward topics, controversial issues, and even potentially abrasive accentuations of genre and style must be avoided. A safe strategy for maximizing sales, box-office and ratings, in short, is to go mid-market and assiduously hug the middle-of-the-road.

Of course, if the entertainment industry, throughout all its branches, exhibited nothing but this entropic tendency, then its equally important need for constant thematic and stylistic innovation could not be met. But in this dialectic, the experimenter's licence to practice is granted in return for bearing all the economic risks, and successful novelties are rapidly co-opted, converted into mannerisms, and embalmed for later recycling as pseudo-historical nostalgia.

Only in popular music has this controlled oscillation ever gotten at all out of hand. The reason is not hard to find. Because of its intimate relation to ritual, emotion and physicality, music as the least directly representational art-form is also the least susceptible, whatever the technological and economic mode, to whole-scale serialization. It is the one sector of mass culture truly haunted by the return of symbolic exchange, and its history has constantly intertwined with that of the national, class and generational movements whose tragic, rebellious or celebratory moods it has been able, with fluctuating degrees of immediacy, to express. A central thread in this story has been the emergence of Afro-American music and its phased appropriation by successive layers of white working and middle class youth as a quasi-Dionysian dance cult. However, the point should not be over-emphasized; for even at this relatively organic level the major ruptures with middle-of-the-roadism — rag-time, jazz, swing, rock, reggae, punk — have been ambiguous in their meaning and ultimately subject to absorption by, or even *as*, the industry-dominated mainstream.

While the entertainment industry's penchant for self-censorship, cultural compromise and normative conventionalism has been a genuine expression of its own bad essence, these tendenices have of course been strongly reinforced by its ties with the whole machinery of mass media advertising. The degree to which advertising revenues directly pay the costs of mass entertainment varies from medium to medium, although given the extent of financial and functional interlock these differences may be misleading. In the limit case, American network TV and radio, the subsidy is total, and so too is the revenue-dependence of the medium on the size (and to a lesser degree the mix) of the audiences its programming can command; for it is on the ratings that advertising rates themselves rigidly depend. Here also, where they are compulsory, the conservative ideological implications of popularity values are most rigidly in evidence. Even less than media programmers, commercial sponsors cannot afford to alienate potential slices of their market. In effect, a double vigilance must therefore be maintained: on the one hand to ensure that only acceptable cultural risks are taken in satisfying and competing for the medium's own audience; and on the other to ensure that the advertising material itself hits absolutely the right consensual spot when addressing its target market.

In its actual functioning, advertising in fact represents the degree zero of show business audience technique. The flattery of the performer was at bottom always a form of self-promotion. In consumer advertising, however, the trick is refined by naturalizing and in the full sense normalizing the conventional cultural values which that flattery sought to confirm, and which, *mutatis mutandis*, are here invoked to valorize the product. The sales aim of commodity semiosis is to differentiate the product as a valid, or at least resonant, social totem, and this would be impossible without being able to appeal to taken-for-granted systems of cultural reference.

In this sense advertising must go even further along the path of popularity than entertainment. The latter, faced by embarrassing cultural divisions, can retreat to jokes and good humour. In so far as conventionality is torn or contorted by ongoing ideological contradictions advertising, however, is constrained to at least construct the appearance of a non-contradictory value-consensus. This is obviously the case where the product's intended market, e.g. for "feminine" cigarettes or "masculine" perfume, is by definition ambivalent toward the cultural codings *prima facie* associated with it. But in a more diffuse sense, the whole discourse of publicity, including, by extension, the subsidized programming which colonizes the mass consumer market as an audience, absolutely requires a normality-pole. The creative genius of advertising and its platforms of associated messages is that it is able to establish one, mythically; and in such a way, moreover, as to occlude the consumerist ontology that anchors it, to reconcile all the cultural antinomies of an unstable ideological universe, and then — through an iconography that adheres even in its most stark typifications to the canons of realist representation — to pass the whole thing off, despite its uncanny resemblance to the familiar world in which we live, as a wistful dream.

IV

Breaking the circle

During the 1960's advertising was the most, perhaps the only, stable medium of mass ideological communication. Besides the downplaying of technological futurism and the increased use of sexual themes (the latter a cause of disturbance in itself), publicity's ideological feathers seemed hardly ruffled by the culture-storm[18] blowing, apparently, all around. Yet that storm did break out; and, as I have tried to indicate, the superstructural *decallage* within which it brewed and grew to hurricane force expressed a determinate historical moment of that same dialectic of culture and commodity which was also responsible for the spell-binding integration of the commercialized sign.

POWER AND SEDUCTION

Baudrillard, who ignored the mediations by which both these moments are connected to capitalism's commodification drive, was transfixed by the Manichaean absoluteness of their opposition. Had the mediations been attended to, the operations of artificial semiosis would doubtless have seemed less omnipotent and the mass outbreak of the Symbolic less conjuncturally mysterious than he made them out to be. Of course, it is hardly surprising that the Edenic epiphanies and street-fighting psycho-dramatics of 1968 nowhere ushered in the New Age: the requisite programme, organization and political forces were altogether lacking. But what that temporary breakdown of normal cultural controls did demonstrate, against all the end-of-ideology soothsaying of the previous decade, is that at the ideological level *par excellence* the development of post-industrial capitalism is as conflictual as it is consensualist; and, indeed, that under the right circumstances accumulated cultural tensions can even engender a global social crisis.

Theory and the evidence of history thus combine to provide grounds for hoping that the circle of the commodity-form's normative self-regulation can indeed be broken. To what extent such a fateful outcome can be deliberately strategized is, however, a different question. Because of the complexity of the process wherein cultural politics arise, the rectilinear relation its issues bear to matters of class hegemonic control, and the potentially self-undermining character of any transparently instrumental invervention into hot zones of consciousness, we may doubt the feasibility of anything so ambitious as a co-ordinated, multi-level, plan of cultural campaign. But in a more circumspect and *ad hoc* sense, Marx's directive to enter the "real battles" of the world in order to "show it what it is actually fighting about"[19] does retain here its moment of activist truth.

Of course, for us it is the commercial media more than organized religion which require demystification; and within the field of cultural politics considered in this paper demystification is hardly enough. The positive deployment of transcapitalist discourse and symbology is also necessary, indeed crucial, since unlike the recognition struggle of master and slave which underlies Marx's concept of class conflict the cultural dialectic of commodification has no truly inner principle of sublation. This, on the plane of trade-union consciousness, and leaving aside its Jacobin inspiration, is presumably what Lenin meant by saying that revolutionary consciousness had to come "from without." On the plane of normative consciousness and in a spirit of preparatory *attentisme* an even more idealist formula could easily be proposed: the stronger and richer the transcendental cultural resources lying to hand at the moment when some fresh round of superstructural troubles break out, the more likely it is that something truly human will strive to emerge — and the greater the chance, perhaps, that we finally will.

Peter Robinson College
Trent University

Notes

1. See V. Descombes, *Le Même et l'Autre* (Éditions de Minuit, Paris 1979), translated as *Modern French Philosophy* (Cam. U. Press, 1980).

2. In this essay I am focussing mainly on Baudrillard's early writings, particularly *Le Système des Objets* (Gallimard 1968); *La Société de Consommation* (Dengel 1970); *Pour une Critique de l'Économie du Signe* (Gallimard 1972); *Le Miroir de la Production* (Casterman 1973); and *L'Échange Symbolique et la Mort* (Gallimard 1976). For English translations of the latter, see *Mirror of Production* (Telos 1975); *For A Critique of the Political Economy of the Sign* (Telos 1981), and the excerpts from *l'Échange Symbolique* in J. Fekete (ed.) *The Structural Metaphor* (Univ. of Min. Press, 1984).

    It would require a whole separate analysis to consider whether, in switching from a sociological to a metaphysical exploration of nihilism in the later texts like *Oublier Foucault, La Séduction* and *Stratégies Fatales*, Baudrillard's social ontology of sign and commodity has remained basically the same.

3. This is the basic motif of *L'Échange Symbolique et la Mort*.

4. Pessimism about proletarian consciousness and correlative elevation of (critical) theory's role within the social dialectic, while absolutized in this 1944 text, was an explicit theme of Frankfurt thinking from the early 30's. See M. Horkheimer, *Critical Theory* (Herder and Herder, 1972) pp. 211-216.

5. Baudrillard, *L'Échange Symbolique*, pp. 118-28.

6. *Ibid.*, p. 73.

7. Baudrillard, *Pour une Critique de l'Économie Politique du Signe*, pp. 194-99.

8. The lament simulates what it projects, and for neo-Kantians (aren't we all?) there can be no escaping the fictitious character of the world. For Baudrillard's most explicit attempt to place himself outside this circle, see *L'Échange Symbolique*, pp. 7-10 and pp. 110-17.

9. The classic statement is to be found in E. Durkheim, *The Division of Labour in Society* (Free Press, 1964) Chap. 7.

10. For a brilliant traditionalist critique of the modern evolution of leisure see J. Pieper, *Leisure: The Basis of Culture* (Pantheon, 1952).

11. D. Bell, *The Cultural Contradictions of Capitalism* (Basic Books, 1976).

12. Ecclesiastical ecumenicism, from the angle of religion's absorption into the culture industry, represents a movement towards cartelization between the largest enterprises. The perverse Paisley protest has its moment of truth here.-

13. B. Friedan, *The Feminine Mystique*.

14. For the notion of 'dominance' in this context see L. Althusser, Ideology and the State' in his *Lenin and Philosophy* (NLB, 1971). Althusser's formulation is much too rigid, however. It is crucial, especially, to disentangle dominance (of an apparatus) vis-à-vis *individual* formation from the question of inter-institutional influence and power within society *as a whole*.

15. For a good social psychological elaboration of this ultimately Sartrian distinction see A. Esterson, *The Leaves of Spring* (Tavistock, 1970).

16. Baudrillard, For a Critique of the Political Economy of the Sign, p. 169.

17. Although they do not elaborate the point, a recent essay by G. Murdoch and P. Golding, 'Capitalism, Communication and Class Relations' states the main issue very well:

   ". . . the determining context for production is always that of the market. In seeking to maximize this market, products must draw on the most widely legitimated central core values while rejecting the dissenting voice or the incompatible objection to a ruling myth. The need for easily understood, popular, formulated, undisturbing, assimilable fictional material is at once a commercial impertive and an aesthetic recipe". Curran, Gurevitch and Wollacott, (eds.) *Mass Communication and Society* (Edward Arnold, 1977) p. 40.

18. This evocative phrase was coined by H. L. Nieburg in his insightful anthropological study of 1960's counter-culture, *Culture Storm: Politics and the Ritual Order* (St. Martin's, N.Y., 1973).

19. Letter from Marx to Ruge 1843. See D. McLellan (ed.) *Karl Marx: Early Texts* (Blackwell, 1979).

BAUDRILLARD, CRITICAL THEORY AND PSYCHOANALYSIS

Charles Levin

Introduction

This essay presents a condensed version of an argument about the sign, the object and the symbol.[1] Its purpose, then, is to suggest how psychoanalytic thought, particularly "object-relations theory", may provide a way out of the stalemate in critical theory.[2]

The theory of reification, although essential to critical theory, is itself based on intellectualized reifications of what it means to be a "subject" and not an object.[3] The traditional theory of reification is described in the light of Baudrillard's work and then rejected in favour of another which views reification as an obsessional project of closing down or emptying out "potential space".

The phrase "potential space" was coined by D.W. Winnicott to refer to a dimension of "transitional" phenomena intermediate to subjectivity and objectivity. My most basic theoretical assumption is that the "space" of the "transitional object" is a place where people actually live, where they are creative, where they interact in depth, and where things are invested with meaning.

I

The best general approach to Baudrillard is through the philosophical tension in his work between structuralist social theory (Lévi-Strauss, Barthes) and critical theory (Lukacs, Marcuse). These are the two modern traditions, dragging their French and German antecedents with them, which are most obviously at work in Baudrillard's early texts. It would be a mistake, however, to think that he ever synthesized them, although it is true that the interplay of structuralism and cultural Marxism determined, to some extent, Baudrillard's own distinctive way of choosing a post-structuralist position. The net theoretical effect is more like the introduction of two corrosives which, having devoured each other, leave nothing behind but a luminous theoretical vacuum. Baudrillard's writing has, since *L'Échange symbolique et la mort*,[4] increasingly approximated a blank surface reflecting only the awful terror of what it had once tried to name.

What is interesting about critical theory and structuralism together (at least, in the medium of Baudrillard) is the dilation of their theories of the *object*. A reading of Baudrillard makes one want to return to these traditions simply to listen to the way objects are talked about. Baudrillard caught this element in their discourse early on,[5] and developed it rapidly. Armed with just the two theoretical languages, the neo-Marxian and the structuralist, he abandoned himself to the world of things.

Jean Baudrillard has a knack for a kind of McLuhanesque "in depth participation," and he turns the two theoretical languages into quite precise tools of description which evoke the object world with amazing poetical force and tension. Although in the end he virtually destroys both structuralism and critical theory (something Baudrillard does to almost everything he touches), he has managed to extract and deliver a lot of what is interesting in the two traditions before bringing them into mutual disrepute. Most of this material has to do with *objects*.

Before Baudrillard critical theory had a great deal to say explicity about objects, which is odd because critical theory has always claimed to be more concerned with the fate of subjects. It can be argued, however, that critical theory has very little of value to say about subjects. According to critical theorists, subjects are beings that make things; they experience a world (usually one they have made themselves without knowing it); they transfer their feelings onto the world, and they internalize authority. In other words, subjects are beings who (according to critical theory) produce, project and introject.

Structuralists aren't much better on this score, although on the surface they may appear to be more sophisticated. Usually, a structuralist begins by arguing that the subject is not an ontological category. There is some value in this argument. But then the structuralists go on to imply that subjects are not epistemological categories either. They do this by arguing that the subject is "decentered". This is true, but not very interesting by itself, and not very different from what critical theory has already said. After all, what does decentering mean, if not producing, projecting and introjecting? The only difference is that critical theory disapproves of this sort of heteronomy, and wants to get rid of it, whereas structuralism thinks it is a good thing, and wants to extend it. Both traditions agree that the subject's experience is false, but not on the reasons why. There is nothing new in these arguments, taken by themselves, but something quite interesting happens when Baudrillard plays them off, one against the other.

Baudrillard is usually thought of as a structuralist or a post-structuralist thinker rather than as a critical theorist in the tradition of the Lukacs/Frankfurt School. But in fact, he remains deeply involved in the latter tradition. It is true that he has made his name as a debunker of Teutonic theory and is notable for being openly anti-dialectical. But Baudrillard is not just contra Marx: he is also contra Foucault, contra Saussure, contra Levi-Strauss, contra Freud, contra Deleuze, etc. In fact, Baudrillard is against any thinker whose ideas he takes seriously. To use a word of Marx's, he is a "counterdependent" thinker. His arguments nearly always depend on the credibility of the categories of the other thinkers he defines himself against. This feature of Baudrillard's discourse is quite typical of critical theory, and secretly dialectical. Perhaps he is saying that if dialectics are not, in his view, an intrinsic property of the world, they are certainly a feature of discourse about subjects and objects. At any rate, when

Baudrillard launches his critique of critique in *The Mirror of Production*, his tone is not so much that of a dyed-in-the-wool structuralist as that of a critical theorist denouncing himself.

There is another, more fundamental reason why Baudrillard should be considered a critical theorist. In fifteen years, since his first sociological publications, which were a review of McLuhan's *Understanding Media*[6] and his own *Le système des objets*, Baudrillard has not written a single thing which was not an attempt to elaborate a theory of reification à la Lukács, Horkheimer, Adorno, Marcuse — with a strong dose of Benjamin. The theory of reification is of course a story about a struggle between subjects and objects in which objects appear, if only temporarily, to have gained the upper hand. Broadly, a theory of reification is not only a theory of misplaced concreteness or of false objectivity (which implies a false subjectivity, of course); it goes further and claims that when objects are misunderstood in this way, they return to haunt the subject and spoil his whole experience. The theory of reification which Baudrillard works with has definite roots which go all the way back to Georg Lukacs and Karl Marx. Like Lukacs' important work, all of Baudrillard's work is a meditation on Marx's theory of commodity fetishism. This makes Baudrillard a critical theorist. There is nothing more essential to cultural Marxism than the theory of reification, which at root is always based on the idea that the structure of the commodity is in some way the abstract essence of capitalist life. If in his later work Baudrillard seems to part more and more with the rationality of critical theory and its interest in the emancipation of subjects, I think it is because his theory has developed gradually into something quite different from the traditional critical theory of reification: it has turned into what Baudrillard now calls "simulation". But this is still a theory of reification.

In order to explain this development, it is useful to return to Baudrillard's very clear analysis in *Critique of the Political Economy of the Sign*.[7] The argument is quite complex, and it depends first of all on a reading of Marx's theory of commodity fetishism.

Marx argued that objects (i.e., produced goods, or use values) are turned into commodities when they acquire through a complicated socio-historical development the additional characteristic of exchange value. Apart from the details which make this development specifically capitalist, one can say that, in Marx, to the extent that objects seem to become pure exchange values, they enter into a system, the commodity system, which appears to act independently of their producers and consumers. The origin of objects in labour and their purpose in satisfying needs tend to be obscured from public view. This is the argument that Lukacs elaborated into the theory of reification.[8] It claims that this false and borrowed power of objects can operate on three and perhaps even four levels: 1) the socio-economic; 2) the epistemological; 3) the practical; and 4) sometimes also the erotic.

Through the lens of critical theory, Marx can be read as having said or nearly having said: 1) that social beings are deprived of their social ground by a process of *extraction*, which robs them of economic power; 2) that they are thereby also

172

deprived of their (social) knowledge by a process of *abstraction* which is induced by the systematic and objectivistic quality of exchange value; 3) having been economically reduced and cognitively seduced, people begin to forget how to respond: they can no longer act or reciprocate. They can only react to what is "given", as if what is given were an intractable "second nature".[9] And finally, 4) we might add, following the arguments of many critical theorists, that there is a fourth dimension to the effects of reification — the one that I have described as erotic. Social beings not only tend to lose their power to be, to perceive and to act: reification also neutralizes or restricts or damages their ability to fantasize, which lies at the very root of everybody's ability to think.

Of course, this last dimension owes something to Freud. All told, reification amounts to a very serious charge to make against anybody, let alone a whole society. It means that commodity fetishism — or if you like, falsely perceived objects — are such a powerful force that they penetrate deeply enough into the lives of individual subjects to control their inner worlds. It sound like a paranoid fantasy, like something Judge Schreber might have thought up.

Now there are two things about this theory of reification that are important to note. The first is that it is hard to imagine how critical theory could ever do without it, for the notion that the commodity form somehow congeals all the bad contingencies of an historical era is fundamental. How can critical theory continue to be critical in the absence of some such hypothesis? The second is that it is hard to imagine how the theory of reification could possibly be true.

Now, these questions have been raised in a way that is obviously slanted for the purpose of discussion Baudrillard's work. Some detail may be distorted, but the underlying issues are fundamental, and Baudrillard has responded to them in a highly original way which is still coherent with the critical tradition. Equipped with the theoretical language of structuralism and some insights from French writers such as Bataille and Foucault, Baudrillard waded into some very deep water indeed in the mid 1970's, and he took critical theory along with him.[10] There was something quite innocent about this at the beginning. In his 1967 review of McLuhan, he said that when you generalize the slogan "the medium is the message" you have the "very formula of alienation in a technical society". He was interested in looking at the commodity as a medium of social values and as a model of public discourse. The idea was very simple.

All that Baudrillard did, in fact, was to point out that the object becomes a commodity not only by virtue of being an exchange value, to be measured and exchanged against other exchange values; the object is also and especially a commodity *because it is a sign*.[11] (This seems so obvious to many of us now that perhaps it should be disputed in order to make the whole discussion more interesting.) It means of course that the commodity is a signifier and a signified, with all the features of abstraction, reduction, equivalence, discreteness and interchangeability implied in the Saussurean theory of the sign. A commodity is not just an exchange value which obscures its origin in labour as an object of, by and for utility; it is an object which has been inserted as an arbitrary term into a purely self-referential system of signifiers which decides the object's meaning before anyone can possess it or consume it or give it away. The commodity is an object in a system of objects; it is consumed as a sign of that system.

Baudrillard calls this phenomenon the "sign-object". He replaces Marx's notion of the commodity form (which is a social form tending to obscure the object's content) with the idea of an "object-form". This object form is also a social form, like Marx's commodity, but it has much deeper implications. What it "veils in mystery" is not the object's real value: *its* origin in labour and its finality in the moment of consumption — i.e., its use value. What the object form conceals is the object's own "nullity". The commodity is a *res nulla*: a *symbolic* absence. Or to put it another way, the object form (the commodity as sign) exhausts and evacuates the social space it occupies. It hides the fact that its meaning does not exist in a relationship between people (what Baudrillard would call Symbolic Exchange), but in the inner relations of signs and commodities among themselves.[12]

As a structural model of reification, this "object-form" is a much more radical hypothesis. It cuts deeper and gets to the 'real' sub-stratum of the social object: its use value. With the logic of signification as his tool, Baudrillard pries apart the bundle of relations which constitute the commodity, only to discover that use value does not designate the otherness of political economy at all, but its ideological groundwork. For included in the object form is precisely the assumed functionality and utility of commodities that Marx had wanted to restore to society by liberating the means of production and abolishing exchange value. According to Baudrillard, use value is simply a product of the alienated system of exchange itself. It is not the meaning of the object, anymore than the signified is the meaning of the sign; it is the effect of the play of signifiers. To use a phrase of Adorno, use value is not the "non-identical side" of the object; it is not a moment of particularity or of quality, such as might be found outside the form in the 'real' act of "consumption". Perhaps this explains the somewhat strained atmosphere of the Frankfurt School's attempts to explain the fetishization of culture in terms of exchange value.[13] For use value turns out to be an alibi for the exchange value system, rather than its hidden or repressed truth. It does not escape the logic of reduction, equivalence and fungibility imposed by political economy. On the contrary, it *is* political economy — its ideal and ideological referent.[14]

The consequence of this argument, of course, is gradually to shift the stance of traditional critical theory away from anti-objectivism to an intensified critique of naturalism. Eventually Baudrillard will carry this forward from the naturalism of Political Economy and Marx's critique of it to the functionalism of the Bauhaus, to the naturalism of the unconscious in various schools of thought, from Surrealism on to Deleuze, and finally to the "hyper-reality" (as Baudrillard calls it) of constituted self-regulating systems, which range from the naturalization of coded difference in molecular biology (DNA) to the cybernetic design of social life itself.[15]

But the critique of the political economy of the sign remains the centrepiece of Baudrillard's work. One cannot read his earlier books on objects and consumption without anticipating this re-evaluation of all socio-economic values. The new model of reification that emerges transforms the whole problematic of the commodity, which has been the core of critical theory and cultural Marxism since Lukács. And all of Baudrillard's subsequent work flows from this conceptual realignment. The key to it, of course, was to read semiology right into the process of political economy, to find the logic of signification in the very structure of the commodity. What is important to grasp, however, is that this is not just another synthesis. There have been plenty of attempts to combine Marx and Freud. Baudrillard's inspiration was different. He wanted to use structuralist theory as the mimetic description language of reification as such. In Baudrillard, the Saussurean model of language really *becomes* the *action* language of the commodity; and the apparent self-sufficiency of the structuralist model of the sign delineates for him the form of reification as a social phenomenon. An interesting consequence of this in the later books, beginning with *L'Échange symbolique et la mort*, is that the equation *commodity = sign = reification* evolves with the internal transformations of the theory of the sign. As semiology begins to devour its own tail in post-structuralist discourse and in the work of Derrida in particular, the theoretical description language of structuralist discourse is no longer projected into the commodity, but hypothetically reembodied as the pure medium of reification, so that the opaque involutions of theoretical language come to serve as the perfectly transparent and unwitting surface of social reality.[16] Baudrillard calls this involution, "simulation", which is nothing other than reification as total semiosis, which now includes the body — or corpse — of social theory itself.

II

If the cutting edge of this conceptual reconfiguration is Baudrillard's attempt to introduce the question of meaning to Marxian discourse, this does not mean that he is able to tell us so much about the nature of social life today that we might not already have guessed. For this cutting edge is turned almost completely inwards, toward critical theory. Looking through the closing pages of *Le système des objets* or *La société de consommation*, the early works, we already find a host of disclaimers which testify, sometimes in a brilliant way, to the profound moment of self-doubt in the act of critique. What is relatively new in Baudrillard is the recognition that this moment of doubt redeems the recalcitrant object, and that there is no salvation without the object. The analysis of consumption *begs* the question of interpretation; it forces critical theory up against the consequences: it's interpretation or die. Échange symbolique or la Mort.

The fact that critical theory has systematically avoided this question is nowhere more obvious than in the traditional theory of reification, or more precisely, in the doctrine of commodity fetishism, which underlies all of critical theory's and cultural Marxism's vision of the modern age. Marx was never interested in the interpretation of commodities. He was concerned with their "historical character", but not with their "meaning", which he dismissed as an illusion in the early chapters of *Capital*.[17] We can hardly blame Marx for not being attracted to the problem, but it is difficult to forgive the Frankfurt School, which professed to be concerned with culture. For what they fail to achieve, on the whole, is any charitable understanding of the role of things in the lives of people. Instead, the standard discourse of critical theory is laced with old Christian sentiments about people destroying their souls by worshipping powers they do not understand because they have projected them onto material objects. This is another way of saying that people are worshipping a false god, a graven image. Adorno was something of an exception to this at the theoritical level, but he was just as intolerant in practice. He described jazz enthusiasts as "temple slaves" prostrating themselves "before the theological caprices of commodities". He described people going to a Toscanini concert as worshipping the money they had spent on the ticket. This is the theory of commodity fetishism. It is part of a kind of religious or moral controversy, a sort of monotheistic attack on animism.

When critical theory is at its worst, what it wants, what it strives for, is a world without objects. The projected ideal is a kingdom of ends, the end of mediation. There is nothing outside absolute spirit anyway. It does not interpret; it decrees. The traditional theory of reification implies that so long as the totality remains inaccessible in its totality to the subject, the subject has been deprived of its essence. It is a vision of social reality which tends to equate emancipation with omnipotence.

Interpretation is impossible for critical theory during these bad theoretical moments because it does not approve of people endowing objects with magical properties, or projecting human qualities onto the world of things. Instead, they are expected to exercise magical control over objects. This is written directly into the theory of commodity fetishism. Objects can only have use value; everything else is mystification. As soon as people attach meaning to things, they plummet into false consciousness. The end of reification would amount to rational knowledge of the totality. People would have totally transparent relations with each other, either because there would be no objects to get in the way, or because objects would only exist insofar as they were rationally distributed according to need (presumably from a centre), or because they are only objects of disinterested aesthetic reflection, a type of relationship to an object which presumably does no harm to the spirit. This is why Marx must have preferred capitalism to feudalism: it was more rational, it made the real social relations clearer, there was less meaning to cloud the vision.[19] On this view, commodity fetishism is simply a residue of the old barbaric consciousness. The commodity ellicits a sort of social projection which disguises the real relations underpinning it. The object hides social reality. It must be eliminated.

Baudrillard's critique of the sign tries to cut through all this metaphysics. Reification ceases to be a mystical veil, a trick of consciousness, an alienation of the subject's power, the robbery of an essence, or a primitive projection based on ignorance. Instead it is a positive presence in its own right. It is physical and it is organized in a describable way. It doesn't hide social relations; if anything, it is a tendency to prevent them from occuring. The self-sufficient object demands a self-sufficient subject. This autonomization and social isolation is achieved through what Baudrillard calls the "semiological reduction", which erodes the possibility of symbolic exchange. Where the commodity is, there the subject shall not be. But this is not the same as Marxian fetishism. It is the opposite, for the problem with the commodity as a systemic object is not, according to Baudrillard, that people attach emotional importance to it, but precisely that they cannot, because the commodity is already a sign. The logic of signification is no longer something to be ignored because it is a superstructural aspect of things which conceals a more profound economic logic, as critical theory once believed; the logic of signification lies, as Baudrillard writes, at the "very heart of the commodity". And because the sign-object is systemic, it comes with its play of meanings already coded. So the problem of reification, at least at the cultural level, is not that people have projected their powers onto things, but rather that objects have become increasingly closed off from human interaction in their systematic self-referential play. People probably have an incorrigible tendency to "fetishize" objects anyway; but the logic of signification blocks even this symbolic relation, and invites people to fetishize *systems* of relationship which are abstract and without much personal significance. This, I believe, is what Baudrillard means by the paradox that consumption has turned into a "system of interpretation" without meaning.[20] There is no meaning because there is no symbolic exchange. The symbolic is always about the potentiality of a relationship. The semiurgy of social objects reduces the availability of things for mediating social relations (symbolic exchange) and assigns them to mediating systems of signs instead. If commodity fetishism exists, it is because in our culture the object has become too rational: commodities come pre-fetishized.

III

Traditional critical theory has tended to parody the pattern of reification that Baudrillard describes to the extent that it holds out the vague promise of returning to a world of simple objects administered by simple subjects. But there can be no such world. In the sphere of culture, objects are never objective — but then they are usually not subjective either: they are neither neutral or natural facts nor hallucinations. This is even true for the real fetishist. For the interesting thing about a fetish, presumably, is that it is never clear what it is — whether it is really an object or whether it is part of the self. A fetish is probably undecidable, and for this reason, it can be thought of as existing in a free space between the subject and the object. But for the fetishist, this space is charged with an extraordinary amount of tension. The fetishist cannot tolerate his object's ambiguity, and wants to resolve it. What might have been a symbol, the symbol of a connection, has turned into a curse of sorts. The fetishist is like a lover who doesn't have a lover and therefore, in a sense, cannot have an object either. He cannot share his failed desire to merge with his lover with his lover's failed desire to merge with him. He is alone with a thing that is not a thing — neither an other nor himself. He cannot wholly possess it because it is not self and he cannot abandon it because it is not other. The space between the subject and object where the fetish object oscillates so painfully is simply too dangerous. he wants somehow to close this space, but he cannot, because neither subjectivity nor reification are ever complete except in the moment of suicide.

The new model of reification changes our view of the subject. The subject is no longer a theory-praxis construct whose perception is clouded by the trickery of things. The subject is now an ambivalent psychological being whose space for living is gradually being closed off. Another way of saying this is that the subject cannot be, and has not been, strictly demarcated from the object — découpé. The realm of freedom cannot be abstracted from and separated from the realm of necessity, except as a sign — but this sign happens to be the ultimate illusory referent of the industrialized world, capitalist and communist. On this question, the only difference between the great blocks of political economy lies in their theories of distribution: the bureaucratic version is quite a bit more obsessive about controlling objects in the name of freedom.

The subject and the object cannot finally be distinguished. They overflow into the ambiguous space that exists between them, where people actually live, and things have meaning. This is where culture takes place. It cannot be wished away. It cannot be completely destroyed in a whole society, even by reification. It can only be more or less restricted, attenuated, under threat. We have lived in this ambiguous space ever since we were children, and we will never succeed in completely sorting it out into the categories of what is properly subject and what is object, or of what we actually made or thought up and what we simply found by luck or accident. Critical theory demands of us an impossible and debilitating maturity. We rationalize the ambiguous space as much as we can and as much as we have to, but we never do away with it because then we would not be able to live, we would have no where to play. This is what Baudrillard originally meant by symbolic exchange, and what he meant when he argued that the logic of the sign eradicates the social symbolic. (I cannot find any other meaning for it.) So reification ceases to be anything like the object's stolen powers returning to haunt the subject, and becomes more like the relative closure of a psychosocial space where, to borrow another phrase of Adorno, we might live in "harmony with the object", and with our own ambivalence.

The psychoanalyst Winnicott called this intermediate area "potential space" — it is where the transitional object exists for the child, between the more or less "me" and the more or less "not me". The transitional object is not an elimination of difference. It just leaves the paradox unresolved.[21] "This potential space is at the interplay between there being nothing but me and there being objects and phenomena outside omnipotent control".[22] The child is not challenged as to the logic of the situation. It is not expected to decide whether it really conceived this thing, or whether it just found a trivial piece of the objective world that it suspects it cannot control. The child is allowed to have its intense symbolic experience. Nobody tries to define the object. Nobody tells the child, "that's just your imagination", or "that's just a bit of dirty old stuffed cloth". The child is allowed to play.

The tragedy of critical theory is that it has never been able to theorize this potential, transitional, symbolic space, although it has always been concerned with it. Critical theory expects so much from the subject that it can only explain away the damage by attributing fantastic, demonic power to the object. It leaves nothing human in between. There is no possible resolution but the destruction of one or the other: the death of the subject or the nihilating absorption of the object.[23] It is ironic that it was the greatest of critical theorists, Theodor Adorno, who presented these abstract alternatives to us most forcefully; and yet it was also he who grasped the life-saving compromise in the "nonidentical side of the object". The nonidentical side of the object, or symbolic exchange or the potential space of the transitional object are all names for a possibility which must be kept open, and opened further if reification is to be defeated.

Let me suggest, briefly, an extension of this thesis. The term potential space implies that there is a dynamic gap between the two relative poles that Winnicott — but also Habermas — call the subjective world and shared objective reality — or, in Habermas' terms, the "inner, private world" and the "outer, public world". My additional reflection is that this intermediate dimension, the world which grows out of the transitional object, has to be enriched and expanded *before* any idea of a publicly shared objective world such as Habermas envisions can be constituted in a genuine and healthy way. This is a crucial issue for cultural politics because there can be no "ideal (public) speech situation" without a foundation that openly and honestly embodies the pre-logical, symbolic root of action, relationship and meaning. Reification is ultimately nothing more than a betrayal or denial of this social symbolic root — which is why structuralist formalism makes such a good model of reified culture.[24]

The main battle among critical theories and cultural Marxisms today seems to be over the definition of this potential space. French theory has occupied it and called valuable attention to it. My criticism of the New French Thought is simply that in having called attention to intermediate areas of social experience, it has had a tendency to autonomize them as unbounded media (without subject and object), as pure media where signs literally devour their own meaning. So what I have been calling transitional space and what Baudrillard used to call symbolic exchange, Foucault now calls power, Deleuze and Lacan call desire, Derrida calls text and Baudrillard calls simulacrum. There is little effort in these trajectories to recover the constructive potential of the pre-logical symbolic dimension of experience. There is alternatively a tendency to stress the equivalence of three all-embracing terms: power = totality = irrationality, full stop. Foucault and Baudrillard and Derrida ultimately fail to solve the problems of critique because they reproduce, in their autonomous theoretical models of "power" and "text" what Baudrillard had originally described as the "very formula of alienation in a technical society" — The Medium is the Message. Instead of articulating an alternative, they reembody the old Hegelian theory of reification they attack.

The problem with Baudrillard's later work — the books that follow the *Critique of the Political Economy of the Sign* and *The Mirror of Production* — is that what began as a critique of naturalistic categories has grown steadily into an obsession, a kind of desire to expunge nature itself, or more precisely, to convert it into an enormous and meaningless cycle of collapsing culture. Baudrillard's simulation is just another word for reification; it is a type of reification bearing no reference to any subject or object, without any counterpraxis. The consequence is that theory — even critical theory — is always faltering behind: it can only mirror what passes it by, with the same aimlessness of simulation itself. Simulation means the death of play in the total omnipresence of play. Baudrillard has autonomized the intermediate area and gotten lost in it, forgetting the virtual difference between the me and the not me which structures human play. He has turned culture inside out and made it a natural process. Play has become simply the function of the universe. And so you have the French Ideology, and Jacques Derrida. Against this catastrophe, Baudrillard has only one strategy left: symbolic exchange, which finding that it can no longer define itself in opposition to the sign, abandons exchange for absolute irreversible reversibility in death; in other words, nihilism.

Baudrillard's argument that reification is not false consciousness but the systematic closure of autotelic signifying systems probably leads fairly inevitably to this nihilism. But it is still an interesting argument because it forces critical theory to begin theorizing the area of transitional phenomena. Whether it is the commodity alone which produces the social effect of reified constriction or whether the commodity has only been the most convenient theme for a critical hermeneutic is another question. There is no inherent reason why the problem of reification should be posed exclusively in terms of consumption. The point of Baudrillard's argument is that we feel not so much mystified by the commodity as excluded by it. We feel excluded from the sign object in much the same way that we feel excluded from (and even hostile toward) a closed group with its exclusively internal system of reference. We tend to get lost in such systems, however, because we feel we have no choice: we have to have objects, partly because we have to have meaning, and sometimes we will take whatever we can get, even though nowadays we often don't expect it to be very significant.

IV

The intention of this paper can be summarized in a slightly different set of terms.

Critical theory has tended to skirt around the issue of interpretation. There are plenty of exceptions, work that comes out of Benjamin for example, but on the whole this at least has been my experience of critical discourse. What this means in knowledge terms is that critical theory won't come to grips with the fact of uncertainty. Hence the tremendous reluctance, until recently, to open up Marx's categories for cultural interpretation.

POWER AND SEDUCTION

In psychoanalytic terms, interpretation probably means learning how to live with oneself after one has tried to destroy the object. We all try to destroy the object, even if only in fantasy. The wisdom of Melanie Klein and others is that if the object survives our bitter attack, then we can not only love the object, but learn to use it as well. But before we can achieve all this, we have to grant the object just enough independent existence so that the possibility of its loss is real, and we can learn to mourn this possible loss.[25]

True, this means a kind of depression. But depression is not so bad — if we have the courage to repair the damage it was caused by. After all, we ourselves have already imagined this destruction, perhaps willed it, without realizing what we were doing. The very idea of our own destructive potential makes us paranoid, because we didn't know what it meant until we had tried it. But if we can be so violent without meaning it, then so can others, even when they don't mean it. This is the essence of paranoid thinking: they're out to get me, even though I know they aren't.

Depression is much less catastrophic, though it is very painful. Recent critical theory is a case in point. Think of the titles: Negative Dialectics . . . The Tragedy of Enlightenment . . . The Dialectic of Defeat . . . The Critical Twilight . . . L'échange symbolique et la mort . . . La Stratégie fatale. It all sounds depressed. But this is probably a healthy depression, a reparative one, perhaps a depression that will lead critical theory to shift its attention away from all the bad things it wants to get rid of in the world, and onto the new things it wants to put into it. This is not just a therapeutic suggestion, it is a tactical necessity, because certain things will never go away completely, they can only be crowded out by something better. Pornography is an excellent example.

Critical Theory must try to find ways to open up transitional areas of experience, so that we can all breathe more freely. And so that eventually paternalistic systems will not be able to trap us with the impossible decision whether we made our own lives and language, or whether we just found them or got them from somebody else and owe them back. But Critical Theory won't achieve this level of creativity until it admits it is (metaphysically?) depressed — because only then will it have the impulse to repair the damage.

Adorno probably understood this. He was so impressed by his own violence as he saw it mirrored in the violence around him that he wanted all of us to get down off our "royal thrones" and commune with the object. But Adorno couldn't translate this theoretical understanding into practice. Neither have we — though in certain ways as a generation we may have begun in the 1960's, with the counterculture, and feminism. At any rate, Adorno was probably too old, and reluctant to give up his rage.

The possibility of any future practice, and the key to interesting interpretations, will depend on our realization that objects are never simply there to be used in the way we merely choose — for in the last, depth-psychological analysis, they always represent another person, and the idea of a relationship with another person.

Appendix: Theses on Critical Theory

I

After Marx, Freud revived the whole idea of bad animal nature as a kind of psychic myth, and resurrected evil as the political problem of human self-definition in history. Marx was right to have concentrated his attention on social relations instead, but Freud's regression was also very fruitful: in the end, he saved the imagination. After Freud, bad animal nature could be construed even more fundamentally as 'bad' relations between internal objects and their split-off, repressed ego counterparts. This does not mean, as a Marxist would say, that bad social relations are simply "reproduced" in the individual. Although bad animal nature is certainly a kind of myth, a hypostatization of bad relations in history, the ego defenses are quite real.

Sometimes the "bad object" has to be taken inside if the possibility of future love and pleasure is to be preserved somewhere in the imagination. We blame ourselves to save others and their love; and then we blame others to save ourselves. In all this effort to control and eliminate pain, love can wither. This is a tragedy that Marx overlooked.

The ego defenses are part of the distinctive organization and energy of psychic reality. They are not 'created' by bad relations, they are provoked, nurtured, encrusted, moulded — and they are powerful in their own right. At relatively crude levels, the form and perhaps even the content of social life are recognizably those of the ego defenses, and this is especially true during early emotional maturation. They are catalyzed prefigurations of human relations, and psychoanalysis is very little or nothing at all if they cannot ultimately be distinguished from the behaviourist thesis.

II

Critical theory should be more playful.

The inner world is fantastic. It is already in formation before cognition and emotion are prepared to join intelligently with the environment. The inner world, or psychic reality, is composed not of impulses or "instincts", but of internalized relations, which are not easily changed. Very early on in this inner world, there are at least good and bad. Neither the good nor the bad can develop into anything real or reasonable in life if they are not allowed to play. But the fantastic opposition of the good and the bad can generate so much anxiety that play seems impossible.

III

Critical theory is insufficiently fantastic.

Fantasy is thought and action before the imagination and the world have mutually adapted. Melanie Klein, following Freud, linked fantasy and play, and then demonstrated an inverse relationship between fantasy and anxiety. The more of one, the less of the other. But the relationship is not balanced. An inhibition in play is a sign of anxious rigidity; but it is never clear how one reverses the alignment in favour of fantasy and play: why elaborate a fantasy that provokes anxiety? Perhaps it will come true?

182

POWER AND SEDUCTION

In this way, psychoanalysis restores the imagination to the life of the body politic — but at the price of its *de*-idealization.

IV

Freedom can increase.

There is no longer much reason to doubt that early experience (which is thankfully still beyond direct social control) is decisive in the formation of a reactive self governed by a compliant ego — or in the formation of its alternative, an active self centred on a critical ego. The problem is that where the alternative is not well-grounded in psychic reality, it is difficult to choose it (often for the best of reasons). Yet Sartre was probably right that the alternative is still a real choice. It is even a kind of choice in a deathcamp. Still, pure expressions of freedom, however modest, are very hard to reconcile with the continuities of psychic and social reality. The therapeutic lesson of psycho-analysis has been from the beginning that every recognition or understanding of determinism implies an act or experience of freedom and vice versa. There is no necessity to determinism, but it is necessary to be determined to be free.

V

Critical theory is generated within a very narrow band of human experience; it doesn't create enough space for itself.

An unusual environment is required if the active, wanting, willing tendencies of a baby are to be reconciled with the emotional challenge of separation and individuation. In the absence of such a tender environment, action, wanting and willing are likely to be split-off and hidden away, remaining for ever infantile and sorely helpless.

Nobody outlives the pleasure of being alone, yet still in the safe presence of the (m)other, once they have had it. We are always in transition and we always create some kind of "space" for this process. It cannot be played out.

VI

The fragility of the potential space between the subject and the object can be so attenuated in life that play becomes a desperate effort to sustain the meaning of a few hardened symbols which are easily coerced and harnessed. The space in which the unity of earlier and later experience is preserved as the growing fund of the self's life in the world and the psyche's life on the planet can be overrun by the conquering drive of subject or object, or collapsed in pathological identity, omnipotent fusion, and the logic of defensive control, none of which ever outlast what they destroy. Critical theory should be much more aware of all this.

VII

On the other hand, the unusually tender environment which fosters the growth of the active self is precisely what makes the prospect of separation and indivuation so painful. It is very hard to learn to create this environment for oneself, and harder for society. A certain amount of "aggression" is needed on all sides if the process is to be carried through — a fact observable in mammals generally. But the human psyche is initially so adaptive and responsive and innately intricate in potential that its birth is never easily achieved. "Nature" has refined a process of specialized differentiation to the point where not only its meaning but its substance are astonishingly symbolic.

The price of intelligence is probably symbolism which thrives on indefinition which reflects difficulty but the higher forms of pleasure too.

VIII

Critical theory has made a great deal of fuss about (what should be called) *secondary* adaptation — as if this is some sort of recognition of psychoanalytic truth. Over and over again, we hear that the individual is "produced" by the culture. In the same breath, psychoanalysis is dismissed as conformist because its theme is the adaptive growth of the individual. Critique is cheap when it ignores or laughs at the needs and strategies of the child. Human beings are always dependent — either in an infantile or a nature way — but dependent nevertheless.

IX

Coercion can be brutally external and social but its conditions of possibility are usually laid down in subtler ways. To achieve a genuine integration of psychoanalytic insight, critical theory must see how primary psychological adaptions are not always in detail directly concerned with the culture at large: they are not political decisions, they are obscure movements within the immediate psychic environment in a context of infantile dependency. Such awareness would weaken the grandiose illusion that critical dialetic can so easily penetrate the social veil; but it would strengthen understanding immeasurably.

X

Nature is perfectly capable of pathology, which is contained grossly in the painful difficulty of choice. Choosing and symbolizing are perfectly natural — we only pretend that they are opposed to nature because we forget that choosing is living, symbols are breathing, and neither choice nor symbol flicks on and off in dimensionless moments of pure rationality and morality. Nature can decide itself, but it often does so in painful and difficult ways, and a lot of this is localized in us. Being human is like being told that the result depends on you but fie on you if you think you know what the process is.

As painful, difficult, deciding parts of the universe, we need mediations. For this reason, critical theory should pay a great deal more attention to the symbolic and to the pressures and limits of the symbolic because it is at this deep level that we actually play out the limits of nature. We create the mediations we need ourselves and we are responsible for the quality of the mediations we create. Or to put it another way, we are almost entirely symbolic in our difference, but this is a responsibility rather than a transcendence: symbols are natural beings.

XI

We should not be overly ashamed of our feeble-mindedness with regard to the Symbolic, however. Critical theory continues to elaborate its fantasy without imagining too seriously that it can ever bring the Symbolic to heel. That is probably a good thing, for the exciting alternative is only an illusion: the illusion of Power, the hallucination of the elimination of the object — all in the name of personal or collective transcendence. People are liable to call for the end of the object (which might be another person) because as everybody knows it is so easy for us to project the unwanted onto the object. But not only can nature not be transcended, it cannot even be tricked. Obsessional control, paranoid vigilance, schizoid detachment, psychotic misery — all are relatively useless paralyses of human fantasy.

The bad object has its place; it may be the loser, but it never ceases to exist as a possibility which must be accounted for in the existence of the good object. If prolonged, splitting, perhaps the most basic form of control, destroys the mediating power of symbolization. This is why potential space cannot easily be divided up in a worthwhile way. The bad, after all, is every bit as symbolic as the good.

Montréal

Notes

1. This is a slightly altered version of a paper delivered at the CJPST's "1983 Theory Workshops" University of British Columbia, Learned Societies, June, 1983.

2. The trend away from classical mechanistic atomism in psychoanalytic theory has been developing in Britain since the 1930's in a variety of quite different ways which have been grouped together under the heading "Object-Relations Theory." The object-relations theorists include, notably: Melanie Klein, Joan Rivière, and Hanna Segal (all of whom have never been able to give up the idea of a "death-instinct"); W.R.D. Fairbairn and Harry Guntrip (theoretically the most coherent group); and D.W. Winnicott and Marion Milner.
    The term "Object-relations theory" can be extended to include the work of some American psychoanalysts, such as Edith Jacobson and Otto Kernberg, and more remotely, the late Heinz Kohut. But this important American work has been hampered by clinging to dubious orthodoxies such as "primary narcissism" and "narcissistic libido."
    A prominent Canadian member of the British school is W. Clifford M. Scott, in Montreal.
    It is difficult to summarize briefly the object-relations point of view. It involves a clinically-inspired shift away from concern with instinctual development and management to an exploration of the emotional layerings of emerging ego-object structures. The potential ego is no longer viewed as inherently the "servant of three masters" — the somewhat schizoid defense centre of classical Freudian theory. Very often, however, so much of the ego is split off or repressed during development that a detached, reactive surface structure is all that remains of the outwardly functioning personality.
    (Some reflections on critical theory from an object-relations point of view are sketched in the Appendix to this article.)

3. The fundamental anxiety which underlies this ever-collapsing distinction is discussed from a psychoanalytic and ecological point of view by Harold F. Searles in *The Nonhuman Environment* (New York: International Universities Press, 1960).

4. Jean Baudrillard, *L'échange symbolique et la mort* (Paris: Gallimard, 1976).

5. In *Le système des objets* (Paris: Denoel-Gonthier, 1968) and *La société de consommation* (Paris: Gallimard, 1970).

6. "Compte Rendu de Marshall MacLuhan (sic): *Understanding Media: The Extensions of Man,"* *L'Homme et la société,* no. 5 (1967), p. 230.

7. *For a Critique of the Political Economy of the Sign,* trans. and introd. Charles Levin (St. Louis: Telos Press, 1981).

8. One can see how this is rather like an historicized reading of Kant's thing-in-itself problem. For interesting discussions on this theme, see, among other works of Theodor W. Adorno: "The Actuality of Philosophy," *Telos,* no. 31 (1977), p. 128; *Negative Dialectics,* trans. E.B. Ashton (New York: Seabury Press, 1973), Part 111; and "Subject and Object," in *The Essential Frankfurt School Reader,* ed. and introd. Andrew Arato and Eike Gebhardt (New York: Urizen Books, 1978), passim.

9. The deep inner connection between this short-circuiting of social communication and the structure of the commodity is analysed by Baudrillard in *For a Critique of the Political Economy of the Sign,* Ch. 8.

10. I am referring to the fact that since *L'échange symbolique et la mort,* Baudrillard has made a nonsense of critical theory as it is understood by most of its practitioners, especially the followers of Habermas.

11. For Baudrillard, the rise of the commodity coincides historically with the passage from symbolic to semiological societies. The recent development is not the rise of the sign (consumerism), but the collapse of the rationality of signification, which has shifted the problem of the social object away from the commodity and onto simulated totalities.

12. It should be pointed out that this argument by itself does not commit Baudrillard to radical indeterminism. On the contrary, his argument seems to be, not that there is no longer any referentiality in neo-capitalist culture, but that there is altogether too much of it: reference is no longer an *act;* it is something received in combinatory forms.

13. See, for example, Theodor Adorno and Max Horkheimer, *Dialectics of Enlightenment,* trans. John Cumming (New York: Seabury Press, 1969), p. 158.

14. See the article, "Beyond Use Value" in *For a Critique of the Political Economy of the Sign.*

15. See "Design and Environment," in *For a Critique; L'échange symbolique et la mort* and all subsequent works by Baudrillard.

16. See *L'échange symbolique et la mort,* where Baudrillard's expressions of utter despair at the involution of post-modern social life can be read as brilliant parodic critiques of Derrida, Deleuze, Barthes, Foucault and Kristeva. Baudrillard's *Oublier Foucault* (Paris: Éditions Galilée, 1977) is perhaps the best example of his technique of dilating a mimetic theoretical description language.

17. Karl Marx, *Capital,* 1, trans. Samuel Moore and Richard Aveling, ed., Frederick Engels (New York: International Publishers, 1967), p. 75.

18. Theodor Adorno, "On the Fetish-Character in Music and the Regression of Listening," in *The Essential Frankfurt School Reader, pp. 278-279.*

19. See any edition of the *Communist Manifesto* or Karl Marx, *Grundrisse: Foundations of the Critique of Political Economy (Rough Draft),* trans. Martin Nicolaus (Harmondsworth: Penguin, 1973), passim.

20. Jean Baudrillard, *La société de consommation* (Paris: Gallimard, 1970), passim; and "The Ideological Genesis of Needs," in *For a Critique.*

21. "I am drawing attention to the *paradox* involved in the use by the infant of what I have called the transitional object. My contribution is to ask for a paradox to be accepted and tolerated and respected, and for it not to be resolved (by) flight to split-off intellectual functioning..." D.W. Winnicott, *Playing and Reality* (Harmondsworth: Pelican, 1971), p. xii.

22. Winnicott, p. 118.

23. "Once radically parted from the object, the subject reduces it to its own measure; the subject swallows the object, forgetting how much it is an object itself." Theodor Adorno, "Subject and Object," *The Essential Frankfurt School Reader*, p. 499. Congealed fantasies of devouring the other or of being devoured by the other are of course often discovered at the roots of persecurory anxiety and guilty thinking.

24. See my "Introduction to Baudrillard" in John Fekete, ed., *The Structural Allegory* (Minneapolis: University of Minnesota Press, forthcoming).

25. Winnicott, "The Use of an Object and Relating through Identifications," in *Playing and Reality,* pp. 101-111. For the Kleinian point of view, see Hanna Segal, 'Notes on Symbol-Formation," *International Journal of Psychoanalysis*, vol. 38 (1957), pp. 391-397.

26. These reflections owe something to a midsummer night's conversation with John Fekete on Prince Edward Island.

III

DEMON POLITICS

HOBBES AND/OR NORTH:
THE RHETORIC OF AMERICAN
NATIONAL SECURITY

Frederick M. Dolan

Manhattoes, Eric Fischl
Mary Boone Gallery

Thus Satan, talking to his nearest mate,
With head uplift above the wave and eyes
That sparkling blazed; his other parts besides
Prone on the flood, extended long and large,
Lay floating may a rood, in bulk as huge
As whom the fables name of monstrous size,
Titanian or Earth-born, that warred on Jove,
Briareos or Typhon, whom the den
By ancient Tarsus held, or that sea-beast
Leviathan, which God of all his works
Created hugest that swim the ocean-stream.
Him, haply slumbering on the Norway foam,
The pilot of some small night-foundered skiff
Deeming some island, oft, as seamen tell,
With fixed anchor in his scaly rind,
Moors by his side under the lee, while night
Invests the sea, and wished morn delays.

— Milton, *Paradise Lost*, I

1

Paradise Lost, completed little more than a decade after the publication of Thomas Hobbes's *Leviathan* (1651), reasserts the sea-beast's sinful deceptiveness. For Hobbes, the dissolution of the metaphysical underpinnings of rule by divine right occasioned the construction of an "Artificiall Man . . . of greater stature and strength than the Naturall . . . ."[1]

Although the breakup of the *ancien régime* appeared to cast man out of his Christian, eschatological "paradise" and into a world bereft of sure moorings, man might build a landing of his own, if only he rid himself of the scholastic fantasies that kept him ignorant of his powers as a God-like *artificer. Leviathan* performs this task in part by ironically inverting the story of Genesis: Eden, in Hobbes's optic, is the harsh and unruly state of nature, of which to be cast out is a blessing; and "that sea — beast/Leviathan," classic symbol of Satan, becomes man's true and only Savior. In Milton's epic, the shifting, unreliable leviathan is mistaken for "some island" — literally *land*, or a *ground* — to which a sailor adrift might anchor himself, escaping the turbulent winds and the dangers of the night. Man's attempt to anchor himself in the ground — in matter, that is, rather than spirit — binds him intimately, Milton suggests, to Satan's revolt against God, and so in reality to a perpetual de — anchoring, a permanent *méconnaissance* of the profane for the sacred. Hobbes aims to show that the Satanic revolt was well — considered, for what man left behind when dismissed from paradise was nothing other than God's "natural" world ("Nature . . . the Art whereby God hath made and governes the World" (81)), in which, as Hobbes tells us, man's life was in fact solitary, poor, nasty, brutish, and short. The state — man's artificially created ground — is the truly limitless power, greater, potentially, than God's nature.

The leviathan-state cannot *simply* replace the anchor of God, however, because Hobbes's attempt to *invent* a new anchor and a new ground relies upon the privileging of capacities that are adrift owing to qualities inherent in the ground-creating, world — interpreting being, Hobbes's "natural" individual. With the same gesture that liberates man's creativity, Hobbes takes it back by insisting on total obedience to his self-created state, reinvesting in the notion of sin and the baleful consequences of revolt — not against God, now, but against the state. Despite their chronological order, *Leviathan* might profitably be read as a Satanic backward masking of *Paradise Lost* — a kind of black mass in which the punishment for disobedience is being cast out of the paradise of a well-ordered society and into God's stateless, indeed hellish, "Nature." With the grounding of the only possible paradise in the deceptive sea-beast of human art, the ground is no longer a ground. Like Milton's Satan, man with his artificial leviathan has been driven into the deep, into Nietzsche's "darkly chopping sea" of uncertainty.[2] Sea changes in this groundless ground are to be expected; the covenants out of which human societies are made will respond to the constant seductions of man's own nature, or what Hobbes calls his "passions." Obedience to state authority emerges as both absolutely necessary and absolutely impossible to guarantee: the artificer that makes the leviathan can always undo it. Hobbes's solution to this politico-metaphysical problem is an elaborate and delicately balanced network of disciplines, constraints, and controls as the condition of man's "freedom" and "power."

Hobbesian man, then, is like the "doublet empirico-transcendental" of Michel Foucault's *Les mots et les choses*: absolutely sovereign and utterly disciplined. An analogous "undecidability" is central, I shall suggest, to the vocabulary of "containment," which has dominated American discussion of foreign affairs since World War Two. Although said to be a Lockean society devoted to maximizing individual freedom, American public and quasi-public figures have promulgated a discourse that tacitly specifies the conditions under which the United States must put aside its Lockean commitments. Ronald Reagan, Oliver L. North and his cabal, and anonymous Pentagon planners have built a discursive bridge leading back behind Locke to Hobbes. They have disclosed — in a Heideggerian sense — an America in which Lockean categories of thought and action are indiscernible, but, as we shall see, they have not fixed the groundless ground that haunts Hobbes's project. Instead, they have pushed to the limit the American anxiety over our schizophrenic coupling of radical freedom with subjection to nature, or what North calls our "dangerous world." For what must strike anyone who followed the debates surrounding the Iran-contra affair was their enigmatic incoherency. Watching Congress's passionate defense of the public's right to know, coupled with careful avoidance of any leads suggesting improper actions by the Central Intelligence Agency, it was difficult not to conclude that most members of the committees investigating the Iran-contra affair sensed that their world no longer reflected, and could not reflect, the theory of constitutionally limited representative democracy they all-too-hesitantly invoked. It was as if the rhetoric of democracy itself had been placed *sous rature*: the committee members could not *not* speak of democracy, but neither could they fully convince themselves of the contemporary relevance of democratic principles. What haunts America now is a political identity crisis: Are we a Lockean or an Hobbesian society?

2

Hobbes's "natural" subject of knowledge and power poses a curious (though for the postmodern sensibility, familiar) dilemma: it can ground itself only in what it creates out of its own resources, yet the world that it thereby discloses, if it is to be compelling, must appear to it as the discovery of a privileged natural object, sign, or kind. To be sure, Hobbes's attempt at epistemological recovery cannot simply be assimilated to "Platonism." For Hobbes, whose model of inquiry derives from Euclidean geometry rather than Platonic dialectic, "*truth* consisteth in the right

ordering of names" (105) and not in the direct mirroring of an uninterpreted reality. The very idea of an uninterpreted reality is, for Hobbes, a
legacy of the "Vain Philosophy, and Fabulous Traditions" that he attacks
in Chapter 46 of *Leviathan*. "Vain Philosophy" teaches that from a statement such as "Man is a living body" we must infer the existence of three
ontologically distinct essences: man, living body, and being itself. In fact,
terms such as *"Entity, Essence, Essentiall, Essentiality"* are "no Names of
Things; but Signes, by which wee make known, that wee conceive the
Consequence of one name or Attribute to another" (691). Nonetheless,
Hobbes is very far from putting all discourse on the same level: the doctrine of separated essences, for example, involves taking literally what are
in fact only "empty names," as opposed to Hobbes's nominalism which
attends scrupulously to the *nature* of language. Making good the Hobbesian critique of separated essences depends upon constituting a subject
of knowledge who can "remember what every name he uses stands for,"
and who can "place it accordingly" (105); it depends, that is, upon fixed
definitions and unambiguous distinctions purged of figural language. In
constructing his rigorously unambiguous and logically consistent system,
however, Hobbes relies upon the suppressed figural dimension of terms
that are crucial to his discussion of man and society. Attention to Hobbes's rhetoric — in particular, the tropes with which he appears to mobilize the authority of nature to compel obedience to discourse — reveals
the shifting ground of Hobbesian politico-linguistic authority.

As a subject of scientific knowledge that transcends that of the "Schoole-
men," Hobbes's natural man needs a long memory to support his
"Knowledge of Consequences." Nevertheless, as a subject capable of abandoning the state of nature and entering into political covenants, such a subject must be able to reinterpret political meanings effortlessly. The subject
whose memory of nature is long demands a correspondingly short *political* memory. How can these epistemological figures be combined in one
subject? Hobbes reconciles the two by founding knowledge on what he
calls "fancy," a word that can refer both to an accurate mental representation of an external object, and an invention, caprice, delusion, or fictional
image. As an *ambiguous* sign, "fancy" performs essential functions in Hobbes's science of politics, despite the latter's alleged dependence upon words
"purged from ambiguity." To avert the impotence of "Insignificant Speech,"
the subject must avoid the "Absurdity" of words severed from their *"Definitions"* — the dark vocabulary of scholastic fantasy that, for Hobbes, has
affinities to immaturity and madness. This is no mere epistemological
problem, for it is the regulation of the passions by thought, as refined,
ideally, into a *method*, that enables individuals to perceive their long-term
interest in security and therefore sacrifice the unlimited exercise of natural rights to the stability of a social contract.

Consider first Hobbes's evocation of the mechanics of "Sense," which
in turn explain the origin of "Thoughts." Thoughts, he writes, are "every

one a Representation or Apparance." A representation designates an "Object, ... a body without us." The relation of thought to its object, then, initially appears as the classical epistemological puzzle concerning the possibility of knowledge of the external world. Hobbes proposes, of course, a mechanical solution: the movement of objects in space produces a corresponding movement in the senses. The "cause of Sense," Hobbes tells us,

> is the Externall Body, or Object, which presseth the organ proper to each Sense . . . which pressure, by the mediation of Nerves, and other strings, and membranes of the body, continued inwards to the Brain, and Heart, causeth there a resistance, or counter-pressure, or endeavour of the heart, to deliver itself: which endeavour because *Outward*, seemeth to be some matter without. And this *seeming*, or *fancy*, is that which men call *Sense* (85).

Although this theory shows the method by which the subject can have thoughts of the "body without," it cannot account for the possibility of *reflection* upon objects that are not immediately present to the senses. If representations are caused by "pressure" on the sense organs from the "body without," how is memory possible? How can the object be present in the imagination when it is not exerting pressure on the senses?

Hobbes's answer is that the "counter-pressure," or the movement of the sensory organ, reverberates for some time after the original pressure of the object has ceased, though not indefinitely; the reverberation gradually "decays." Since the movement of the sensory organ outlasts the movement of the object, without, however, outlasting it indefinitely, a kind of thought not under the immediate sway of desire becomes possible, namely deliberation. The mechanism of "decay" ensures that the subject may entertain, in the imagination, a "fancy" or "relique" of the object's impact, thus establishing the possibility of knowledge of the connections between past events and, therefore, of instrumental action oriented towards the future.[3] This foundation has been secured, however, at the cost of constituting the knowledge of events as "fancy." The mental representation of a thing, a fancy, can also be an invention or caprice, and as such tends to blur the distinctions between the names that Hobbes strives to keep carefully "placed." The depiction of knowledge of the past as the remains of an originally fully present (but now decaying) "fancy" necessarily renders knowledge opaque, vague, and ambiguous.

This becomes clearer if we consider that for Hobbes, the mechanism of decay is not only the dwindling of sensory motions set off by the pressure of an object, but rather the interference of *other* objects, nearer in time, which obscure, muffle, and cover over the previous movement. If fancies did not decay and could not be pushed aside by the pressure of other objects, the subject would, after all, be confined to a perpetual present — or past. Ironically, the mechanism that makes possible the *growth* of knowledge is a continuous layering process that might equally well be said to yield a *loss* of knowledge, as the apprehension of the "body without" is complicated by a continually revised mass of experience that has the status of an ambiguous fancy, caprice, or invention. Such a view of experience is crucial, of course, to Hobbes's vision of an unconditioned invention of the political order: the subject of political action must be free of past contingencies and traditional values, viewing the accumulation of knowledge as raw material for creative manipulation. At the same time, however, knowledge of the connections between past events is essential to a scientific subject who abandons scholastic fantasy in favor of exact knowledge of causal relations. "Fancy" is a term whose dual meanings are equally necessary to Hobbes's derivation of sovereign power.

The contradictory character of "decay" appears again in Hobbes's discussion of how rational speech wards off the error threatened by the unavoidable layering of fancy in knowledge. In Hobbes's genesis of the natural individual, a crucial property of speech is its capacity to offset the unreliability and insubstantiality of ambiguous sensory phenomena. The signs of language, Hobbes says, attenuate or "delay" the decay of signs long enough to enable these "reliques" of external motion to perform as the objects of an intelligible discourse of deliberation and explanation. Decay cannot and must not be eliminated, but thanks to rightly ordered speech it can be postponed long enough for the accumulation of "Knowledge of Consequences," or memory. This stable language of consequences, in turn, provides the foundation in the natural individual for those effects of power specific to Hobbes's "Artificiall Man": for without this faculty of knowledge, as Hobbes puts it, "there had been amongst men, neither Common-wealth, nor Society, nor Contract, nor Peace, no more than amongst Lyons, Bears, and Wolves" (100). If, however, the delay afforded by linguistic signs is the mechanism that lends stability to a self-invalidating sensory apparatus, Hobbesian language itself raises, albeit in a different form, the very difficulties bound up in the ambiguities of fancy. For Hobbes, the horizon of clear and distinct ideas is populated by dream-like visions, absurdity, giddiness, and finally madness. Speech, which enables memory and the knowledge of consequences, is in itself no guarantee of reason. Hobbes's vivid examples of intellectual error are governed by the figure of a subject who has lost control over speech, trapped in a meaningless show of vain images that are incapable of reaching the real world. The discourse of the "Schoole-men" aptly symbolizes this mad speech in which words are juggled for purely ornamental effect. Far from having mastered language to escape the uncertainty of fancy, the subject of dogmatic fantasy is literally dissolved into the signs of language themselves, a plaything of discourse rather than an agent who orders the world by "settling on . . . definitions." So radically impotent a subject, absorbed not in the strict calculation of consequences but by the contemplation of a display of representations, is in no respect the stuff of the "Artificiall Man."

The emergence of a Hobbesian subject of power is linked to the invention of a language "purged from ambiguity," but how does one move from the aesthetic play of signs to a discourse of empirical causes and effects, when the very condition of thought and representation is the permanent possibility of decay, layering, and substitution? Hobbes deals with the ambiguities that arise here by referring them to other domains, via the textual strategies that Jacques Derrida has isolated under the rubric of "supplementation."[4]

We have noted how the gradual decay of sensory motion establishes both the possibility of thought and the layering over of its object. Hobbes insists that "There is no conception in a man's mind, which hath not first, totally, or by parts, been begotten upon the organs of Sense" (94). Mental representations are derived from the pressure of bodies upon the senses, as we have seen, but since the latter persist as "reliques" and "fancies," representations can be linked together by the mind in a virtually unlimited variety of combinations. An event can be mentally attached to any other event, therefore becoming imaginatively tied together; and, as Hobbes notes, they can as easily be untied, dissolved, and recombined. If this vertiginous option is extended, it "comes to pass in time," Hobbes says, "that in the imagining of anything, there is no certainty what we shall imagine next."[5] The terror of unregulated thought is articulated through images of variance and eccentricity: persons friendless and alone, wills empty of desire, disharmonious, and caught in the "wild ranging of the mind." This "uncertainty about what we shall imagine next," Hobbes says, is delirium. Sanity, of course, consists in experiencing ourselves as enduring subjects acting in time. Since, on Hobbes's account, it is in the nature of human beings as speakers that delirium remains a constant possibility — that thought might become "*unguided, without Designe, and inconstant*" — some principle is required to establish how the subject avoids falling prey to the anarchic play of imagination. Speech, whose resources were introduced to correct the ambiguities of sense, is now itself felt to require similar treatment.

"Passion," "desire, and designe" are the figures that Hobbes now introduces to discipline the paralyzing chaos of memory, imagination, and fancy unleashed by a disorderly language. Desire accomplishes this task by positing some aim for the subject, lending direction to the associative spontaneity of thought by organizing it according to a teleological movement towards the real world of consequences. "Thoughts," when ordered by desires, become organized as "Scouts, and Spies, to range abroad, and find the way to the things desired." Not only does desire supply direction and coherency to the imagination, it also increases the sense of substantiality attached to its representations: "The impression made by such things as wee desire," in Hobbes's pithy phrase, "is strong and permanent" (95). Desire and speech reinforce one another, prolonging the life of a given impression despite the constant intrusion of fresh experience. Yet in a sense,

Hobbes is exploiting still another meaning of the metaphor with which he began his genealogy of the natural individual: "fancy" can mean not only a mental representation, but also something desired by an individual. In appealing to passion to regulate the chaos of sense and thought, Hobbes is relying upon the multiple significations of his original metaphor.

Desire allows for the creation of a kind of subjective ontology, singling out and investing with special significance a particular class of impression. More importantly, it is what provokes the subject to make connections between the desired object and the performances required to attain it, as well as to collect in memory and recall all the effects associated with such objects. At this point, the term "power" acquires some concreteness, for it is by proceeding backwards in the chain of means towards some desired end that one arrives at a "beginning within our own power" (96) and can construct a practical syllogism relevant to the subject's actual situation. With this concept, Hobbes links thought and power by constituting thought as a tool for attaining the end desired by a concrete, situated subject, as opposed to fancies divorced from practice.

Yet Hobbes's vocabulary of desire, no less than that of sense and speech, generates multiple meanings whose effects must be taken into account. As a regulator of errant signs, the figure of desire we have just isolated plays a positive role in Hobbes's project, bringing order to the "wild ranging" of the mind and constituting a necessary step in the genealogy of a subject of power. Nevertheless, *Leviathan* offers a different picture of desire, emerging as Hobbes looks more closely at the nature of the passions and which again engenders ambiguities it was designed to foreclose. Passion too, it seems, contains its own principles of disharmony and excess, so that the same disability — the failure to master a discourse of causes and effects — and the same problem — how can this excess be limited or regulated? — emerge again. The discipline of instrumental thinking can be upset by what Hobbes calls "the more or lesse Desire of Power," marking passion too with an inconstancy that once again culminates in madness:

> For as to have no Desire, is to be Dead: so to have weak Passions, is Dulnesse; and to have Passions indifferently for every thing, GID-DINESSE, and *Distraction*; and to have stronger, and more vehement Passions for any thing, than is normally seen in others, is that which men call MADNESSE (139).

Hobbes comes full circle by linking to madness the "Insignificant Speech" of the "Schoole-men," who "speak such words, as put together, have in them no signification at all" (146). The category of passion, whose unity, it was hoped, would temper the Hobbesian mind's "wild ranging," emerges as an ambiguous new source of error.

To the dangerous entanglement of desire and language, Hobbes envisages a radical solution: replace the common vocabulary with one "purged from ambiguity" that allows the deduction of complex passions from simpler, self-evident elements, as demanded by Hobbes's conception of scientific method. With passion disciplined by an unambiguous language — that is, with an impersonal *method* — the subject can hope to ward off the aesthetic pull of fanciful representations, invent a true discourse of causes, and enjoy the effects of power. The hazards of this project reach their zenith, of course, in Hobbes's vision of a body politic. An association of acquisitive individuals requires a sovereign power that can never quite be guaranteed, because the fabrication of the "Artificiall Man" relies upon an "Inconstancy" that persists in haunting it. What is striking about the state of nature is less the fear engendered by the unrestrained exercise of natural rights than the relative absence of *logos*. Life is not only "solitary, poore, nasty, brutish, and short," but also it is unintelligible: "In such condition, there is . . . no Knowledge of the face of the Earth; no account of Time; no Arts; no Letters; no Society" (186). The absence of speech disciplined by *logos* means that individuals in the state of nature are "dissociate(d)" from one another, so that their actions are "governed" only by the anti-logic of the passions. The individual delirium that Hobbes forecasts when passion overcomes thought re-emerges at the level of collective life as the "war of each against all." The state of nature is a state of generalized "madnesse."[6]

To overcome this pandemic madness, an undivided sovereign power must coordinate the anarchic play of desire-cum-delirium. Even though covenants without the sword are meaningless, this is to be accomplished not only by force of arms, but by supplying the *logos* that the state of nature lacks: the sovereign power discharges its duties by pronouncing *laws* to regulate and regiment the passionate pursuit of individual interests. The sovereign power, as "Judge of what is Commodious, or Incommodious to the Common-wealth," must, as Hobbes puts it, promulgate "*good* Lawes"[7] (327), i.e., regulations that ensure commodious living. While subjects, then, have a duty of "simple obedience," the sovereign's duties are more subtle and demanding. The Hobbesian sovereign must *teach* obedience, and learn the arts that Foucault studies under the name of "discipline."

While the sovereign's injunctions aim to endow society with certainty and predictability, the capacity of the sovereign power to do so depends in turn on its "constancy." The figure of the sovereign, however, opens the door to the same problem of *inconstancy* that we saw in the delirium of passions and the chaos of the state of nature. If the sovereign power takes the form of an assembly, it will be threatened, Hobbes fears, by disagreement among those who comprise it (accordingly, Hobbes advises against democracy and aristocracy). Even when vested in an individual, inconstancy may spring from human nature, i.e., from the passions: the sovereign power might fail to perform its duties owing to excessive timidity or arrogance. The sovereign is, after all, a "*mortal* god,"[8] "compounded of the power of all *men*" (227), and thus fully subject to the dialectic of desire and language we have already adopted. Here again, the invention of an impersonal discourse is necessary to correct for this excess of desire, in this case the knowledge of how to govern and be governed: educating subjects to adhere to the prevailing form of government, to dismiss competing claims of authority, to obey established authority, to memorize the duties of citizenship, to respect parental authority, to nurture the habits of compliance, and to adjust their "designes and intentions" to the law. Knowledge of how to rule is an all-embracing pedagogy of obedience in which "thought" is removed from the world of airy abstraction and concretized as a mechanism of political control.

The system of concepts organized by the sovereign's laws are subject, however, to a chaos of their own. The sovereign, as we have noted, performs its duties "by a generall Providence, ... and in the making, and executing of good Lawes. . . ," but laws may be misunderstood. The need to interpret the sovereign's commands is another source of inconstancy, threatening the commonwealth. Neither brevity nor verbosity are of any use:

> The written Laws, if they be short, are easily mis-interpreted, from
> the divers significations of a word, or two: if long, they be more
> obscure by the divers significations of many words (322).

By multiplying the senses of a text, interpretation creates more problems than it resolves:

> For Commentaries are commonly more subject to cavill, than the
> Text; and therefore need other Commentaries; and so there will be
> no end of such Interpretation (326).

Misunderstanding the sovereign can be mitigated, for Hobbes, only by insisting on the "literal" sense of the law: "that, which the Legislator intended, should by the letter of the Law be signified." Disputes over the scope and meaning of laws, of course, are to be settled by the sovereign power alone. More than brute force, however, lies behind the sovereign's authority over the meaning of its words. It is not simply the sheer power of sovereign intention that adjudicates disputes over interpretation, but his "perfect understanding of the finall causes, for which the Law was made" (322). The sovereign's intention, obscured by the "divers significations" of his words, can be saved, once more, only by a political science "purged from ambiguity" and embodying a "perfect understanding." The problem of interpreting the commonwealth's laws, then, is referred to sovereign intention as the content of the law, while the problem of interpreting sovereign intention is referred to the "laws" of a new political science. The mainspring of the civil order remains as fragile as the ever-threatened line between passion and delirium — no more, finally, than a "*Fiat*," as Hobbes puts it in the Introduction to *Leviathan*.

DEMON POLITICS

Leviathan attempts to establish an unambiguous political vocabulary on the basis of figures whose multiple meanings necessarily thwart any such project. At each stage, the hoped-for "constancy" — political, psychological, metaphysical — appears compromised by the resources of the figures in which Hobbes chooses to state it, and must be guaranteed by supplementary measures. Political action is concentrated as much as possible into the sovereign's law-making duties; law-making, to circumnavigate the passions, must attain the status of a science; and finally, the imperative of guaranteeing a "felicitous" sphere of individual action necessitates a comprehensive education for obedience. This route, however, merely returns us to the passions, and to Hobbes's recognition that the artificiality of covenants among self-sufficient individuals requires that these be enforced by the sword, by a power able to "keep them in awe."

That the indispensable unity of the sovereign rests on a delicate weave, easily unraveled, helps to explain Hobbes's hostile reaction to the suggestion that the sovereign be subject to the law. This idea is "repugnant," he says, because it would lead to an infinite chain of equivocation, "continually without end, to the Confusion, and Dissolution of the Commonwealth" (367). This properly Hobbesian repugnance towards executive power being subject to law is now voiced with increasing shrillness in what is commonly supposed to be the most authentically Lockean political culture, the United States.

3

America was promises . . .

Archibald MacLeish

The conundrums following Hobbes's demand that individuals make an almost *unconditional* grant of authority to the state appear less problematical for Locke, for whom the people's power is held conditionally, on trust. Hobbes's unholy coupling of human power with the despotic state, we like to think, is simply an expression of bourgeois pessimism that more reasonable thinkers, upon whom we rely for our political identity, saw through. But Lockean liberalism encounters its own problems of undecidability. At the center of both Hobbesian and Lockean accounts of politics, of course, is the contract, the *promise* — the individual's promise not to use his unlimited natural right to invade others as long as all other individuals make the similar promise. Accordingly, the great fear of contractarian experience is that one or more of the parties to the contract might make a *lying promise*, a circumstance that pushes hermeneutics close to the center of politics: now, political life demands ways of discerning sincerity, and liberalism demands a political semiotic that can tabulate the reliable signs of the sincere promise.

Precisely this riddle of promising and keeping promises, in fact, was en-countered early in the history of semiotics by Umberto Eco, who defined the field as "a theory of the lie."⁹ Semiotics, which treats "sign-functions" abstracted away from their referential dimension, is the study of whatever can be used to *depart* from the real. Eco's paradoxical definition of a dis-cipline devoted to telling the truth about lies captures the character of modern political theory as Hobbes sees it. For Hobbes, sheer human ar-tifice could fashion a simulacrum of the "natural" ruler, but the coopera-tion upon which this art depended relied in turn on promises that were likely to be overwhelmed by the passions. Since promises are so thin, on-tologically speaking, the necessary partner of consent is state coercion, which at its roots is that which moors us to the deceptive sea-beast, Levia-than, the only ground for which we may hope. This dialectic of consent and coercion was analyzed by Nietzsche in his early draft "On Truth and Lies in a Nonmoral Sense," where he emphasizes the conformity implied by the notion of a social contract.¹⁰ Individuals "by themselves," Nietzsche writes, will in the ordinary course of events rely on subterfuge, camouflage, and the lie for survival. Through "boredom and necessity," however, they might contract to live according to certain rules, i.e., promises. The essence of the social contract is to tell the truth, but also to define truth as the conformity to the conventions of the group, to "lie according to fixed conventions." Later, in *On the Genealogy of Morals* and elsewhere, Nietzsche detailed the forms of discipline required to produce a creature — the modern, guilt-ridden individual — with a memory capa-ble of keeping promises. Like Hobbes, Nietzsche emphasizes the paradox of the promiser: the language of commitment, stability, and trust most lends itself to deception and ruses. Contractarian societies, therefore, encourage ambivalence towards the promise, alternately grounding it in a dangerous-ly unmanageable human will and in a nature that can overcome the haz-ards of the former. The founding document of the American polity, Jefferson's *Declaration of Independence*, conforms to this pattern: it celebrates the capacity of individuals acting with others to alter, invent, and establish new forms of political association, but it is careful to ground these capacities in "the Laws of Nature" and "Nature's God," consistent with a theory of the individual's natural right to be against and control nature.¹¹

The most vivid recent expression of liberal anxiety over the promise is the discourse of Ronald Reagan. Indeed, for Reagan our enemies are those who cannot keep their promises. Referring to the leaders of the Soviet Un-ion, Reagan claims that "they reserved these rights to break a promise, to change their ways, to be dishonest, and so forth if it furthered the cause of socialism. . . . (P)romises are like pie crusts, made to be broken."¹² Ac-cordingly, Reagan's objections to the Sandinista government in Nicaragua center not on the government's human rights violations, but on the claim that the Sandinistas *broke a promise*: they, Reagan alleges, "literally made a contract" with the Organization of American States for support in return for "true democracy."[13] In such statements, the emphasis is less on the absence of true democracy in Nicaragua than on the alleged fact that the Sandinistas broke a promise — that is, that they violated a principle that is central to legitimate government as we understand it. At the same time, the state over which this Lockean liberal presides relies overwhelmingly on what one of his operatives calls "great deceit":

> I think it is very important for the American people to understand that this is a dangerous world; that we live at risk and that this nation is at risk in a dangerous world. And that they ought not to be led to believe ... that this nation cannot or should not conduct covert operations. By their very nature covert operations or special operations are a lie. There is great deceit, deception practiced in the conduct of covert operations. They are at essence a lie.[14]

For Lt. Col. Oliver North, its is imperative that Americans understand that this nation can and should engage in "great deceit," even though such action violates the principles of legitimate government embodied in the U.S. constitution. The "dangerous world" in which we live demands that we resort to "covert actions" or "special operations" that "are at essence a lie." The covert action, however, has the epistemological and moral status of a noble lie, forced upon the liberal democracies by the difficult choice between "lives and lies" and by the fact that those, such as North, who possess an esoteric knowledge of the nature of the threat to American freedom, are hampered by an unwieldy bureaucracy, a misinformed Congress, and an apathetic public.[15]

Still, North's testimony, taken by itself, leaves unclear the basis upon which the representative of a polity dedicated to open contracts and serious promises can instead devote himself to "great . . . deception." A complete answer to this question would require a study of the rhetoric of the great documents of containment, such as George Kennan's "Mr. X" essay, National Security Council Memorandum #68, Henry Kissinger's *Nuclear Weapons and Foreign Policy*, and the Pentagon Papers. Some insights, however, can be gained from a close reading of one of those hundreds of ignored government planning documents: "Prospects for Containment of Nicaragua's Communist Government," dated May 1986 and issued by the U.S. Department of Defense. Read not as a prosaic planning study but as political allegory, the Defense Department document bridges the gap between Locke and Hobbes, showing *why* the character of our "dangerous world" is such that our principles of legitimacy no longer apply. It provides the theory that North did not explicitly pronounce, but upon which he acted.

"Containment" refers broadly to the postwar commitment of the United States to prevent the spread of Communism.[16] In the debate, however, over how to accomplish this goal, two camps quickly emerged. The document's title refers to the debate between proponents of "rollback" and a less extreme variant that became known simply as "containment." In this sense, containment envisaged a political deal in which the Soviet Union and the United States enjoyed tacitly recognized spheres of influence, and it assumed that both parties were capable of honoring treaties, i.e., making contracts and keeping promises. Proponents of rollback understood the Soviet Union as incapable of such behavior — in Reagan's terms, it reserves the right to lie, cheat, and steal in pursuit of Communist expansion. In addition, rollback, by its nature, involves military conflict because an adversary that does not recognize the sanctity of contracts cannot be a party to a political solution. In arguing that the prospects for merely *containing* Nicaragua's communist government are bleak, the study is an implicit call for a military solution: rollback.

The document begins by noting differences of opinion in Congress over U.S. policy towards the Sandinista regime, differences that came to the fore after Reagan's lurid speech in March of 1986 about Nicaragua as a "safe haven" for terrorists from around the world caused some to call for political compromise rather than military conflict:

> The President's request to Congress on aid to the Nicaraguan Democratic Resistance has led to an extensive debate in Congress. There is a difference of views as to how effective an agreement would be in providing the needed security for Central America.

The document begins, in other words, by stressing the liberal, democratic context of U.S. policymaking: the "difference of views"; but it subsequently emphasizes that despite differences over policy, all parties to the debate agree that the Sandinistas are a threat to be combated, and that while some in Congress "maintain that a greater effort should be made to secure a political agreement which would serve to contain Communism in Nicaragua," "Many . . . recall the failure of previous treaties and agreements with the Communists." "Prospects for Containment," then, will jog the short political memories of those who forget that treaties with "the Communists" are mere scraps of paper.

This is accomplished in a section misleadingly entitled "Historical Perspective." The title is misleading not because the accounts historically inaccurate (they are, in fact, grotesquely oversimplified), but because the study purports to deal with U.S. policy towards Nicaragua, but not a word is devoted to relations between these two countries. Rather, "Historical Perspective" means reviewing situations in which the United States entered into political agreements with "the Communists," who, in the vernacular of the document, are a kind of Jungian archetype that everywhere and always remains the same. (I can recall childhood memories of TV news broadcasts about the "Viet Cong," which I dimly imagined must be an ethnic group different from the Vietnamese we were defending.) Since "the Communists" are always the same, it follows that the behavior of any one Communist entity is entirely predictable. If the further assumption that the Sandinistas are Communists is also made, no further inquiry is necessary into the historical peculiarities of U.S.-Nicaragua relations: Sandinista policy is determined by their being part of "the Communists," and not as Nicaraguans.

The document then contains discussions on violations of treaties with Communists entered into by the United States, which amount, of course, to Communists' breaking their promises, just as, according to Reagan, they affirm their right to do. In the case of Vietnam, for example, North Vietnam "began illegal subversive operations in South Vietnam immediately after signing the 1954 Geneva Accords," although "Communist military violations of the Geneva Agreement began to escalate sharply only in the late 1950's, when Hanoi started to infiltrate armed cadres and supplies into Vietnam." The same is true, according to the document, of "communist belligerents" in Korea, other Indochinese countries, and Cuba. True to form, the Nicaraguan Communists "literally made a contract," in Reagan's words, with the Organization of American States to establish "true democracy," only to violate it after assuming power. The Communists, then, are *hoi barbaroi*, a group that cannot keep promises and hence is not fit to enter into the sort of contractual arrangements familiar to Lockean liberals.

Not only do Communists fail to keep promises, they actively, intentionally utilize the rhetoric of promising — likely persuasive for liberal polities — to pursue the expansion of Communist power. As Reagan has it, for Communists promises are made *in order to be broken*. Equally alien to liberal sensibilities is the fact that the Communists *plan* to break their promises: the Nicaraguans "never intended to honor the pledge" they made to the Organization of American States, and the Vietnamese and Korean Communists "were planning the infringements even as they were negotiating." The mere fact that the Communists *plan* is a mark of their difference from us. Strictly speaking, a liberal polity cannot plan; it only creates a framework of order within which individuals contract with one another and thus determine their fates. Planning in a liberal polity is possible only on an individual, not on a collective, basis. The Communists, with their Five Year Plans and historical inevitabilities, even plan to break promises.

The Communists, then, plan with no regard for past promises, and use promises only as a rhetorical device with which to manipulate liberal polities. The Sandinistas, therefore, can be expected to violate a Central American peace treaty. The questions then become: What would a Central American treaty call for, and what Sandinista violations are likely to occur? The key element of any such treaty, the Pentagon emphasizes, is the stipulation that the governments of the region refuse to allow foreign troops or military advisors on their soil, and refrain from supporting insurgencies in neighboring countries. This entails that Soviet and Cuban advisors leave Nicaragua, and that the United States discontinue its support for El Salvador, Guatemala, and Honduras. On the theory that the Communists plan to break promises, there can be only one reason for the Sandinistas to agree to such an arrangement: to induce the United States to withdraw from the region while they secretly pursue a military build-up that would enable them to become master of the region. As the Pentagon imagines it:

> The Nicaraguan government would sign a Contadora agreement . . . the Nicaraguans would circumvent and violate the agreement in order to maintain or increase their military strength and to . . . support . . . Communist insurgencies throughout Central America. Nicaragua would seek to conceal its violations as long as possible. The U.S. and other Central American nations would fully abide by the agreement. . . .

Constrained by contractarian principles, the United States would abide by its promises while the Nicaraguans secretly break theirs, resulting ultimately in the Communist conquest of Central America. What, under the circumstances, can a liberal polity do? The United States could not simply announce its refusal to abide by a treaty supported by the governments of the region. Yet to abide by the agreement while the Communists secretly subvert it is to accept Communist rule over Central America, in the long run. Although the Pentagon stops short of drawing this consequence explicitly, the rhetorical context of the document encourages the conclusion that the United States must, like the Communists, secretly violate the agreement by supporting what it calls the "Democratic Resistance Forces" (the contras) covertly with the methods developed by North. Faced with an entity incapable of participating in contractarian life, the United States has no choice but to resort to "great deceit."

The rhetorical strategy that North adopted in his testimony to the Congressional committees investigating the Iran-contra affair was to present the great deceit as natural, realistic, and self-evidently justified. Although the U.S. Constitution grants the executive branch limited powers in foreign affairs, North speaks as if it were self-evident that the president is "in charge" of foreign policy. Congress need not be informed of government action in that area, according to North, because the president is accountable directly to "the people."[17] North makes it clear that the great deceit is not limited to the Communist enemy, but includes all elements of the liberal polity (e.g., the press and Congress) that threaten the implementation of the covert policy: the deceit was staged in part, according to North, "to limit the political embarrassment."[18] North asserts that to prevent political embarrassment, members of the executive branch can destroy official documents or fail to inform Congress of current policy ("deceit by omission"). All of this is, by definition, legal, because it is done at the behest of the "Commander-in-Chief," who, once again, acts in the interests of the nation as a whole and not in the parochial interests represented in Congress.

DEMON POLITICS

The logic of containment, as expressed both in North's testimony and the Pentagon study, specifies the conditions under which the United States moves from Lockean commitments of limited, open government to an Hobbesian state of near-total authority and detailed administration of citizenship, for what were North's slide shows — and indeed his testimony — other than an exercise in "nurturing the habits of compliance"? Yet a nagging politico-epistemological question remains: If state policy must be secret, how can it be ratified by the people? Senator Mitchell raised this issue in the course of his questioning of North: "if, by definition, covert action is secret and (the president) doesn't tell them about it, there's no way the American people can know about it to be able to vote him out of office. . . ."[19] Covert action emerges as a vulgar Platonism in which a system of hierarchical, Hobbesian state authority is masked for the multitude by a display of images staged for the purposes of ratifying the people's sense of living in a Lockean society of maximum individual freedom and government on trust. Thus, the inescapable duplicity of North's presentations, emphasizing Soviet designs on Central America while at the same time implying that the United States was doing no more for the "Democratic Resistance" than allowing them to die for their country. In public, North offered a rhetoric in which the citizen of a liberal polity might comfortably dwell, making arguments in favor of a particular policy; while privately carrying out a war his "intelligence" told him was necessary but towards which the public remained unsupportive.

Containment depicts a "dangerous world" in which liberal principles are put "at risk" to the precise extent that liberal polities adhere to them. Containment — in both its moderate and extreme versions — sees the postmodern political condition as demanding private Hobbesian action coupled with public Lockean rhetoric. At the limit, containment even threatens to dissolve the difference between public and private upon which liberalism thrives. Many of North's associates, such as Richard V. Secord and Albert Hakim, were private individuals implementing state policy, which resorted to private funding and operatives because what it wanted to do was illegal. The implosion of the private into the public enabled all to claim a lack of responsibility: government officials could say that no appropriated funds were going to support the contras, even though the policy of support was worked out in the White House; while citizens, violating the law at the behest of the executive branch, could say they were doing so as patriots coming to the aid of their president. Perhaps North, Secord, Hakim, and even Reagan are neither private nor public figures, but an undecidable, postmodern amalgamation of these terms, figures capable of simulating the public and the private according to necessity. In a complementary way, containment gives us a new American state that is neither Lockean nor Hobbesian, but both in the sense that it is committed to staging itself in either mode according to the demands of state power. In the last analysis, the Iran-contra affair (like the affair of Gary Hart, which condensed similar confusions over the difference between public and private) is but a symptom of an American identity crisis — a crisis, precisely, *of* identity: the repressed Hobbesian identity of freedom and control.

Department of Rhetoric
University of California

Notes

Several individuals read and responded to earlier versions of this essay. I would like in particular to acknowledge the generous comments, criticisms, and leads supplied by: Philip Kuberski; the faculty and graduate students of the Department of Rhetoric, University of California, Berkeley; and two anonymous readers for the *Canadian Journal of Political and Social Theory*

1. Thomas Hobbes, *Leviathan*, ed. C.B. Macpherson (Harmondsworth, Middlesex, England: Penguin Books, 1985), p. 81. Further quotations from this text will be parenthetically referenced in the main body of the essay.

2. Friedrich Nietzsche, "On Truth and Lies in a Nonmoral Sense," in *Philosophy and Truth: Selections From Nietzsche's Notebooks of the Early 1870's*, trans. and ed. Daniel Breazeale, (New Jersey: Humanities Press, 1979).

3. Hobbes's use of "relique" to refer to sensory experience may be innovative. The word normally refers to the physical objects of a saint, and more generally to the physical tokens of a past civilization, practice, or experience. According to the Oxford English Dictionary, however, its reference seems to have been restricted to external physical or material objects. By naming ideas and sensory experiences as "reliques" (traces, remnants, residue) of past motion, Hobbes extends the word's range and ironically harnesses its honorific connotations to his project. Just as a relic provides a link with venerated persons or practices, and is considered especially valuable owing to the connection it establishes between a physical, temporal entity and a spiritual one, the depiction of sense as a relic of actual movement provides a firm ontological foundation for the "seemings" of the imagination, allowing Hobbes to combine in one figure the laws of mechanics and the preservation of the sacred.

4. See Jacques Derrida, *Of Grammatology* trans. Gayatri Spivak, (Baltimore: The Johns Hopkins University Press, 1976), p. 150ff.

5. Ibid. Hobbes notes that the course of apparently undisciplined "fancies" in the imagination is in fact determined by the *original* succession "made in the Sense."

6. It might be objected that this characterization overstates the absence of a *logos* in the state of nature, without which it is difficult to imagine how its inhabitants could ever contract to make over their rights to a sovereign power. On the other hand, the transition from the state of nature to political society has always presented problems for contractarians, who have generally taken the position that the idea of an original contract does not describe an historical event at all.

7. Emphasis added.

8. Thomas Hobbes, *English Works*, ed. Sir William Molesworth, (London: Bohn, 1839-1845), Vol. 6, p. 251. Emphasis added.

9. Umberto Eco, *A Theory of Semiotics*, (Bloomington: Indiana University Press, 1976), pp. 6-7.

10. Nietzsche, Section 1. See also *On the Genealogy of Morals*, trans. Walter Kaufmann and R.J. Hollingdale, (New York: Vintage Books, 1967), Second Essay, Sections 5, 19, *et passim*.

11. "A Declaration by the Representatives of the United States of America, in General Congress Assembled," in *Thomas Jefferson: Writings*, (New York: The Library of America, 1984), p. 19.

12. Ronald Reagan, speech of January 20, 1983, quoted in *Reagan's Reign of Error*, ed. Mark Green and Gail MacColl, (New York: Pantheon Books, 1987), p. 41.

13. Ronald Reagan, speech of July, 1983, quoted in Roy Gutman, "America's Diplomatic Charade," *Foreign Policy*, Fall 1984. For a discussion of the substance of Reagan's claims, see the above essay and Noam Chomsky, "Nicaragua," *The Chomsky Reader*, ed. James Peck, (New York: Pantheon Books, 1987), p. 352.

14. Lt. Col. Oliver L. North, quoted in *Taking the Stand: The Testimony of Lt. Col. Oliver L. North*, (New York: Pocket Books, 1987), p. 12.

15. For documentation of North's views, see the section entitled "Reasons for the Deception" in the *Report of the Congressional Committees Investigating the Iran-Contra Affair*, (Washington, D.C.: Government Printing Office, 1987), p. 150, et passim.

16. Primary documents relating to the containment and rollback doctrines can be found in *Containment*, ed. Thomas Etzold and John Lewis Gaddis, (New York: Columbia University Press, 1978).

17. On the significance, in this context, of the president's direct accountability to the people, see Sheldon S. Wolin, "Democracy and the Welfare State: The Political and Theoretical Connections Between *Staatsrason* and *Wohlfahrtsstaatsrason*," *Political Theory*, Vol. 15, No. 4 (November 1987). Wolin argues that Locke's defense of "Prerogative," or "the power to act . . . for the Publick good, without the prescription of Law, and sometimes even against it," provides the means whereby Lockean political leaders can "inherit the same right of Reason of State to summon the full power of society, but now it is not for simple defense or domination but for the good of all" (p. 488). The result is that the overwhelming need to control disorder that is characteristic of the state of nature is imported into domestic society in the person of the executive. The bridge between Locke and Hobbes, in Wolin's reading, is provided by Locke himself.

18. *Taking the Stand*, p. 525.

19. Ibid., pp. 674-680.

THE DARK NIGHT OF THE LIBERAL SPIRIT
AND THE DAWN OF THE SAVAGE

Michael A. Weinstein

I propose to undertake a critique of contemporary American liberalism, specifically what is commonly called "neo-liberalism," from the foundation of a phenomenological reflection on modern consciousness. Liberalism, as a political formula for self-consciously organizing society, is fatefully bound to the continuance of the modern understanding of life and cannot survive the failure to instantiate that understanding into consciousness, to make it the very constitution of consciousness. The current talk about a postmodern historical period appears, therefore, to be an admission that liberalism is a thing of the past. Yet the very term "postmodern" is empty of any positive content, subsisting tensely to signify a craving for its own transmutation into something fundamentally new, a fresh description of the structure of life that would carry with it a transfigured politics. There is also a radical uncertainty in the postmodern mind, a suspicion that there is no transformation on the horizon, that consciousness is incarcerated in the categories of modernity and must face the realization that the human self has at last become fully lucid to itself, that now is the time to learn to live within a final self-understanding and not to escape into new visions. Taken together the craving for radical novelty and the nagging doubt that it is a genuine possibility make postmodernism another instance of *avant-garde* modernism, perhaps the last one, the final modern irony.

Postmodernism is the modern reflection on the loss of dynamism in modernity, its self-closure, and the inability to get beyond it: postmodern consciousness bounds the boundless, but the "dynamic insight" of continuous change, as Karl Mannheim called it, has been inextricably associated with modernity. Thus, postmodern consciousness is the pure dialectical negation of modern consciousness, locked in an embrace with it, decreeing that it must assent to just what it is most unwilling to hold close to itself, its own being as a static form. Postmodernity is the most acute instance of the "unhappy consciousness," an empty craving for liberation, for the unlimited, crashing against the success of self-determination. Politically, it is decomposed or deconstructed liberalism, a spasmodic hope for progress unhinged from life by a corrosive, nostalgic doubt.

Postmodernism is the most recent of the "waiting philosophies" that have characterized twentieth-century Western culture, the most profound of which is Martin Heidegger's effort to open himself to the voice of Being, undertaken within an "interregnum." I shall initiate a phenomenological reflection on modern consciousness by questioning waiting philosophy, which is constituted by the pure intentionality of a receptive strain towards that which does not appear and the appearance of that which is held in doubt. The intentionality itself cannot be criticized on its own terms: it is a possible structure of consciousness that is not self-contradictory; that is, one can form one's being-in-the-world according to uncertain expectation. Thus, a critical approach to the unhappy consciousness of postmodernity will have to proceed by treating it as a symptom of an act of evading a more primary intentionality, as a form of neurotic compromise between a judgment of the truth about personal existence and a wish that the judgment was false. The life of uncertain expectation is a form of dissociated existence in which one carries out all daily activities according to the requirements of social function and legal fiction, while experiencing these activities as detached from any unifying significance. The sense of importance is fully transcendentalized into the experience of waiting — the round of life becomes reduced to killing time, whereas inwardness is intensified into a restless tension and dis-tension, according to the vicissitudes of doubt. Such a consciousness wrenches itself into a groundless hopefulness through nostalgia for a lost unity, translating deprivation into craving for novelty. It is the breakdown product of the religious will, the historicized wish for salvation divested of its object and even of any symbolization of a questionable object. The waiting attitude is based on the judgment that it is better to hold on to the religious intentionality than it is to become coincident with life, verifying Max Weber's observation that the modern life that they had created for themselves was too much for human beings to bear. Postmodern consciousness is the very thinnest, almost transparent veil thrown over the modern understanding of life, a nisus towards the beyond superadded to finite mundanity and, therefore, the most austere of the modern cultural neuroses. As the pure wish for a transformation that is held to be questionable or even, more purely, impossible, it discloses its other, its dialectical reciprocal, without any necessity of interpretation. That other, detached from the vacantly straining expectation, but always juxtaposed to it, is the formed content of modern life itself.

Modern consciousness may be grasped most generally through the act by which the self seizes itself from within in a declaration-deed; that is, the self actualizes its own being through a declaration. My paradigm here is the Cartesian *cogito* through which the self is realized partially as a "thinking substance" though not yet as a complete life. Indeed, the phenomenology of the modern mind is a remorseless, uncompromising process of enriching and intensifying the inward center of individuated life until it reaches the limit of its empire, and must then either try desperately to transcend itself or learn to live within the boundaries that it has made lucid to itself. The historical moments of modern consciousness are familiar. From the Cartesian starting point of the thinking ego one passes to the self-legislating will of Kant and finally to Nietzsche's passionate and personated flesh, best captured by Unamuno's designation, "the man of flesh and bone, who is born, suffers, and dies." One of the great ironies of postmodern consciousness is that it recreates the Cartesian starting point through an inversion. When Descartes, frustrated in his efforts to discover certain knowledge that would enable him "to walk with confidence in this life," finally was impelled to make himself the object of inquest, he seized a thinking ego from which no linkages could be made to his daily life. Indeed, his only connection to the other-than-self was transcendental, was to the idea of perfection. Lacking a bridge to mundanity, he devised a "provisional morality" that enjoined him to live with good will according to the usages of those around him. For Descartes there was hope that genuine and satisfactory connections would be made to the world through rational investigation, so his was a patient waiting. Now with the modern closed in upon itself the waiting returns, only it is desperate and impatient. There is the same detachment of life from spirit, but it is not the pregnant suspension filled with expectation of the unfolding of a new age; it is bitter nostalgia ungirdled from perfection, craving for miracle: the *cogito* has become the *pour soi*, thought has become the manipulation of signs, and only the barest interiority remains at the very margin. This interiority is necessary to express the judgment that interiority is a useless passion or, in a flight of bad faith, a word functioning to legitimate racial, patriarchal, capitalistic, or, most radically, linguistic domination.

The burnout of modernity is the scorching of the desire to live as a finite individual. What came between Descartes and the postmoderns was a daring growing-into life: Descartes needed a way into life; the postmoderns crave for a way out. The mainstream of modernity wanted life and followed Goethe's dictum: "Become who you are." The self-closure of modernity is the success of this great pedagogical project: a complete self-understanding through the inwardly grasped self is now available to anyone who is strong enough to tolerate it, and, as in the case of any foundation, it is all too simple to express, all too obviously true to those who grasp it, and all too difficult to bear. When I grasp myself from within, now, as the twentieth century moves to its close, with all the modern self-discoveries suffused through my being, I seize myself concretely as conscious flesh, as a sensible, desiring, and self-interpreting body. And that is the modern truth, the end of the search for the *res vera*, the richly-laden truth, bearing the purest pleasure and the most agonizing hatred within it; that all I can assent to primordially is an utter surd, a failure by its own requirements, yet the very plenitude of being itself and the generator of all of the interpretative projections that take it away from itself — restless, conscious flesh. Yes, I acknowledge that I sprang from a womb. But I feel the tensions of my organs destroying me and I feel the pleasures that are fuller than any ideas of perfection. My immanence is immediate, my transitivity phantasmic. I cannot be grateful for being born, nor can I feel any obligation to that which sustains me, because my existence is a great tease: life is too marvelous to surrender and too horrible to affirm.

For Dostoevsky, living in the period between the Kantian moment of moral will and the present horizon of carnal consciousness — the transitional moment of the arbitrary, irrational, and, for him, spiteful will — everything was possible because nothing was forbidden. Now Dostoevsky's consciousness has split in two. Those who are wounded by the absence of prescription yearn for a new order. Those who live in the plenitude of possibility know that nothing is necessary — they have no obligation, only a default drive, the body living them. And here is the curse that plagues and haunts liberalism — the restless monkey who is revealed through the insistent demystification and concretization of life, who has finally demystified society sufficiently to objectify it as an aspect of the natural environment, a simple opportunity structure. Each individual in the West today lives in conscious or unconscious tension with the finality of the finite flesh, acknowledging or suppressing the enormous idea that everything about life's conduct is a matter of strategy and that nothing is a matter of duty. Indeed, an examined life is so difficult to live that it is tempted, nay, compelled, to tell itself that there are no moral restraints on it because the great tease is a dirty trick — individuated life is a losing proposition, but it is the only game in town. Who can swallow the deromanticized Nietzsche? Who can acknowledge themselves to be the savage, the true savage who is the secret of modernity; not the noble savage, but the civil savage, the one who knows civilization as an animal knows its ecological niche, as a wilderness? This is the wild card of liberal society and it is dealt to every hand. But who does not try to domesticate it by converting it to a regular member of the deck? And in doing so liberal society is made to suffer its death agony. But it is an interminable death. The civil savage, the fruit of modernity, the masterless man disposing of his estate, his body, dwells with a crowd that has committed itself to the hospice called liberal society. Would that it were a half-way house, but hospice it must be for the legions who cannot live with the finite eschatology of the modern process.

Liberalism cannot tolerate the Nietzschian fulfillment of modernity, the appearance of a dis-banded ape who returns to his wits after a long romance with reason. And this ape cannot tolerate himself, unless gifted with massive infusions of Hume's "moral sentiment," the emotional lithium for dispelling autism. But moral sentiment has never been in sufficient supply to sustain a civilization and today even less so than ever with the disappearance of its traditional supports in customary community. The famous "cake of custom" of Walter Bagehot has once and for all been broken beyond repair and mild cases of schizophrenia are increasing at a faster rate than are cases of AIDS. Liberalism's immune system, the sense of duty, has broken down, dividing society into two life-forms, predators and parasites, both of which symptomize an intolerance for the living modern truth, the civil savage, and from that intolerance fall into a chronic demoralization. The predators are those who are fortunate to be in a social position in which they can exploit the less favored, so they declare their independence from any obligation to serve others. Yet they are poisoned by guilt and must perform the disgusting and unedifying rite of justifying themselves: Ivan Boesky pontificated, "You can be greedy and still feel good about yourself," and the crowd of students at UCLA cheered. The parasites are the unfortunates who are ever reminded of their dependence on others and seek, therefore, to make everyone servants. They mewl about community or snarl about alternative life-styles, but their aim is to place everyone in their position of social failure, which is why their intellectual advocates scream that the ego is a linguistic fiction. Calculating and consuming egos versus linguistic fictions is what the fashionable Nietzsche/Marx debate comes down to on the street-level of academia, the convention floor. Liberalism has imploded and two illiberalisms have been sucked into the void, the old anarcho-capitalism strutting in the black mask of Nietzsche and the even staler Jacobinism parading under the red flag of Marx. And sitting on the imperial throne of the West as 1986 ends is the predator-parasite, Ronald Reagan, the logical successor of the parasite-predators, Hitler, Stalin, Mussolini et al.

Modern life has developed beyond liberalism, beyond its own social support system of institutions, and confronts radical human weakness, which is expressed as the specious independence of the dependent exploiter and the resentful dependence of the anxious exploited: it inscribes the fulfillment of the master-slave dialectic without the saving grace of the servant's self-overcoming. The life of strength, which is the demand of an overripe modernity, is based on the simple acknowledgment of irremediable human frailty and failure without any superadded compensation. From there one makes do, creating the social bond out of sentiment and sensibility, whether it is a more primary erotic feeling or a more reflective sympathy. Strength is assent to weakness followed by the determination to hang on tenaciously and, perhaps, to find and cultivate the Epicurean garden, not behind walls but in the streets. And street life has become ubiquitous, if only in the bizarre simulacrum of video. The modern romance has come full circle, returning to the ground of all civilization, to the recognition of the insufficiency of the flesh, but without any symbolic escape from it and promising only the disturbing tubes and switches of the intensive-care unit. And everywhere the signs intrude and indicate that human beings cannot tolerate such an existence. People clutch and claw each other, seek completion in the other, an effort doomed to failure because in the other they confront themselves, though this is the one thing that they will not admit. This is not the war of all against all but the ramshackle play-room of the bourgeois man-child, Disneyland after the rides have rusted out and the parents have gone home. Modernity is the deconstruction of civilization itself, demystifying the symbols of transcendence and leaving only the reflection of human fallibility and all of the desperate attempts to avoid owning up to it.

It is far more accurate to call the present era postliberal than postmodern. For the great liberals, such as Hobhouse, Dewey, Croce, and Ortega, the statement would be a contradiction in terms, because in their time modernity had not yet deconstructed itself, had not found its basis in the individuated flesh which is resistant to and unassimilable by any institution. The high point of liberalism was reached at the second great moment of modernity, that of the Kantian moral will. Before the turn of the nineteenth century liberalism had been a counterpoint to absolutism, but lacked a foundation for organizing social life, opening restricted spheres of autonomous activity such as commercial enterprise, scientific investigation, and secular art. Under the sign of the Cartesian ego, the modern spirit filled itself out in each special area of life, but had no thematic organization of its own save the passive reflection on totality through reflective thought — rationalist metaphysics and empiricist epistemology. The notorious split in Locke's thought between an empiricist theory of knowledge and a voluntaristic political philosophy epitomizes the adolescence of liberalism, an incipient ideal for social life not yet interiorized by the self as essential to itself. Kant undertook that interiorization by making the will intrinsic to the self, determining it morally. Kant liberated the will from religious mystification, thereby removing the traditional supports for social relations, such as, Edmund Burke's "pleasing illusions", and leaving as their distilled essence a principle of conduct, known as the categorical imperative, which he believed to be inherent to human thought. Suddenly the Cartesian ego was transformed into a moral self, capable of constituting society out of its own resources, at least in principle. At this point, liberalism encounters its sustaining truth, its principle of self-organization, which is revealed to be an ideal: liberal society is constituted by the project of universalizing the moral will, that is, of creating a voluntary solidarity of human beings based, most profoundly, on practical assent to the imperative to treat others as ends-in-themselves, never as means only; thus it is the moralization of politics.

Viewed historically, the failure of liberalism is the failure of the duty to sustain modern society. At the root of the Kantian revolution is the bold dare to live with others in a disposition of forbearance, to sacrifice the pursuit of objects of one's own inclinations when that pursuit would deprive others of their freedom to create a life. Kant, in the dawn of the democratic age, did not believe that the moral will actually could constitute a social order. He discoursed about a rational being, not a man of flesh and bone, and was clear about the distinction, affirming most of the early-modern realism about the necessity of external threat and punishment for disciplining his concrete individual, the "unsociable social being." His realism, however, had no inward foundation and was merely the mirror image of Locke's voluntarism — the counterpoint had become the melody. In the generations succeeding Kant, liberals were left with the task of showing how society was, could be, or inevitably would be constituted on the basis of voluntary solidarity. Hegel's notion of voluntary solidarity as a self-conscious affirmation of rational necessity, Stirner's proclamation of the union of egoists, and Marx's sublime principle "from each according to his abilities, to each according to his needs" are the great expressions of the liberal ideal. And all of them founder on the rock of the end-in-itself, which is progressively revealed to be the "ill-construed organism" of Alfred North Whitehead.

As in the case of every dialectical process, the negation of the liberal moment began almost simultaneously with its affirmation. Kierkegaard, with a desperate nostalgia, challenged the fundamentality of the moral will, just as Pascal had earlier attacked the Cartesian ego, because it did not express the claims of his inwardness for a satisfaction unavailable in mundanity. But even more fateful was Schopenhauer's proclamation of the insatiable and ever-frustrated will to live, so astutely understood by Georg Simmel to be the result of the first pure reflection of life upon itself, the moment at which life itself becomes fully its own object. This is the appearance of the wild card in modernity, of its deconstructing element, which renders any principle of social organization gratuitous by bringing to lucidity that which can never be socialized, but which can only be suppressed or repressed in the interest of common life, if it is not self-limited in an act of compassionate humility. Modernity now begins to outrun liberalism, to blast its synthesis of will and morality, the rational being as citizen. It is only a short run from Schopenhauer through Dostoevsky's "underground man," who will not be a piano key for others to play upon and who asserts with futility the "freedom to be free," to Nietzsche's mendacious animal who will not face the truth of his constitutive imperfection and ends up avoiding it by the spiritual surgery of the "last man," the blinking consumer. Through Nietzsche's conduit streams the modernist understanding of the conscious flesh — Freud's mordant insight that the conflict of Eros and Thanatos is resolved for the individual through the will to die at one's own proper biological time; Sartre's gasp of the useless passion, so chilling that it transmutes into the purest liberal *ressentiment*, the terroristic decree that "none is free until all are free," inverts voluntary solidarity, the grimacing mask of intolerance; and finally, the philosophy of the nursery, the current fascination with the Nietzsche of the devolutionary dialectic of camel, lion, and child. Liberalism was a passing phase of modernity, its young adulthood, and not its permanent structure, a hope and never a fulfillment, as much a romanticism, a mystification, as the totalitarianisms it destroyed and the chiliasms that have overwhelmed it, especially the ultimate chiliasm of the overman as bionic man. Liberalism is burned out because the crawling flesh does not aspire to be a moral being, the liberal substitute for the immortal soul. It has (passed that wish by in) favored biological romanticism. Nazism was not an enormous aberration, nor was it the revelation of the depth of "man's inhumanity to man," nor the culmination of modernity, capitalism, German idealism, the modern state system, or desacralization, but merely an instance of life reflecting upon itself with intolerance, with hatred. It is the precursor of the substitution of tubes and switches for the flesh, of the laboratory for life.

Prior to the French Revolution, liberalism was a leavening agency in absolutist institutions. Now, in the Nietzschian moment, it is a *trompe d'oeil* covering techno-bureaucratic organization. During its own time, liberalism fought to concretize the moral universal. Indeed, the institutions of liberal democracy may be understood as neurotic compromise formations between the ideal of voluntary solidarity and the predatory and parasitical wills. Such is a post-Freudian interpretation of constitutionalism, bills of rights, representative government, checks and balances, separation of powers, rule of law, loyal opposition, competitive party systems, and all of the other devices of liberal political mechanics — all of which are neuroses synthesizing the Kantian super-ego and the old Adam. Of course, they are not as such for liberals, who clutch them as earnests on the fulfillment of the ideal, as hard-won victories in the struggle for liberty that warrant appreciation and gratitude, and that should incite to fresh efforts at reform. Whether or not one is a liberal depends, in the terms I am using here, on how one values these institutional devices and the whole project of spinning out mediations between morality and organized predatory-parasitical lust. A mediation between conflicting intentionalities becomes neurotic when the wishes that must be restrained and reshaped become too refractory to be satisfied in a sublimation and begin to infect and transform the blocking wish into a distorted representation of themselves; in this case the moral will is impressed into the service of the exploitative will and, thus, becomes demoralized, taking such forms as *ressentiment*, projection, rationalization, splitting, displacement, and reaction formation — the defense mechanisms. And then a deadly repetition proceeds, a slow downward cycle of corruption marked by ever-new "adaptive structures," ever-more mechanisms — boards, committees, agencies, special prosecutors, consultants — to rectify the failure of the older mechanisms. Finally, as E.M. Forster wrote, "The machine stops," but probably not for a long time. The liberal will say that there is nothing else to do but keep working on the system because it's still the best mechanism around — one-half of a cheer for democracy, maybe? The alternatives are worse, aren't they? Liberalism with a fascist streak looks better than socialism with an inhuman face, doesn't it? There's no harm in trying; something good might come of it. Anyway we have our whole world to lose and it doesn't look like there's anything else to win. Richard Rorty looks around and finds nothing better than bourgeois democracy. His imagination fails him. The civil savage maps the new wilderness and applies his imagination to strategy and tactics — Lenin interiorized, with all the projections withdrawn from the liberal ruins.

As a compromise formation, liberalism undergoes a continuous process of alteration as the relation between the super-ego, the Kantian moral will, and the desires that ever threaten to dissolve public order change. Desire here is understood not merely as an inward experience of individuals, though it is most primordially that, never shedding its subjective root, but as the entire organization of the pursuit of objects in the public field of social action. Thus, the project of mapping the wilderness takes the form of presenting a "diagnosis of the times," as Mannheim called it. The civil savage is the heir of the "free-floating intellectual," the living precipitate of the burned-out liberal polity; not a hyper-civilized functionary composing social conflict into a putative harmony, as such mature liberals as Mannheim and Ortega envisioned, but a genuine negation, the dialectical other, of his spiritual progenitor. The free-floating intellectual, aware of all the possibilities of programmatic social change, performed a secondary reflection on them, creating an ideal synthesis, an image of a comprehensive order that allowed for the preservation of every value backed by organized power. This reflective operation is the final moment of the Kantian procedure of receiving the culturally-formed given and eliciting the ground of its possibility through a transcendental move. In contrast to Kant's transcendental critique, which results in the separation of the forms of the given from their contents, however, the free-floating intellectual's reflection eventuates in a new formed-content, a reconciliation of ideology and utopia, a compromise formation at a second remove from the conflict of lust and morality, a sublimated neurosis. As the negativity of the free-floating intellectual, the civil savage retains the hyper-civilized awareness of the multiplicity and relativity of programmatic possibility, but appropriates the sociology of knowledge as a means to mapping and charting, not as a springboard to totalization. Instead of that totalization, he undertakes a deconstruction, an analysis that brings the given of programmatic political thought back to the elements out of which it was composed, those forces that created its being as political neurosis; that is, the dialectical other of the free-floating intellectual's reconstruction is deconstruction. The civil savage is as much a healer as his forebear, but he is not society's physician: he takes seriously the dictum of Lev Chestov: "Philosopher, heal thyself." Wholeness, for the civil savage, cannot be reclaimed within the bounds of the liberal-democratic machinery but only through the recovery of corporeality, which is accomplished by radically objectifying all social images of the self, appropriating them as masks, personae, or better, as the masks of the primitive. The new social therapy is the withdrawal of projection, the reversal of inserting the self into a greater whole, of investigating how the many individuals become one social order. Now it is a matter, as Nietzsche understood, of what the flesh can assimilate from civilization, of treating civilization according to the standards of nutrition.

There is a new liberalism rising in the United States amid the collapse of the right-wing reaction that followed the suppression of the "liberation movements" in 1968. In order to chart that liberalism it is necessary to understand what the reaction signified, which is now easy to do, since it reveals its essence in its demise. I shall begin with the figure of Ronald Reagan, the representative man of the reaction, the negation of Machiavelli's Prince and all of his offspring, the social type of leader. In the dialectic of the modern spirit Reagan is determined as the purest individuation of Nietzsche's "last man," the predator-parasite, a gutless blinker, a creation of public relations, void of will, existing at the margins of Machiavelli's discourse, attempting, unself-consciously, to make the appearance of virtue stand completely for its reality. The phenomenon of Reagan can be understood only through the insight that modernity has outrun liberalism. From the very start neither he nor his advisors evinced any respect for the legal mechanics of a liberal society. Perhaps his great joke on constitutionalism was to offer Gerald Ford a "condominium" over the Presidency in return for his accepting the place of Vice-President on his ticket. But Reagan was never intended to be a President, in the sense of governing anyway. The man who would not even broach the question of trade with Nakasone, because he didn't want to argue with a "friend," who hates conflict and is, therefore, the man who is well liked by everyman — the incarnation of Willie Loman — styles himself as a "marketer" of policy, not as an executive, that is, an executor. The man who needs cue cards to think, who reads political fantasies and watches movies to prepare for summits, who calls his wife "Mommy" and keeps a Nancy doll with him in the hospital, embodies the consciousness that the social world is a second nature, made for him, which takes care of itself. Far more deeply than a negation of liberalism, Reagan represents the negation of modern politics itself, which is predicated on the figure of the protector, the Prince, Hobbes's sovereign. He is what the media call a "disengaged" President, their euphemism for the predator-parasite who feeds upon a civilization unaware of the virtue required to sustain it, the fulfillment of Josiah Royce's "viciously acquired naiveté."

The President as salesman, as cheerleader, and — most deeply — as rationalizer of his constituents' predatory and parasitical lusts is the measure of citizenship in the contemporary United States. Indeed, Reagan's Presidency symbolizes the American mind because, unlike the modern leader, who has qualities of will and determination that distinguish him from the followers, Reagan is but the public image of the ordinary self-understanding of the mass. The long-observed splitting of Reagan's mentality into "ideologue" and "pragmatist," again a euphemistic characterization, is merely the structure that is encountered in every panelled den, cocktail lounge, coffee shop, cafeteria, and meeting room in the United States, where the "cheap grace" deplored by Dietrich Bonhoeffer is dispensed with political flavoring. Everyday political consciousness in the postliberal era employs political ideas primarily as incitements to feeling good about oneself, specifically through the stimulant-depressant of *ressentiment*. The noble savage becomes the noble sucker and is proud of himself for being so. What can be more self-flattering than to take pot shots at the Evil Empire, to degrade "Washington" while being at its center — the blind eye of the hurricane — and to rail against parasites when one is the parasite king? That is the so-called "ideological side" of the Reagan mind, but it does not comprehend ideology in the conventional senses of vision or apology. It is politics serving neurosis, the thought of the "good man" who excuses his failures and vents his hatreds by pretending that the wicked have stomped all over him only because he was too nice a guy to fight them in the gutter. But now, the good man will tell you, things are going to be different — we're going on a crusade. Of course, that is all talk and meant to be no more. The predator-parasite is fundamentally a parasite, not a predator like Hitler was. As parasite, he intends that his thought be taken seriously only as provocative of emotion. What he really wants is to live his ordinary life as comfortably as possible, strictly defining his obligations to the bare minimum, leaving maximum "quality time" for the enjoyments of mass consumption, like the supreme gratification of televised football. And this is what passes for "pragmatism." But, of course, it is not that, not even expediency. It is sheer flaccidity, letting things go, doing no more than what one is intimidated into doing because one hates to fight, which is why, in the Reagan era, it has frequently been so difficult to determine just what governmental policy is: it is not that Reagan is a "yes man," rather he can't say "no." Strutting around as the apostle of anti-terrorism and then dealing arms for hostages is not, essentially, an instance of hypocrisy or of self-conscious mendacity, as the liberal mind must understand it, but an evidence of a neurotic splitting, the moral equivalent of a stroke, in which the right hand does not know what the left hand is doing. The unity of the Reagan mind is not ideational, but is constituted by his impulse to feel good about himself, to desperately give a hopeful emotional cover to his own inadequacy, and it is this passion that unites him to the public-at-large. The crusade against "state-sponsored terrorism" is not meant to be undertaken, but to make Americans experience the feeling of moral strength and resolve. Dealing arms for hostages was the easiest thing to approve when some parasite-predators proposed it: it was too hard to say "no," or even to think of saying "no," and far too easy to whip up sufficient enthusiasm and rationalization to say "yes." Therefore, direct action, which Ortega identified as the negation of liberalism, became the essence of American politics, in the form of "loose cannons," the cute media euphemism for adventurism.

Reagan's is the postmodern mind encountered at the level of the panelled basement den, the preferred "site" of his mass constituency. Ensconced in his easy chair, nibbling on snacks with his cronies in front of the TV, he is free to turn political program into the quip, soothing the wounds of his masculine pride left by all of the craven concessions he made to the ambitious exploiters who weaseled their ways into access to him during the day. Then he appears with those same viciously naive quips on the screens of TVs in dens across the country. Life goes on in its everyday round and so does the englobing fantasy of the externalized imagination, the bizarre simulacrum of TV. Here pop culture becomes fully coincident with *avant-garde* modernism. For what is the Reagan mind but the child-man's waiting philosophy, the last man's embrace of everyday life with a transcendental reflection superadded to it? The Presidency is a retirement village, the office is part-time work, execution is pure delegation. Only now, at the end of 1987, the mass rebels against its own image — it doesn't really want a President who wants to be protected by others; it wants a protector. It also wants to keep dreaming: it doesn't want a protector who will demand anything from it but one who will keep dispensing cheap grace to it — it doesn't want a parasite-predator who will put it to work and war, because it wants to remain a predator-parasite. It wants the impossible, a liberal fascism ruled by a benevolent protector; someone who likes it — since it is incapable of feeling love — just for what it is. And above all, the mass wants to feel good about itself.

"You can be greedy and still feel good about yourself." Ivan Boesky, that other representative man of the late '80's, the parasite-predator, the arbitrageur who epitomizes the self-cannibalization of corporate capitalism, is the legacy of the "me generation" to the emerging neo-liberalism. The military science fiction of "Star Wars" and the financial science fiction of "supply-side economics" may pass with economic recession, but the degradation of modern consciousness, the dark night of the liberal spirit will not go away. In the current social-science blockbuster, Robert Bellah's *Habits of the Heart*[1], a trenchant analysis of the standard interpersonal relation in the United States today is depicted as a therapeutic connection; that is, the common ground of meeting the other is the implied contract — "I'm OK, you're OK." Each offers to the other an affirmation of sanity and asks in return that nothing more be requested but that which is required by conventional and minimal expectations. All individuals are free to create a self-satisfied self out of whatever they can scrounge from the environment, as long as they don't bother others in the pursuit of the same — everyone a bag lady, the yuppie as bag lady, the bag lady as yuppie. If the pursuit of a lonely self-consumption fails, one must suffer in silence, because if one gives way to overt discontent there is a place waiting in that fast-growing service industry, the private psychiatric hospital or in a half-way house or mass shelter. There is nothing worse for the predator-parasite than to miss the "good" experiences that he or she "deserves" from life. Moral grace is bestowed on those who "do something for themselves." The predator-parasite is a weak ego, ever-slipping into the lonely despair of the dying flesh, ever-looking to inflate itself with what it has acquired, especially the empty "strokes" that others give it. Just this type of mentality believes Ronald Reagan to be a "nice" man. It, indeed, lives in dread of the "not nice," the reminders of everything that goes wrong with life. The formula for the mind of the United States is a strong sense of self and a weak ego, the deep feeling of me-ness and the deeper insecurity about one's ability to cope with the trials of life. Enthusiasm that masks fear is pervasive; this is how Ronald Reagan has cast his spell for years. Now that the spell has been broken, what will restrain the parasite-predators? This is the question that neo-liberalism addresses; it is the popular alternative to fascism and, therefore, the way in which modern politics drags itself along as it lives out its prolonged death agony.

There are no paradigmatic texts expressing the new liberalism, just statements of Democrats plotting appeals for 1988, overviews of journalists, and fragments of opinion writers. This absence of programmatic content is symptomatic of liberal burnout, but it is surely intelligible in light of the spoliation wrought by the late reaction, because liberalism today has the unhappy and thankless task of building upon scorched earth, of imposing austerity on a debt-ridden society that has glutted itself with imports; of scaling back its military might and, therefore, retreating from spheres of influence; of saving a service economy when the rest of the world has learned the secret that anyone can sell insurance. The United States, king of the debtor nations, is the new Argentina: it will be handed over to the liberals now that it is going broke and has suffered humiliation in foreign affairs at the hands of the right wing. But the children who inhabit this rusted Disneyland want nothing to do with austerity; they don't want to be wakened from their dream. This is the terrible dilemma of the new liberalism, why it has no program, no totalizing vision: it must impose pain while seeming to provide pleasure. In the wake of the bankruptcy of the public treasury through the "arms buildup" it must become the loyal friend of capitalism rather than its friendly adversary, as it has been since the Great Depression: liberalism must become fascism with a human face merely to save a severely weakened society, constituted by a corrupt mass, from the rigors of the classical corporate state of the 1930s. Its mediation between morality and desire must therefore be more strained than it ever was in the past; it must resort to compulsion or simply become the precursor of fascism. If Ivan Boesky and Ronald Reagan are the problem, then the solution must be the fabrication of a "we generation" out of the scant materials of "Live Aid," "Farm Aid," and "Hands Across America." People must be convinced to "feel good about themselves," as Joan Baez claimed that she "felt good" about herself after participating in "Hands," by joining a sacrificial community. The political formula of neo-liberalism is the capitalistic community of sacrifice, the jamming together of the tension of modern liberalism in the apotheosis of therapeutic fantasy. The rhetorical device of the new liberalism has been sounded by Mario Cuomo: Americans are one big family and must treat one another as good relations. Try it, you'll like it. The civil savage laughs without any bitterness at this vain posturing. It is more sad than disgusting. There will have to be a new crusade, a new dream, but how uninspiring — America must get itself into shape to ... win the trade war. Will it be World War II all over again?

Understandably, the new liberals resist being forced to thematize a program. They have in common only a concern with keeping the less fortunate in the fold of the Democratic Party as they broaden the coalition to include the good people of the broad middle class and gain sufficient financial support to mount a successful campaign. The essence of their mediation may, indeed, never be expressed in any popular forum, because it juxtaposes anarcho-capitalism and Jacobinism far too closely, without any buffer to comfort the ordinary mind. That essence has been described by Mickey Kaus, a journalist for *The Washington Monthly*, in his reply to Randall Rothenberg's overview, *The Neoliberals*.[2] According to Kaus, his brand of neo-liberalism has two principles:

> First, instead of tolerating capitalism, neoliberalism champions its positive virtues — risk-taking, creativity, and the excitement of change and accomplishment.... Second, instead of trying to muffle the material inequalities generated by the marketplace neoliberals would restrict the world in which these inequalities matter. They would carve out a communitarian sphere where class distinctions are dissolved, where the principle of equal dignity in citizenship prevails, where it is recognized that money is, after all, only money. The idea of national service and the neoliberal insistence on saving the public schools should be seen as attempts not just to help out the economy, but to preserve a community life where a kid from the ghetto and a kid from Beverly Hills meet as equals.[3]

This is the prescription for capitalist Jacobinism or Jacobin capitalism, depending upon which of the two principles is made the dominant theme and which the counterpoint. Or, it might best be called liberal fascism, a managed capitalism in the context of a compelled community, under the motto "dignity in citizenship."

Neo-liberalism is the romance of reindustrialization, the fantasy of industrial policy. Most deeply, though it is liberalism that has outrun itself, that has lost its footing in voluntary solidarity and has at last surrendered to the state as the basis of community, an action which political thought must do when traditional solidarities have been worn away and there is no longer any hope for voluntary solidarity. From Kaus's principles follow all of the specific neo-liberal policies — a revived NRA, a new CCC, subsidization of entrepreneurship in growth industries, workfare rather than welfare, restoration of the draft, university-industry research centers, education for skills, worker participation in management, and the scaling back of entitlements. Some of these measures will surely be enacted, others will be diluted, and others passed by, depending upon the severity of economic conditions and the degree of fear within the population; but what appears clearly on the horizon is the appeal to state-sponsored community, enjoining sacrifice and holding out safety under the cover of the joy of serving together in a grand national effort to catch up and pull ahead in the great technological race. The predator-parasites will acquiesce more or less in this kind of program — they are already frightened, now that the Reagan myth is being dispelled, and need more togetherness than the "new patriotism" provided. They will, of course, be refractory, which only means that the new liberalism will be a holding action against the day in which Jacobinism and capitalism finally fuse into techno-fascism. There will be plenty to manage in the coming order for the parasite-predators, who will bring the manipulation of consent to a high art. The civil savage will exist in the interstices of the new order, feasting on the leavings of the old liberal civilization while building up a tolerance for the humiliation of the flesh.

Department of Political Science
Purdue University

Notes

1. Robert Bellah et al., *Habits of the Heart: Individualism and Commitment in American Life* (Berkeley: University of California Press, 1985).

2. Randall Rothenberg, *The Neoliberals: Creating the New American Politics* (New York: Simon and Schuster, 1984).

3. Mickey Kaus, "Too Much Technology, Not Enough Soul," *Washington Monthly*, 16, 8 (September, 1984), p. 53.

A THOROUGHLY HIDDEN COUNTRY: *RESSENTIMENT*, CANADIAN NATIONALISM, CANADIAN CULTURE

Michael Dorland

The object is to explore the huge, distant and thoroughly hidden country of morality

Nietzsche, Genealogy of Morals

...the Canadian cultural obsession with victimization is the flip side of a belief in total superiority

B. W. Powe, The Solitary Outlaw

Introduction

...the most terrible antidote used against...people is to drive them so deep into themselves that their re-emergence is inevitably a volcanic eruption

Nietzsche, Schopenhauer As Educator

With the distinguished yet qualified exception of George Grant and the writings of some Canadian historians, the theme of *ressentiment* as such has been all too neglected in the critical literature on Canadian culture. Not because the theme is not a major one in the Canadian discourse, but on the contrary perhaps because it is so massively pervasive by its absence. For in this negative form, ressentiment presents profound problems in the development of cultural expression, and the formation and application of a cultural politics that would include artistic practices, their institutional orientation and critical interpretation — in short, for the problems of Cana-

dian culture. If as will be argued here, ressentiment does, in fact, constitute a dominant theme explicitly in Canadian political and cultural practices and implictly in the administrative practices of their institutional
orientation, its non-recognition hitherto in Canadian critical writing might
indicate if not interpretive timidity, then at least a strategy of avoidance
worth examining in greater detail.

Ontology of Canadian ressentiment: the discourses of Canadian silence

> I had come to see that everything was radically connected with po-
> litics, and that, however one proceeded, no people would be other
> than the nature of its government made it
>
> Rousseau, Confessions

Reflecting, forty years ago, on his "unhappy experiences" at academic
conferences, Harold Innis had discerned a rhetorical pattern at such meet-
ings, namely that Americans and Englishmen, "quickly made aware of our
sensitiveness", spent much of their time commenting on how much better things were done in Canada than in Great Britain or the United States.
As Innis observed, "The demand for this type of speech implies a lack
of interest in a Canadian speaker who might say something distasteful about
domestic affairs."[1]

As Innis would go on to explain, the "lack of interest" came not from
foreign guests, in any event invited only to praise, but from Canadians and
so suggested, as Innis was aware, the presence of something more
problematic than mere lack of interest. In fact, it suggested something deeply rooted in Canadian experience, the presence, as he put it, of "a continuous repression"[2] of "a very great fear of pronouncements" by Canadians,
indeed, that there was something, possibly dreadful, about Canada that
only a Canadian might be able to utter "since . . . non-Canadians . . . could
not make statements about Canadian affairs which would be taken
seriously."[3]

But if tasteful statements about domestic affairs by non-Canadians would
not be taken seriously and there was such a great fear of distasteful
pronouncements on the part of Canadians such that, if they were actually
going to attempt to say something, their only recourse was, as Innis put
it of his own experience, "writing in such guarded fashion that no one
can understand what is written"[4], what was being maintained in silence,
and silenced to such an extent as to suggest, again, something possibly
more considerable than lapses of taste?

The notion of a distasteful statement, however, provides a clue as to what
might be involved, since the idea of taste suggests, narrowly, that which
goes into or comes out of the mouth (as food, drink or words) and so more
broadly an idea of politeness, manners, i.e., culture. The distasteful statement, then, would be the expression of a form of culture (or perhaps, more
precisely, non-culture) whose 'taste' has been so affected or altered in such

226

a way as to have become 'distasteful'. As for the nature of that distaste, suffice it for now merely to indicate its lack of specificity by way of a potentiality that could range from the merely unpleasant through the bitter to the extremities of the poisonous or even the monstrous. More important, however, might be the question of what happens when the mouth, i.e., the organ of communication and culture, is filled with unpleasantries to the point of becoming so unspeakable that these cannot be expressed openly, or whose public forms of expression must, therefore, be subjected to rigorous policing or strict morality? What happens when a nation, i.e. a territorial configuration of mouths, establishes silence as the cultural norm for domestic affairs?

This paper will attempt to begin to account, by means of a theory of ressentiment, for the discrepancies between the very great fear of unauthorized pronouncements by Canadians that Innis indicated, and the mere talk of an officialized nationalist and culturalist discourse whose *precondition* is silence, i.e. the security that comes from knowing that nothing can ever be contradicted because nothing will ever be said. And this principally because, in William Kilbourn's grim formulation, *Canadian nature* "dreadful and infinite has inhibited the growth of the higher amenities in Canada": "Outnumbered by the trees and unable to lick them, a lot of Canadians look as though they had joined them — having gone all faceless or a bit pulp-and-papery, and mournful as the evening jackpine round the edges of the voice, as if...something long lost and dear were being endlessly regretted."[5] Such an account must then begin with an interrogation of the nature of Canadian silence.[6]

Writing last year some months after the opening of the current (and largely secret) round of Canada-US free-trade talks, *Report on Business Magazine* editor Peter Cook remarked that "There is probably no better sign of our own maturity than the fact that the average Canadian spends twice as much on imported goods as the average American without feeling bitter or resentful about it."[7] The valorization of an absence of ressentiment is what one might term, after Innis, a tasteful Canadian statement about domestic affairs, especially when, according to Cook, Americans by contrast are not only bitter and resentful but in addition "pugnacious" and "xenophobic" as a result of *their* trade deficit. However, Cook went on, if Canadians display remarkable maturity by their absence of resentment and bitterness, American "tantrums and tirades" are nevertheless "particularly vexing" for Canadians who in opening the free-trade talks "made the decision that America is the trade partner with whom they want to share their future."[8]

Cook's statement at a remove of forty years illuminates what Innis meant, at least in part, by the "distasteful", namely, bitterness and resentment. But if, on Cook's account, Canadians today possess such maturity as to not feel bitterness and resentment on economic questions, they are still capable of feeling particularly vexed on other accounts, such as being rebuffed by the *trade* partner with whom they want to share their future. In other words, and contrary to what Cook writes explicitly, Canadians *do* implicitly feel economic bitterness and resentment, and so much so that in addition they feel emotionally vexed as well. But vexation, like resentment, is an emotion or a form of expression that does not suddenly surface; rather, it is slow-burning and long-term: to say of something that it is vexed, as in 'a *vexed* question', is to say that it has occurred again and again, that it is tormenting, and that it is something that needs to be much debated and discussed. Like resentment, and perhaps this becomes clearer in its French form as *re-sentiment* (lit., feeling again), vexation is experienced repeatedly, repetitively, compulsively, and obsessionally: "a gruesome sight is a person single-mindedly obsessed by a wrong" (Nietzsche).[9] Furthermore, Cook's use of metaphor suggests that Canadian vexation or resentment arises from a perception of intimacy and (fear of) the rejection of that proposed intimacy by a chosen partner. As for the gender of the chosen partner, Cook makes clear, by two references to American films (RAMBO and CONAN THE BARBARIAN), how he regards at least one partner in the future relationship. The gender of the Canadian partner, however, is ambivalent: "...if the deal is not... rushed through Parliament and Congress, we will face a fresh administration in Washington which, like a spoilt child, will have to be tutored in the ways of the world anew."[10]

Canadian *denial of ressentiment* — the cultural celebration of silence as the highest form of our modernity — thus conceals a complex interlocking of multiple resentments: 1) a resurfacing of economic resentment that is 2) then displaced to a general emotional resentment where it recharges itself as vexation and 3) is displaced again as an interpersonal relationship in which fear of (and resentment of) rejection causes it to shift once more to 4) a moral plane now, where, from rebuff to rejection, Canada emerges radiantly as master of the ways of the world. In addition, Cook's use of what one could term a gender-bound metaphor (of the family, in which resentment is processed by morality and transformed into love, the rejection of which becomes an occasion for self-pity and so further resentment) evokes similar such recurrences in Canada's past that, as with the 1987 round of free-trade talks, involved fundamental relationships and orientations in Canadian history, internal and external, in which metaphors of the family encode far greater violences. The first example is internal and refers to the long and never-declared civil war between Canada and Quebec or what Hubert Aquin in 1964 called "the theme of the shotgun marriage" in Confederation, namely "the coexistence between two nations [might this not equally apply to Canada and the US?] [that] seems to form a venereal relationship pushed to a paroxysm of disgust, when it is not [in] the very image of a Christian marriage, indissoluble and in ruins...."[11] The second example is external (Canada's place in imperial relations) and thus entails a reversal in venereal relationships, from the aggressive waging of internal civil war to a more passive form of commodity-transfer, here from one pimp (the British Empire) to another (the American Empire). As William L. Grant put it in a 1911-1912 address on "The Fallacy of Nationalism": "I have no desire that this country of mine should be either the kept woman of the United States, or the harlot of the Empire."[12] A third example from the time of Canada's entry into the Second World War sees an American writer describing Canada as "the problem child of the Western Hemisphere", a typical product of family estrangement with an Oedipus complex with the mother country that prevents her ever growing up. As the writer puts it: "'Canada,' exploded one of her resentful intellectuals, 'is in international affairs not a man but a woman!'"[13]

In other words, and in a concretization of George Grant's "listening for the intimations of deprival,"[14] attending to intimations of *ressentiment* becomes a way of hearing Canadian silence speak. Instead of mere silence, following the chains of Canadian resentment soon unconceals discursive fields that extend from the landscape to economics, to politics, to sociology, to technology, to the intimacies of sexuality, and to the "higher amenities" of culture. What I'm suggesting here, in fact, is that there are few areas, if any, of Canadian experience where one is not struck by the extent to which the discourse upon that experience, whether acknowledged or repressed, whether official (government and press), intellectual (academic), or cultural (literary and artistic), to make some possibly arbitrary distinctions, is a discourse of *ressentiment*. This may sound a lot more overwhelming than it might actually turn out to be; in fact, this may simply be a guarded way of saying that, so far perhaps, Canadian experience has been intensely given over to nursing the petty wounds of the small, as Denys Arcand has suggested in films such as LE CONFORT ET L'IN-DIFFERENCE and LE DECLIN DE L'EMPIRE AMERICAIN or Harold Town in his painting "Canadian Retirement Dream" or the many other Canadian artists who, like Nietzsche's Zarathustra, may have sighed for a homeland where they need no longer "stoop before those who are small." But Canadian artistic expression may be just as imbricated with resentment as any other dimension of Canadian existence. The point is simply that, at the outset, we do not know this without, first, a better grasp of Canadian *ressentiment*: what is it? how prevalent is it? how does it articulate itself? what have been its effects? and lastly how does one overcome it? since, according to Nietzsche, *ressentiment* does not disappear without being overcome.

Ressentiment as a concept for cultural studies

As a concept for contemporary cultural studies, *ressentiment* has been curiously under-employed, though I suspect that as Nietzsche increasingly comes to be seen as *the* philosopher of (the overcoming of) *ressentiment*[15], this is likely to change. For certainly, in some of its earlier applications including Nietzsche's, *ressentiment* would appear to offer an infinitely rich terrain for cultural studies. Thus, for instance, Nietzsche's own characterization of the entire Judeo-Christian tradition as "the very seat of *ressentiment*"[16], or Michelet's and Taine's use of *ressentiment* as the motive of the French Revolution[17], or Simmel's ascription of *ressentiment* as "for all time the most solid support of bourgeois morality"[18] or Max Scheler's observation that "There is no literature more charged with *ressentiment* than Russian literature."[19] Or, in more recent studies, Fritz Stern's identification of "the ideology of Resentment" as having appeared almost simultaneously in almost every continental country in the last decades of the nineteenth century, including as well in certain aspects of American Populism[20]. And, in film studies, historians of Hollywood (such as the British writer David Thomson or the American businessman Benjamin Hampton) ascribe to *ressentiment* one of the key drives in American popular culture[21].

In other words, even a brief overview of some of the applications that have been made of *ressentiment* might potentially at least indicate a concept for the study of cultural formations (eg., religion, secular ideology, forms of popular culture such as literature and cinema) in the wide range of countries or continents that could be embraced within such notions as "the Judeo-Christian tradition" or "bourgeois morality" or the Western tradition of political, social and cultural modernity.

On the other hand, it is perhaps the very all-embracingness of *ressentiment* that has militated against its wider use in recent scholarship, at least until the broader development of all-embracing fields such as the humanities and/or cultural studies. Indeed, in an extension of the Michelet-Taine hypothesis that *ressentiment* is the content of revolution, Jameson argues that "the theory of *ressentiment, wherever it appears*, will always... be the expression and production of *ressentiment*" (emphasis added)[22]. This is to say that *the production of ressentiment as a theory* cannot be distinguished (or at least only with difficulty) from *the production(s) of theorists*. According to Jameson, these are "the intellectuals... — unsuccessful writers and poets, bad philosophers, bilious journalists, and failures of all kinds — whose private dissatisfactions lead them to their vocations as political and revolutionary militants [who]...will furnish the inner dynamic for a whole tradition of counterrevolutionary propaganda from Dostoyevsky and Conrad to Orwell...."[23] However, making of some intellectuals, whether revolutionary or counterrevolutionary, the producers of *ressentiment* is only restating the theory (or phenomenon) of *ressentiment* whereby, in Jameson's concept, 'authentic *ressentiment*', once stripped of its bad faith, "may be said to have a certain authenticity"[24], i.e., that *ressentiment*, like the rose by any other name, is *ressentiment*.

But what exactly is *ressentiment*, this word which has no exact correspondence in German, but which a German thinker (Nietzsche) introduced into philosophy "in its technical sense"[25]? If of Nietzsche and *ressentiment*, it might be possible to say, as Nietzsche remarked of Schopenhauer, that "He had only one task and a thousand means of accomplishing it: one meaning and countless hieroglyphs to express it"[26], it could perhaps be said that there are also a thousand ways of defining *ressentiment* in its technical or any other sense. It is thus interesting that Walter Kaufmann, for instance, finds it impossible to define *ressentiment* other than quoting Nietzsche who in turn variously sketches *ressentiment* as "hatred," "tyrannic will", or "picture-hating drives" (Heine)[27]. Similarly, Scheler whose book is a refutation not so much of *ressentiment per se*, which like Simmel he considers the basis of bourgeois morality and modern humanitarianism, as of Nietzsche's charge that *ressentiment* is the content of Christian (or more precisely Catholic) love; but Scheler at least sidesteps Nietzsche to the extent of providing a working definition of *ressentiment* as:

> the experience and rumination of a certain affective reaction directed against an other that allows this feeling to gain in depth and penetrate little by little to the very heart of the person while at the same time abandoning the realm of expression and activity

and

> this obscure, rumbling, contained exasperation, independent of the activity of the ego, [that] engenders little by little a long rumination of hatred or animosity without a clearly determined object of hostility, but filled with an infinity of hostile intentions. (emphasis added)[28]

This is to say, then, that *ressentiment* is not so much a theory (or at least not to begin with) as a (silent) feeling. To say of what, however, requires transforming *ressentiment* from an emotion into a theory, in other words, reducing Nietzsche to a philosopher or theorist of *ressentiment* when, if anything, he was its greatest dramatist, i.e., not a preacher of *ressentiment*, but the poet of its overcoming. Be that as it may, the Nietzschean definition of ressentiment that I will employ here is that where ressentiment becomes a revolt that turns creative:

> The slave revolt in morals begins by rancor turning creative and giving birth to values — the rancor of beings who, deprived of the direct outlet of action, compensate by an imaginary vengeance....Slave ethics...begins by saying "no" to an outside, an other, a non-self, and that no is its creative act. This reversal of the direction of the evaluating look, this invariable looking outward instead of inward, is a fundamental feature of rancor. Slave ethics requires...a sphere different from and hostile to its own...it requires an outside structure in order to act at all; all its action is reaction.[29]

However, let me elaborate that a little by suggesting after Nietzsche that *ressentiment* is the emotional content of the catastrophe of modern culture whose advent — in the form of what Nietzsche called the three M's:

Moment, Mode and Mob[30], and to which we can add a fourth, namely, Mood (and later perhaps a fifth: Movies) — entails a great silencing of every-thing else that was or might have been. If for Nietzsche, Western culture is the progressive advent of ever-larger *adiaphora* — spheres of non-determinacy or the neutralization of difference (*diapherein*, to differ) — *ressentiment* is the mood of the *adiaphora* of the "absolute silence" of any other cultural possibility save (totalitarian) Modernity, its History, its Culture and its multi-national organization as States which "In their hostil-ities...shall become inventors of images and ghosts, and with their images and ghosts they shall yet fight the highest fight against one another"[31].

In what follows, however, rather than extrapolating Nietzsche quotations, I would like to illustrate this theory of *ressentiment* with particular refer-ence to the forms of the 'creative no' developed by one modern state, name-ly Canada, in its experience with the adiaphora of the history, culture, and multinational organization of modernity.

Ressentiment in Canadian discourse: cultural implications

...there is a sort of mixture of inquisition and censorship which the Germans have developed into a fine art — it is called absolute silence
Nietzsche, Schopenhauer As Educator

The greatest melancholy of the will, even the liberating will, and thus the source of its *ressentiment* and revenge-seeking, is its inability to change the past: "Powerless against what has been done, he [the will] is an angry spectator of all that is past."[32] As a result, according to Nietzsche, history, justice, willing itself and "all life" become a form of suffering or punish-ment, i.e., revenge-seeking but with a good conscience. In such a form of suffering or punishment — not so much a theory but "as an almost in-tolerable anxiety"[33] — this corresponds to the *written* experience of Canadian history and literature, in a word, the Canadian experience of cul-ture, primarily in the form of chronicles of the (usually deserved) adminis-tration of punishment. Thus, to take what would be, in effect, the first of innumerable Royal Commission Reports, Lord Durham's (1839) recom-mended the "obliteration" of the nation (here French-Canada) out of fear that "the mass of French Canadians" would otherwise succumb to the "spirit of jealous and *resentful nationality*" (emphasis added).[34] Crushing the 'resentful nationalities' of North America (first French Canada, then — unsuccessfully — the Thirteen Colonies, and thirdly English Canada) "seems... to have been...the policy of the British Government [:] to govern its colonies by means of division, and to break them down as much as possible into petty isolated communities, incapable of combination, and possessing no sufficient strength for individual resistance to the Empire."[35] The absence, in Canadian experience, of any kind of revolutionary (or mere-

ly combinatory) disruption (of isolation) meant that the tradition of punitive administration assumed a deep and uninterrupted development in the
form of "a continuous repression" (Innis) of Canadian cultural expression
as resentful nationality (or in the more modern administrative discourse
of the Canadian state, 'narrow nationalism'). What nationalism and culture
there would be in Canada would thus be i) firmly Erastian, i.e. under the
authority of the State, both in character and in organization[36], ii) and if
not under the control of the state, either marginalized, fragmentary or non-
existent, or if neither of the above, iii) imported. Which is to say that, in
Canada, *ressentiment* takes the form of the administrative practice of an
absent discourse on the relationship between nationalism and culture. This
absence is structured around a) its preservation by b) the denial of the relationship between nationalism and culture instituted as c) three separations:
i) an administrative separation (known in the discourse of cultural policy
as "arm's length") of state cultural agencies from both nation and culture,
ii) an economic separation by the state of culture into public and private
administrative realms, and iii) a cultural separation by nationality in that
the content of the public realm is officially (and incrementally) Canadian
whereas that of the private realm is unofficially (and exponentially) American.[37] Put slightly less rebarbaritively, Canadian *ressentiment* articulates itself as the three absent discourses of a social structuring of cultural
contempt: that of the administrators for those whom they administer: "Inside every Canadian, whether she or he knows it or not, there is, in fact,
an American"; that of middle— and upper-class Canadians "concerned with
the health and viability of Canadian culture"; and thirdly, that of lower-
class Canadians who express their *ressentiment* in preferring American
popular culture: "...the more low-brow an American cultural activity, the
wider its appeal in Canada."[38]
    What characterizes these absent discourses as absences is that each forms
a discursive whole whose rhetorical strategy, but not its practices, consists in the denial of its own *ressentiment*. Thus, the discourse of Canadian cultural policy is always meliorative, though its punitive characteristics
do transpire. To take but one example from the cultural policy area that
has had the longest history of official Canadian preoccupation, namely cinema, Peter Pearson, current head of the principal state agency with responsibility for feature-film and television series production, reported in a
speech last winter before the Canada California Chamber of Commerce
that "We, the private sector and Telefilm now are fulfilling our joint goal:
to be on network primetime and playing the mainstream, not only in Canada, but like the Hollywood studios, all over the world." I won't discuss
the validity of the claim other than to note its similarity to Peter Cook's
vision of Canada as master of the ways of the world; suffice it here that,
according to Pearson, this worldwide expansion of Canadian cinema is
predicated upon and made possible by the silencing of the nationalism
that had, until this point, been the content of Canadian films, though the

blame for this is attributed to Canadian youth who must now be punished: "Now this 'national glue theory' is coming unstuck. The reality is that teenagers in Canada won't go to a Canadian movie if you pay them. Unless of course they want to." But as they don't want to, making them **want to** would henceforth be the thrust of Canadian policy; as Pearson put it, "Canadian fannies are going to have to fill the theater seats, and Canadian eyeballs watch the programs."[39]

Similarly, the discourse of Canadian literary culture denies its double *ressentiment* (which would otherwise be directed upwards at the literary patron, the state, and downwards onto the antinationalist and uneducated masses, the cultural consumers) and instead replaces it with theories of victimization, i.e., *ressentiment* turned in upon itself as self-punishment. As I shall below offer in greater detail an analysis of the workings of this, the clearest form of Canadian *ressentiment*, let me for now give one brief example, from Margaret Atwood's classic, *Survival*: "Let us suppose, for the sake of argument, that Canada as a whole is a victim...." The supposition, of course, soon becomes self-fulfilling: "...stick a pin in Canadian literature at random, and nine times out of ten you'll hit a victim."[40] If the perspectives of victim-production seemingly provide Canadian literature with a discourse that is not about ressentiment, the problem with victims as a literary natural resource is that supplies run out unless consciously produced. As Atwood notes, the productive resources of victimization over time only become depleted and increasingly obscure, thus creating the (state-supported) demand that makes of CanLit the producer of another Canadian staple, like fur, wheat or hydro-electricity: namely, the culture-victim:

> In earlier writers these obstacles are external — the land, the climate, and so forth. In later writers these obstacles tend to become both harder to identify and more internal; ...no longer obstacles to physical survival but...spiritual survival, to life as anything more than a minimally human being.... and when life becomes a threat to life, you have a moderately vicious circle. If a man feels he can survive only by amputating himself, turning himself into a cripple or a eunuch, what price survival?[41]

With that question— what price survival? — we come to the third and most literally absent discourse in Canadian *ressentiment*, namely the absolute silence of the Canadian public itself: glacial, inert, and so totally impenetrable that it can only be represented: "Have you no public opinion in that province?" a British statesman once asked Ontario's equivalent to Duplessis, Sir Oliver Mowat, while Sir Richard Cartwright, minister of finance, commented severely on the worthlessness of public opinion in the same province.[42] This absolute silence, however, is presumed by the other Canadian discourses of *ressentiment* to be the one most driven by revenge-seeking and so most to be feared and despised. For here is the (presumed) source of the 'resentful nationality' that, in the administrative discourse (Durham), "would separate the working class of the community from the possessors of wealth and the employers of labour"[43] : namely, the inhabitants of North America who, in Canadian historical discourse, "sometimes found their greatest and most malicious pleasure in the 'freedom to wreak upon their superiors the long locked-up hatred of their hearts'"[44]; a people who in Canadian literary discourse "make up for the[ir] meekness [in the province of public criticism]... by a generous use of the corresponding privilege in private"[45]; and that Canadian philosophical discourse (George Grant) has designated as the majority population of the continent, the last men of an achieved modernity.

To dwell in modernity might thus be assumed to be the animus of Canadian *ressentiment*. The signs of modernity (eg., population, urbanization, technologization, or in its cultural form, Americanization) would then be experienced with something akin to panic, an unbalancing and literal dislocation that Northrop Frye, in a profound insight, states perfectly when he writes that: "...Canadian sensibility has been profoundly disturbed, not so much by our famous problem of identity...as by a series of paradoxes in what confronts that identity....less...the question 'Who am I?' than...some such riddle as 'Where is here?'"[46]. Understanding Canadian *ressentiment* as precisely such a dislocation, this would suggest, with the advent of modernity, an acceleration of the inability to change no longer the past now (as in Nietzschean *ressentiment*) but an intensification of *ressentiment* to include the present and future as well. As William Norris, a Canadian author of the 1870s, expressed it, half-seriously: "Under the present system [in Canada] there is no past to be proud of, no present to give reliance, and no future to hope for. Devoid of national life the country lies like a corpse, dead and stagnant; but not so bad as it has been"[47]. This fear of loss —of one's place in time or history and in the space of community, of nation, of culture; in short, of group values— is what Frye calls "the real terror" of the Canadian (garrison) imagination, namely, the individuation that is also part of modernity, in which the individual is confronted with nothingness: "The real terror comes when the individual feels himself becoming an individual, pulling away from the group, losing the sense of driving power that the group gives him, aware of a conflict within himself far subtler than the struggle of morality against evil," a struggle which Frye does not identify but which we may suggest is that of *morality as ressentiment denied*. Instead of engaging with this struggle, as Frye remarks, "It is much easier to multiply garrisons, and when that happens, something anti-cultural comes into Canadian life, a dominating herd-mind in which nothing original can grow. The intensity of the sectarian divisiveness in Canadian towns, both religious and political, is an example..."[48]. Denied, *ressentiment* proliferates, rooted in the Canadian social structure —"The garrison mentality is that of its officers: it can tolerate only the conservative idealism of its ruling class, which for Canada means the moral and propertied middle class"[49] —garrisons multiply, the anti-cultural herd-mind dominates and "from the exhausted loins of the half-dead masses of people in modern cities" (as Frye puts it in a rare display of his own *ressentiment*[50]), the literature the garrison (but now metropolitan) society produces "*at every stage*, tends to be rhetorical, an illustration or allegory of certain social attitudes" (emphasis added).[51] And it is rhetorical, as opposed to poetic, (historical as opposed to mythic, documentary as opposed to imaginative, and single-mindedly obsessed with assertion as opposed to an autonomous literature) because, according to Frye, it avoids the theme of self-conflict[52], i.e., the theme of *ressentiment*, preferring instead the self-inflicted punishment of a good conscience.

Ressentiment and the Canadian Mind: Innis, McLuhan, Grant

If Canadian *ressentiment* can thus be understood as strategies for the avoidance of the (national and cultural) implications of modernity, even though as Frye remarks, "Canada is not 'new' or 'young': it is exactly the same age as any other country under a system of industrial capitalism"[53], does Canadian intellectual discourse share in the avoidance of *ressentiment*? Taking the three "emblematic figures in Canadian thought"[54] of Innis, McLuhan and Grant, one would have to say that they too practice survivalist strategies of avoidance, but primarily by way of attempts at displacing Canadian *ressentiment* onto larger transnational and technological entities. If Innis, McLuhan and Grant write always guardedly of Canadian *ressentiment*, their occasional lapses are, therefore, all the more powerful.

Innis

Innis' most unguarded text, and perhaps his most blunt, is his 1947 "The Church in Canada:" "...in this country [w]e are all too much concerned with the arts of *suppressio veri, suggestio falsi*. 'The inexorable isolation of the individual is a bitter fact for the human animal...and much of his verbalizing reflects his obstinate refusal to face squarely so unwelcome a realization.'"[55] Thus the Canadian preference for public lies, the inertia of public opinion, the notorious longevity of the political life of public figures, and the settling of "all great public questions" on the basis of petty, personal prejudices had for Innis "particular significance for the fundamental corruption of Canadian public life."[56] The uninterrupted and counter-revolutionary tradition of the dominance of church and state bureaucracies in both English and French Canada, which allowed the British to govern New France, brought Quebec into Confederation and thirdly made possible Canadian resource development by government ownership of canals, railways, hydro-electric and communications facilities, had also profoundly imprinted Canadian cultural development with what Innis termed "ecclesiasticism." This comprised a Puritanical repression of art and other expressions of cultural life, dogmatism, heresy trials, fanaticism, and supination before the state's incipient totalitarian encroachments upon civil liberties in general and intellectual freedom in particular[57]. These aspects of the corruption of Canadian public life thus made it "not only dangerous in this country to be a social scientist with an interest in truth but...exhausting:"

> On a wider plane it is a source of constant frustration to attempt to be Canadian. Both Great Britain and the United States encourage us in assuming the false position that we are a great power and in urging that we have great national and imperial possibilities. From both groups we are increasingly subjected...to bureaucratic tendencies dictated by external forces. We have no sense of our limitations.[58]

Without once using the word, Innis manages in this text to provide what amounts to a model or research agenda for understanding Canadian *ressentiment*.

McLuhan

Though McLuhan did not at any length write specifically on Canada, in *Counterblast* (1954) he offered the following poem on Canadian culture:

> Oh BLAST
> The MASSEY REPORT damp cultural igloo
> for canadian devotees of
> TIME
> &
> LIFE
> Oh BLAST....(t)he cring-
> ing, flunkey spirit of canadian culture, its
> servant-quarter snobbishness
> resentments
> ignorance
> penury
> ....
> BLESS
> The MASSEY REPORT,
> HUGE RED HERRING for
> derailing Canadian kulcha while it is
> absorbed by American ART & Technology.[59]

In other words, Canadian culture, as one particularly resentment-charged idiom in the residues of European nationalist print-culture, would be (deservedly) punished for its *ressentiment* by being joyously ground into "cosmic talc" by the American crusher of art and technology. McLuhan's flight into the cosmos of the technological Pentecost of universal understanding and unity[60] is thus but another version of the denial of Canadian *ressentiment* by a moralizing fantasy of world (or now cosmic) proportions. In this sense, McLuhan, as Arthur Kroker has written, by the time "he became fully aware of the nightmarish quality of...his thought....was...,in the end, trapped in the 'figure' of his own making....In a fully tragic sense,...he was the playful perpetrator, and then victim, of a sign-crime."[61]

Grant

In Grant, Canadian *ressentiment* is not denied qua *ressentiment*; on the contrary, it is universalized as the psychology of the "last men who will come to be the majority in any realized technical society".[62] (Saved perhaps by the "nemesis" of its aspiration to nationhood or at least protected by religious remnants of an identification of virtue and reason, Canada for Grant, as for Frye, is not a realized but a "decadent" technical society[63].) The will's despair at being unable to reverse or change the abyss of existence —life experienced as public and private fields of pain and defeat— becomes the spirit of revenge against ourselves, against others, against time itself. But the central fact about the last men is that because they cannot despise themselves, they can thus inoculate themselves against existence: "The little they ask of life (only entertainment and comfort) will give them endurance"[64]. Because they *think* they have found happiness, the last men of the northern hemisphere in the modern age have not overcome *ressentiment*, but "want revenge...against anything that threatens their expectations from triviality"[65]: impotent to live in the world, "in their self-pity (they) extrapolate to a non-existent perfection in which their failures will be made good." They are the last men because they are the inheritors of a decadent rationalism, the products of (resentful) Christianity in its secularized form.

Thus, Grant's celebration of the defeat of Canadian nationalism in *Lament For A Nation* — "I lament as a celebration of memory"[66] — might be seen as a model for the overcoming of *ressentiment*, a Nietzschean exercise in *amor fati*: a willed deliverance from the spirit of revenge. For, in the realization that this "last-ditch stand of a local culture"[67] was not a trivial issue (unlike the branch-plant culture of the last men) but involves "the diamond stuff of which nationalists must be made in these circumstances," Grant suggests a heroic or noble acceptance of defeat:

> Perhaps we should rejoice in the disappearance of Canada. We leave the narrow provincialism and our backwoods culture; we enter the excitement of the United States where all the great things are being done. Who would compare the science, the art, the politics, the entertainment of our petty world to the overflowing achievements of

New York, Washington, Chicago and San Francisco?....This is the profoundest argument for...break [ing] down our parochialism and lead[ing] us into the future.[68]

But is this acceptation not, as Grant remarked of his "incomprehension" of Nietzsche, simply too much to demand? Would the defeat of Canada's local culture be, in fact, an overcoming of ressentiment or, on the contrary, by its defeat the generalization of ressentiment to the core of modern, technical civilization? For Grant, amor fati "seems to me a vision that would drive men mad — not in the sense of a divine madness, but a madnesss destructive of good."[69] In this sense, Grant implies that accepting the defeat of Canadian nationalism would be such a form of madness — destructive of the good. But what then would be the "good" of Canada's local culture? Here, rather than further exploring Grant's writings, I would like to submit that such a definition would be the (gratuitous) undertaking of Canadian culture itself, in the Applebaum-Hebert Report's sense that "the largest subsidy to the cultural life of Canada [has] come... not from governments, corporations or other patrons, but from the artists themselves, through their unpaid or underpaid labour."[70] Defining the good of Canada would thus be a 'gift' to the nation from its artists (e.g., novelists, painters, filmmakers).

However, before turning specifically to an examination of these discourses, I would like to begin with a category of literary practitioner not currently considered an artist —namely, the historian— but who can, I think, be so considered here.[71] For one because of the literary origins of Canadian historical writing; for another because Canada's historians (at least until the mid-1960s) have all been nationalists; and thirdly because "there are hidden and unsuspected factors behind any national tradition of historical writing, and these need be raised as far as possible to the level of consciousness...."[72] In other words, what has "the diamond stuff" of Canadian nationalism consisted in?

Ressentiment and Canadian History

L'histoire est cultivée au Canada plus peut-être qu'en aucun autre pays au monde

Remy de Gourmont (1893)

Until the mid-1960s, Canadian historical writing, French and English, was predominantly and unproblematically nationalist.[73] In 1971, Ramsay Cook articulated a criticism of English-Canadian historical nationalism that English-Canadian historians had long levelled against the nationalism of French-Canadian historical writing, namely "misusing history for nationalist purposes."[74] While there would be something to say about Cook's conflation of nationalism, survivalism and historicism, his main argument for repudiating the nationalism of (English-) Canadian historians was that:

because of their common commitment to the nationalist criterion
of survival...(t)his has meant that the conflict has been a battle of
patriots...for national greatness. And...there is no war more bitter
than...a war between patriots, even if the battle is restricted to a battle
of the books.[75]

In other words, that there was a particularly fearful bitterness to Canadian expression, whether in literary or scholarly books, relative to not one
but three separate realms of self-definition: a) a common commitment, b)
survival, c) national greatness. To put it more bluntly, is this not simply
a fearful way of stating the truism that Canadian politics (common commitment), economics and culture (survival), and statecraft in both domestic and foreign affairs (national greatness) have been bitter? If so, then what
is at issue would be less the biases of Canadian historical scholarship than
a quality of Canadian history itself.

By way of illustration, let us take Ramsay Cook's 1963 general history
of Canada, *Canada: A Modern Study*[76], in the preface to which Cook
presents all the biases of (English-) Canadian historical nationalism that he
would repudiate several years later: eg., the 'miraculous' survivalism of
Canadian history. Thus "If Canada's history is distinguished by anything
it is a determination to survive and live according to the dictates of our
historical experience." However, a close reading of Cook's history might
suggest instead that if Canada's modern history is distinguished by anything, it is the bitterness and divisiveness of the historical experience he
describes from, on the first page, the "tragedy" for French Canadians of
Britain's conquest of Canada to, on the last page, the nation whose four-
teenth prime minister found facing "serious economic problems..., was
sorely divided between city and country, between French and English, and
still had not solved the...problems of foreign and defence policy" — in
short, whose "problems...taken together seemed to challenge the continued
and healthy existence of the nation itself" (pp. 260-1).

In such a light, Canadian history would appear as a form of resentment-
management, a controlling of the complex play of linguistic, class, region-
al, national and inter-national ressentiments that constitute Canadian historical experience. Thus, taking from Cook's text only those examples where
he specifically uses the verb "to resent" (and one could substantially
broaden the sampling by use of such cognates of ressentiment as 'fear',
'bitterness', 'envy', 'irritation', 'unhappiness', 'obnoxiousness' etc.), we find
the following:

"The Presbyterians, Methodists and Baptists deeply resented the
privileges granted to the Anglicans" (p. 44); "The farmers resented the high
rates charged by the Canadian Pacific Railway for carrying grain to market" (p. 121); "...in 1914 Canada was not an independent state and Britain's
declaration of war was made on behalf of all the Empire, including Canada. Few Canadians resented this fact" (p. 165); "When the depression threw
thousands of French Canadians out of work, smouldering resentment ex-

DEMON POLITICS

ploded into anger against 'foreign' employers" (p. 200); "This slight feeling of resentment at the attitude of the United States to the Seaway was part of a growing anxiety in Canada about the degree of influence which the United States seemed to exercise in Canadian affairs" (p. 243); and "The Liberals had been particularly worried about their ability to retain the support of Quebec, for the French Canadians had resented the conscription policy of 1944" (p. 250). Thus, even in the writings of a historian who would come to identity "the lack of 'sound thinking on the national question'" as "one of the most serious weaknesses of Canadian intellectual life"[77], one finds levels of Canadian ressentiment that are not attributable to nationalism. On the basis of the examples above, religious, economic and domestic political ressentiment would appear on their own to offer sufficient grounds for divisiveness without the added ressentiment provided by nationalism. Curiously, in Cook's examples of the two instances where nationalism is directly a factor, the level of ressentiment is less than it is with the non-nationalist forms: Canada's 1914 lack of independence vis-a-vis Britain caused little resentment among Canadians, and the growing early to mid-1950s suspicion of United States influence in Canadian affairs caused only slight resentment.

However, if one turns to the writings of avowedly (as opposed to uneasily) nationalist Canadian historians such as Creighton, Lower and W.L. Morton, the relations between ressentiment and nationalism become more pronounced and at the same time more complex. Indeed, Creighton, of the Alaska boundary dispute, writes that "the background of brutal imperialism on both sides of the Atlantic...produced a nationalist reaction in Canada more violent and sustained than anything in the history of the country.... this double resentment...so characteristic of Canadian nationalism."[78] Creighton's notion of the double resentment of Canadian nationalism is immensely suggestive of the complex interplay of ressentiment and nationalism in Canada in its double articulations: 1] a) an external ressentiment of English Canadian nationalism towards both British and American imperialism and 1] b) similarly of French Canadian nationalism towards its former metropolis as well as Anglo-Canadian imperialism; and 2] an internal ressentiment that is itself double: a) directed downwards onto the populations of Canada and b) reflected back up again as the regionalisms, separatisms or other forms of alienation that have constituted the permanent crisis of the Canadian confederation.

If the writings of Creighton and Morton[79] are invaluable for understanding external ressentiment in Canadian nationalism, those of A.R.M Lower display a similar candour in giving voice to internal ressentiment: "The weakness of Canadian democracy has lain not so much in its leaders as in its followers....Canadian nationalism was formed from the top. The farther down the scale one went, the less consciousness there was of the whole country...."[80] That the "followers" only returned this kind of ressentiment, of course, was not lost on Lower: "Secession talk and other

241

phenomena of disintegration proceeded either from economic disappoint-ment or its by-product, partisan sniping. Of the former there was much and it was graven deep in the failure of the country to grow."[81] Lower ex-presses a Canadian nationalism made up of interlocking ressentiments that, in Morton's view, conveyed the colonial fixation of an entire generation: "They love the nation Canada, but they hate it also. They hate it because they hate its colonial origins, which they wish to deny but cannot, and must therefore tramp on endlessly in ever less meaningful frenzy."[82] Thus, in Lower's words:

> ...English Canadians...are a dour and unimaginative folk. Having failed to find a centre in themselves, they borrow the heroes, the history, the songs and the slang of others. With no vividly realized res publica of their own to talk about, they take refuge in silence, unable to formulate their loyalties, confused over their deepest aspi-rations. Yet they...must surely have an intuitive faith in the unex-pressed essence of their traditions....If the Canadian people are to find their soul, they must seek...it, not in the English language or the French, but in....the land.[83]

For Lower, however, the failure of Canadian nationalism, always choked back into silence on its ressentiment, meant the possibility that the Cana-dian artist might succeed where the historian could not.

Ressentiment and Canadian Literature: Susanna Moodie and Sara Jeannette Duncan

> Her resentment was only half-serious but the note was there
> Sara Jeannette Duncan, The Imperialist

If in Lower, ressentiment of the soullessness of the Canadian people is deflected onto the landscape whose distinguishing characteristic thus be-comes the celebration of what is in effect a punitive absence of popula-tion, he was only repeating a strategy practiced by Canadian letters in a long tradition of embittered or ironic criticism of Canadian society since Haliburton. As I don't propose to review that tradition here, I will restrict myself to the examples offered by Susanna Moodie's *Roughing It in the Bush* (1852), together with a brief discussion of Sara Jeannette Duncan's *The Imperialist* (1904).

In Moodie, the social basis of ressentiment precedes emigration to Cana-da. Emigration is forced "upon the proud and wounded spirit of the well-educated sons and daughters of old but impoverished families." That res-sentiment, while acknowledged as a component of the Old World, is however denied as constitutive of the New World:

> But there is a higher motive [to emigration]...that love of indepen-dence which springs up spontaneously in the...high-souled children

of a glorious land. They cannot labour in a menial capacity in the
country where they were born and educated to command. They
can trace no difference between themselves and the more fortunate
individuals of a race whose blood warms their veins, and whose
names they bear. The want of wealth alone places an impassible
barrier between them and the more favoured offspring...and they
go forth to make for themselves a new name and to find another
country, to forget the past and to live in the future, to exult in the
prospect of...the land of their adoption [becoming] great.[84]

Revenge against the past, ie., ressentiment, thus fuels the vision of greatness (independence) promised by the idealized and moralized Canada. In
the encounter between the ideal and the impoverished reality, not only
is there disappointment, but the bitterness of that disappointment releases
the ressentiment that was "the ordinary motive" for emigration: "Disappointment, as a matter of course, followed...high-raised expectations...."
but the disappointment is due to the "disgusting scenes of riot and low
debauchery...[the] dens of dirt and misery which would, in many instances,
be shamed by an English pig-sty."[85]

Not only does the populace compare unfavorably to British pigs, but
the state-apparatus and its industrious pamphleteers and hired orators,
whose glowing descriptions of Canada had produced a "Canada mania"
in the middle ranks of British society, were scarcely better:

Oh, ye dealers in wild lands — ye speculators in the folly and credul-
ity of your fellow-men — what a mass of misery, and of misrepresen-
tation productive of that misery, have yet not to answer for! You
had your acres to sell, and what to you were the worn-down frames
and broken hearts of the infatuated purchasers? The public believed
the plausible statements you made with such earnestness, and men
of all grades rushed to hear your hired orators declaim upon the
blessings to be obtained by the clearers of the wilderness."[86]

By contrast, the land itself, as wilderness, i.e., once emptied of its corrupt inhabitants, presents the standard jouissances of the Burkean sublime
as repertoried by Chauncey Loomis: "sound and silence, obscurity, soli-
tude, vastness and magnificence as sources of sublime astonishment and
terror."[87] Thus Moodie writes of Canada's "awful beauty," "excess of beauty," "astonishing beauty" whose "effect was strangely novel and imposing...where the forest has never yet echoed to the woodsman's axe or
received the imprint of civilization, the first approach [to which]...inspires
a melancholy awe which becomes painful in its intensity."[88]

If the sight of Canadian shores produces in Moodie a culturally distinct
response — "I never before felt so overpowering my own insignificance"
(p.29) — the fact that the same shores produce a radically different cultural response among the lower classes only brings out Moodie's ressentiment
in which cultural and class differences are fused into the landscape:

> It was a scene over which the spirit of peace might brood in silent
> adoration; but how spoiled by the discordant yells of the filthy be-
> ings who were sullying the purity of the air and water with con-
> taminating sights and sounds!
> The sight of the Canadian shores had changed them into persons
> of great consequence. The poorest and worst-dressed, the least
> deserving and the most repulsive in mind and morals exhibited most
> disgusting traits of self-importance. Vanity and presumption seemed
> to possess them altogether.[89]

She continues:

> Girls, who were scarcely able to wash a floor decently, talked of
> service with contempt, unless tempted to change their resolution
> by the offer of $12 a month. To endeavour to undeceive them was
> a useless and ungracious task....I left it to time and bitter experience
> to restore them to their sober senses.[90]

Moodie's resentful observations of the effects of Canadian shores upon
the lower classes had already been noted some thirty years earlier by John
Howison in his 1821 *Sketches of Upper Canada*:

> Many of the emigrants I saw had been on shore a few hours only,
> during their passage between Montreal and Kingston, yet they had
> already acquired those absurd notions of independence and equal-
> ity, which are so deeply engrafted in the minds of the lowest in-
> dividuals of the American nation.[91]

In Moodie, ressentiment becomes the basis of a vision of Canadian nationalism (pp. 29-30) in which she urges Canadians to "remain true to your-
selves", ie., to the (silent) landscape ("Look at the St. Lawrence...that great
artery...transporting...the riches and produce of a thousand distant climes").
Instead of becoming a "humble dependant on the great republic," Canada
should "wait patiently, loyally, lovingly" for the day when Britain "will
proclaim your childhood past, and bid you stand ...a free Canadian people": "...do this, and...you will...learn to love Canada as I now love it, who
once viewed it with hatred so intense that I longed to die..."

It is perhaps appropriate that Moodie's book aroused resentment in Canada — as she put it, "a most unjust prejudice...because I dared give my opinion freely" — and would not be reprinted in Canada until 1871, or almost
twenty years after its first edition.

In contrast, if Sara Jeannette Duncan's journalistic ressentiment of the
population of Ontario whom she described collectively as "Maoris" and
a "giant camp of the Philistines" has been documented[92], the absence of
any such outspoken ressentiment in her novel *The Imperialist* is noteworthy. Duncan's novel affects an almost clinical detachment in which ressentiment has simply become naturalized, i.e., it's merely part of the landscape,
and so there are no descriptions of the landscape, other than the social
topology of the town of Elgin, until pp. 70-71:

...he had nothing to say; the silence in which they pursued their way was no doubt to him just the embarrassing condition he usually had to contend with. To her it seemed pregnant, auspicious; it drew something from the low grey lights of the wet spring afternoon and the unbound heartlifting wind....They went on in that strange bound way, and the day drew away from them till they turned a sudden corner, when it lay all along the yellow sky across the river, behind a fringe of winter woods, stayed in the moment of its retreat on the edge of unvexed landscape.[93]

For the young Englishman, Hugh Finlay, the Canadian silence is just the embarrassing condition he usually had to content with; for the Canadian, Advena Murchison, ("occupied in the aesthetic ecstasy of self-torture",p.184) her feelings are drawn from the ordinary landscape: what they suddenly see and share in, however, is not the ordinary landscape, but the extraordinary landscape; in Duncan's words, the unvexed landscape. Duncan continues:

They stopped involuntarily to look, and she saw a smile come up from some depth in him.
"Ah, well," he said, as if to himself, "it's something to be in a country where the sun still goes down with a thought of the primaeval."
"I think I prefer the sophistication of chimney-pots," she replied. "I've always longed to see a sunset in London, with the fog breaking over Westminster."
"Then you don't care about them for themselves, sunsets?" he asked, with the simplest absence of mind.
"I never yet could see the sun go down, But I was angry in my heart," she said, and this time he looked at her.
"...It's the seal upon an act of violence, isn't it, a sunset? Something taken from us against our will. It's a hateful reminder, in the midst of our delightful volitions, of how arbitrary every condition of life is."[94]

For Finlay, the sunset is, as the depopulated Canadian landscape was for Moodie, an instance of sublimity. For Advena, if the landscape was "involuntarily" and momentarily unvexed, vexation or ressentiment immediately returns such that she prefers an imaginary landscape (a sunset in a London she's never seen) to the (populated) one she can see (and lives in) since this is a hateful reminder of the cultural anger in her heart (the poem she quotes), of the violence of unsophistication, i.e., the ressentiment of the will's inability to alter the past. That ressentiment (something taken from us against our wills) is further reinforced by the discussion they have as to where the light goes: "Into the void behind time," Finlay suggests; "Into the texture of the future," Advena answers.

However, it's Advena's brother, Lorne, the imperialist of the novel's title, who defines the texture of that future in language that would be reminiscent of Grant's ressentiment-filled last men with their trivial desire for entertainment and comfort: "...it's for the moral advantage [of belonging to an empire]. Way down at the bottom, that's what it is. We have the sense to want all we can get of that sort of thing. They've developed the finest human product there is, the cleanest, the most disinterested, and we want to keep up the relationship...."[95]

In comparing these two moments in the development of Canadian literature, Moodie's vision offers an unvexed natural landscape, but a vexed social landscape, while Duncan blends the one into the other. As Lorne Murchison's words suggest, the advent of mechanical means of reproduction such as photography or cinema (the finest product, the cleanest, the most disinterested) might at last provide a path around the vexacious Canadian literary landscape, be it that of its philosophers, historians, or novelists.

Ressentiment and Canadian Visual Arts: The clicheization of the landscape

> One must guess the painter in order to understand the picture. But now the whole scientific fraternity is out to understand the canvas and the colours — not the picture"
>
> Nietzsche, Schopenhauer As Educator

Dennis Reid has suggested that "of all the arts in Canada, painting is the one that most directly presents the Canadian experience."[96] However, if there is any consistency to Canadian experience (and this paper has argued that there is), that experience has been predominantly characterized by ressentiment and the quest for its relocation by distancing in i) a *meta*-Canadian moralism, ii) a pan-Canadian nationalism, and iii) a *trans*-Canadian landscapism. In this sense, Canadian art rather than most directly presenting Canadian experience would continue along the same trajectory of relocation that we have encountered in Canadian philosophy, historical writing and literature. As Vancouver artist Robert Kleyn has put it:

> Plagued by questions of identity, Canadian art often proposes prescriptive frameworks which easily lead to deciphering rather than interrogating the authority of the representation behind the presentation. This identity is posed in terms of recognition, recognition outside Canada.[97]

That recognition, however, would only be made possible, in Creighton's bitter observation, "by abandoning a part, or the whole of [the artist's] own tradition or special point-of-view....A Canadian artist...could either leave Canada for the metropolitan centre of his choice, or he could give up Canadian themes, except those...regarded as quaint or barbaric, and therefore interesting, in the artistic and literary capitals of Western Europe and America."[98] But, in fact, there was another, and more intricate, possibility for the development of Canadian art as a strategy of avoidance of Canadian ressentiment, and I'd like to term this *the clicheization of the landscape*.

Between Confederation and the end of the century, Canadian art followed no direction save that of 'pleasing the public.'[99] If most Canadian artists approached painting in the spirit of the age— to become rich fast— that spirit would increasingly be one marked by the development of mechanical (or photo-chemical) means of reproduction. The impact of the camera on Canadian art would be decisive as part of the "pragmatic materialism and commercialism [that] permeated the *whole fabric* of Canadian life (emphasis added)"[100]. As indicative elements in a total transformative process affecting Canadian art, I'll single out three: i) the *institutionalization* of art, ii) the *commercialization* of artists, and iii) the *mechanization* of vision.

i) The institutionalization of art as of the 1870s, begun with the Ontario Society of Artists, the Royal Society, and the Royal Canadian Academy of Arts, would be directed by the state (the Marquis of Lorne as Governor-General) and modelled on the recreation of "little replicas of British cultural organizations"[101]. The process of statification would be distinguished by outbursts of ressentiment or a "marvelous amount of bitterness and bad language; half the artists are ready just now to choke the other half with their paint brushes".[102]

ii) The commercialization of art amounted to the subordination of painting to photography and the rise of photographic firms such as William Notman of Montreal, Notman and Fraser of Toronto, and later the other commercial studios such as Toronto's Grip, the Brigden Organization and Phillips-Gutkin Associates in Winnipeg, and Graphics Associates in Toronto, all of which played essential roles in the development of modern Canadian art and film.[103] To take but one sign of the general subordination of painting to photography (though photography would "indirectly encourage... the spread of painting through Canada" [Harper]), the Ontario Society of Artists' first exhibition (1873) would be held at the Notman and Fraser Photographic Gallery in Toronto.

iii) The aesthetic of Erastian institutionalization on the one hand and commercialization on the other was a photographic vision or realism that, at its best, aspired to be "a precise clear reflection of the world" which, in Canadian terms, meant the search for ever wilder Canadian terrain that would reach its fullest expression in the Group of Seven. At its worst, such photographic realism was "pedestrian and laborious"; and, in between, lead to a Canadian national style whose beginnings would be the production of the double volume entitled *Picturesque Canada* (1882) by which a "veritable army" of artists, including American newspaper illustrators who had worked on the earlier *Picturesque America*, "made available to public and artists alike the first great series of locally produced Canadian scenes...at a time when nationalism was being aroused on all sides."[104]

For the problem posed by the clicheization of the landscape involves a major (and I'm tempted to say absolute) displacement. In part, this displacement is the mediumistic problem of the shift from landscape as a literary figure to landscape as backdrop or cliche (from the German, *klitsch*, lump or mass, and thus its aesthetic, *kitsch*); in other words, the shift from figure to image that Walter Benjamin understood as the annihilation of metaphoricity by the advent of "the long-sought image sphere...the world of universal and integral actualities, where the 'best room' is missing — the sphere, in a word, in which political materialism and physical nature share the inner man."[105] To put it another way, the transition from literary to mechanized medium involved a double displacement of the Canadian landscape: firstly, the *objectification* of the vacant landscape (whose evacuation, as we have seen, is an effect of ressentiment) as 'reality'; secondly, the deterritorialized non-specificity or *universalization* of a vacant reality by mechanical means. If American newspaper illustrators could readily produce Canadian scenes, American film crews would within a few years produce 'Canadian' features shot entirely in the U.S., just as Canadian film producers would one day come to specialize in making 'American' features shot entirely in Canada.

The annihilation, or at least unidimensionalization, of metaphoricity by the clicheization of the landscape thus naturalized Canadian silence to a degree Canadian letters (or any literary medium, including newspapers) could never. Like the ownership of the land by the Crown, the development of Canadian communications would be a state-monopoly. But before further reference to modern media, it is necessary to conclude this discussion of Canadian visual arts by examining the ressentiment produced by the Group of Seven's attempted revolt against the cliched landscape.

If the members of the Group were "the first to speak loudly as consciously national Canadian painters,"[106] the search for something Canadian in painting had been the objective of several Toronto painters since the 1890s. But as MacDonald said of one of his teachers ("the Canadian in him is not quite dead"), this objective kept getting "switched off the tracks..."[107], and the Group was no exception: eg., the 1914-1918 war; Harris' training in Germany; Thomson's dependency on photographs; or the "tremendous" impact on Harris and MacDonald of a 1913 exhibition of Scandinavian painting seen in Buffalo. The actual origins of the Group's "cult of Canadianism" (Harper) need not concern us here; what matters was i) that they felt they were painting 'Canada', and ii) the ressentiment that such a presumption unleashed.

As Harper puts it, "Toronto critics in particular were so indignant that an observer could but assume they had been personally insulted"; Harper also writes of an "incredible flood of adverse publicity," "massive criticism", and cites Harris' claim that the first Group show (May 1920) produced whole pages in newspapers and periodicals of "anger, outrage and cheap wit [such as] had never occurred in Canada before."[108] Critics (and writers like Hugh Maclennan) saw in their work alarming expressions of terror and violence. Hector Charlesworth felt that the Group's work was detrimental to Canada's foreign image because it was likely to discourage immigration.

Members of Parliament joined in the bitter criticism, hurling abuse and humiliation at the head of the director of the National Gallery of Canada for his choice of Group of Seven paintings to be sent to the British Empire Exhibition at Wembley (1924).[109] The Royal Canadian Academy "resented the Gallery's involvement in the organization of an international exhibition..."[110] But the collective resentment suddenly evaporated when overseas critics pronounced the Group's work the most vital painting of the century. Within two years the Group were the acknowledged center of serious art activity in Canada; by 1931, the year of their last group exhibition, "their supremacy was acknowledged — both grudgingly and willingly — right across the country."[111]

For perhaps the most problematic effect of the clicheization of the landscape, and in this sense Group 'Canadianism' failed, in becoming by the 30s and well into the 50s a suffocating artistic orthodoxy, is that it was the neutralization of the only valid emotional outlet for Canadian ressentiment. Thus contained, what resulted was the dramatic intensification of ressentiment that constitutes the entire history of Canadian cinema.

Ressentiment and Canadian Cinema or 'Le mepris n'aura qu'un temps'

As the most successful Canadian feature film ever, that LE DECLIN DE L'EMPIRE AMERICAIN should be a film about ressentiment is clearly visible on a number of levels: 1) the (*intellectual*) ressentiment of the film's historians or last men of history who, because they know they will never amount to Braudels or Toynbees, can generalize into the future and the past the social and cultural decline they *already* inhabit: the loss of a social project, (to activate ressentiment, one makes separate factors causative: thus, **as a result of**) the institutional and institutionalized cynicism of elites, and (**caused by**) the effeminization of a culture they resent; 2) the (*emotional*) ressentiment of men today toward women (*and* of women toward women: eg., Dominique vis-a-vis Louise; 3) the (*inter-elite*) ressentiment which the film articulates on two levels: that of Third World intellectuals and more locally of untenured *chargés de cours* for the privileges (economic and sexual) of the First or Second World tenured professorate that the film describes as having the best labour contract in North America; 4) the (*class*) ressentiment of the uneducated toward the educated who do not do anything but only talk, and 5) Arcand's acknowledgement of Canadian (*cultural*) ressentiment in expunging from the script all specific reference to Canada or Quebec — all, that is, but one.

And that is the landscape of Lake Memphremagog and the nature footage of the water, reeds and later the snow-bound house at the film's end; in other words (and as Pierre, the cynic, says: the only reality that will remain once all the[se] people have died), the romantic primal of the Canadian landscape where, since Moodie, Canadian artists have sought refuge from (and discharged) the accumulated ressentiment of Canadian social existence.

It is thus possible to make two observations: 1) LE DECLIN, as a film about ressentiment, renews (and legitimizes) the ressentiment thematic in Canadian (cinematic) culture as explored by such films as, for instance, Michel Brault's LES ORDRES, Arthur Lamothe's LE MEPRIS N'AURA QU'UN TEMPS, or Gilles Groulx's NORMETAL, going back to, at least, that extraordinary post-Griersonian moment of the self-revelation of the Canadian psyche, in Robert Anderson's "Mental Mechanisms" series for the National Film Board of Canada (1947-1950). The series identified, in order, the four principal drives of the Canadian sensibility: THE FEELING OF REJECTION; THE FEELING OF HOSTILITY; OVER-DEPENDENCY; and FEELINGS OF DEPRESSION.[112] And yet while signalling that Canadian cinema may, and with considerable historical justification, be legitimately a *cinema of ressentiment*[113], LE DECLIN is, I think, attempting something more.

2) In part because of the landscape primal but also because of the film's humour and diegetic sympathy for its characters (since as a student of Canadian history and a filmmaker in both state and private industry for some 20 years now, Arcand understands that Canadian ressentiment is double and so includes French and English, male and female, etc.), the film is seeking, though not without hesitations, to include *within* its landscape human characters in a way that Canadian literature or history or painting has not. In other words, LE DECLIN attempts a path beyond ressentiment. If that attempt fails — by the film's offering in conclusion only the solace of another vista of the depopulated Canadian landscape — it does bring to the fore once again the clicheization of that landscape that has been a, if not the only, constant of Canadian cinema since its earliest years.

This is to say, then, that the first Canadian features from, for instance, EVANGELINE (1914) to BACK TO GOD'S COUNTRY (1919) were cliches, as were the Hollywood 'northerns' set in Canada through the mid-20s, as was the first indigenous radio drama broadcast by the CNR in 1930 (*The Romance of Canada*) since "Audiences never tired of viewing Canada's stereotyped image."[114] Peter Morris has summarized the films of these early "years of promise" as follows:

> If there was a definable quality...and it was a tentative one...it lay in relating fiction and reality, in the idea that stories should be filmed not on set but in natural locations, in applying a documentary approach to drama. Such an approach characterized many of the most successful films of the period...those of Ernest Shipman [eg., BACK TO GOD'S COUNTRY] and was to find its most potent expressions in three quasi-Canadian films: Nanook of the North, The Silent Enemy and The Viking.[115]

As producer Ernie Shipman explained it, this naturalistic or documentary quasi-realism originated in Canadian life, in "a demand for Canadian-made motion pictures as real and free and wholesome as...Canadian life."[116] However, as Barthes remarks in *S/Z*: "...realism consists not in copying the real but in copying a (depicted) copy of the real. This famous *reality*, as though suffering from a fearfulness which keeps it from being touched directly, is set *farther away*, postponed."[117] In other words, Canadian realism originates not in the wholesomeness of Canadian life, but in the fearfulness of it, ie., in ressentiment and its avoidance by duplicity, specifically the deceptive immigration advertising, bitterly commented on by Susanna Moodie, that began in the 1830s as part of public (ie., State) effort — a government Bureau of Immigration would be formally established in the 1850s — and would continue with the creation of the National Film Board in 1939 (and, indeed, has characterized every stage of state involvement in Canadian cinema from the teens of the century to the present). From the films of the CPR with their interdiction against showing snow or ice scenes[118], to Beaverbrook's propaganda War Office Cinematographic Committee, to the Canadian Government Motion Picture Bureau whose film publicity aimed to "make Canada known, as she really is", the 'realism' of Canadian filmmaking is inscribed within a state-supported tradition of deceptiveness. As a result, the relationship between fiction and realism in Canadian image-production has, at every stage, been problematic, whether one considers the post-Grierson documentary, Canadian cinema direct, Carle-Owen's (re)discovery of the feature under the cover of documentary, Peter Pearson's and the CBC's lawsuits over THE TAR SANDS, or the more recent experiments of the NFB's Alternative Drama Program.[119] And yet for all that, there was never any doubt in Canadian philosophical realism (cf. John Watson: "we are capable of knowing Reality as it actually is....Reality when so known is absolutely rational") and its derivatives in Canadian documentary, especially Canadian experimental cinema, as to the epistemological validity of its realism. Or none until the contemporary Canadian philosopher (and filmmaker) Bruce Elder retheorized Canadian realism as the awareness of an absence: "only when the absence of the represented object is acknowledged can representation actually occur."[120]

Elder thus suggests a Canadian contribution to the critical theory of representation in which presentation or the present that can be re-presented is problematized by the absent concept of 'resentation', not a present that can be re-presented but an absent present that cannot: namely, the 'resent' or *ressentiment* that George Grant has defined "At its simplest...[as] revenge against what is present in our present."[121] In any event, as Peter Morris has remarked, excellence in the documentary form developed because Canadians "were denied access to producing feature films."[122] At the end of this study, Canadian cinema, like literature or painting, becomes visible as just another part of the ressentiment-filled discourse of the continuation of an absent present in the evacuated landscape of indefinite cultural postponement in the administration of the non-existent reality of Canadian culture.

Conclusion: Modernity, the reactionary landscape and the bias of *ressentiment*

On a wider plane, it is a source of constant frustration to attempt to be Canadian

H.A. Innis

At the conclusion of this study of Canadian cultural forms, is it possible to at least begin to situate Canadian *ressentiment*? I believe it is, if only to attempt to put the tormented question of Canadian *ressentiment* to a, by now perhaps, much deserved rest.

Since the Second World War, ie, since Canada's full-scale integration into the American empire after a decade of proto-nationhood, there developed in Canadian literature and in literary criticism principally — more broadly speaking within the instrumentalization of the humanities— a largely southern Ontario school with a curious kind of awareness of the Canadian literary landscape. "I have long been impressed in Canadian poetry, " wrote Frye in his 1965 conclusion to a literary history of Canada, "by a tone of deep terror in regard to nature."[123] Compare that with an observation of Emily Carr's: "I have often wondered what caused that fear, almost terror, of New York before I saw her."[124] I would like to suggest, therefore, that in the Canadian imaginary 'nature' and 'modernity' are one and the same, and both evoke an identical response: terror experienced as *ressentiment*. Terror in some cases admitted but more often in what Gaile McGregor terms 'the wacousta syndrome'[125], denied because *it is* terrible. However, the awareness of this, I would suggest, makes of *ressentiment* the primary characteristic of the Canadian imaginary, ressentiment which i) is displaced or projected onto the landscape and ii) denies this. Given that the landscape, or rather representations of the landscape, by their indexicality or referentiality can claim to point to, refer to, or show a 'natural' or 'objective out there', it may be possible to say that the landscape is the least mediated or non-institutionalized form of Canadian ideas of modernity itself. Thus, the Canadian 'identity' can only be said to be "fully integral to the question of technology," as Arthur Kroker has written,[126] in the sense of being dissimulated therein in the attempt to displace itself beyond the *ressentiment* occasioned by modernity. For if McGregor is correct in defining Canadian being as "a kind of normalized duplicity"[127], it becomes almost impossible to make a distinction between a threatening externality (for instance, technology or modernity or nature) and the internal core of that being itself (terror); indeed, is it possible to assign limits to an imaginary?

But, for the sake of argument, taking the external threat as so (nature as terrifying), what this produces is Frye's garrison mentality or the reinforcement of institutionalization. If space is, as McGregor says, "*the* identifying feature of the Canadian interior"[128], then it is space-binding institutions and techniques (nationalism, the state, communications and culture) that are privileged as a result — but only to silence that space by binding it. For the institutions of overcoming space are themselves subject to the same normalized duplicity. McGregor, analyzing Canadian literature, uncovers a similar ambivalence or as she terms it "institutionalized ambivalence" with respect to institutions: "The state," she remarks, " is simply alien, and that's what makes it dangerous...'society' in Canada is viewed as fearful specifically because it is not machinelike, predictable, mechanical but [because it is] prey to confusion and disorder...in Canadian literature...the public world is somehow demonic, an utterly foreign element...." (p. 173)

If nature in Canada is terrifying and the Canadian social world is demonic, then what is safe? What becomes completely safe is precisely what is *genuinely* foreign, "machinelike, predictable, mechanical" — technology, or the empty will to will, but just to be absolutely preserved from experiencing Canadian ressentiment, that technology and that willing are preferable in their imported as opposed to the indigenous (i.e, absent or silenced) forms. For, as McGregor puts it, "Judging by our literature...many Canadians believe...that for us...symbolic capitulations to the victimizing forces is liberation"[129] — because capitulation, symbolic or real, is liberation from Canadian *ressentiment*.

I said earlier that these views of nature were characteristic of a largely southern Ontario school, i.e., were formed in the intellectual and cultural center of Canadian modernity. However the "stable and restrained society of Ontario," as geographer Cole Harris remarked in an essay on the myth of the land in Canadian nationalism, "developed in an environment which has been less a challenge than a neutral backdrop."[130] If "The land," as Harris insists, "did not create tensions," then the landscape itself becomes the primary cultural myth of Canadian avoidance of *its own* modernity; namely, what the Canadian art historian David Solkin has termed "the landscape of reaction"[131]. Canadian *ressentiment* would thus be the fullest form of the expression of Canada's *reactionary modernity*; that is to say, a form of nostalgia that is itself a (purely mythical) dimension of modernity.[132]

If this is so, and in the light of what we've examined here, it may be enough to raise some questions both in terms of the regnant interpretations and practices of Canadian cultural existence. Such a questioning would clearly, I think, bring to the forefront what I have argued is the dual displacement of the nature and institutions of modern Canadian nationalism and culture by a reactionary *ressentiment*.

If Canadian thought has excelled in comprehensive analyses of the biases of communications (Innis) and technology (Grant, Kroker), it would seem that this enterprise could only be fruitfully complemented by an understanding of the bias of the culture that connects them. Then, and only then, might something of this huge, distant and thoroughly hidden country of ressentiment emerge finally into view.

Communications Studies
Concordia University

Notes

1. *Essays in Canadian Economic History*, ed. Mary Q. Innis, (Toronto: University of Toronto Press, 1956), 383.

2. Ibid., 386.

3. Ibid., 387.

4. Ibid.

5. *In Canada: A Guide To The Peaceable Kingdom* (Toronto: Macmillan of Canada, 1971), xiv.

6. This is as well the starting point for Marc Henry Soulet's recent study of the Quebec intelligentsia, *Le Silence des Intellectuels: Radioscopie de l'intellectual québécois* (Montreal: Editions Saint-Martin), 1987.

7. *ROB* Magazine, September 1986, 15.

8. Ibid.

9. "On the Adder's Bite," Thus Spake Zarathustra, in Walter Kaufmann, ed. *The Portable Nietzsche* (Harmondsworth: Penguin, 1959), 180.

10. ROB, op. cit., 16.

11. Hubert Aquin, "Le Corps Mystique," in *Blocs erratiques*, (Montreal: 10/10, 1982), 105.

12. In Carl Berger, ed. *Imperialism and Nationalism, 1884-1914: A Conflict in Canadian Thought*, (Toronto: Copp Clark, 1969), 60-61.

13. John MacCormac, *Canada: America's Problem* (New York: The Viking Press, 1940), 32.

14. *Technology and Empire*, (Toronto: Anansi, 1969), 141.

15. Cf., Fredric Jameson, "Nietzsche's whole vision of history, his historical master narrative is organized around this proposition [ressentiment]," in "Authentic Ressentiment: Generic Discontinuities and Ideologemes in the 'Experimental' Novels of George Gissing," *The Political Unconscious*, (Ithaca: Cornell UP, 1981), 185-205.

16. *The Will To Power*, trans. Walter Kaufmann and R.J. Hollingdale, (New York: Vintage, 1967), 100-101.

17. Jameson, op. cit., 201.

18. Georg Simmel, *Le Bourgeois*, trans. Jankelevitch, (Paris: Payot, 1926), 411-412.

19. *Uber Ressentiment und Moralische Werturteile* (1912) translated in French as *L'Homme du ressentiment*, (Paris: Gallimard, 1970), 49, note 1.

20. Fritz Stern, *The Politics of Cultural Despair* (Berkeley and Los Angeles: University of California Press, 1961), xx-xxi.

21. See David Thomson, *America In The Dark: The Impact of Hollywood Films on American Culture* (New York: William Morrow, 1977), passim, and Benjamin B. Hampton, *History of the American Film Industry: From Its Beginnings To 1931* (New York: Dover, 1970), esp. ix-x.

22. Jameson, op. cit., 202.

23. Ibid.

24. Ibid., 205.

25. Max Scheler, *L'Homme du ressentiment*, op. cit., 11.

26. In *Schopenhauer As Educator* (South Bend, Indiana: Regnery/Gateway, 1965), 91.

27. See Walter Kaufmann, *Nietzsche: Philosopher, Psychologist, Antichrist* (New York: Meridian, 1956), esp. 319-325.

28. Scheler, 11.

29. *The Genealogy of Morals*, trans. Francis Golffing, (New York: Doubleday, 1956), 170-171.

30. See *Schopenhauer As Educator*, op. cit., 69.

31. Zarathustra, op. cit., 213.

32. Ibid., 251.

33. Margaret Atwood, *Survival: A Thematic Guide To Canadian Literature* (Toronto: Anansi, 1972), 33.

34. Cited in Tony Wilden, *The Imaginary Canadian* (Vancouver: Pulp Press, 1980), 71.

35. *Durham Report*, 1839, also cited in Wilden, 43.

36. See Innis, op. cit., 384.

37. See for instance the Report of the Federal Cultural Policy Review Committee (Ottawa: Information Services, Department of Communications, Government of Canada, 1982), 15: "We start from a view of Canadian society that sees it as an aggregate of distinctive spheres of activity. Each of these has its own values and purposes and its own network of institutions, interacting with one another in myriad ways but equal in their social importance. The political order — the state — is one of these great spheres and institutional systems; the cultural world is another." See also Theodor W. Adorno, "Culture and Administration," *TELOS* No. 37, Fall 1978, 93-111.

38. John Meisel, "Escaping Extinction: Cultural Defence of an Undefended Border," *Canadian Journal of Political and Social Theory*, 10. 1-2, Winter/Spring 1986, 248, 252.

39. "Telefilm Fund Ready To Make 'Movies,' Not 'Films,' Sez Pearson," Variety, Dec. 3, 1986, 32. A certain sense of déjà vu or perhaps déjà entendu was echoed by the Variety writer's lead paragraph: "As it makes its decades-old pitch again to 'strike a new deal' in the international film industry and unhitch the 'old hegemony' of Hollywood, Canada is getting ready to make 'movies' rather than 'films'....".

40. Survival, op. cit., 35, 39.

41. Ibid., 33.

42. See Innis, op cit., 386, also A.R.M. Lower, *Colony To Nation* (Toronto: Longmans, 1946), 399.

43. Wilden, op. cit., 71.

44. D. G. Creighton, *Dominion of the North* (Toronto: Macmillan of Canada, 1967), 217.

45. Sara Jeannette Duncan, *The Imperialist* (Toronto: McLelland and Stewart, 1971), 61-62.

46. In *The Bush Garden: Essays on the Canadian Imagination* (Toronto: Anansi, 1971), 220.

47. *The Canadian Question*, 1875, cited in Wilden, op. cit., 123.

48. *The Bush Garden*, op. cit., 226.

49. Ibid., 236.

50. Ibid., 135.

51. Ibid, 231.

52. Ibid.

53. Ibid, 135.

54. Arthur Kroker, *Technology and the Canadian Mind: Innis/McLuhan/Grant* (Montreal: New World Perspectives, 1984), 15.

55. Innis, op. cit., 386.

56. Ibid.

57. Ibid, 385-389.

58. Ibid., 392.

59. Cited in Wallace Clement and Daniel Drache, *A Practical Guide To Canadian Political Economy* (Toronto: James Lorimer & Co., 1978), 24. The poem does not appear in the Canada Council grant-supported subsequent editions of *Counterblast*: Toronto (1969), New York (1969) and Montreal (1972).

60. See Kroker, op. cit., 80.

61. Ibid., 86.

62. George Grant, *Time As History* (Canadian Broadcasting Corporation, 1969), 33.

63. See *Time As History*, 34-35; also George Grant, *Technology and Justice* (Toronto: Anansi, 1986), 100, and Joan E. O'Donovan, *George Grant and The Twilight of Justice* (Toronto: University of Toronto Press, 1984), 4, 87.

64. *Time As History*, op. cit., 33.

65. Ibid., 40.

66. *Lament For A Nation: The Defeat of Canadian Nationalism* (Toronto: McClelland & Stewart, 1965), 5.

67. Ibid., 66, 76.

68. Ibid., 88.

69. See *Time As History*, 46-47.

70. Op. cit., 4.

71. For such a "superlative" view of the historian, see Emery Neff, *The Poetry of History: The Contribution of Literature and Literary Scholarship to the Writing of History since Voltaire*, (New York and London: Columbia University Press, 1947).

72. See Carl Berger, *The Writing of Canadian History: Aspects of English-Canadian Historical Writing: 1900 to 1970*, (Toronto: Oxford University Press, 1976), ix, 259 and passim.

73. "Canada's historians have all been nationalists," Berger, op. cit., 259.

74. "La Survivance English-Canadian Style," in *The Maple Leaf Forever: Essays on Nationalism and Politics in Canada*, (Toronto: Macmillan of Canada, 1977), 144.

75. Ibid., 126.

76. Written with John T. Saywell and John C. Ricker (Toronto and Vancouver: Clarke, Irwin & Co. Ltd.).

77. Ibid., p.xi.

78. Op. cit., 409.

79. On the depths of Canada's "long-accumulated" and "suppressed resentments" towards the United States, see Morton's "Canada and the United States," in *The Canadian Identity* (Toronto and Buffalo: University of Toronto Press, 1972), 58-87.

80. See *Colony To Nation* (Toronto: Longmans, Green & Co., 1946), 399-401.

81. Ibid., 404.

82. Cited in Berger, op. cit., 252.

83. *Colony to Nation*, 560.

84. Susanna Moodie, *Roughing It in the Bush or Forest Life in Canada* (1852), (Toronto: McClelland and Stewart, 1962), xv.

85. Ibid., xvi.

86. Ibid., xvi-xvii.

87. Cited in I.S. Maclaren, "The Aesthetic Mapping of Nature in the Second Franklin Expedition," *Journal of Canadian Studies*, 20:1, Spring 1985, 41.

88. Moodie, op. cit., 22,23,24.

89. Ibid., 26,31.

90. Ibid.

91. Cited in Wilden, op. cit., 3.

92. See Karen Davison-Wood, *A Philistine Culture? Literature, Painting and the Newspapers in Late Victorian Toronto*, PhD Dissertation, Concordia University, 1981, pp. 267-8.

93. Duncan, op.cit., 70.

94. Ibid., 70-71.

95. Ibid., 98.

96.   *A Concise History of Canadian Painting* (Toronto: Oxford University Press, 1973), 7.

97.   Robert Kleyn, "Canadian Art or Canadian Artists?", *Vanguard*, February 1985, 29.

98.   Op. cit., 578.

99.   J. Russell Harper, *Painting in Canada: A History*, 2nd ed. (Toronto and Quebec City: University of Toronto Press and Les presses de l'université Laval, 1977), 180.

100. Ibid., 181.

101. Ibid., 183.

102. W. Stewart McNutt, *Days of Lorne* (Fredricton, 1955), cited in Harper, 184. See also Davison-Wood, op. cit., 121.

103. See Harper, 182-183; Gene Walz, "Flashback: An Introduction" in Gene Walz, ed., *Flashback: People and Institutions in Canadian Film History*, (Montreal: Mediatexte Publications, 1986), 9-15; John Porter, "Artists Discovering Film: Postwar Toronto," *Vanguard*, Summer 1984, 24-26.

104. Harper, op. cit., 180, 183, 194.

105. See "Surrealism: The Last Snap-shot of the European Intelligentsia," in *Reflections*, ed. and intro. Peter Demetz, (New York: Harcourt, Brace, Jovanovitch, 1978), 192; also Abraham Moles, *Psychologie du Kitsch: L'art du bonheur* (Paris: HMH, 1971).

106. Harper, op. cit., 288; see also Ramsay Cook, "Landscape Painting and National Sentiment in Canada," in *The Maple Leaf Forever*, op. cit., 158-179.

107. Cited in Harper, 264.

108. Ibid., 263, 279.

109. Ibid., 288.

110. Reid, op. cit., 151.

111. Ibid., 152.

112. See Peter Morris, "After Grierson: The National Film Board 1945-1953," in Seth Feldman, ed. *Take Two: A Tribute To Film in Canada* (Toronto: Irwin, 1984), 182-194.

113. In a comment on part of this paper presented at the Film Studies Association of Canada/Association québécoise des études cinématographiques Annual Conference (May 21-24, 1987) in Montreal, Professor Paul Warren of Laval suggested that, of all modern art forms, cinema might be the one whose content is most directly and literally 'pure' ressentiment, ie., a matter of the re-experiencing of feelings.

114. Peter Morris, *Embattled Shadows: A History of Canadian Cinema, 1895-1939* (Montreal: McGill-Queen's University Press, 1978), 37.

115. Ibid., 93.

116. Ibid, 95.

117. Roland Barthes, *S/Z* (New York: Hill and Wang, 1974), 55.

118. Morris, op. cit., 33.

119. See Seth Feldman, ed. *Take Two*, op. cit., passim, but especially his very important article, "The Silent Subject in English Canadian Film", 48-57.

DEMON POLITICS

120. See R. Bruce Elder, "Image: Representation and Object — The Photographic Image in Canadian Avant-Garde Film" in *Take Two*, 246-263.

121. *Time As History*, op. cit., 40.

122. Op. cit, 93.

123. Op. cit., 235.

124. Cited in Cook, Maple Leaf, op. cit., 158.

125. *The Wacousta Syndrome: Explorations in the Canadian Langscape* (Toronto: University of Toronto Press, 1985), passim.

126. Op. cit., 12.

127. Op. cit, 53.

128. Op. cit., 13.

129. Op. cit., 229.

130. In Peter Russell, ed. *Nationalism in Canada* (Toronto: McGraw-Hill, 1966), 27-46.

131. See Neil McWilliam and Alex Potts, "The Landscape of Reaction" in A.L. Rees & F. Borzello, eds., *The New Art History* (London: Camden Press, 1986), 106-119.

132. See R.K. Crook, "Modernization and Nostalgia: A Note on the Sociology of Pessimism", *Queen's Quarterly*, LXXIII: 2, Summer 1966, 289-283.

PROMOTIONAL CULTURE

Andrew Wernick

The division of labour, from which so many advantages are derived...is the necessary, though very slow and gradual,consequence
of a certain propensity in human nature which has in view no such
extensive utility; the propensity to truck, barter and exchange.
Adam Smith

The wealth of modern societies in which the capitalist mode of
production prevails appears as an immense collection of comodities.
Karl Marx

In societies where modern conditions of production prevail, all of
life presents itself as an immense accumulation of spectacles. Everything that was directly lived has moved away into a representation.
Guy Debord

1: Promotion and culture

With the industrialisation of publishing in the late nineteenth century, "writing" wrote Innis "becomes a device for advertising advertising."[1] Most immediately, the great Canadian media historian was thinking of newspapers,
circulation wars, and the role of Hearst-type journalism in promoting ads
for industrialism's new consumer goods. But he also had in mind the
growth of the publishing industry's own promotional needs, by virtue of
which even serious and seemingly autonomous forms of writing became
deeply tangled up in the advertising function as well. Hence the enhanced

"importance of names" a marked tendency in all corners of the literary market towards topicality, faddism, and sensation.

Nor was Innis only concerned with print. As scattered references to other media make clear,[2] his aphorism was intended as a broader comment on the fate of commercialised "writing" in all its forms. In that light, the (Victorian) assimilation of literature to advertising on which he focussed can be read as a figure for a longer-term structural tendency — one that culminated in his own day with the rise to cultural power of a multi-media communications complex that was more saturated with promotion than the one it had technologically surpassed.

The main purpose of the following reflections that follow is to see to what extent Innis's point can, in fact, be pushed. Summarily expressed, the thesis I want to explore is that North American culture has come to present itself at every level as an endless series of promotional messages; that advertising, besides having become a most powerful institution in its own right, has been effectively universalised as a signifying mode; and that this development goes far to explain such characteristic features of the contemporary ("post-modern") cultural field as its pre-occupation with style, its self-referentialism, its ahistoricity, and its vacuous blend of nihilism and good cheer.

So totalistic a formulation, in line with the exhausted character of our age, may seem to imply historical closure. If so, that is not my intent, which is simply to disentangle one aspect of modern society's culturo-economic logic, and, for the moment, leave other levels of determination (and contradiction) to one side. Even in itself, moreover, the rise of a promotionally dominated culture has not been exactly conflict free. As the "ideological" revolt of the sixties attests, the structural shift in the relation of culture to economy with which the rise of promotion has been associated has brought new tensions and, indeed, new opportunities for the formation of an emancipatory will.

It would be wrong, at the same time, to overcorrect. Movements can die from the attention they seek. Where all the channels have been colonised by exchange, the most oppositional discourse gets easily blunted and the Novum itself ("the Revolution," as we used to say) rapidly becomes just one more (self-)promotional sign.[3] What is true for radical action, moreover, is truer still for radical thought. Publication means publicity, and these very words, in being published, cannot avoid being part of what they seek to overcome.

One last opening remark. In contemporary usage, "advertising," "publicity," and "promotion" have become virtually interchangeable. But if their referents are the same their ways of grasping the concepts are not, and for present purposes, as the title of this piece indicates, I have a marked preference for the latter of these terms.

"Advertising" is literally the act of catching someone's attention; and "publicity" (Berger's term from the French[4]) emphasizes the quality of obtrusive visibility. Both are descriptive labels that approach the phenomenon from the concept of reception — without reference to the whole backstage circuitry of distribution and exchange to which its existence, as a prominent form of communication, is fundamentally tied. The word "promotion," by contrast, is abstractly operational and in its derivation (from the Latin *pro-movere*) conveys very precisely the sense of what promotion/advertising/publicity actually does: it at once anticipates, stands for and propels forwards those other circulating entities to which its messages severally refer.

In addition, more than in the case of its terminological rivals, modern usage has stretched "promotion" to cover not just ads as such but the whole field of public relations, including religious and political propaganda, as well as the more informal kinds of boosterism practiced in everyday life. In an analysis concerned with stressing the growth of salesmanship not just within but beyond the strictly commercial sphere, this greater generality provides a second ground of choice.

The enlarged referential meaning of "promotion" corresponds, in short, to the phenomenon's real expansion in the world, which in turn corresponds to "the penetrative powers of the price-system"[5] and to the spread of analogous relations into every aspect of social life. The end result has been the emergence of an all-pervasive configuration that might fittingly be called promotional culture. In posing the question of this complex's meaning, logic, and constitutive power let me now retrace the movement that brought it into being, along with the ever more convoluted forms of expression to which the extensions of promotion have cumulatively given rise.

2: Commodities and Communication

The spectacular development of advertising as a distinct apparatus, and the wider permeation of culture by promotion ultimately derive from the primordial characteristic of commodity that its classical theorists, from Adam Smith to Karl Marx, tended to overlook: the dependence of any money-mediated market on a functionally specific type of communication. For goods and money to exchange, information must be exchanged also. Buyers must know what is for sale, when, where, and at what price, and sellers must know what goods can be marketed and on what terms.

In the pre-capitalist case, where production and distribution are local and communication is face-to-face, this double exchange of commodities and information takes place all at once, at the point of sale. The designated site for such activity — the Roman forum, the Turkish bazaar, the Medieval fair — typically has the added character of a public institution for general social intercourse. But this coincidence of functions should not be misread. Whether it is street vendors crying their wares or ancient textile traders haggling over price and supply, the informational aspect of the market always has its own modalities and represents a form of social practice in itself.

The second circuit, like the first, is formally constituted as a system of exchange, but there is also a crucial difference. For even in the primitive case, where the two processes overlap, each act of money/goods exchange is consummated at once, whereas the two moments of information exchange are typically separated in time. Information about supply precedes purchase, but information about demand remains incomplete until the purchase is complete. Besides making it possible for each half of the information transaction to go its own specialised way(in modern parlance: advertising and market research), this difference also means that, however perfect the market, the communicative relation will tend to favour the vendor. For the latter gives mere assurance, but on completion of the sale gets hard data in return. The old tag "buyer beware" signposts this inequality, whose significance is not exhausted by the bad deals to which it may evidently lead.

From the earliest days of capitalist development, as commodity production begins to expand, ousting natural economy and involving local markets in a far-flung nexus of trade, the communicative activity associated with it not only expands as well but also undergoes a number of qualitative changes whose effect is to actualise the latent imbalance just sketched out.

First, the greater the distance of goods from their market the more that information about them has likewise to be communicated from afar. While this by no means abolishes either retail activity or the face-to-face ("oral") culture that surrounds it, the more geographically extended the market the more such direct forms of information exchange become only the endpoints in a chain of communication whose decisive links are anything but face-to-face. In the Old World the steady displacement of localised culture began in the "age of discovery" with printing and the port town shipping manifests that were the forerunner of the modern newspaper. Since then, the ever-widening market has stimulated technical improvements in communications to the point where, with telegraph and telephone, the movement of information has become materially independent of the movement of people and tangible goods.[6] But even at an earlier stage — where information had to travel via ship, horse, and handbill — the impact of geographically extended trade on commercial communication was rupturable. Gone was the simple overlap of commodity and information exchange, leaving the latter free (within the limits of its economic function) to develop a luxuriant life of its own.

As a further consequence of de-localisation the two halves of the information transaction — that is, from the sides of demand and supply — themselves begin to split, and in doing so their social character as communication likewise begins to diverge. The largerand more dispersed the market, the more that sales information, as advertising, becomes anonymously public. Information provided by the buyer, on the other hand, in the first instance as raw sales data, increasingly comes to have a private character as privileged communication within and between the profit-making enterprises involved.

With this step, finally, the whole circuit of commercial communication comes under the singular control of those who control supply — wherewith its very quality as exchange begins to disappear. No doubt the reception of print-age advertising, as of commercial broadcasting later on, was never wholly passive; and, on the other hand, the acquisition of demand information must always start with the consumer's own wants and needs. But a system in which data about the latter is appropriated by the same agency which transmits the self-interested messages constituting the former is clearly unilateral, implying a monopoly of knowledge where it does not, in any case, rest on a monopoly in the goods being sold.

At the level of media history it was the establishment of the popular press (the first regular American daily was the New York Sun in the 1830s) combined with the growing use of social statistics[7] which first brought such a system into being, paving the way for the more general establishment in this century of a media environment that has been flatly described as "speech without response."[8] Response, in the dialogical sense, has in effect now been replaced by feedback which, at the alienated limit — in the mute and automatic form of sales curves, product testing, and polls — merely registers the effects of a promotional monologue spoken from elsewhere into the dispersed vacuumland of mass opinion and taste.

3: Mass Production and Managed Demand

The precondition for this and the more general emergence of promotion as a distinct cultural force was industrialisation, or more precisely: the development of a capital intensive manufacturing sector, corporately organised and oriented to the mass-production of finished consumer goods.

Beginning in the early nineteenth century with food, clothing, and patent medicines, and then moving on to furniture, kitchen appliances, cars, and leisure goods, mass production methods swept through the capitalist economy like a wave, each advance representing at once a new incursion of standardised production into the needs structure of everyday life, a new substitute for domestic labour, and a new way to capitalise on the demands and desires (e.g., for relief from stress and for perpetual youth) created by the exigencies of industrial re-organization itself. Setting aside other dimensions of this complex shift to consumer capitalism,[9] its most important implications for the development of promotion can be summarized as follows.

First, (and most obviously,) mass production, implies mass consumption which, in turn, implies mass distribution and mass marketing. In this new ensemble, advertising in fact comes to play a strategic economic role.

For if industrial technology vastly increases the productivity of labour it also increases competitive risk by tying up the larger amounts of capital that have to be invested in each phase of the production cycle. Capitalists in the industrial age have thus become faced with a recurrent problem of surplus realisation; and this has required a sustained effort, on their part, to ensure that the ever greater abundance of manufactured goods gets to market and then actually gets to be sold.[10]

The obstacles to be overcome are both physical and cultural. Concerning the former, distribution and marketing must be organized on a trans-regional scale. Concerning the latter, the demand for what is being mass-produced must be continuously cultivated among the population reached by the manufacturer. Hence with mass production not only does the information circuit associated with commodity exchange undergo a prodigious expansion — to the point where it becomes a major industry in itself — but it is also forced to become pro-active. Manufacturers must survey consumers to know what they are likely to buy before production begins; and for the flow of any existing product, the requisite demand must be created or at least channelled so as to absorb available supply.

The cybernetic circularity of advertising and market research, each systematically complementing the other in the manipulative practices of the modern advertising agency, is a familiar target of humanist critique.[11] But questions of freedom aside, the paradox represented by the very existence of such a system for demand management is also worth pondering.

In effect, the larger our productive capacity, the higher the proportion of resources that have to be devoted to the "non-productive" domains of distribution and exchange. According to Stuart Ewen,[12] over 40% of the cost of producing assembly-line automobiles in the boom years of the twenties was spent on the dealerships and advertising campaigns used to market them once they left the plant. In the contemporary fragrance industry, this figure rises to over 90 per cent. Overall, in consequence, an obsessively productivist form of economy has made consumption its most salient objective, while the enhanced power of its productive apparatus has been expressed in the even greater development of its communications apparatus which, though parasitic on profits of the former, has in fact become the most mass-productive sector of all.

A second cluster of implications concerns the nature of advertising itself, both with respect to its rhetorical mode and in the changed relation ads have come to bear to the goods they are meant to promote.

The fact that mass produced consumables have to be continually offloaded, that they must compete with the virtually identical products of their rivals, and that product promotion and innovation, the conquest of new markets, requires constant consumer education to break the hold of old habits, all mean that advertising in the age of mass production must go far beyond the mere provision of notice and information if those products are to sell. This excess of meaning primarily condenses in that panoply of images commodities are laboriously given to maximise their consumer appeal.

This is not to say that earlier forms of advertising were always purely and neutrally informative. Sales talk, however simple, immediate, and low-key, has always had a demonstrative element (Hey you! This is for sale...), and the practice of hyping and profiling the wares had its origins in the street cries, store signs, and carnival pitches of petty commodity traders long before J. Walter Thompson turned it into a corporate art.[13] The pre-industrial Molly Malone, we may recall, sang — sang! — about her shell-fish and took good care, as in any modern jingle, to emphasise their saleable quality of praeternatural freshness.

The specific novelty of modern advertising lies not in its mere departure from some foresaken rationalist norm but, first, in the way that its demonstrative function has expanded to the point where buy-me signs get to be posted not just at the point of sale but everywhere; and, secondly, in the particular kind of non-reason to which these signs make appeal. In the image-making companies of Madison Avenue, advertising moves beyond hard sell insistence on the product's performative qualities, beyond even simile (Bovril: as strong and nutritious as the ox from which it is supposedly made) to the stage of outright symbolic identification. It follows that a cultural threshold is also reached: by representing the product as the embodiment of some existing cultural or psychological value — Coke is it; Pepsi the choice of a new generation — modern mass promotion at once etherealises the product and turns it into a cultural totem.

From this momentous change in advertising technique a number of consequences follow. At a textual level, advertising messages have become less verbal, discursive, and argumentative, and more figurative, allusive, and pictorial. Without discounting radio (whose use of narrative word-pictures allows it to function as a kind of visual medium at one remove), the most prominent advertising media have therefore been visual — from bill-boards and magazines to TV — for which the crucial technical breakthrough, more than a century and a half ago, was the development of photography, together with related improvements in the capacity of printing to mass-reproduce graphic design.

The visual ad, at once a mirror and a screen for the consumer's own projections, achieves a power and economy that the abstractions of verbal language can never match. Its main trope is metaphor, and its motivational force relies less on persuasion than on mimetic magic: we are invited to want the product as a way to re-unite with our fantasy selves. To gain this effect, the visual ad places at its signifying centre a euphoric, connotationally saturated image of the product proferred for sale; an image that is at once naturalistic (or at least set among images we will recognise as "real") and symbolically endowed, so that we will read the verbal and pictorial references to the product as signifiers in turn for the myth or desire the product is made to connote.[14]

Multiplied a million-fold and considered at the level of the whole cul-turescape, the effect has not only been our ubiquitous encirclement by messages enjoining us to buy, but our sensory implication in a fantastic web of signification which, before our very eyes, duplicates and redupli-cates the very commodities it presents for sale. Everyday life, without the exertion that a trip to the stores would normally involve, has in this way come to resemble one long and semi-continuous round of window-gazing. And overall, to use Situationist phraseology, advanced capitalism has given rise to a "society of the spectacle," culturally constituted by that "immense flotation of signs" which the machinery of commercial promotion has been driven to generate and set into general circulation.[15]

The signs which so circulate, be it noted, are themselves signs of signs. For the commodity which industrial promotion insistently represents as the image of a myth becomes mythic in the actually imagined relation the purchasing consumer has with it. What this means is that modern promo-tion effectively joins together two distinct signifying chains — those denot-ing products and those connoting values — and that both of these domains, stylised and conventionalised to render them fit for mainstream consump-tion, come to circulate via the same messages and the same media channels.

Advertising thus comes to serve as a major transmission belt for ideolo-gy. But ideology itself undergoes an important change to the same extent. The closed system of loaded concepts is replaced by the moving code of the ultra-conventional; and in the discontinuous kaleidescope of endless ads the components of this normality-based value system are shredded into little stereotypical bits. These too, like the commodities they help circu-late, and precisely because of their placement in promotional messages, become exchangeable tokens in a world where value of all kinds is being undermined by the inflation of hyper-productivity.

The conjunction in the imagistic advertising of ideology and product signification also changes the character of commodities themselves. To the extent that such promotion succeeds, the mythic, psychological, or status-related meaning that ads associate with the commodities they depict be-comes transferred to them, so that from the standpoint of consumption the ads merely reflect (and reinforce) what has actually become the case: that to its users Chanel No.5 is not just a sweet-smelling transparent liquid but bottled Parisian chic, that Smirnoff really does "mean friends," and that Marlboroughs, over and above their quality as addictive carcinogens, are the very embodiment of Frontier toughness.

Only a lingering nostalgia for what Veblen called "the instinct for workmanship"[16] could lead us to imagine that the use-value of commodi-ties has ever been reducible to their practical function. Apart from the fact, however, that human goups always attach symbolism to things, the exigen-cies of mass marketing such marginally differentiated (and similarly priced) products as shoe polish, beer, or soap make their mere performance charac-teristics recede even more as a mark of identifiable difference while their immaterial features as tokens of status, ideology or desire, become ever more pronounced.

As an important corollary, the initially distinct worlds of promotion and production begin to intersect, wherewith the relation between them begins to undergo a strange reversal. Promotion feeds back into the product's concept and design so that what is produced has already been conceived from the vantagepoint of the campaign wherein it will be promoted. Conversely: the campaign to promote the product, far from being a mere add-on, becomes itself the main productive activity at the centre of the whole commodity process.[17]

Roland Barthes provides a classic instance in his celebrated analysis of the Citroen DS, designed in shape and appurtenaces to resemble the seductive goddess of technology that its name (De-esse) punningly connotes.[18] A more contemporary example is provided by all the ballyhoo surrounding Coca Cola's ill-considered 1985 decision to promote a new formula for its leading beverage. Problems of image not taste dictated the change, and even the humiliating reversal of Coca Cola's decision in the face of consumer resistance was recuperated (one is tempted to see this too as planned) in the massive free publicity that re-launching the original formula instantly gained.

4: The Culture Industry

So far I have only considered the extension of promotion in relation to material goods, that is, in relation to those commodities whose use-value is not exhausted by their symbolic function. Nevertheless, the production of symbols has also been commodified leading to the growth of a vast industry for the production and dissemination of culture, consciousness, and information. The latter, moreover, has become crucial to the former since those who control the culture industry also control the major channels through which all mass disseminated promotion must flow.

The interdependence, at once technological and financial, between advertising and popular culture has changed the character of both — most importantly, by dissolving the boundary between promotion and the wider world of expressive communication. Through this breach, which coincided with the rise of the mass media, advertising messages have swirled into every corner of commercialised culture, transforming the latter, as a more or less integrated totality of ads, entertainment, and news, into one gigantic promotional vehicle.

Before considering the wider implications of this, however, it should be noted that the media industries were themselves promotional in character before, and independently of, the way in which their programmes came to piggy back on other people's ads.

For one thing, the modern rendering of popular culture as a publicity-seeking display belongs to a tradition of ritual entertainment that reaches back to the spectacles of the ancient world. Such "art for exhibition value"[19] advertised (at least) itself from the very start — even when "free" as a state-sponsored occasion, and well before the time when plays, competitive sport, music concerts, etc., became fully commodified. In addition to (and in the face of industrialism's own myths of which we constantly need to be reminded), the whole history of mass production, and of mass marketing itself, began three centuries before Wonderbread and the Model T with Gutenberg's printing press: that is, with the mass production of signs. From publishing to television, the culture industry has, in fact, not merely followed but pioneered the whole development that led, via industrialisation, to the greater prominence of distribution and promotion, and finally, to the conversion of the mass produced product into a promotional sign of itself.

Moreover, the tendency of mass production to issue in self-promoting products has been reinforced in the case of the culture industry by the very nature of the activity in which it is engaged: precisely because its business is communication, the mechanism for distributing the product is the same as the one for distributing promotional messages about it.

Self-advertising by and in the media has taken many forms, ranging from the direct insertion of spot ads (e.g., for "other books in the series") to the use of audience build up for the sequel (Richardson's *Pamela*, Stallone's *Rocky I-IV*). More generally, the mass cultural artifact advertises itself through the sheer visibility that the organs of mass communication automatically confer on whatever they transmit. Such visibility, indeed, can create the success it feeds on; and in just that spirit every mass medium, from music and literature to theatre, film, and broadcasting, has developed (and constantly updates) its own roster of stars, hits, and classics. Like the registered trade-mark whose prototype they are, the function of these big names and titles is at once to ratify and push to the centre of the stage the products which the industry believes can most readily be sold. The game of celebrity also provides a ready-made market for the secondary cultural products (literary gazettes, fanzines, talk shows, etc.) which help to sustain it. These products' whole lottery-like saga of instant fame, which replaces the oral mode of gradual reputation, only fans the flames of that envious identification which gives the celebrated works and stars their prodigious power in the first place to move the merchandise and to keep it moving.

The promotional activities of the culture industry fan out along all its media branches, binding them together in a spreading system of inner references that converts the whole into a single promotional intertext. Authors appear on TV, newspapers publicise movies, and radio, supplemented first by film and later by television, provides a vital advertising outlet for the recording industry. Nor is all this intermedia promotion incidental to programme content. Where the product is designed for appropriation through a set of repeated acts, the presentation of an extract, chapter, or episode can double both as an ad and as first-order programming. Besides the pure case, exemplified by the publication of book extracts in magazines, or by the broadcast media's use of records and music video, culture industry news and gossip about itself comes to serve as a staple-of its own entertainment fare.

As a further effect of popular culture's integration with advertising, the rise of new media technologies, from the rotary press to recording and broadcasting, has combined with commercial logic to systematically subordinate some forms of media presentation to others, as their anticipatory promotion. Since a printed text, photograph, record, or broadcast has a larger audience and is easier to valorise as a commodity than the (staged) performance on which it is based, the latter tends to be transformed into an advertisement for its replica. Not only, as a result, do live events, even when commodified through a gate, come to be staged expressly for their mass-mediated reproduction (Bruce Springsteen, Live!); but also, where such fabricated reproduction has already occurred, the "live" is itself reduced to simulating the "original" transcription, and the aura of its "liveness" becomes just a promotional device for investing the studio recorded performance with a pseudo-auratic resonance of its own.

For this reason, pop stars, poets, and publishing academics are periodically encouraged by their commercial handlers to take their product out on the road. Whether in the form of a rock concert or a public lecture the result in every case is an ambiguous performance, delivered on two levels, in which the aspect of immediacy essential to a culture's living substratum is continuously nullified by the promotional role which the live performance is contextually called upon to play.

All in all, then, the union of culture and advertising has done more than just colonise the former by extending the sway of the latter: it has brought about the interfusion of what are already two extremely dense promotional apparatus. The forms of promotion and promotional culture that have resulted from this union have tended correspondingly, therefore, to become even more convoluted and complex.

Let us first consider some of the ramifications of what Smythe, Bagdikian, and others have dubbed the "free lunch".[20] Setting aside the vexed question of the "audience commodity and its work," the economic principle denoted by this term is simple enough. In the marriage of convenience between advertising and the information/entertainment industry, the latter attracts an audience for the former in return for its subsidisation through the sale of space and time. To the extent of this subsidy, media production and delivery costs are born by the sponsor and the consumer gets a "free lunch" — in return for the latter's voluntary subjection to the ads carried along with the paper, event, or programme. Price subsidy varies from medium to medium, rarely total in the case of print and 100% in the case of radio and network TV. With broadcast media, the requisite reception equipment has to be privately paid for, with a further gain for the electronic companies that spawned the media in the first place. Nonetheless, once you have your set, the programming comes (gratis), any amount of it, ultimately supported by a hidden charge built right into the price of all advertised consumer goods.

As concerns content, the most obvious effect of media dependency on advertising is to create a situation where not only are ads designed with available advertising opportunities in mind, but the non-advertising component itself, i.e., the space between the ads, is also fashioned to suit the ads within its space. To some degree the objectives of advertising and regular programming already coincide in the latter's pursuit of high ratings. By attracting a mass audience to itself a programme or publication also clearly attracts attention to the bill-boards in its midst. At this level, perhaps, the carrying of paid ads only serves to reinforce the inherent tendency of all commercialised culture, from news to the serious arts, to embrace the values of popularity, diversion, and fun.

The effect, however, goes deeper. What matters to advertisers is not just the scale but the composition of their audience. This is partly a question of optimising the mix in terms of the average disposable income. (A spectacular instance, in the early 1920s, was the fate of the British Daily Herald. Despite breaking all circulation records, the paper went broke because its largely working-class readership was too down-market to attract sufficient advertiser support.[21] With growing affluence, however, and the mass market's envelopment of more and more social layers, the problems of audience composition have become more complex. Advertisers, in response, have sought to target the specific markets they want, adopting campaign strategies which, with the rise of demographics and psychographics, have become ever more sophisticated and statistically precise.

A similar dynamic has led to a process of differentiation among the media channels as well, so that thematically, ideologically, — and stylistically the non-advertising contents of TV shows, magazines etc., have come to be angled and coded in terms of the same economically functional group identities (of age, sex, income, "life-style," etc.) as those underlying the ads themselves. Not all products, however, have such singular target markets. As a result, cross-cutting the tendency to audience fragmentation, a mid-market middle-of-the-roadism has also come to be suffused, whose overarching effect, beyond torpor, has been to anchor the false universal it projects everywhere: that great mass cultural mirage of the normalised "middle class."

The resemblance between ads and their media surrounds spreads also to style. Linguistic, acoustic, and pictorial compression has shaped the language of television as profoundly as it had earlier shaped the sensory and ideational texture of newspapers and radio. Hence, the prevalence within popular media of quick-fire and laconic forms of communication, their sensory play with visual and auditory puns, their inconsequential sequencing of one message after another, and their magazine-type formats which reconfigure life and its experience into an ever-shifting mosaic of disparate shiny bits. Modernist poetics, as the literary and visual art of the early twentieth century explicitly attests, transformed the results into a now triumphant point of aesthetic principle — whose prosaic basis continues to lie in the high cost of media space and time, and the compressional effects of this on the syntax and semantics of all forms of mass-mediated talk.

At a deeper level, though, the free lunch comes to resemble its — accompanying ads not just because of the common repertoire of signifying forms and elements they both put into play, but because, precisely as a free lunch, it is equally promotional in intent. In its capacity as an audience magnet for a particular ad-carrying channel, the sports page of the newspaper, or an episode of Dallas, or rock concert simulcast effectively advertises the whole channel in which it appears. In so doing, it serves as an ad for other ads. Indeed, since mass-mediated inscription, even on a first order level, tends to double as promotion for itself, what presents itself on the surface as the literal and self-evident content of mass media programming, is actually constituted as a form of advertising raised to at least the power of three.

The requirements of modern mass marketing thus reverberate within the convoluted hype circuits of the commercialised sign to produce a mass cultural environment that is not just promotional in feel and function, but promotional in depth. At every point in its programmatic flow, layer upon inter-connected layer of advertising activity is always happening, and every layer refers us to another layer, and so on in an endless dance.

Within this self-reflecting vortex even the commodity, as advertising's real-world referent, loses its anchoring finality. Some ads are ads for other ads as well for immediately purchasable commodities, and some products (especially cultural ones) do double-duty as ads for other products as well. Thus when Michael Jackson did a video for Pepsi, Pepsi was in the same process boosting Michael Jackson; and their mutual promotion, each time the ad was broadcast, also helped boost the ratings of the network carrying it by attracting, with some predictable follow-through, a proportion of the channel-flippers who happened to be looking out for just such images at the time.

Underlying the feeling of profound, if fascinating, hollowness that the deceptively legible surfaces of mass-mediated culture tend to evoke is the curious structural development they instantiate. This is the fact that the mass production of culture via audio-visual media has brought about not just the merger of circulating signs and circulating commodities, but the merger of both with the advertising activity that was originally their mediating term. What commodity production has severed its further development has re-united, though not in the same way. For this time, not social instinct and everyday convenience, but the extruded circuit of commercial signification, with its ever-extending promotional activity, has provided the principle of unity, and only on condition that the rejoined spheres of culture and commerce, signification and commodity production, both submit to its empty embrace. Empty, because promotion always defines itself by reference to something else, in relation to which its own perpetual presence is the perpetuation of a lack, a continual reminder of the unsatisfied desire it is designed to provoke. Promotional culture is thus inherently nihilistic because sustaining this artificial and unbridgeable gap — cultivating demand, moving the commodities, stimulating circulation — is the whole and only point of the exercise.

5: General Exchange

To complete the picture, there are two final extensions of promotional activity that I must mention. Both have already been alluded to, but their fuller significance in the unfolding dialectic of culture and economy could not be clearly stated till now. With their development, in fact, promotional activity is brought into line with yet a further stage in the evolution of commodity production: that of the commodity's universalisation as a social form, wherein the modalities of commercial circulation, having completely permeated the mass cultural field, begin to generalise beyond the boundaries of commerce in the ordinary sense.

The French sociologist Jean Baudrillard has termed this ultra-commodified order the society of "generalised exchange".[22] To which one need only add that, with the arrival of generalised exchange, the promotional activity that has always been intrinsic to commodity production, and that has become increasingly prominent as that mode has spread, has likewise begun to generalise; and that, as it has done so, the entire space of signification has begun to be reconstituted as one vast, implosive and multiply inter-connected promotional culture.

The first of these extensions concerns the way that promotionalism has come to shape, not just the commercial output of media, but public discourse as such. The new element here is not simply that public information channels have been increasingly used to transmit commercial messages, for the histories of the assembly and the market-place have long been intertwined. Nor is there any novelty to the way in which news and opinion have themselves become commodities, for in this the contemporary media have simply followed a trajectory newspapers had already set. What is new, however, is that the doubling and redoubling of promotional activity within commercial media, which qualitatively intensified as the tie-in between product advertising and the culture industry grew, has transformed the whole process of public communication to the point where the interchange of political and cultural ideas has itself come to resemble nothing so much as a permanent advertising contest between rival brands and firms.

This has involved more than a tactical shift. Mainstream electoral politics, and indeed the competitive propaganda of international relations as well, have come to be conducted not only by means of advertising but to an increasing degree in terms of who can manage the whole business of advertising best. Nor is this criterion of suitability entirely irrational, since in a promotional culture the capacity to promote becomes an objective attribute of political leadership. The head of state is automatically a media star and, as we know, media stars who know how to manage their own image can also become heads of state.

A whole analysis would be needed to show how other institutional agencies that similarly compete for public attention, favour, or funds — churches, schools, hospitals, charities, professional groups, ideological lobbies, etc. — have similarly come to recast their propagandistic activities along quasi-commercial lines. Suffice to say that, just as the mass-mediated scene of public opinion comes to be reconstituted as a simulacrum of the mass comsumer market, so all its players, whatever their political or ideological objectives, come to modify their means and ultimately their ends in line with the public relations mode this implies. From both directions, then, politico-ideological, and commercial discourses have begun to interpenetrate. In place of their difference an inter-related complex of media circuits, public and private, for (what one might call) generalised promotional exchange has arisen.

The second way in which promotional activity has extended to signifying practices beyond the strictly commercial sphere is as an outgrowth of the process in which the human individual, as well, has been caught up in the expanding system of exchange. To this process there have been three distinct moments, each of which has generated its own forms of inter-individual competition, and its own level of related promotional practice.

Most immediately commercial in character is the competition that market-based society has set up between all "free" individuals as owners and traders of their own labour power. Of special significance, bracketing all the material dimensions of this contest, is the increasing extent to which the contest for jobs and more genteelly, for positions, has taken on increasingly other-directed forms. The job interview, the resume, deportment at work, the choice of consumption style, the projected family front, all become not just indices of success but permanent zones of competition in the struggle to get ahead. As a social psychological correlate, self-promotional careerism — Hobbes plus Narcissus — has been installed as the normalised form of adaptive behaviour and identity.

The steady intensification of status competition between individuals as consumers is closely related. Again, the contest has a material dimension (the more wealth, the more scope for competitive display) but even more clearly than in the case of positional competition, with its credentialism and lifestyle management, such competition unfolds as a game of staged appearances. Indeed, given the instability of consumption-based hierarchies in the fashion-driven centres of advanced capitalism, the apparent, here, is virtually synonymous with the real. The voguish becomes outmoded, only to be resurrected as high camp — between which there may be the only difference of intention implied by other marks of sophistication (or its absence) which the possessing actor drapes around the stage. The giddier the game, the more it resolves into a mere struggle to establish the dramaturgical credentials of the consumer/actors who conduct it — a promotional parody of the romantic ideal that individuals should re-create themselves as artists, and their own lives as works of art.

The primacy of promotion, however, in inter-individual exchange asserts itself most clearly with the emergence of yet a third form of status contest in which what is at stake is the sign-exchange value of individuals, not as worker/professionals nor as accumulators of status-bearing insignia, but as exchangeable (and consumable) tokens in themselves. Here, above all, the political economist of culture encounters Goffman's impression-managing self, brought to its highest pitch of anxiety and alienation, perhaps, in the rating-dating rituals of high school and beyond wherein the familial couple at the centre of the contemporary kinship system continues to be inter-generationally reproduced.

In effect, the freer individuals have become to form liaisons and attachments, the more they have been constrained by the ensuing competition for suitable partners with whom to strategise their personal lives, careful to cultivate their own associative worth. Since at least Shakespeare's time, it is Romantic Love that has provided the main motive and alibi for this gigantic roundalay,[23] whose objective on all sides is to maximise the self's trade-in value on the marriage/friendship/personality market (via publicity-conscious alliances and self-prestations) and to get as good a bargain in return as one can. The modern de-patriarchalisation of romance and the emergence of an inter-subjective rhetoric of caring and sharing abolish neither the market character of this process nor its mystification as Love. They represent, rather, the enlightened adaptation of such romantic ideology to a more advanced, i.e., more egalitarian, secular, and psychologically self-conscious stage in the development of the exchange system in which it is socially rooted.

In this respect, as in others, the wider commodification of the individual has been reinforced by the spread of market-derived norms concerning the abstract equivalence of persons. With the ascendancy of that principle, the barriers of ascribed status (especially as they affect youth and women) have successively crumbled, leading to a marked liberalisation in terms of interpersonal trade. Singles clubs, dating services, and 'companions wanted' sections in the classified ads represent only the most visible contemporary result of such accelerated circulation, which has necessarily unfolded mainly in the private domain. Yet the fact that the inter-individual quasi-market has here folded over into the capitalist market indicates that, just as generalised exchange establishes deepening lines of continuity between public and commercial communication so, too, does it connect the money economy and its promotional supports with even the most intimate transactions of private life as well.

Such linkages, of course, are not only economic. Beyond the direct provision of advertising services, the commercial sphere also incorporates the promotional moment of inter-indiviudal exchange ideologically, by the way in which its forms and imperatives are embedded in the human interest stories and glossily consumerised environments that comprise the figure and ground of the culture industry's regular programmatic fare. The inscription of generalised inter-individual exchange and its promotional correlate in the pivotal images and ideology of ad-carrying media serves both to naturalise the former and to make the latter seem credible by soaking them in the established forms of everyday life. The primacy of promotion in the private and public realms thus becomes mutually self-confirming, and the incommensurability of these two spheres in classic bourgeois thought ("homme et cityoen") resolves into the illusory two-sidedness of a Moebius strip, on which is inscribed one single and continuous promotional text.

At the level of private interaction, then, as well as at the level of the political process, the extensions of exchange progressively absorb all major dimensions of signifying practice into the discourse of promotion. And with this development, whose origins can be traced to the merger of advertising and entertainment in the formative phase of corporate capital, promotional culture can be said to have become not just hegemonic, but all-inclusive.

6: Beyond Promotion? Beyond Exchange

The further thought to which such reflection leads is that the complex elsewhere dubbed "post-modernism,"[24] and itself held to have become culturally dominant, is, if differently accounted for, the self-same complex, now the term "postmodernism" has its uses. The characteristics it draws together — multi-perspectivalism, de-centering, self-referentiality, etc., — do indeed combine. And the pre-fix ("post-") draws attention to a real difference between this configuration and the more utopian and contestative strains of "high" modernism that flourished earlier this century with Joyce, cubism, and jazz.

It is important, however, neither to overstress the discontinuity nor to concede too much to the culturalist notion that the symbolic somehow develops according to its own transcendant logic. To the contrary, as I have suggested, the endless intertextual contortions that constitute post-modernity are not just rooted in a larger social history: they are the effect of a structural mutation within market society which, by fusing economy and culture together and ushering in a world of generalised exchange, has deprived the cultural moment of even that degree of autonomy which gave its former activist partisans, romantic and avant-garde, their semblance of radical practicality.

Of course, to acknowledge that all signifying activity has been absorbed into a system of expanding sign-circulation to which promotion has become central is not, in itself, to be critical. Art, for example, has long since made its peace with the corporate boardroom, and in the amoral neutrality of contemporary cool — epitomised by figures like Warhol and Bowie — the pervasiveness of the promotional is accepted as an obvious and inescapable fact. Nevertheless, realism is better than misrecognition, and to grasp the essential link between the forms and spirit of our culture and the ascendancy of promotionalism is to gain a perspective, beyond the flat, dissolvent ironies of post-modernity itself, from which a critique, grounded in the possibility of an actual supercession, becomes at least thinkable.

Thinkable? How? The category of promotion directs us to a social form, the commodity, whose dialectical capacity to engender progressive change, Marxism, and a century of upheaval, has been made into an article of faith. Yet if promotional culture is all-inclusive does it not smother its own contradictions? If it expresses a universal development, the generalisation of exchange, is there any historical warrant for positing or striving for a different cultural future? What space, in short, does the tendency to pan-promotionalism — or a critique that projects it — leave for transformative practice, particularly (since that is what concerns us here) in the cultural sphere? In response I would offer just three observations.

The first is that to seize on advertising as the essential mode in which the signifying practices of advanced capitalist society are set is not simply to return the discussion to Marx, still less to certain rote formulae about class conflict and ideology which became associated with his name. It is, rather, to find a new relevance to that broader debate about society and economy which attended the whole birth (from 1750-1850) of modern capitalism, and which centred on the problematic of exchange.[25]

Marx's own contribution to this debate was no doubt path-breaking. But even as an anatomy of economically based social relations, his work was also flawed, and flawed precisely by what made it powerful: its insistence on the social (not just economic) centrality of production.

Marx's productivism was itself in reaction to the over-emphasis in liberal economic theory on distribution and exchange. Whatever the virtues of this correction, at the level of cultural analysis it left a gap that Marx's followers could only fill by developing the domination model sketched out in the *German Ideology* and the base/superstructure notion mentioned later on.[26] The result, for radical theory, has been an anachronism: on the one hand, a map of the cultural relations of advanced capitalism that extrapolates from those of previous class societies, particularly medieval Europe; on the other, an actual form of society in which, precisely as a result of the commodification process that defines it, such a sharply stratified mode of cultural organisation has tended more and more to break down.

Within American thought, it was the non-Marxist Veblen[27] who did most to re-introduce into cultural discussion the importance of circulation and exchange. But Veblen himself was working against the background of an older tradition, and here, at least with respect to the critique of consumerism and status competition, the key voice revived was undoubtedly that of Rousseau.

Rousseau, for his part, absolutised the problem. For him, competitive display — as evidenced in the fopperies and salon culture of eighteenth century Paris — was not only historically prior to the rise of the market, but prior to the institutionalisation of social life as such. It was, indeed, the primal consequence of association itself, the Adamic fall from which all subsequent social evil flowed. Under the circumstances (went the argument in his *Essay on Inequality*) progress meant regress and the most that could be accomplished was a mitigation of the social inequality and cultural hypocrisy that, in a state of developed civilisation, were status competition's entrenched bad effects. Hence his arguments, on the one hand, for a new contract to reconstitute the collectivity as a legitimated power, and, on the other, for a naturalist reform of education/socialisation to maximise the pre-social individual's real moral capacity.

Rousseau's solution has been attacked from all sides. But beyond a sharper appreciation of the property question it cannot be said that progressive praxis has found a better way. At the most radical level, attempts have been made (most recently in China) to abolish competitive circulation as such. These, though, have invariably foundered by exacerbating the contradiction between individual and society they hoped to transcend. The pendulum, in consequence, has begun to swing the other way — with reform movements in socialist societies, like those in capitalist ones, tending to accept that the wheel of exchange cannot be stopped, or even (heresy of heresies) that a modest restoration of the market might have a liberating effect. Radical thought, it seems, is being pressed to adopt the notion of a "self-limiting revolution,"[28] a revolution in which the community gains power, but not without leaving the circulation of goods and signs some scope for play.

It would be wrong to conclude, however, that a dialectical approach must be abandoned altogether. To decouple the problematic of advancing exchange from the (still vital) issues of class, private property, and economic distribution does not at all mean that promotional culture should be regarded as homogeneous or without contradiction.

Conflicts, for one thing, are continually provoked by the unsettling impact of the ever-expanding market on existing values, particularly where these serve as moral restraints to trade.[29] The current controversy over street prostitution, which above all concerns its advertising aspect, is a clear case in point. Such issues — coded as liberal versus conservative, individual versus society, for and against "the family" etc., — create the basis for an ongoing cultural politics which, at the limit, can even combine with other aspects of the situation (Weimar Germany, North America in the 1960s, Iran in the late 1970s, etc.) to provoke a total social crisis.

It is hard to define this dynamic in ways that do not capitulate to one or other of its poles. Suffice to say that while the contradiction is material (in the sociological sense) its expression is cultural; and that the most important zone of combat is at the interface between promotion (as propaganda for trade) and the entrenched values through which a social formation, and, indeed, the social as such, is culturally reproduced.

My final point concerns media. I have already noted that with the development of techniques for recording, simulating, and mass reproducing the live, the latter has increasingly come to be subordinated as promotion for the former; and that this development mirrors and intersects with the promotional reduction (via inter-individual status competition) of everyday life itself. As a philosophical analogue, the Grand Theorists of our culture, morbidly fascinated with the death of meaning that has accompanied the proliferation of cross-referring texts, have declared war on the traditional privileging of the spoken word as the fount of thought and speech. In *Grammatology*, Derrida has insisted that speaking is only a special case of writing and that the authenticity values which romantics, traditionalists, and mystics from Plato to Heidegger have identified with the human voice rest on a mythic view of language — one that modern linguistics has fortunately begun to correct.

Whatever the philosophical merits of this line of reasoning its political value is entirely suspect since it seems only to ratify a movement that has produced a culture based on substitutions, vacuities, and outward show. To dismiss the face-to-face, the immediate, the oral is indeed to devalue a dimension in which values arise counter to promotional culture, ones that can be appealed to, at the very least, as establishing the basis of a critique. Nor does such a critique have to confine itself to nostalgia and lament. For, as every activist knows, talk — for all its impoverishment — is still the least promotionally mediated of media. Not only does it thus remain the oxygen of traditions and institutions; it is also *par excellence* the communicative mode in which new ideas arise and populations can mobilise themselves, if only for an instant, to assert their deepest, most emancipatory desires.

Department of Sociology
Trent University

Notes

1. Note 15/24 reads in full: "Pervasive influence of advertising — writers of one media [sic] place articles in another media and secure advertising for former as well as latter — writing becomes a device for advertising." W. Christian, ed., *The Idea File of Harold Adams Innis* (1980), Toronto, University of Toronto Press,) p.125. For Innis

on the publishing industry, see H.A. Innis, *The Bias of Communication* (1952, Toronto, University of Toronto Press) pp. 142-189.

2. W. Christian (ed.) *The Idea File of Harold Adams Innis* p.72 and *passim*.

3. The phrase is Louis Althusser's. See his essay on May '68 in *Politics and History: Montesquieu, Rousseau, Hegel, and Marx*, (1978, New York, Schocken).

4. John Berger, *Ways of Seeing* (1977, London, British Broadcasting Corporation and Penguin), especially pp. 129-155.

5. The title of a key essay in Innis's *Essays in Canadian Economic History*, (1956, Toronto, University of Toronto Press,) pp. 252-272.

6. "It was not until the advent of the telegraph that messages could travel faster than a messenger. Before this, roads and the written word were closely interrelated." M. McLuhan, *Understanding Media: the Extensions of Man* (1965, New york, McGraw-Hill), p. 89.

7. The two practices were conjointed when Richard Gallup left academia to join the Young and Rubicam agency in 1932. See S. Fox *The Mirror Makers: a History of American Advertising and its Creators* (1984, New York, Vintage) p. 138.

8. J. Baudrillard, *Towards a Critique of the Political Economy of the Sign* translated by Charles Levin (1981, St. Louis, Telos Press) p. 169 and ff.

9. A good account of this shift is to be found in S. Ewen, *Captains of Consciousness* (1976, New York, McGraw-Hill).

10. The classic modern statement of the realisation dilemma is to be found in J. Galbraith, *The Affluent Society*, (1956, Boston, Houghton-Mifflin). For a good discussion of the arguments for and against this view of advertising's larger role see W. Leiss, S. Kline and S. Jhally, *Social Communication in Advertising* (1986, Toronto and New York, Methuen) pp. 13-19 and ff.

11. See especially 'The culture industry: enlightenment as mass deception' in M. Horkheimer and T. Adorno *The Dialectic of Enlightenment* (1972, New York, Herder and Herder).

12. *Op. cit.* pp. 23-30.

13. For the early history of advertising see F. Presbrey, *The History and Development of Advertising* (1968, New York, Greenwood Press) and R. Fox, *op. cit.*

14. The most thorough account of this mechanism is to be found in J. Williamson, *Decoding Advertising* (1978, London, Mario Boyars). See also R. Barthe's essay "The rhetoric of the image" in his *The Responsibility of Forms: Critical Essays on Music, Art and Representation*, (1985, New York, Hill and Wang) pp. 21-40 and A. Wernick "Advertising and Ideology", *Theory, Culture and Society*, 1984, Vol. 2 no. 1. Leiss, Kline and Jhally suggest that imagisitic advertising becomes a dominant motif from the early 1930s on, and that so far it has gone through three psycho-semiological shifts. These they label Symbolism, Gratification and Lifestyle, arguing that each in turn corresponds to a different symbolic mode, respectively Iconology, Narcissism and Totemism. See *Social Communications in Advertising* pp. 259-298.

15. See especially "Requiem for their media" in J. Baudrillard's *Towards a Critique of the Political Economy of the Sign*.

16. T. Veblen, *The Instinct of Workmanship* (New York, Viking, 1914).

DEMON POLITICS

17. Semiological self-consciousness about design can be traced to the earliest days of mass production. See for example the discussion of Wedgwood pottery design in A. Forty *The Objects of Desire*, 1986, New York, Pantheon).

18. See R. Barthe's, *Mythologies* (1973, London, Paladin).

19. *Q.v.* W. Benjamin's celebrated essay "Art in the Age of Mechanical Reproduction", published in the collection *Illuminations*.

20. D. Smythe *Dependency Road: Communications, Capitalism, Consciousness and Canada*, (1981, New Jersey, Ablex); B. Bagdikian *Media Monopoly*, (1984, Boston, Beacon).

21. See J. Curran "Capitalism and Control of the Press" in J. Curran, M. Gurevitch and J. Woollacott (eds.) *Mass Communication and Society* (1977, London, Edward Arnold) p. 225.

22. Especially in earlier works like *Towards a Critique of the Political Economy of Signs* and *L'Echange symbolique et la mort*. One suspects that Baudrillard's formulation was itself derived from C. Levi-Strauss's discussion of modern kinship in *Elementary Forms of Kinship* (1969, Boston, Beacon).

23. For a masterful account of the roots of this complex in the chivalric tradition see C.S. Lewis *The Allegory of Love: A Study in Medieval Tradition* (1939, London, Oxford University Press).

24. J-F. Lyotard, *The Post-modern Condition: A Report on Knowledge* (1984, Minneapolis, Minnesota Unversity Press); H. Foster (ed.), *The Anti-aesthetic: Essays on Postmodern Culture* (1983, Washington, Bay Press); F. Jamieson, "Post-modernism, or The Cultural Logic of Late Capitalism", *New Left Review* 1984 pp. 53-92.

25. Besides Rousseau and the French tradition of anthropology and sociology deriving from him, key figures include Ferguson, Smith, James Mill, and Manderville on the British side and Hegel, Tonnies and Weber on the German.

26. See especially *A Contribution to the Critique of Political Economy* translated from the second German edition by N. Stone (1904, Chicago, Charles Kerr and Co.)

27. The Rousseauian influence in particularly strong in his *Theory of the Leisure Class*, (1899, New York, Viking).

28. This formula is particularly associated with the Polish Solidarity intellectual, Adam Michnik. In a curious way, the Left in the West and reform movements in the East, including Gorbachev's, have come to converge in a rediscovery of the virtues of a 'mixed economy'.

29. I have developed this argument at some length in "Sign and Commodity: Some Aspects of the Cultural Dynamic of Advanced Capitalism", *The Canadian Journal of Political and Social Theory*, Vol. VIII, Number 2 (Winter/Spring) 1984.

IV

... AND THE INSURRECTION OF SUBJUGATED KNOWLEDGE

WE OBJECTS OBJECT:
PORNOGRAPHY AND THE WOMEN'S MOVEMENT

Eileen Manion

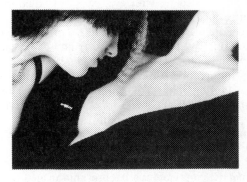

Photo: George Tysh

"A woman has a product and she should use it."
> Chuck Traynor to Linda Lovelace, quoted in *Ordeal*

"All struggle for dignity and self-determination is rooted in the struggle for actual control over one's own body, especially control over access to one's body."
> Andrea Dworkin, *Pornography: Men Possessing Women*

Since the mid-seventies in the United States and the late seventies here in Canada, feminists have been discussing pornography as a problem for women, a danger to women, not just a symptom of misogyny, but also one of its causes. Large numbers of women report that they both fear assault triggered by pornography, and experience pornography itself as violent assault. As Susan Griffin put it: "Pornography is sadism."[2] Its very existence humiliates us.

More and more forcefully women have been demanding that something be done about pornography. Strategies differ. Feminists with civil libertarian backgrounds advocate open discussion, demonstrations, education, consumer boycotts. The more impatient prefer the consciousness raising of direct action, as in the bombing of Vancouver's Red Hot Video. Others look to the state to enforce existing obscenity laws or to frame new legislation which would suppress pornography, not because it is sexual, but because it is hate literature and incites violence. As Susan Brownmiller declared: "Pornography is the undiluted essence of anti-female propaganda."[3]

Though anti-pornography tactics vary, feminists generally agree that pornography is a bad thing, that it does harm to women, and that if we have trouble defining it,[4] we still recognize it when we see it. This is not unreasonable since the pornography most feminists attack does not disguise itself. However, when we look critically at other cultural products — advertisements, mainstream movies and television programs — they often resemble pornography.

One problem with the feminist consciousness raising that has taken place around pornography is that it intends to generate fear and anxiety, or to bring to the surface fears women already experience.[5] In our society, every young girl's developing sexuality is hedged with awareness of frightening possibilities: violent assault and unplanned pregnancy. As adolescents, we learn both to fear men and to mistrust our own amorphous desires, which may betray us. Feminist discussions of pornography address these fears and emphasize pornography's danger to women, epitomized in Robin Morgan's slogan: "Pornography is the theory, and rape the practice."[6] Gloria Steinem makes the same point in her essay, "Erotica vs. Pornography." Following a brief discussion of the feminist movement's having raised issues such as rape, wife battering and enforced prostitution to public consciousness, she says: "Such instances of real antiwomen warfare led us directly to the propaganda that teaches and legitimizes them — pornography."[7]

Pornography makes us nervous for a number of other complex reasons. Beyond the fear that it incites violence, it represents an analogue of what alcohol symbolized for nineteeth century feminists at a time when most respectable women did not drink. Not only was alcohol for them a lower class social evil contributing to domestic violence and public corruption (associated as drinking was with party politics), but it was also, for more powerful men of their own class, a glue, a mucilage bonding males in exclusive enclaves off-limits to "good" women. Nineteenth century feminists imagined that if they could remove the alcohol, these male bastions would open up and admit them. Similarly for feminists today, pornography represents a unifying force in male power groupings. Pornography is quintessential macho culture: one thinks of businessmen enjoying an evening at a strip club — the "good" women who aspire to be partners in the firm might well feel uncomfortable.

We are also uneasy about pornography for it seems to promote isolation of men from women, the substitution of fantasy for relationship. If socialization into macho values denies tenderness and compassion, pornography promises sexual gratification without the necessity of those "effeminate" feelings.[8] "Real men," we sometimes suspect, don't need women at all,[9] or they want only the compliant, pre-packaged woman of the skin magazine. Pornography, like advertising, appeals to a whole range of insecurities, evokes envy by suggesting somehow, somewhere, more pleasure is available.

In addition, feminists fear that pornography not only distorts the portrayal of female sexuality by depicting women as no more than objects-for-men, but that it also blocks exploration of women's "true" sexuality. Just when women were beginning to discuss what a sexuality emancipated from double standards and procreative teleology might mean for them, pornography turned up its volume and drowned out with a quadrophonic blast women's tentative whispers.

Violence against women exists and women must defend themselves against it. Our other concerns about pornography are equally serious. However, focussing analysis of pornography on potential violence or other sources of anxiety makes it difficult to think clearly in the ensuing tense, over-charged atmosphere. I'm not arguing that our anxiety is unjustified. However, I do think there's a real danger that the climate of fear we are helping to create will strengthen repressive social forces and that some of our demands with regard to pornograhy will backfire and result in unanticipated losses for women. Thus as a feminist I'd like to take one step back from the feminist discussion of pornography and look at why we began to perceive pornography as a problem, what some of the contemporary rhetoric about pornography is saying, and how the contemporary anti-pornography consensus[10] fits into the history of feminist causes and demands. Since I am primarily concerned about pornography in relation to the women's movement, I will not deal with the separate though related questions of child pornography or gay male pornography.

Once upon a time there were norms of correct masculine and feminine behaviour. A number of factors — economic and social changes beyond the control of any one group — have ensured that these norms remain unchallenged in very few milieus within North America today. Feminism, needless to say, has been directly involved in overthrowing received ideas about both male and female propriety.[11] Parallel with these changes, pornography, presumably to create and sustain new markets, has extended the bounds of what can, without incurring prosecution, be shown and described. Pornography allegedly breaks taboos of acceptable representation, often in a context which claims to be funny, ironic, self-referential. Pornography provokes the shocked response, the censor in our heads who tells us the image is bad or dirty, and therefore pleasurable. Pornography claims to push back barriers in order to continue to titillate. Perhaps pornography even needs censorship so that it will have norms to violate.

However, an important element in the feminist analysis of pornography has been the argument that pornography does not, in fact, violate norms of male dominance and female submissiveness, but operates to sustain them. In this view, pornography only seems to have a radical, liberatory appeal to the unconscious. In reality, pornography gives us the same old world view we see everywhere else: men are subjects, women are objects, not even objects to be "known," but discrete items to be scanned, viewed, taken in, or exchanged, like bits of information.

But then, so what? Why did feminists become concerned about pornography if its values are just the same as those we see everywhere else in the culture? Why isolate pornography for special attention?

If we're not afflicted with historical amnesia or guilty self-denial, we must remember that in the sixties most of us assumed sexual openness and explicitness had something to do with human liberation: we were creating a joyous emancipatory festival which would liberate us from our fears, timidities, hang-ups, double standards. In the present climate, when so many of us see ourselves as the walking wounded of the sexual revolution, that view at best seems naive, at worst a male-conspiratorial rip-off.

IDEOLOGY AND POWER

Feminists often suggest that the seventies' proliferation of pornography, as well as its increased explicitness and violence, is a male chauvinist backlash to the women's movement. In pornography men take revenge on uppity women. Male consumers buy into the fantasy and keep "their" women off balance by bringing home pornography or by going out openly to view it. Religious fundamentalists blame the women's movement more directly for augmenting the availability and popularity of pornography. Didn't we urge women to be "liberated," independent of men and marriage? Many North Americans can't distinguish the idea of liberation promoted by Gloria Steinem from the one marketed by Helen Gurley Brown. Didn't feminists raise "new" issues related to sexuality to public consciousness? Didn't we say that "the personal is political"?[12] For many that translates into "the private is public" — so there we get pornography taking us at our word and making women's privates publically visible just about everywhere we turn. How can we object to that? might the jeremiahs ask, and how shall we respond to such a nightmarish perversion of our message?

For feminists, there is nothing liberated, liberating, or libertarian in the current availability of explicit sexual images catering to all specialized tastes. At best this wide open market constitutes "repressive tolerance;" at worst, sexist propaganda as nefarious as *Mein Kampf.* On the evilness of pornography, feminists and fundamentalists are at one. They differ, of course, on why it's so bad.

Feminists have isolated pornography as a problem as a result of two parallel trends within the women's movement. One is the focus on male violence, which I mentioned earlier, and the other is the attempt to develop a women's perspective that calls into question male "universal" values. Whether or not connections between pornography and rape can be demonstrated "scientifically" in laboratory experiments with bizarre methodologies and dubious theoretical assumptions, women assert that the degradation of women immediately visible to them in pornography is reason enough to believe that boys and men who regularly consume it must be corrupted. Beyond that, women question the way pornography depicts sexuality, claiming that it's not about sex at all, but only about dominance, or that it represents only male sexuality.

This concern with pornography can be correlated with escalating frustration over the resistance of "the system" to grant our just and reasonable demands. During the late sixties and early seventies, enormous amounts of investigations were done, information was collected, analyses were made; we discovered and demonstrated how empty was the egalitarian rhetoric of our society when it came to men and women's real life privileges and opportunities. Then by the late seventies, many things seemed to be getting worse instead of better. Increased divorce rates and the jump in single parent female-headed households, we realized, were liberating many women into poverty.[13]

However, just as nineteenth century feminists overestimated the potency that would accrue to them with the vote, we also may at first have exaggerated the power of legal change. Historically feminists often conflated legal rights with political power and assumed one devolved directly from the other.[14] Perhaps we also assumed, in the early days of the contemporary movement, that cogent argument, along with tidying up of the law, would be enough, or almost enough, to affect change. Our early optimism has since given way to rage, and we have been forced to examine aspects of our culture which maintain male dominance at the irrational level and undercut our rational demands.

This search has led some feminists like Nancy Chodorow and Dorothy Dinnerstein [15] to take a closer look at mothering and use psychoanalytic theory to explore misogyny and personal/cultural ambivalence toward women. It has led others to pornography, which, insofar as it blatantly sneers at us, tediously insists we are nothing but cunts, bunnies, pussies, and chicks, seems like the grandiose revenge of the (male) infantile imagination. For, adopting the vision pornography presents of women, who would trust us with any authority if all we really want, no matter what our pretensions, is a good lay? But then who would trust the men we see in pornography either? Would we buy used cars from them or elect them to political office? No matter what their pretensions, all they want is a good lay. Suppose we as women really do look at pornography with our own eyes and not as we imagine men look at it. This may seem like a ridiculous, utopian wish, given the power relations of our culture. But then who can endow us with the legitimacy of our own perspective?

If we do look again at pornography, I think we'll see not only women's degradation, but also human pathos and pain. Paradoxically, feminist condemnation of pornography acccepts the brittle male fantasy — that the real-life, unreliable penis is magical, powerful, irresistible — and overlooks the fears and insecurities such fantasy is meant to dissolve.

I realize that I've strayed here from feminist orthodoxy and raised provocative questions which some may regard as frivolous. Nonetheless, in taking up pornography as a political issue, I think we have not taken account of historical parallels with various nineteenth century feminists' moral and political concerns. For a few moments, I would like to explore some of these and then return to contemporary feminism and pornography.

Nineteeth century feminism was not limited in scope to a unidimensional struggle for women's suffrage, as historians would have had us believe for many years. Women's demands for civil rights and expanded participation in the world outside the home were linked with a wide range of other issues, including concerns related to sexuality. Discussions of "voluntary motherhood" raised the possibility of women's sexual autonomy within marriage.[16] A few utopian communities and free love advocates went further, questioned the sanctity of marriage and championed women's right to a sexuality free of marriage's exclusivity. Nonetheless, most feminists foresaw a transformed institution of marriage, purged of both male supremacy and sexual ignorance.[17] However, on the darker side, women did recognize that sexuality could pose a threat, and their fears became organized around various campaigns dealing with prostitution, white slavery and "social purity."

Ellen Dubois and Linda Gordon have pointed out that for nineteenth century feminists the prostitute represented the "quintessential sexual terror,"[18] for she epitomized female victimization at the hands of lustful, exploitative men.

Reformers in both Britain and the United States focussed their energy both on rescuing prostitutes from their degraded life and on opposing state regulation of prostitution. Licensing prostitutes and coercing them into physical examinations, reformers argued, cynically attempted to protect men from venereal disease at the expense of the women's civil rights. Since the definition of prostitution even at the turn of the century was notoriously vague, [19] and could include non-commercial extramarital female sexual activity, the danger of infringement on any woman's civil rights was evident. However, many feminists also imaginatively identified with the actual prostitute and made her outrage their own.

In Britain, Josephine Butler led the feminist wing of the anti-Contagious Diseases Acts movement. The Contagious Diseases Acts, a series of laws passed between 1864 and 1869, provided for the "sanitary inspection" of alleged prostitutes near designated military depots in England and Ireland. Some doctors and politicians wanted to see the Acts extended to the civilian population. Similarly in nineteeth century America, feminists took part in struggles to oppose the passage of such regulatory legislation.[20] In Canada, a Purity Education Association existed in Toronto between 1906 and 1915, and a National Council for the Abolition of White Slavery was founded in 1912, but most of the activity around sexual concerns was connected with the Women's Christian Temperance Union.[21]

The prostitute, however, was not only a symbol for feminists of women's oppression; she was also a symbol for moralists of the social dislocation caused by industrialisation. When we look at the anti-Contagious Diseases Acts campaign in Britain or the anti-regulation campaigns in the United States, we see that moralists and feminists had concerns that both differed and overlapped. Feminists wanted to abolish prostitution by "saving" prostitutes and rechanneling men's sexual impulses into "acceptable" relationships. They rejected the view that the prostitute was a "fallen woman," a perpetual outcast, a potential polluter of men. Instead she was a victim of "male pollution . . . who had been invaded by men's bodies, men's laws, and by that 'steel penis,' the speculum."[22] Feminists deeply resented the sexual license men claimed for themselves and condemned in women. Both feminists and others in the purity movement advocated a "single standard of morality" for both men and women. In addition, feminists could use the assumed moral superiority and "passion-lessness" of good women to argue that they should weild political power to clean up the corrupt public world.[23] However, this strategy undermined attempts to make positive claims for women's sexuality.

Enthusiasm for the temperance, social purity and other reform movements which aimed at moral improvement through legislative intervention was fueled partly by what we might see as feminist concerns, and partly by anxiety over urbanization, commercialization, industrialisation — all the "-izations" that threatened family and rural values with rampant, exploitative individualism.[24] Very often other anxieties were displaced onto sexual issues, which are guaranteed to provoke attention and indignation. However, as we'll see, women did not necessarily benefit from the resulting climate and/or reforms.

SUBJUGATED KNOWLEDGE

By emphasizing the Victorian notion of women's passionlessness and moral superiority women were able to challenge male sexual prerogatives within and outside the family and forge an argument in favor of their own political power. However, this led feminists to sacrifice for several decades an opportunity to define their sexuality on their own terms. (As we know, numerous "experts" rushed in to fill the vaccuum.) Even early birth control advocates ran up against the fear that contraception would leave women more vulnerable to male sexual exploitation. This restricted view of women's sexuality also made it impossible for many feminists to understand the complex reality of the prostitute herself. Consequently they could be shocked by prostitutes who refused to behave like proper victims and accept "rescue." They were also highly suspicious of working class culture and mores, and could take a repressive attitude toward sexual activity on the part of young working girls. One might even go so far as to argue that many ordinary women were put off by a view of female sexuality that did not correspond to their own experience.[25]

Consequently, although feminists succeeded in Britain in having the Contagious Diseases Acts repealed, and blocked in many instances the passage of regulationist legislation in America, they ultimately did not control the direction of the purity movements and their work ironically helped pave the way for legislation aimed at repressing prostitution, which, though it did not eliminate the "social evil," made the life of the prostitute herself lonelier, harder, and riskier.

As long as prostitution had been informally tolerated, prostitutes could live among or on the fringes of the casual laboring poor. They had a degree of autonomy, and were not usually exploited by pimps. However, in Britain the debate over prostitution was raised to a more impassioned level with the publication of W.T. Stead's infamous "Maiden Tribute of Modern Babylon" series in 1885. Stead's documentation of the sale of "five pound virgins" to aristocratic rakes, along with other sensationalistic accounts of "white slave" traffic, led to the passage of the Criminal Law Amendment Act (1885) which raised the age of consent for girls from thirteen to sixteen. However, it also gave the police increased jurisdiction over working class girls and women and enabled them to carry out raids on lodging house brothels. The closing of brothels failed to eliminate prostitution, but it did render prostitutes subject to arbitrary exercises of police power and it forced them to seek protection from pimps and other underworld men. In 1912 Sylvia Pankhurst remarked of the White Slavery Act: "It is a strange thing that the latest criminal Amendment Act, which was passed ostensibly to protect women, is being used exclusively to punish women."[26] It is also worth noting that the earlier 1885 Act prohibited "indecent acts" between male consenting adults, allowing for the prosecution of homosexuals.

Paradoxically, the purity movement, in its efforts to establish "civilized morality," a pre-Freudian notion of the passions under the total control of will and reason, helped to launch an airing of topics formerly untouchable. Ironically in its very desire to suppress passion and disruptive sexuality it contributed to a climate in which such issues could be researched and investigated. Nonetheless, this "openness" also meant behaviour must be more carefully scrutinized. As I have noted, for women, especially young working class women, extramarital sexual activity often became not only unacceptable and immoral, but also criminal, and more likely to result in arrest and imprisonment.[27]

Thus in the United States, nineteenth century evangelical movements to rescue prostitutes gave way to Progressive Era social welfare efforts to "reform" them. During the post-bellum era, former abolitionists turned their attention to prostitution and brought to the crusade against "white slavery" all the energy and moral enthusiasm they'd developed in the fight for black emancipation. However, as in England, legislation passed to eliminate prostitution led to arbitrary police raids, pressuring prostitutes into dependence on pimps. Ironically the new reformatories instituted after the turn of the century to punish deviant female sexual behaviour created conditions whereby girls like Maimie Pinzer, whose life has become known through publication of her letters to Fanny Quincy Howe,[28] might be pushed into prostitution by the very justice/social welfare system designed to redeem them.

The ultimate result of the alliance of feminists and other social purity advocates was that the feminist dimension of the attack on prostitution was lost and only the attack on the prostitute herself survived. This can be seen at its most virulent after American entrance into World War 1. The federal government was so concerned with maintaining a "pure" army that it arrested and detained more than 15,000 suspected prostitutes. In addition, it's worth noting that the social purity campaigns against obscenity in literature, art, and popular culture led by Josiah Leeds and Anthony Comstock created the legislation (1873) under which the Sangers were later prosecuted for sending women birth control information. This legislation also made it difficult for feminists to write openly about topics like rape and incest.

We can see that nineteenth and turn of the century campaigns around sexual themes coagulated anxieties provoked by increased commercialization, commodification, and other types of social change, and ultimately, in order to allay fears, legitimated more government intervention, manipulation and control. Although we must be careful about drawing historical parallels in a facile way, one thing we can note is that public discussions of sexual issues are extremely volatile, encourage displacement, and provoke repression as well as permit enlightenment.

Twentieth century feminists certainly do not claim, as did so many of our nineteenth century sisters, that women are "passionless" or "sexless" and for that reason deserving of more power and authority. However, in the feminist discussion of pornography we find the assumption that men's sexuality is essentially different from women's and more pathological. In Susan Griffin's analysis, sexuality itself is natural and good but men have corrupted it with bad cultural constructions.[29] In Andrea Dworkin's view, pornography lies about female sexuality, representing woman as "a lewd, dissolute brazen thing, a whore always soliciting," but it tells the truth about male sexuality: "That men believe what pornography says about women . . . From the worst to the best of them, they do."[30] To take this point one step further, pornography portrays women and their sexuality as essentially controllable by men (bondage pornography is the logical result); feminist discourse on pornography portrays men and their sexuality as essentially controllable by pornography. This mirroring of what is a distorted idea of our own sexuality ought to give us pause.

Although feminist writers on pornography do not presume women are sexless, they do imply that, left to our own devices, free of male coercive interference, women are reasonable, self-determining beings with a sexuality that is unproblematic, unpathological, gentle and good.[31] In feminist discourse on pornography all dangerous, disruptive aspects of sexuality are projected onto men or "male culture." Interestingly, this projection mirrors what Susan Griffin tells us pornography does with men's "good" feelings; pornography projects men's vulnerabilities onto women so that these feelings can be controlled. We reverse the process and project our unfeminine nastiness and aggression onto men. Insofar as such human nastiness surfaces in pornography, we'd like to suppress it. Lorenne Clark provides a good example of this attitude when she says: "We are not in any way opposed to the manufacture, sale, or distribution of materials which stress the positive aspects of human sexuality."[32] As feminists, can we really set ourselves up as cultural commisars, deciding what is and what is not "positive" enough about sex to be represented?

We may not precisely be passionless anymore, but some of these hidden assumptions about our sexuality are equally distorting. They accompany a notion of the self as an entity distinct from the body; for Andrea Dworkin: "All struggle for dignity and self-determination is rooted in the struggle for actual control over one's own body, especially control over access to one's own body."[33] But, we might ask here, are women embodied beings or are we owners of bodies who make rational decisions about others' rights of way? This is not a frivolous, hair-splitting question, if, after all, we don't like pornography because it markets women as salable objects or male public property accessible to anyone. If we posssess our bodies, surely we can sell them in a commodity culture. Only if, as feminists, we develop a very different view of the self, and argue from that, can self-sale be unthinkable.

Another point of continuity between nineteenth and twentieth century feminists revolves around the word "protection." One of the most important emphases on which feminists and others in the social purity movement agreed was the protection of the family, which seemed threatened by any wayward and/or commercialized sexuality. Given that the nineteenth century family was already an abstraction from the larger community, it's a measure of just how atomized our society has become that we hear little from modern feminists about protection of the family, though we do hear a good deal about protecting women and children from harm resulting directly or indirectly from pornography.

The attempt to demonstrate such harm empirically has been creating the reputations of large numbers of behavioural psychologists these days.[34] Concern shifts from what pornography might encourage men to do to women to what pornography encourages men to think about women and sexuality. All such experiments isolate pornographic images of women and then postulate an extremely simplistic relationship between representation and actions or attitudes. They presume, as do many feminists who base their analyses on similar assumptions, that seeing certain kinds of images "conditions" men to degrade and despise women. Lorenne Clark makes this point when she says: "Pornography is a method of socialization."[35] Such use of the word "socialization" reduces it to the thinnest, most psychologically superficial behaviourist model. In this view sexuality — or more specifically male sexuality — is lifted entirely out of the fabric of family or other deep emotional relationships and is viewed as infinitely malleable. Ironically, this thin, contigent view of human relationships is just the portrait we get in pornography itself.

In addition, experiments dealing with pornography assume that pornographic images and narratives affect viewers/readers in a way that is entirely different from other types of narratives and images so that audiences will treat pornography much more like "information" than they will other types of popular culture, that they will bracket it in an entirely different way from say, westerns or science fiction.[36] Pornography in this view becomes a kind of "how to" manual: "It is a vivid depiction of how to deploy male sexuality in just the way that will achieve maximum effect in maintaining the *status quo*."[37]

Perhaps the underlying concern here is the fear of a kind of epidemic degeneration of interpretive skills. We live in a world which demands an ability to scan material for facts and arguments, which encourages the diffusion of attention or concentration, which relegates "interpretation," formerly at the cultural centre, at least in religion, to the relative periphery of literary criticism and psychoanalysis. Have most people's interpretive skills degenerated to such a degree that they can no longer distinguish, at the most basic level, literal from symbolic meaning? Or is this a peculiarly male foible in the realm of pornography?

If we ask that question, however, we might also ask ourselves how sophisticated feminist critiques of pornography have been? Is there room for improving our own interpretations? Does this matter if what we are engaged in is a struggle for power?

One thing that disturbs me about the feminist discussion of pornography is the way all pornography is lumped together and flattened out. Would we make the blanket statements we make about pornography if we were discussing any other popular genre? Some feminists do distinguish between violent and non-violent pornography, arguing that only the latter is dangerous, but more commonly we see the contention that all pornography is objectifying, degrading, and therefore violent. If a young man begins by subscribing to *Playboy*, he will end with a craving for snuff movies, much the way we were warned about the danger of marijuana's leading us inevitably to heroin addiction.

Certainly the portrayal of women in pornography is, by and large, insulting, irritating and worthy of critique. However, when we invoke more "protection" from the state, we must be careful how we do it. I think that the very word

SUBJUGATED KNOWLEDGE

"protection," given what it implies for women, should make us hesitate, for the historical record of "protective" legislation — whether in the realm of morals or the labour market — is certainly an ambiguous one. When we demand government protection from pornography, given the arbitrary, paternalistic, authoritarian modes such legislation and its enforcement always take, aren't we asking for more of what we don't like in other areas? Insisting on our need to be protected, we hold onto the role of victim or potential victim, the very position from which our efforts as feminists are designed to extricate us.[38] Our status as victims of male violence may seem to give us a kind of moral authority. And the detachment we claim from male sexual pathology may give us an argument for appropriating more power. But historically in the gender battles we have seen how limiting and undermining these tactics were, as well as how they often backfired in their ultimate effects. I think today we should jettison them in our current struggles.

Of course women do suffer real life acts of violence everyday. This is a fact which being fastidious about words like "protection" will not make go away. Certainly a good deal of our anger about pornography results from our fear that we may be victimized either by the man whose free-floating psychotic misogyny has been set off by pornography, or by the more ordinary male who sees rape as a minor peccadillo, for if sex is a commodity, isn't rape just petty theft?

Since our culture constitutes itself to such an extreme degree from images and spectacle, it's inevitable that political struggle will revolve around just such issues. For the image of woman as moronic sex object, we would like to substitute the image of woman as complex person, active subject — someone to be reckoned with and regarded seriously. It's quite obvious that in this struggle over images we can't stop with pornography; we also have the whole domain of advertising to contend with, not to mention a staggering proportion of our television, movies and books. After all, one could argue that many mainstream movies are more dangerous than pornographic ones. Insofar as they are better made, with more talented direction and acting, more sophisticated narration and filming, they ought to be more powerful, more compelling than the low budget drivel regularly turned out by the skinflick trade.

This is not to say that just because humiliating images pervade our culture we ought to forget about pornography as an issue, but we should be careful not to legitimize other sexist images by focussing exclusively on pornography. I don't think we can solve our "image problem" with better definitions of obscenity, inclusion of an acceptable definition of pornography in the criminal code, or more censorship. Instead of demanding more restrictions from the state, we should demand more resources — for women artists, filmmakers, publishers. "Better" censorship will not benefit women, but it will certainly benefit police forces and prosecutors who will see their already fat budgets swell.

A new approach to legislation on pornography has been proposed in Minneapolis by Catherine MacKinnon and Andrea Dworkin. Their ordinance would permit civil litigation against pornographers by women who claimed that harm had occurred to them: that they had been coerced into making

295

pornography; that they had been forced to view it; or that they had been assaulted due to pornography. MacKinnon's purpose is to transfer the debate out of its current legislative *cul de sac* and raise in the courts the issue that pornography violates women's civil rights.

This approach has some attractive features, since it does shift emphasis from the idea that sexual explicitness *per se* is offensive to the notion that certain kinds of sexual representation are harmful because they promote inequality. Nonetheless, I still wonder whether we can or want to legislate only a certain kind of sexual representation — i.e., sex under conditions of mutuality, reciprocity, equality. Do we really want to say that our civil rights include the right to see only certain kinds of images?

Sexuality has shouldered an enormous weight of expectations in our culture,[39] expectations that sexual "fulfillment" will compensate for the sensual impoverishment of urban life, the emotional impoverishment of a culture that promotes thin sociability at the expense of long-term deep connection, the spiritual impoverishment resulting from the abstract quality of most work.[40] Pornography capitalizes on these expectations, inducing us to believe that sexual "fulfillment" is available but elusive, just like the gratification of a Salem, a Budweiser — it's there for sure, in the next, always the next act of consumption.

As women, we are more aware of the fraud here; we not only receive the illusory promise of fulfillment, we are the promise. The terrible irony of female sexuality is that women are expected to embody a oneness with the body, a physical self-confidence associated with ideal motherhood — this they are supposed to give to men. However, it's rare for women to develop a true confidence in their own desire and desirability since female sexual development is so permeated with fear, and everybody's identity is constantly undermined in this culture of envy.

Pornography confronts us not only with male power, but also with male resentment, resentment at what has seemingly been promised and then withheld. We, on the other hand, should know that this sensual pleasure does not belong to us, is not ours to give or deny for it is not a thing, not a product, but, where it exists, is activity, process, feeling, relationship. In sexuality we would like to preserve some privileged area, some space free from the commodification of so much of the rest of our lives. When sexuality seems like the last vestige of our romantic individuality, pornography insists that here too there's nothing but a kind of Eaton's catalogue of images — a restricted code reducing all "self-expression" to grotesque banality.

This paper is meant to be provocative. It may seem like a betrayal of the forces of good, an over-intellectualized sell-out to the pornocrats. However, I'm writing it because as a feminist I'm concerned about our directions, demands and alliances. We should keep in mind when forming political alliances on this issue that, no matter what we say, most people will become indignant about pornography, not because they see it as misogynistic, but because they see it as sexual, and for that reason it raises all kinds of anxieties about "proper" gender relations we call into question in other contexts.

SUBJUGATED KNOWLEDGE

As we saw with the first wave of feminism, sexual issues focussed all kinds of other fears. Today we have even more to be afraid of — acid rain, nuclear reactors, chemical wastes — to name but a few at random. To even the most optimistic, our world seems quite out of control. A re-ordering of gender relations, along with suppression of sexual explicitness, can take on powerful attraction. We see this in American right-wing anti-feminism.

A number of other things disturb me about feminist discourse on pornography. Often we catch an echo of the nineteenth century temperance movement's assumption that eliminating drink would abolish wife beating in modern feminists' notion that suppressing pornography would reduce rape and other forms of actual male violence. In addition, a contempt for "freedom of expression" creeps into many feminists' writings. "Civil libertarian" is becoming an insult, not yet quite equivalent to "fascist." Although we may be disillusioned with liberal political philosophy and agree that "freedom of expression" is at best an abstraction and at worst a cynical defense when we're talking about a multi-million dollar industry like pornography, it still seems to me dangerous to encourage government to get more involved in the business of defining what we are allowed to see or read. If we concern ourselves with pornography as an industry rather than as a purveyor of bad ideas, we might think in terms different from censorship: e.g., unionizing workers in the industry, preventing monopolies, investigating distribution networks, taxing profits more rigorously. We should never lose sight of the fact that the pornography industry could not exist without its women workers. Women who write about pornography must not identify with these women solely at an abstract level, as did many nineteenth century feminists with prostitutes. We know what kinds of pressures drive women into the sex trades; we know how exploited the women who work in the strip clubs, sex acts, and skin flicks are. In making demands on the state, we should be very wary of falling into the same trap as first wave feminists. Instead we need to find ways of supporting these women. Pushing pornography further into a shadow world where, like drugs, pornographic materials are illegal but clandestinely available will only make the lives of the women in the industry more risky, more endangered.[41]

In addition, I think we must be careful as women, who have never had the same "freedom of expression" as men, either because we were not allowed to speak in public forums, or because when we did speak our words carried no authority, were dismissed as hysterical ravings, we must be careful at this juncture, not to denigrate "freedom of expression," but to demand it, seize it, appropriate it, allow it to one another. Historically as women we have been silenced, and today we do not have the access or decision making power in relation to mainstream media we need. Pornography has become symbolic for us of the blatency of male supremacy, acted out, represented and enjoyed. It seems particularly insidious because it directs its appeal to the most vulnerable areas of the psyche. The proliferation of pornography is certainly part of a whole cultural order that undermines our sense of security and authority, but displacing too much anxiety onto it may not only waste some of our time and energy, but also may encourage the state to think it can throw us a censorship sop and keep us happy, may even backfire in an unexpected wave of repression provoked by fears we've helped to generate.

Department of English
Dawson College

Notes

1. For American feminist discussions of pornography, see: Susan Brownmiller, *Against Our Will: Men, Women and Rape* (New York: Simon and Schuster, 1975); Robin Morgan, "Theory and Practice: Pornography and Rape," in *Going Too Far: The Personal Chronicle of a Feminist* (New York: Vintage Books, 1978), pp. 163-169; Kathleen Barry, *Female Sexual Slavery* (New York: Avon, 1979); Andrea Dworkin, *Pornography: Men Possessing Women* (New York: Perigree Books, 1979); Laura Lederer, ed., *Take Back the Night: Women on Pornography* (New York: William Morrow and Company, Inc., 1980); Susan Griffin, *Pornography and Silence: Culture's Revenge against Nature* (New York: Harper & Row, 1981); Gloria Steinem, "Erotica vs. Pornography," in *Outrageous Acts and Everyday Rebellions* (New York: Holt, Rinehart and Winston, 1983), pp. 219-230. For some feminist discussions of pornography published in Canada, see: Myrna Kostash, "Power and Control, a Feminist View of Pornography," *This Magazine* 12:3, pp.5-7; Thelma McCormack, "Passionate Protests: Feminists and Censorship," *Canadian Forum* 59: 697, pp. 6-8; Lorenne Clark, "Pornography's Challenge to Liberal Ideology," *Canadian Forum* 59:697, pp. 9-12; Maude Barlow, "Pornography and Free Speech," *Common Ground* 2:3, pp. 28-30; Jillian Riddington, "Pornography: What Does the New Research Say?" *Status of Women News* 8:3, pp. 9-13; Micheline Carrier, *La pornographie: base idéologique de l'oppression des femmes* (Sillery, Québec: Apostrophe, 1983); Sara Diamond, "Of Cabbages and Kinks: Reality and Representation in Pornography," *Pink Ink* 1:5, pp. 18-23; *Canadian Woman Studies* 4:4 (issue on violence).

2. Griffin, p. 83.

3. Brownmiller, p. 394.

4. David Copp has a useful discussion of the problem of defining pornography in his introduction to *Pornography and Censorship*, ed. David Copp and Susan Wendell (New York: Prometheus Books, 1983), pp. 15-41.

5. Ellen Dubois and Linda Gordon make a similar point in their article, "Seeking Ecstasy on the Battlefield: Danger and Pleasure in Nineteenth Century Feminist Sexual Thought," *Feminist Studies* 9:1, p. 8. According to Dubois and Gordon, "The feminist movement has played an important role in organizing and even creating women's sense of sexual danger in the last one hundred and fifty years." For a discussion of nineteenth century feminists' organizational responses to this sense of danger from male violence, see Elizabeth Pleck, "Feminist Responses to 'Crimes against Women,' 1868-1896," *Signs* 8:3, pp. 451-470.

6. Morgan, p. 169.

7. Steinem, p. 221.

8. Susan Griffin makes this point: pornography "would have sexuality and punish feeling." *Pornography and Silence*, p. 178.

9. According to Kathleen Barry: "One of the effects of widespread pornography has been to introduce movies, books, or pictures as the erotic stimulant between two people, thereby reducing the need for people to relate to each other." *Female Sexual Slavery*, p. 213.

SUBJUGATED KNOWLEDGE

10. Not all feminists have jumped on the anti-pornography bandwagon. In 1979 Ellen Willis wrote a critique of Women against Pornography entitled, "Feminism, Moralism and Pornography," originally published in *The Village Voice* and reprinted in *Powers of Desire: The Politics of Sexuality*, ed. Ann Snitow, Christine Stansell and Sharon Thompson (New York: Monthly Review Press, 1983), pp. 460-467. Deirdre English also published a similar critique, "The Politics of Porn," in *Mother Jones* 5:3, pp. 20-23, 43-49. Betty Friedan dismissed the anti-pornography marches in New York as "irrelevant" in *The Second Stage* (New York: Summit Books, 1981), p. 20. Here in Canada Thelma McCormack has been critical of feminists who advocate censorship of pornography. She makes the point that such advocacy "manipulates women's anxieties about rape and the safety of children while strengthening a system which creates these fears." "Passionate Protests: Feminists and Censorship," *Canadian Forum* 59:697, p. 8.

11. Barbara Ehrenreich in *The Hearts of Men: American Dreams and the Flight from Commitment* (Garden City: Doubleday, 1983) argues that male rebellion against the "breadwinner role" preceded the women's movement. In this context she has an interesting discussion of *Playboy* which, in promoting a "new" consumerism for men emancipated from families, needed the nudes to demonstrate that these men were not effeminate. *Playboy* popularized the notion that "real men" did not need to be heads of households.

12. In *Public Man, Private Woman: Woman and Social and Political Thought* (Princeton, N.J.: Princeton University Press, 1981) Jean Bethke Elshtain has an interesting and critical discussion of this slogan.

13. Deirdre English discusses this in "The Fear that Feminism Will Free Men First," in *Powers of Desire*, pp. 477-483.

14. Elshtain, p. 236.

15. Nancy Chodorow, *The Reproduction of Mothering: Psychoanalysis and the Sociology of Gender* (Berkeley: University of California Press, 1978). Dorothy Dinnerstein, *The Mermaid and the Minotaur: Sexual Arrangements and Human Malaise* (New York: Harper & Row, 1976).

16. See Linda Gordon's discussion in *Woman's Body, Woman's Right: A Social History of Birth Control in America* (Harmondsworth: Penguin Books, 1974).

17. See William Leach, *True and Perfect Union: The Feminist Reform of Sex and Society* (New York: Basic Books, 1980).

18. Dubois and Gordon, p. 9.

19. Mark Connelly discusses the problem of defining prostitution and measuring its extent in *The Response to Prostitution in the Progressive Era* (Chapel Hill: University of North Carolina Press, 1980), p. 16.

20. See David Pivar, *Purity Crusade: Sexual Morality and Social Control, 1868-1900* (Westport, Conn.: Greenwood Press, 1973).

21. See James H. Gray, *Red Lights on the Prairies* (Toronto: Macmillan of Canada, 1971) and Carol Lee Bacchi, *Liberation Deferred? The Ideas of the English Canadian Suffragists, 1877-1918* (Toronto: University of Toronto Press, 1983).

22. Judith R. Walkowitz, "Male Vice and Female Virtue: Feminism and the Politics of Prostitution in Nineteenth Century Britain," in *Powers of Desire*, p. 442.

23. This argument is made by Judith R. Walkowitz with regard to Britain in her book *Prostitution and Victorian Society* (Cambridge University Press, 1980), p. 117, and in relation to the United States by Carl Degler in *At Odds: Women and the Family in America from the Revolution to the Present* (New York: Oxford University Press, 1980), p. 258.

24. Connelly, p. 30.

25. Peter Gay argues that many Victorian women acknowledged and expected sexual pleasure in *The Bourgeois Experience: Victoria to Freud, Volume One: Education of the Senses* (New York: Oxford University Press, 1983).

26. Quoted in Walkowitz: "Male Vice and Female Virtue: Feminism and the Politics of Prostitution in Nineteenth Century Britain," p. 443.

27. See Ruth Rosen, *The Lost Sisterhood: Prostitution in America, 1900-1918* (Baltimore: Johns Hopkins University Press, 1982).

28. Ruth Rosen and Sue Davidson, eds., *The Maimie Papers* (Old Westbury, N.Y.: The Feminist Press, 1977).

29. Griffin, *passim.*

30. Dworkin, p. 167.

31. There has been some feminist exploration of the "darker" sides of female sexuality: see *Heresies* 12 (Sex Issue) and *Coming to Power: Writings and Graphics on Lesbian S/M*, published by Samois, a lesbian feminist S/M organization (Boston: Alyson Publications, Inc., 1981).

32. Lorenne Clark, "Pornography's Challenge to Liberal Ideology," *Canadian Forum* 59: 697, p. 10.

33. Dworkin, p. 203. Dworkin's view resurrects the "possessive individualism" to which many nineteenth century feminists saw themselves opposed in their attempt to fashion a more communitarian social vision. See Leach, p. 10.

34. See Michael J. Goldstein and Harold S. Kant, eds., *Pornography and Sexual Deviance: A Report of the Legal and Behavioral Institute, Beverly Hills California* (Berkeley: University of California Press, 1973); Maurice Yaffé and Edward C. Nelson, eds., *The Influence of Pornography on Behaviour* (London: Academic Press, 1982); David Copp and Susan Wendell, eds., *Pornography and Censorship* (New York: Prometheus Books, 1983).

35. Lorenne Clark, "Liberalism and Pornography," in *Pornography and Censorship*, p. 53.

36. Susan Sontag makes this point in her essay, "The Pornographic Imagination," in *Perspectives on Pornography*, ed. Douglas A. Hughes (New York: St. Martin's Press, 1970), pp. 131-169.

37. Clark, "Liberalism and Pornography," p. 53.

38. Elshtain, p. 225.

39. See Jessica Benjamin's essay, "Master and Slave: The Fantasy of Erotic Domination," *Powers of Desire*, pp. 280-299.

40. Meg Luxton discusses the connection between the work lives and sexuality of her subjects in *More Than a Labour of Love: Three Generations of Women's Work in the Home* (Toronto: The Women's Press, 1980), pp. 55-65.

41. See Anne McLean, "Snuffing Out *Snuff*: Feminists React," *Canadian Dimensions* 12:8, pp. 20-23.

THE END/S OF WOMAN

N.P. Ricci

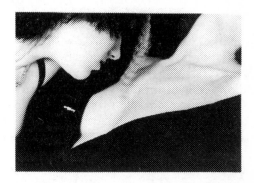

> As the archaeology of our thought easily shows, man is an invention of recent date. And one perhaps nearing its end.
>
> Michel Foucault, *The Order of Things*[1]

With the disappearance of man, what happens to woman? Having only recently gained a voice *as* women, feminists are now confronted with the proposition that to speak as a woman is merely to reinscribe oneself within the logic of an androcentric epistemology, the very logic, in other words, which feminists have been trying to combat. The decentering of the subject advocated by Michel Foucault and other French theorists has moved us, apparently, beyond sexual identity, into a new landscape where men can be women and women men, and where subjects are simply proper nouns. But if the disappearance of 'man,' the dissolution of the sovereign Cartesian ego, ensures that "Men will no longer speak for mankind[, s]hould women, by implication, no longer, i.e. *never* speak as women?"[2] While writers like Foucault have provided women with the tools required to 'deconstruct' the systems of power that have oppressed them, doesn't the current eliding of sexual identity require from feminists a note of skepticism, a wariness that the new polemic does not simply reauthorize old injustices?

I: Subjects and Subjection

> The individual is an effect of power, and at the same time, or precisely to the extent to which it is that effect, it is the element of its articulation. The individual which power has constituted is at the same time its vehicle.
>
> Foucault, *Power/Knowledge*[3]

The question of identity, and hence of sexual identity, arises out of the general poststructuralist critique of humanism and Western metaphysics. In current theory, identity — individuality, subject-hood — is held to be a construct complicitous with certain modes of restrictive logic. What French theorists have been trying to do — writers like Jacques Derrida and Roland Barthes — is to wear away the ontological ground which has traditionally accrued around the "I" of discourse, to question the self-presence of the speaking subject, to show how subjects *are spoken* rather than speak — that is, how they are constituted by a web of forces of which consciousness is the effect rather than the point of origin.

The most thoroughly historical critique of the subject, and perhaps the one most useful to feminists, is that of Michel Foucault. Though Foucault does not specifically pose the question of *sexual* identity, his work on the subject's historical constitution lays out the terms in which such a question might take form. Throughout his research, Foucault has been concerned to show how the individual is constituted "as effect and object of power, as effect and object of knowledge."[4] In a Foucauldian framework, then, the question of woman comes down to a question of knowledge and power.

In his analysis of penal reform in *Discipline and Punish*, Foucault shows how "a refinement of power relations" in the nineteenth century helped foster the growth of those sciences known (aptly, feminists have noted) as "the sciences of man." At the center of these new sciences stood a new object of knowledge, the individual, invested through and through by the systems of power which had created it. Hence the recent vintage of "man": in Foucault's view, "individuality" is a social construction whose origins are traceable to the institution of a new technology of power. By creating new forms of knowledge, power constitutes its own objects; and the objects which power has thus constituted then become the elements of its own articulation. "It is a double process, then: an epistemological 'thaw' through a refinement of power relations; a multiplication of the effects of power through the formation and accumulation of new forms of knowledge" (*DP*,224). Thus the human sciences, which grew out of a web of power relations spanning everything from medicine, psychiatry and education to military training and penal reform, helped perpetuate those very relations by constituting the individual as a new object of knowledge.

Foucault's perspective on subject-hood, then, is decidedly polemical: to become subject means to be subjected. "We should try to grasp subjection in its material instance as a constitution of subjects" (*P/K*,97). The human sciences, by reordering our ways of knowing and focussing our attention on the individual, have made it possible for power to entrench itself more firmly into the social body. Foucault gives the example of the homosexual, who arose as 'a species' at the point where homosexuality was characterized "less by a type of sexual relations than by a certain quality of sexual sensibility" — when, in other words, emphasis shifted from the act to the individual.[5] But it has been this very sort of shift, according to Foucault, through which individuality has been constituted. Around this new object arise new discourses — in the realm of medicine, psychiatry, criminology — and through them "power reaches into the very grain of individuals, touches their bodies and inserts itself into their actions and attitudes, their discourse, learning processes and everyday lives" (P/K,39).

But in Foucault's view it would be wrong to imagine that power simply acts *against* individuals, in the form of prohibition and oppression. On the contrary, "individuals are the vehicles of power, not its point of application" (P/K,97); in other words, power passes *through* individuals, using them to further its own ends. Thus the "I" which power and knowledge have jointly constituted is also the "eye" of power and knowledge, that which subjects everything to its normalizing, hierarchizing gaze. To become subject, then, also means to subject, to give priority to identity, to authorship, to ownership, to situate consciousness at the origin of truth while excluding everything that is different and 'other.'

It is this aspect of the subject which Foucault attacks in his critique of traditional historicism. In his preface to *The Order of Things*, Foucault dissociates himself from the "phenomenological approach" to history, that "which gives absolute priority to the observing subject, which attributes a constituent role to an act, which places its own point of view at the origin of all historicity — which, in short, leads to a transcendental consciousness" (OT,xiv). The same technology of power which has created individuals as objects of knowledge also situates them as subjects of knowledge. This "sovereignty of the subject" has led to what Foucault calls "continuous history":

> Continuous history is the indispensable correlative of the founding function of the subject: the guarantee that everything that has eluded him may be restored to him; the certainty that time will disperse nothing without restoring it in a reconstituted unity; the promise that one day the subject — in the form of historical consciousness — will once again bring back under his sway, all those things that are kept at a distance by difference, and find in them what might be called his abode.[6]

Totalizing and totalitarian, continuous history, the history of "transcendental consciousness," strives to situate itself at the privileged source of truth, and so "to preserve, against all decenterings, the sovereignty of the subject, and the twin figures of anthropology and humanism" (AK,12).

Thus the subject emerges in Foucault's work as the nexus of certain "mechanics of power" — as both effect and vehicle of power, as that which subjects and is subjected. Foucault's task has been to write a history without a subject, "to get rid of the subject itself" (*P/K*,117), and so to expose the complicities of knowledge and power which have led to the subject's historical constitution.

II: Foucault and Feminism

> Interviewer: Do you feel that your 'History of Sexuality' will advance the women's question? I have in mind what you say about the hysterisation and psychiatrisation of the female body.
> Foucault: There are [a] few ideas there, but only hesitant ones, not yet fully crystallised. It will be the discussion and criticism after each volume that will perhaps allow them to become clarified. But it is not up to me to lay down how the book should be used (*PK*,192).

Foucault's critique of humanism and of the subject offers obvious points of convergence with feminist interests. Throughout his work, Foucault has been concerned with marginal groups, the insane, the delinquent, the sexually perverse — groups which, like women, have been traditionally silenced by the powers-that-be, and excluded from the privileged realm of "truth." But truth, in Foucault's view, as the end point of knowledge, "is linked in a circular relation with systems of power which produce and sustain it, and to effects of power which it induces and which extend it" (*P/K*,133) — thus those groups which are barred from it will always be forced to the margins of discourse. Women have traditionally occupied that margin, and the androcentric humanism which Foucault deconstructs — with its "universals," its canons, its privileging of (an overwhelmingly male) tradition — has certainly been one more link in a long history of women's oppression.

But a thoroughly Foucauldian analysis would have to proceed at the level of the "micro-techniques of power" through which woman has not only been silenced, but *constituted* as object of power and knowledge, much as delinquents, the insane, and the sexually perverse have become "species" which power has used for its own ends. What historical determinants have moulded what we understand by the term "woman"? What nexus have women occupied in the web of power relations within a given epistemé, what functions have they served? Foucault gives the example of how the creation and medicalisation of female sexuality served part of a larger strategy for the policing of families and populations.

> It is worth remembering that the first figure to be invested by the deployment of sexuality, one of the first to be 'sexualized,' was the

'idle' woman. She inhabited the outer edge of the "world," in which she always had to appear as a value, and of the family, where she was assigned a new destiny charged with conjugal and parental obligations (*HS*,121).

A Foucauldian history of women, then, would begin at the point where "woman" is revealed to be a social construction.

But it would be wrong, therefore, to see in Foucault merely a project for the reclamation of lost voices. While Foucault's own studies are often exempla of the recuperation of marginal or seldom considered materials, feminist histories which concentrate solely on filling in the gaps and lacunae of traditional history, on giving a voice to women's silenced "sisters," may find themselves firmly reinscribed within the tenets of humanistic historicism, substituting, for example, a "great women's" history for that of the "great men." One of the buzz words of humanism which Foucault deconstructs in *The Archaeology of Knowledge* is "tradition." "The problem," writes Foucault, "is no longer one of tradition, of tracing a line, but one of division, of limits; it is no longer one of lasting foundations, but one of transformations that serve as new foundations, the rebuilding of foundations" (*AK*,5). Once "woman" is seen as a social construction, the question of "tracing a line," of reclaiming women's lost history, becomes somewhat anachronistic.

But on what "new foundation," then, is feminism to build its abode? As feminists begin to examine their own work in the light of a Foucauldian critique, they are finding that what Foucault may offer is not so much an extension of works-in-progress as a change in direction.

III: De-sexualisation

The real strength of the women's liberation movements is not that of having laid claim to the specificity of their sexuality and the rights pertaining to it, but that they have actually departed from the discourse conducted within the apparatuses of sexuality. These movements do indeed emerge in the nineteenth century as demands for sexual specificity. What has their outcome been? Ultimately a veritable movement of de-sexualisation, a displacement effected in relation to the sexual centering of the problem, formulating the demand for forms of culture, discourse, language and so on, which are no longer part of that rigid assignation and pinning-down to their sex which they had initially in some sense been politically obliged to accept in order to make themselves heard (*PK*,219-220).

Among French women theorists, the writer who seems to have come closest to Foucault's ideas on de-sexualisation is Julia Kristeva. In her article "Women's Time," Kristeva isolates two phases in the women's movement's strategies for dealing with women's traditional exclusion from the social contract.[7] In the first, women "aspired to gain a place in linear time as the time of project and history" (*WT*,36) — in other words, to right the fact of their exclusion by making central what had been marginalized, by bringing women in, on an equal footing with men, to a system which would not be fundamentally changed by the fact of women's inclusion. In the second phase, "linear temporality has been almost totally refused, and as a consequence there has arisen an exacerbated distrust of the entire political dimension" (*WT*,37). In this phase women have rejected traditional sociopolitical and cultural models as inimical to women's needs, since such models are permeated through and through by the male libidinal economy which has created them. Instead, women of this second generation have sought alternative cultural models which will be more expressive of a unique feminine identity.

The danger of these strategies — and I think Kristeva and Foucault would agree here — is that both can be easily reappropriated by the systems of power they struggle against. The first most clearly, since it strives not so much to change the system as to find a place for women within it. But the second also, despite its rejection of male-centred models, since in positing a feminine *identity* it tends to elide the question of social construction and take refuge in a precarious essentialism. Proponents of a unique feminine identity have usually had to resort to a theory of biological difference which triumphs female sexuality as the basis for the subversion of male-dominated systems.[8] But it has been precisely on the basis of biological difference that women have been traditionally oppressed; any theory which resorts to such difference as its ground merely reinscribes itself within an old logic and risks perpetuating old stereotypes. And Foucault's analysis of the deployment of sexuality should alert feminists to the dangers of seeing any great liberating potential in female sexuality; sexuality itself, according to Foucault, is a social construct, one which has been deployed for the ends of power. "The irony of this deployment," Foucault writes in the last lines of *The History of Sexuality*, "is in having us believe that our 'liberation' is in the balance" (*HS*,159).

An essentialist position can only perpetuate an oppositional logic which many French theorists — most notably Jacques Derrida — have been trying to undo. Such a position posits a notion of "difference" as "absolute otherness" rather than as an "alterity" which can be shown to be internal to the system which has excluded it. Traditionally, oppositions like speech/writing, presence/absence, culture/nature, man/woman, have implied a hierarchy, with privilege being given to the first term. A notion of alterity, however, displaces the hierarchy by showing the second term to be the necessary condition of the first — not as absolute other, but as a difference at the very heart of the privileged first term. In Foucauldian terms, hierarchized oppositions can be seen as another instance of the complicity of knowledge and power. Thus woman's constitution as man's other — passive rather than active, emotional rather than rational, secondary rather than primary — has served to solidify male domination. The problem with essentialist views which emphasize the positive qualities of "woman" against the repressive aspect of male-centred systems is that they tend to reverse the hierarchy without displacing it — that is, they place "woman" in the privileged position — and thus remain caught up in the very logic they are trying to subvert, a logic which is complicit with the systems of power that have traditionally silenced women.

Kristeva recognizes the necessity of these first impulses of the women's movement — both the attempted insertion into the system and the rejection of that system in the name of absolute difference; they may be seen to correspond roughly to what Foucault calls "that rigid assignation and pinning-down to their sex which women had initially in some sense been politically obliged to accept in order to make themselves heard." But Kristeva sees herself as part of a "third generation" — existing in parallel rather than chronological relation to the other two — for whom "the very dichotomy man/woman as an opposition between two rival entities may be understood as belonging to *metaphysics*. What can 'identity,' even 'sexual identity,' mean in a new theoretical and scientific space where the very notion of identity is challenged?" (*WT*,51-52). Here is the "movement of de-sexualisation" which Foucault identifies as the most positive element of the women's movements, the "displacement effected in relation to the sexual centering of the problem." This displacement pushes the issue of "woman" outside the restricted logic of metaphysics and opens it up to the question of social construction, to questions of knowledge and power. But is this, then, the end of woman?[9]

IV: New Woman/Old Stereotypes

The Germans are like women. You can never fathom their depths. They have none.

Friedrich Nietzsche[10]

... Nietzsche revives that barely allegorical figure (of woman) in his own interest. For him, truth is a woman. It resembles the veiled movement of feminine modesty.

Jacques Derrida, *Spurs*[11]

We enter now the new landscape, beyond sexual identity. How have things changed? For one thing, Nietzsche now looks like a proto-feminist — at least in the treatment he receives in Derrida's *Spurs*, where he appears to have pre-figured woman as the "untruth of truth," as that which undermines truth from within (*Spurs*,51).[12] But after all it is not biological women Derrida is talking about here; woman for Derrida is the supplement, différance, the lack at the center which displaces the center, and if there is any *body* involved in all of this, as Alice Jardine points out, it is the body of the text as *écriture*.[13]

Woman, then, has not disappeared in the poststructuralist landscape, though she has apparently changed her form. For one thing, she has shed her body; for another, she is no longer the absolute other but precisely the point of alterity, the internal exclusion which undermines the system. Simply speaking, woman has become, under several headings — supplement, *écriture*, feminine jouissance, seduction, the unconscious, the *vreél* — a trope, a metaphor for that which bursts through the boundaries of traditional codes.

Of course, in this new order of things, biological women have not entirely dropped out of the scene. Precisely because they have been traditionally marginalized, women may have special access to what has been now coded as a "feminine operation," the act of subversion. For Kristeva, for instance, women, because of their incomplete accession into the social order, are always "*le sujet-en-procès*," the subject in process/on trial, on the threshold between selfhood and its dissolution; they are thus in a privileged position to question the social construction of identity. But it is not a biological difference which thus distinguishes women, only a social one.

The case with someone like Hélène Cixous is more problematic. At times she tends towards a biological essentialism, suggesting that women's bodies are the basis for a subversive practice: "women must write through their bodies, they must invent the impregnable language that will wreck partitions, classes and rhetorics, regulations and codes, they must submerge, cut through, get beyond the ultimate reserve discourse . . . ." (*NFF*,256). Yet she is willing to allow that someone like a Genet can write from the feminine (*NFF*,255), and she shows an allegiance to a Derridean deconstruction of opposites: "sexual opposition, which has always worked for man's profit to the point of reducing writing, too, to his laws, is only a historico-cultural limit" (*NFF*,253; see also *NFF*,90ff). Nonetheless, it would seem that women, that is women with bodies, are in a better position to take hold of feminine writing than men. "More so than men who are coaxed toward social success, toward sublimation, women are body. More body, hence more writing" (*NFF*,257).

But despite the recoding of the feminine as "the untruth of truth," as that which bursts "partitions, classes and rhetorics, regulations and codes," we might ask, as Jardine has, in what ways the New Woman — with or without a body — is so different from the old.[14] Though Derrida's woman, for example, is (as one expects with Derrida) highly problematic, there are sentences in *Spurs* which wrench as sharply as any of the old stereotypes. "A woman seduces from a distance," Derrida writes. "In fact distance is the very element of her power. Yet one must beware to keep one's own distance from her beguiling song of enchantment" (*Spurs*,49). Here, certainly, is a depiction of woman as old as Genesis: woman as seductress, woman as sorceress. And again: "Because woman is (her own) writing, style must return to her. In other words, it could be said that if style were a man (much as the penis according to Freud is the 'normal prototype of fetishes'), then writing would be a woman" (*Spurs*,57). The problem with this equation of woman with text is that it exactly reiterates a paradigm which has long helped keep women silent: woman is she who is written, not she who writes. "The model of the pen-penis writing on the virgin page," writes Susan Gubar, in another context, "participates in a long tradition identifying the author as a male who is primary and the female as his passive creation — a secondary object lacking autonomy, endowed with often contradictory meaning but denied intentionality."[15] But finally Derrida also has a word or two for the feminists: "And in truth, they too are men, those women feminists so derided by Nietzsche. Feminism is nothing but the operation of a woman who aspires to be like a man .... Feminism too seeks to castrate" (*Spurs*,65).

We have to ask: does Derrida's deconstructive intent justify comments that in another context might be seen as blatant chauvinism? Granted it may be unfair to take Derrida's statements out of context, but perhaps to do so demonstrates the potential danger of this new appropriation of woman. To pose a very Foucauldian question, to what old uses might these "new" representations of woman be put? Whose interests do they serve? What are the dangers of a theory of woman that can elide Nietzsche's blatant misogyny? Even if Derrida is not referring to "real" women when he uses that name in his writing, Nietzsche (despite all the theoretical baggage that accrues around a word like "real" nowadays) certainly was. And for all the rigours of Derrida's thought, the line between deconstruction — the wearing away of old ontological ground — and reconstitution — the point at which subversive concepts crystallize into essences — is often rather thin. One need only look at the American appropriation of the Derridean concept of *mise en abyme* to see how radical concepts can be used to justify old institutions.[16]

Even Cixous's depiction of the New Woman sounds suspiciously like an old tale. For Cixous, woman is "a giver": "She doesn't 'know' what she's giving, she doesn't measure it; she gives, though, neither a counterfeit impression nor something she hasn't got. She gives more, with no assurance that she'll get back even some unexpected profit from what she puts out" (*NFF*,264). Elsewhere, woman is a mother: "In women there is always more or less of the mother who makes everything all right, who nourishes, and who stands up against separation; a force that will not be cut off but will knock the wind out of codes" (*NFF*,252). Woman as giver, woman as mother — Cixous might be describing a positive ethos, but what is troubling is that she doesn't question the social construction of these two fairly standard depictions of woman, or look at them in terms of what role they have served in perpetuating women's oppression. Perhaps it is not enough simply to assert that the mother in women "will knock the wind out of codes."

One of the ironies of this poststructuralist reappropriation of woman is that most of the leading theorists of the feminine — apart from Derrida, there is Lacan, Barthes, Baudrillard — are male.[17] Even Kristeva and Cixous take their basic framework from male theorists — Kristeva from Lacan and Cixous from Derrida — and both of them, when invoking paradigms of subversive or "feminine" writing, refer back to a male tradition (typically Mallarmé, Genet and Joyce). If these facts are not suspicious, they are certainly curious. Where, in fact, are *women* in the midst of all this talk about *woman*? It seems men, on top of everything else, are even better at being women than women are. And what, for example, does history look like when we get beyond sexual identity, and "woman" becomes an attitude rather than a signature?

V: Women and History

> What is a woman? I assure you I do not know. I do not believe you know.
>
> Virginia Woolf[18]

From the perspective of those who have moved beyond sexual identity, feminism, as a *women's* movement, cannot help but seem outdated, "nothing but the operation of a woman who aspires to be like a man" — who, in other words, remains caught up in the systems of power defined by the ruling (predominantly male) hegemony. Feminists are thus faced, as Peggy Kamuf admits, with "the erosion of the very ground on which to take a stand."[19] If feminism rests on a biological distinction, it remains open to charges of essentialism: the "feminine," writes Derrida, should not "be hastily mistaken for a woman's feminin*ity*, for female sexual*ity*, or for any other of those essentializing fethishes which might still tantalize the dogmatic philosopher, the impotent artist or the inexperienced seducer who has not yet escaped his foolish hopes of capture" (*Spurs*,55). But if feminism rests on a *social* distinction, then it becomes very difficult to say who, under what circumstances, is a woman. Feminists who try to have it both ways will find themselves tangled in thorny methodological problems.

To take one example: in an article on the image of Eve in *Paradise Lost*, Chritine Froula, alluding to a passage from Woolf's *Jacob's Room*, defines "woman" as someone who divines "the priest" of cultural authority, and so calls that authority into question.

> This definition identifies 'woman' not by sex but by a complex relation to the cultural authority which has traditionally silenced and excluded her. She resists the attitude of blind submission which that authority threatens to imprint upon her; further, her resistance takes form not as envy of the 'priest' and desire to possess his authority herself but as a debunking of the 'priestly' deployment of cultural authority and a refusal to adopt that stance herself. Women, under this local rule, can be 'men,' and men can be 'women.'[20]

But one problem with such "local rules," clearly, is that they are self-serving: if definitions of woman are up for grabs, there is little to stop one from choosing a definition that is tailor-made to fit one's own arguments. Another problem, within the specific context of *Paradise Lost*, is that one might conceivably make a case — though Froula's definition does seem to be trying to avoid this possibility — for Satan as a woman. And one could certainly make a case for the author of "On the New Forcers of Conscience Under the Long Parliament" and *Areopagitica* — that is, for Milton himself.[21] Perhaps, after all, Milton was of woman's party without knowing it, and he might take his place next to Nietzsche as one of history's misogynists reclaimed for the feminist ranks by new definitions of woman.

Little attempt has been made to show what a "history of women" would look like from beyond sexual identity. We have to ask, in fact, whether such a history would be possible. If we take Foucault as a model, then much of the historical work which has been done by feminists to date — the tracing of a women's heritage, the establishment of a women's "canon" — would have to be regarded as caught up with an old, essentially self-defeating, historicism. Jeffrey Weeks has outlined some of the problems confronting a history of homosexuality conducted within a Foucauldian frame;[22] a history of women would face the same kinds of problems. If "woman" is a social construction, then women can claim no universal essence which has united them through the ages, no "tradition" they can claim to follow in the line of. And in fact, even any synchronic movement based on a common sexual bond would have to be seen as rooted in an outmoded concept of sexual identity. Hence the move among some women in France today towards "anti-feminism," i.e. the rejection of a stance which takes sexual solidarity as its base.[23]

Yet it is Foucault himself who has made us sensitive to the subtle machinations of power, to the way power almost seems to plan ahead for the reappropriation of its own failures — as Foucault demonstrates, for example, in his analysis in *Discipline and Punish* of the "failure" of prison reform: prison reform has failed, in Foucault's view, not through an inefficiency of power, but as a strategy of power, as a means of creating a class of "delinquents" which power can then use for its own ends. So it would be timely to ask what interests this "beyonding" of sexual identity might serve. Why is it, for instance, that sexual identity is being elided at the very point at which women, after centuries of subjugation, have been emerging as a potent political force? Certainly any move which could effectively undermine women's solidarity could easily be reappropriated by the very systems of power which have traditionally worked to oppress women. And the "new" representations of woman which have arisen as a result (as a symptom?) of this eliding of sexual identity should also be examined in the light of a Foucauldian critique. We might ask of the new discourse on woman the questions which Foucault poses at the end of "What is an Author?":

> What are the modes of existence of this discourse?
> Where does it come from; how is it circulated; who controls it?
> What placements are determined for possible subjects?
> Who can fulfill these diverse functions of the subject?[24]

There is no guarantee that the new discourse will be "liberating" for women. Foucault himself warns that discourses can "circulate without changing their form from one strategy to another, opposing strategy" (*HS*,102) — for example, from a strategy of subversion to one of suppression.

But this logic also suggests — and Foucault's own analyses, despite his call for "de-sexualisation," support this argument — that resistances can also operate *within* a given discourse. Thus Rosalind Coward, for instance, is not quite correct to say that Foucault's *History of Sexuality*, in denying that there has been any sudden change from repression to liberation over the past century in the discourse on sexuality, implies also a denial of the important changes in representations of female sexuality which have occurred during recent years.[25] "We must make allowance," Foucault writes, "for the complex and unstable process whereby discourse can be both an instrument and an effect of power, but also a hindrance, a stumbling block, a point of resistance and a starting point for an opposing strategy." Foucault again gives the example of homosexuality, which "began to speak in its own behalf, to demand that its legitimacy or 'naturality' be acknowledged, often in the same vocabulary, using the same categories by which it was medically disqualified" (*HS*,101). A similar analysis would pertain, certainly, to the women's movement and its fight for changes in the representation of female sexuality.

One matter I have not yet addressed is the shift which occurs in Foucault's later work, when he moves away from the classical period in France to classical antiquity. In this later work, we find a continuing concern with the question of the subject, but while Foucault speaks of the subject in relation to the Greeks, speaks, for example, of "the mode of subjection" by which "the individual establishes his relation to [a] rule and recognizes himself as obliged to put it in practice," of a Greek boy's attempts to transform himself from "object of pleasure into a subject who was in control of his pleasures," of Greek ethics as "the elaboration of a form of relation to the self that enables an individual to fashion himself into a subject of ethical conduct," it seems he is talking here of a fundamentally different phenomenon than the subject he earlier defined as a product of the human sciences.[26] "Because no Greek thinker ever found a definition of the subject and never searched for one," Foucault has said, "I would simply say that there is no subject."[27] The Greeks, in Foucault's view, had developed what he calls an "aesthetics of existence," a system of ethics which allowed more room for individuality and self-creation than the later juridical ethics of Christianity. It is in the dawning of Christianity that Foucault sees the first move towards subject-hood, with the beginnings of a code-oriented morality which specified much more distinctly the limits of ethical behaviour, with the introduction of confession as a means of subjecting the very soul of an individual to the gaze of authority, and with the development of conscience as a way of turning that authoritarian gaze inward, of turning self against self as a mode of subjection.

But if we follow Foucault in this formulation of the subject's genealogy, then some limits in a feminist appropriation of his critique of the subject as a point of entry for analyzing woman's construction as "other" become apparent. As Nancy Miller points out, "society did not wait for the invention of man to repress 'woman' or oppress women"[28] — did not wait, in other words, until the subject was constituted by humanism before creating the categories of gender opposition which have served to solidify male domination. While Foucault's analysis of homosexual relations in ancient Greece, for example, shows they were viewed then in a fundamentally different light than in the modern era, his considerably less thorough and less satisfying analysis of women in that society reveals what seems to be a fundamental continuity: women were viewed by the Greeks as inferior by nature, to be ruled over and controlled, much as they were viewed later by the Christian church fathers, and much as they have been viewed almost up to the present day. Foucault does suggest a point at which representations of gender identity may have undergone an important shift, when the emphasis on the relationship between men and boys as "the most active focus of reflection and elaboration" in classical Greek thought gave way, in the Roman and early Christian era, to the emphasis on relations between men and women, on virginity, and on "the value attributed to relations of symmetry and reciprocity between husband and wife" (*Use*,253). But even taking into account such a shift, an important residue remains. If Greek women were not "subjects" in Foucault's sense of the word, they were certainly subjected, and the main terms of that subjection — that is, a fundamental gender split, and a hierarchical organization of that split — are the same ones that feminists are dealing with today. The history of women, then, may in some respects be a continuous one, in that both the fact of their oppression, and the theoretical terms which have been used to justify that oppression, have demonstrated a tremendous staying power from era to era.

But Foucault's theories do not necessarily preclude this kind of continuity. Foucault himself has bemoaned the emphasis which commentators have placed on his notion of *dis*continuity:

> My problem was not at all to say, '*Voilà*, long live discontinuity, we are in the discontinuous and a good thing too,' but to pose the question, 'How is it that at certain moments and in certain orders of knowledge, there are these sudden take-offs, these hastenings of evolution, these transformations which fail to correspond to the calm, continuist image that is normally accredited? (*P/K*,112).

Yet only recently has the status of women shown signs of being in the process of a *fundamental* transformation, one which is shaking the roots of sexual differentiation and discrimination. And while it would be reductive to deny that any changes have occured in the image of woman from era to era, many of these changes — for example, the "medicalisation" of the female body which Foucault has pointed to — have merely served to reaffirm women's marginal status. Thus while relations of power may alter according to the kinds of major transformation which Foucault has noted, certain strands in each era's web, specifically those which have accrued around gender oppositions, have remained strong throughout the long history of women's oppression. The forces which have held these strands in place will also have to be looked at before we have finished with the question of woman.

VI: Intellectuals and Power

> The intellectual no longer has to play the role of advisor. The project, tactics and goals are a matter for those who do the fighting. What the intellectual can do is provide the instruments of analysis (*PK*,62).

Foucault's "toolkit" view of theory should help put him in perspective for feminists. While he seems to sympathise with the move "beyond" sexual identity, his work still provides tools for those feminists still fighting, as women, in the trenches, where the battle is far from over. As Biddy Martin points out with respect to the current eliding of sexual identity, "the projects of male" (and, I would add, some female) "critics and feminist critics are necessarily non-synchronous despite commonalities."[29] Feminists have only just begun the work of reclamation and production necessary to guard against women's being eclipsed once again at the very moment of their emergence into history. Would a move away from sexual oppositions towards a more epistemologically "correct" position imply, for instance, that women academics should stop lobbying to get more women's work included on course lists? That reading Joyce (whose own views on women are far from trouble-free) may bring one closer to the "feminine" than reading, say, Virginia Woolf? Someone like Derrida (after all a man) may rejoice in the subversive potential of a woman who is "a non-identity, a non-figure, a simulacrum" (*Spurs*,49); but such "non-identity," as countless feminist analyses have shown, has been precisely the status of women since time immemorial, and this status — for all its supposedly subversive potential — has been the main source of their oppression.

I am not suggesting that feminists reject the new discourses on "woman" out of hand, or that they ignore the epistemological concerns which have prompted those discourses. Instead they should get the lay of the land, see what old faces lurk in the new landscape, judge what is germane to the political reality they face. Next to the Marxist "always historicize," we might add the very post-modern "always problematize."

At the end of *The Order of Things*, Foucault writes that if the arrangements which led to the birth of the human sciences were to disappear, "then one can certainly wager that man would be erased, like a face drawn in sand at the edge of the sea" (*OT*,387). But before that happens perhaps woman's face will have to be etched firmly beside it, if only as a network of scars on a once-smooth surface.

Montréal

Notes

1. Michel Foucault, *The Order of Things* (New York: Vintage Books, 1973), p. 387. Hereafter cited as *OT*.

2. Biddy Martin, "Feminism, Criticism, and Foucault," *New German Critique*, 27 (1982), 17. Emphasis added.

3. Michel Foucault, *Power/Knowledge: Selected Interviews and Other Writings, 1972-1977*, trans. Colin Gordon et al., ed. Colin Gordon (New York: Pantheon Books, 1980), p. 98. Hereafter *P/K*.

4. Michel Foucault, *Discipline and Punish: The Birth of the Prison*, trans. Alan Sheridan (New York: Vintage Books, 1979), p. 192. Hereafter *DP*.

5. Michel Foucault, *The History of Sexuality*, trans. Robert Hurley (New York: Vintage Books, 1980), p. 43. Hereafter *HS*.

6. Michel Foucault, *The Archaelogy of Knowledge*, trans. A. M. Sheridan Smith (New York: Harper & Row, 1976), p. 12. Hereafter *AK*.

7. Julia Kristeva, "Women's Time," trans. Alice Jardine and Harry Blake, in *Feminist Theory: A Critique of Ideology,* ed. Nannerl O. Keohane et al. (Chicago: University of Chicago Press, 1982). Hereafter *WT*.

8. See, for example, Luce Irigaray, "This Sex Which is Not One," trans. Claudia Reeder, in *New French Feminisms*, ed. Elaine Marks and Isabelle de Courtivron (New York: Schocken Books, 1981), pp. 99-106. Hélène Cixous, in "The Laugh of the Medusa," (trans. Keith Cohen and Paula Cohen, *New French Feminisms*, pp. 245-264) also suggests a difference between male and female sensibility grounded in differing sexual economies, but the case with Cixous, as indicated below, is problematic. (*New French Feminisms* will hereafter be cited as *NFF*.)

9. Among American critics, Peggy Kamuf has used a specifically Foucauldian framework to arrive at a position similar to Kristeva's. See her article, "Replacing Feminist Criticism," *Diacritics*, 12, No. 2 (1982), 42-47. Though Kamuf does not acknowledge any debt to Kristeva, she also seems to see herself as part of a "third generation"; she isolates two feminist strategies, strikingly similar to the two "phases" Kristeva identifies, which are doomed to perpetuate the system women have been trying to subvert: "on the one hand an expansion of institutions to include at their center what has been historically excluded; on the other hand, the installing of a counter-institution based on feminine centred cultural models" (Kamuf, p. 45).

10. Quoted in *The Great Quotations*, comp. George Seldes (Secaucus, N.J.: Castle Books, 1960), p. 530.

11. Jacques Derrida, *Spurs: Nietzsche's Styles/Éperons: Les Styles de Nietzsche*, trans. Barbara Harlow (Chicago: The University of Chicago Press, 1979), p. 51. Hereafter *Spurs*.

12. Derrida, anticipating objections to his rather "eccentric" reading of Nietzsche, summarizes his own position thus: "Must not these *apparently feminist* propositions be reconciled with the overwhelming *corpus* of Nietzsche's venomous anti-feminism? Their congruence (a notion which I oppose by convention to that of coherence), although ineluctably enigmatic, is just as rigorously necessary. Such, in any case will be the thesis of the present communication" (*Spurs*, 57). It is impossible to do justice to the rigours of Derrida's analysis here; what concern me more are the potential *uses* of that analysis.

13. Alice Jardine, "Gynesis," *Diacritics*, 12, No. 2 (1982), 64. Jardine gives a good overview of the role of "woman" in current French theory, though she concentrates mainly on Lacan and his followers. I take her article as a point of departure for what follows.

14. Jardine, p. 64.

15. Susan Gubar, "The Blank Page and the Issues of Female Creativity," in *Writing and Sexual Difference*, ed. Elizabeth Abel (Chicago: The University of Chicago Press, 1982), p. 77.

16. For the best critique of this appropriation, see Frank Lentricchia's chapter on poststructuralism in *After the New Criticism* (Chicago: The University of Chicago Press, 1980), pp. 156-210; also his chapter on Paul de Man, pp. 282-317. Paul A. Bové provides a similar analysis in his essay "Variations on Authority: Some Deconstructive Transformations of the New Criticism," in *The Yale Critics: Deconstruction in America*, ed. Jonathan Arac, Wlad Godzich and Wallace Martin (Minneapolis: University of Minnesota Press, 1983), p. 2-19. See also Wlad Godzich, "The Domestication of Derrida," in the same volume, pp. 20-40.

17. See Jacques Lacan, *Encore* (Paris: Editions du Seuil, 1975); Roland Barthes, *Roland Barthes by Roland Barthes*, trans. Richard Howard (New York: Hill and Wang, 1978); Jean Baudrillard *De la séduction* (Paris: Galilée, 1980).

18. Virginia Woolf, "Professions for Women," in *The Norton Anthology of English Literature*, Vol. 2, ed. M.H. Abrams et al. (New York: W.W. Norton & Company, 1979), p. 2047.

19. Kamuf, p. 42.

20. Christine Froula, "When Eve Reads Milton: Undoing the Canonical Economy," *Critical Inquiry*, 10 (1983), 321-347. The Woolf passage alluded to is from *Jacob's Room* (1922; New York, 1978), pp. 40-41.

21. Edward Pechter, in a response to Froula ("When Pechter Reads Froula Pretending She's Eve Reading Milton; or, New Feminist Is But Old Priest Writ Large," *Critical Inquiry*, 11, 1984, 163-170) notes the fact of Milton's own anti-authoritarianism, though he does not take specific issue with Froula's definition of woman.

22. Jeffrey Weeks, "Discourse, desire and sexual deviance: some problems in a history of homosexuality," in *The Making of the Modern Homosexual*, ed. Kenneth Plummer (Totowa, N.J.: Barnes & Noble Books, 1981), pp. 76-111.

23. Jardine discusses French anti-feminism in "Gynesis."

24. Michel Foucault, "What is an Author?" in *Language, Counter-Memory, Practice*, trans. Donald F. Bouchard and Sherry Simon, ed. Donald F. Bouchard (Oxford: Basil Blackwell, 1977), p. 138.

25. Rosalind Coward, "Are Women's Novels Feminist Novels?" in *The New Feminist Criticism*, ed. Elaine Showalter (New York: Pantheon Books, 1985), p. 234.

26. Michel Foucault, *The Use of Pleasure*, trans. Robert Hurley (New York: Pantheon Books, 1985), pp. 27, 225, 251. Hereafter *Use*.

27. Michel Foucault, "Final Interview," *Raritan*, 5, No. 1 (1985), 1-13.

28. Nancy Miller, "The Text's Heroine: A Feminist Critic and Her Fictions," *Diacritics*, 12, No. 2 (1982), 49. Miller's article is a response to Kamuf's "Replacing Feminist Criticism," in the same issue.

29. Martin, p. 21.

Printed on paper
containing over 50%
recycled paper including
5% post-consumer fibre.

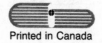

Printed in Canada